Healthy Ide

Improving Global Health and De
in the 21st Century

by
Devi Sridhar and Igor Rudan

Published in the United Kingdom by JoGH.

JoGH is an imprint of the Edinburgh University Global Health Society.
Edinburgh University Global Health Society
Teviot Place, Edinburgh EH8 9AG
Scotland, United Kingdom

Printed in Croatia by LaserPLUS, Ltd.

ISBN-13: 978-0-9933638-1-8

Photo on book cover:
Credited to Ewan D. Kennedy, the University of Edinburgh Medical School

Citation:
Sridhar, Devi* and Rudan, Igor*. Healthy Ideas: Improving Global Health and
Development in the 21st Century. Edinburgh: JoGH, 2015, pp. 1-440.

*The authors contributed equally. Therefore, they agreed that the hard cover edition of this
book should list IR as the first author and the paperback edition should list DS as the first
author. This order was determined by tossing a coin.*

Healthy Ideas

Improving Global Health and Development in the 21st Century

by

Devi Sridhar and Igor Rudan

JoGH, Edinburgh, 2015

To G. V. and Lalita Ramakrishna, with admiration and love.

To Diana, Božidar and Klara Rudan, with devotion and love.

Table of contents

PART 1. Improving available evidence

PART 2. Improving policy formulation

PART 3. Improving development assistance for health

PART 4. Improving governance and legislation

PART 5. Improving international organizations

PART 6. Improving research prioritization

List of abbreviations

ACP	African, Caribbean and Pacific Group of States
ADI	Alzheimer's Disease International
AHC	Ad Hoc Committee on Health Research Relating to Future Intervention Options
AIDS	Acquired Immune Deficiency Syndrome
AMC	Advance Market Commitment
ASEAN	Association of South-East Asian Nations
BMGF	Bill and Melinda Gates Foundation
BRICS	Brazil, Russia, India, China and South Africa
CAM	Combined Approach Matrix
CAO	Chief Administrative Officer
CARICOM	Caribbean Community
CARMEN	Collaborative Action for Risk Factor Prevention & Effective Management of NCDs
CCDCP	Chinese Center for Disease Control and Prevention
CCM	Country Coordinating Mechanism
CCO	Chief Communications Officer
CEO	Chief Executive Officer
CFO	Chief Financial Officer
CHERG	Child Health Epidemiology Reference Group
CHNRI	Child Health and Nutrition Research Initiative
CHOICE	Choosing Interventions that are Cost-Effective
CIDA	Canadian International Development Agency
CIVET	Colombia, Indonesia, Vietnam, Egypt and Turkey
CNKI	Chinese National Knowledge Infrastructure
CoATS	Coordinating AIDS Technical Support
COHRED	Commission on Health Research for Development
COO	Chief Operating Officer
CSO	Civil Society Organizations
DAH	Development Assistance for health
DALY	Disability-Adjusted Life Years
DCPP	Disease Control Priorities Project
DFID	Department for International Development
DGAP	Diarrhoea Global Action Plan
DHS	Demographic and Health Surveys
DNA	Deoxyribonucleic Acid

DOTS	Directly Observed Treatment, Short-course (for tuberculosis)
DQA	Data Quality Audits
ECDPC	European Centre for Disease Prevention and Control
EHCP	Essential Health Care Package
ENHR	Essential National Health Research
EPA	Economic Partnership Agreements
EQUIST	Equitable Impact Sensitive Tool
FCTC	Framework Convention on Tobacco Control
GAIN	Global Alliance for Improved Nutrition
GAPP	Global Action Plan for Pneumonia
GAPPD	Global Action Plan for Pneumonia and Diarrhoea
GATHER	Guidelines for Accurate and Transparent Health Estimates Reporting
GAVI	Global Alliance for Vaccines and Immunization
GBD	Global Burden of Disease
GFHR	Global Forum for Health Research
GHERG	Global Health Epidemiology Reference Group
GHI	Global Health Initiative
GHRS	Global Health Research System
GIST	Global Implementation Support Team
GPA	Global Program on AIDS
GTZ (GIZ)	German Agency for International Cooperation
GWAS	Genome-Wide Association Studies
H8 (or H-8)	The Health Eight
Hib	Haemophilus influenzae type B
HIF	Health Impact Fund
HIV	Human Immunodeficiency Virus
HLE	Healthy Life Expectancy
HMN	Health Metrics Network
HNP	Health, Nutrition and Population Sector (of The World Bank)
HPSR	Health Policy and Systems Research
HSS	Health System Strengthening
IARC	International Agency for Research on Cancer
IBRD	International Bank for Reconstruction and Development
ICD	International Classification of Diseases
IDA	International Development Association
IDF	International Diabetes Federation
IFFIm	International Finance Facility for Immunisation
IGME	United Nation's Inter-Agency Group for Child Mortality Estimation

IHME	Institute for Health Metrics and Evaluation
IHP+	International Health Partnerships Plus
IHR	Instrument of Health Research
IMCI	Integrated Management of Childhood Illness
IMF	International Monetary Fund
INCLEN	International Clinical Epidemiology Network
IRC	Independent Review Committee
ISS	Immunisation Services Support
LDC	Least Developed Countries Group
LIST	Lives Saved Tool
LMIC	Low and Middle-Income Countries
LRG	Larger Reference Group
MBB	Marginal Budgeting for Bottlenecks
MDG	Millennium Development Goals
MDR-TB	Multidrug Resistant Tuberculosis
MERS	Middle East Respiratory Syndrome
MI	Myocardial Infarction
MICS	Multiple Indicator Cluster Surveys
MNCAH	Maternal, Newborn, Child and Adolescent Health
MNCH	Maternal, Newborn, and Child Health
MSF	Medecins Sans Frontieres
NACO	National AIDS Control Organisation (in India)
NACP	National AIDS Control Projects (in India)
NCD	Non-Communicable Diseases
NGO	Non-Governmental Organization
ODA	Official Development Assistance
OECD	Organisation for Economic Co-operation and Development
OECD-DAC	OECD's Development Assistance Committee
P3G	Public Population Project in Genomics
PAHO	Pan American Health Organization
PC	Pneumococcus (Streptococcus Pneumoniae)
PCB	Programme Co-ordinating Board
PEPFAR	President's Emergency Plan for AIDS Relief
PIP	Pandemic Influenza Preparedness
PLANET	Planning, Monitoring and Evaluation Tool
PneumoADIP	Pneumococcal Vaccines Accelerated Development and Introduction Plan
PRSP	Poverty Reduction Strategy Paper(s)
R&D	Research and Development

RAND	Research and Development (corporation)
RCC	Rolling Continuation Channel
RPS	Research Priority Score
SARA	Service Availability and Readiness Assessment
SARS	Severe Acute Respiratory Syndrome
SDG	Sustainable Development Goals
SME	Small and Medium Enterprises
SUS	Sistema Unico de Saude
SWAPs	Sector-Wide Programmes
TAC	Treatment Action Campaign
TB	Tuberculosis
TRIPS	Trade Related Aspects of Intellectual Property Rights
TWG	Technical Working Group
UHC	Universal Health Coverage
UN	United Nations
UNAIDS	Joint United Nations Programme on HIV/AIDS
UNASUL	The Union of South American Nations (synonims: USAN, UNASUR)
UNDP	United Nations Development Programme
UNFPA	United Nations Population Fund
UNICEF	United Nation's Children Fund
UNODC	United Nations Office on Drugs and Crime
USAID	United States Agency for International Development
USCDCP	United States Centers for Disease Control and Prevention
VIP	Chongqing VIP Information Company
VoI	Value of Information
WDR	World Development Report
WHA	World Health Assembly
WHO	World Health Organization
WHO RPC	WHO's Department for Research Policy and Cooperation
WHOSIS	WHO Statistical Information System
WTO	World Trade Organization

Preface

The world of global health and development has undergone dramatic changes in the 21st century. The United Nation's Millennium Development Goals, adopted in the year 2000, marked the beginning of a new era that drew an unprecedented number of players, funding commitments and popular interest towards making the world's population healthier. A proliferation of international organizations, non-governmental agencies, private philanthropic foundations and many high profile individuals which all focused on various issues in global health and development created an entirely new world. However, the arisen complexity led to many new challenges that now require effective solutions.

In this book, we identify the key challenges, analyse their roots and interpret their evolution throughout the 21st century. Moreover, we offer our ideas on how to potentially address these challenges to make investments in health and development more effective. The book is a compilation of both of our past and current thoughts and ideas relevant to problems that the global health and development community faces today. We published these contributions over the past decade in some of the leading international journals focused on the area of global health and development. The book also explains three tools that we developed to assist decision-making processes: CHNRI, EQUIST and PLANET.

We organized our writings systematically, based on six major themes: (i) improving available evidence; (ii) improving policy formulation; (iii) improving development assistance for health; (iv) improving governance and legislation; (v) improving international organization; and (vi) improving research prioritizaton. In doing so, we only included the articles to which we made a major contribution, either as leading, co-leading or corresponding authors. However, this does not mean that we derived all of the ideas on our own: collaboration with many inspiring and well-minded colleagues shaped our thinking and writing. We would therefore like to acknowledge great help, support and friendship from each and every one of our co-authors, listed here in alphabetical order, followed by the number of chapter(s) to which they contributed:

Davies Adeloye (2, 6), Shanthi Ameratunga (39, 43, 44), Yurii Aulchenko (8), Rajiv Bahl (45), Manuela Balliet (12), Abdullah H. Baqui (8), Rajaie Batniji (22), Claudia Beiersmann (28), Zulfiqar A. Bhutta (8, 39, 44), Maureen Black (39, 44), Robert E. Black (39, 41, 43, 44, 46), Claire E. Brolan (27), Kenneth H. Brown (39, 44), Harry Campbell (2-4, 7, 8, 11, 14, 19, 25, 39, 41, 43, 44), Josip

Car (25), Ilona Carneiro (39, 43, 44), Kit Yee Chan (1, 2, 6, 43, 44, 45), Daniel Chandramohan (39, 44), Mickey Chopra (8, 12, 19, 25, 39, 43, 44, 46), Chelsea Clinton (15, 26), Barney Cohen (12), Simon Cousens (39, 44, 45), David Craig (20), Gary L. Darmstadt (39, 44), Shireen Durrani (27), Jennifer Edge (27), Karen Edmond (8), Shams El Arifeen (39, 41, 43, 44, 46), Julio Frenk (34), Eric Friedman (28), Julie Meeks Gardner (39, 44), Jennifer L. Gibson (39, 43, 44, 46), Lawrence O. Gostin (9, 27, 29, 32, 33, 34), Eduardo J. Gomez (24), Hebe Gouda (28), Liz Grant (6), Karen Grepin (13), Sonja Y. Hess (39, 43, 44), Peter Hill (27, 28), Adnan A. Hyder (39, 44), Bernardo L. Horta (8), Albrecht Jahn (28), Lydia Kapiriri (12, 39, 43, 44, 46), Keith P. Klugman (8), Ivana Kolčić (6), Margaret Kosek (39, 44), Claudio F. Lanata (8, 39, 44), Mary Ann Lansang (39, 43, 44), Joy E. Lawn (39, 44), Shabir A. Madhi (8), Anthony Maher (17), Jose Martines (45), Ana Marušić (2, 3, 4, 6, 7, 11), Martin McKee (27, 28), Suerie Moon (34), J. Stephen Morrison (37), Harish Nair (2, 3, 4, 8), Gorik Ooms (28), Peter Piot (37), Zeshan Qureshi (8), Craig Rubens (8), Tami Tamashiro (38), Evropi Theodoratou (2, 4, 8), Mark Tomlinson (12, 39, 43, 44, 46), Alexander C. Tsai (43, 44), Cesar G. Victora (8), Wei Wang (8), Martin W. Weber (8), Jayne Webster (39, 44), James F. Wilson (8), Ngaire Woods (9, 25), Derek Yach (32), Sachiyo Yoshida (45) and Lina Zgaga (8).

We extend our gratitude to our teachers, mentors and other colleagues committed to improving global health and development who have guided, influenced and inspired us through our careers and contributed to the ideas expressed in this book.

Devi Sridhar and Igor Rudan

PART 1.

Improving available evidence

CHAPTER 1.

Global health metrics needs collaboration and competition

The most recent update on the global, regional, and national causes of death, presented in The Lancet by the GBD Mortality and Causes of Death Collaborators (1), a large international consortium of researchers led by the Institute for Health Metrics and Evaluation, includes an unprecedented amount of data. The Global Burden of Disease Study (GBD) 2013 has provided internally consistent estimates of the causes of death for 1990–2013. The yearly number of deaths worldwide increased as a result of population expansion, from 47.5 million in 1990, to 54.9 million in 2013. In relative terms, mortality rates have steadily decreased, leading to an increase in global life expectancy from 65.3 years to 71.5 years (1).

The clearest progress was in reduction of global child mortality from infectious causes such as pneumonia and diarrhoea, accompanied by decreasing mortality rates from cardiovascular diseases and cancer in high-income regions. The HIV/AIDS pandemic was the greatest challenge to overall progress during this period, resulting in substantially shortened life expectancy in sub-Saharan Africa. Non-communicable diseases gradually emerged as the most prominent contemporary threat to global public health. The ageing global population has increased the absolute number of deaths related to non-communicable diseases, although relative mortality rates improved for most diseases. A small number of non-communicable diseases, including pancreatic cancer, atrial fibrillation and flutter, diabetes, chronic kidney disease, and drug use disorders, ran counter to these trends and became increasingly deadly in both absolute and relative terms (1). The authors present fairly precise estimates of the number of deaths owing to 240 different causes in 188 countries over a 23-year period; an astonishing number of outputs, based on far more input data (1).

In many fields of modern science, collection and analysis of so-called "*big data*", generated by collaborations between hundreds of scientists, has become a major driver of new discovery. Notable examples include the Human Genome Project, the search for the origin of mass at the Large Hadron Collider, the Sloan Digital Sky Survey in astronomy, and genome-wide association studies in genomics and personalised medicine (2). Such science generates new information on a large scale that fills many gaps in knowledge and enables further scientific progress. It is not surprising that such efforts have come to dominate evaluations of research impact in recent years (3). Modern science is benefiting from massive collaborations. However, big data science is also associated with risks. Research projects can become so large that they acquire a political dimension, mainly because of their anticipated effect on subsequent policies and funding decisions. Once a network of researchers achieves a monopoly over an area of research, incentives to perform might fade, while incentives to preserve that monopoly rise. When the slow-moving, publicly funded Human Genome Project suddenly had competition from the privately funded Celera Genomics, a dramatic race began to complete the human genome sequence, which accelerated and improved both efforts (4). Similarly, thousands of scientists working at the Large Hadron Collider were arranged in the two parallel experiments – ATLAS and CMS – that were expected to confirm each other's findings independently. For genome-wide association studies, replication of findings is a norm before results can be seriously considered (5).

As an emerging field of science, global health metrics seems to be following a similar evolutionary path to other big data disciplines. Estimates of the causes of the global burden of disease, disability, and death are important because they guide investment decisions that, in turn, save lives across the world (6). Historically, the responsibility for those estimates rested largely with WHO and its academic partners. Although WHO's team of experts have been doing fine technical work for many years, its monopoly in this field had removed incentives to invest more time and resources in continuous improvement (7). The emergence of the Institute for Health Metrics and Evaluation, generously supported by the Bill & Melinda Gates Foundation, has changed the science of global health metrics in a similar way to Celera Genomics' competition with the Human Genome Project.

It is hardly surprising that the publication of GBD 2010 sparked controversy (8). The Institute for Health Metrics and Evaluation struggled to generate support, legitimacy, and acceptance for their findings. Their many invited collaborators expected unrestricted access to all input data, sharing of methods, clear timelines, fair and transparent distribution of funding support, and agreement on the acknowledgment of credit. Researchers outside the GBD 2010 collaboration expected provisions for independent replication of all results. Some collaborators withdrew from the GBD 2010 project over those concerns. Moreover, WHO chose not to acknowledge the GBD 2010 estimates because of similar concerns, thus creating open competition (9). Some feared that the existence of parallel global health estimates would confuse policy makers in low-income countries and reduce pressure on non-performing governments to improve health of their jurisdictions (10).

The initial concerns are now being attenuated by the benefits of competition. WHO mobilised their staff and collaborating academic expert groups to revise their methods and consolidate the estimates for which they are traditionally strongest – e.g., on child and maternal health, malaria, tuberculosis, and HIV/AIDS (11). They launched a series of meetings to develop clear guidelines for reporting global health estimates that could be officially endorsed by WHO (9). Those meetings included scientists from the Institute for Health Metrics and Evaluation, ensuring communication between the two groups and possibly suggesting a future change in policy towards the GBD estimates. Meanwhile, the Institute for Health Metrics and Evaluation responded to criticisms and improved its practices. The new GBD 2013 estimates show the vast expansion of collaborators, acquiring primary information even from countries that traditionally provide little data, such as China, Mexico, Turkey, and Russia (1). The description of methods is more detailed and transparent, and the instruments of analysis – many of which are now available online – are becoming increasingly sophisticated. Particular care was taken to address the key weaknesses, correcting questionable estimates from GBD 2010. Unfortunately, the GBD 2013 estimates fall short of allowing full independent replication of all results.

A comparison of the GBD 2013 estimates to those of WHO and its affiliates suggests that we should expect the grand convergence between two sets of estimates to begin this year, with the global causes of child deaths being a prime example (11,12). The remaining differences are, in fact, useful because they point to the most important data gaps or the most controversial sources of data used. They will help focus subsequent debate on an increasingly specific set of questions. Therefore, the competition between WHO and the GBD has benefited the entire global health community, leading to converging estimates of the global causes of death that everyone can trust.

The GBD initiative has emerged as a well-organised and rapidly growing collaboration that is now seriously challenging WHO's role in generating global health estimates. WHO maintains its position for several key strengths, for which it benefits from collaboration with affiliated groups of external academics. However, it will need to rethink its own role and massively scale up its capacity to generate global health estimates to remain competitive. WHO's indecision over investment in global health metrics, or over the role it should have in the long term, will help the GBD collaboration to gain widespread support for its estimates. Idleness by WHO might even lead to a new monopoly in global health metrics, with the centre of activity moving from Geneva to

Seattle. Such a scenario might again simplify global health politics but, in the absence of healthy competition, science could be the poorer.

Acknowledgement: Originally published as: Igor Rudan and Kit Yee Chan: Global health metrics needs collaboration and competition. Reprinted with permission from Elsevier (Lancet 2015; 385:92-94).

References

1. GBD Mortality and *Causes* of Death Collaborators. Global, regional, and national age-sex specific all-cause and cause-specific mortality for 240 causes of death, 1990–2013: a systematic analysis for the Global Burden of Disease Study 2013. Lancet 2015; 385:117-171.
2. Visscher PM, Brown MA, McCarthy MI, Yang J. Five years of GWAS discovery. Am J Hum Genet 2012; 90:7–24.
3. Thomson Reuters. The world's most influential scientific minds 2014. New York: Thomson Reuters, 2014. (Available from: http://sciencewatch.com/sites/sw/files/sw-article/media/worlds-most-influential-scientific-minds-2014.pdf; Accessed: 3 Oct 2014).
4. Gunnison Ballen K. Decoding our DNA: Craig Venter vs the Human Genome Project. Minneapolis: Twenty-First Century Books, 2012.
5. Kraft P, Zeggini E, Ioannidis JPA. Replication in genome-wide association studies. Statist Sci 2009; 24:561–573.
6. Rudan I, Marušić A, Campbell H. Balancing investments in existing and emerging approaches to address global health priorities. J Glob Health 2012; 2:010101.
7. Levine R. Open letter to the incoming Director General of the World Health Organization: time to refocus. BMJ 2006; 333:1015–1017.
8. Cohen J. A controversial close-up of humanity's health. Science 2012; 338:1414–1416.
9. Horton R. Offline: the darker corners of our world. Lancet 2012; 381:612.
10. Victoria CG. Causes of child deaths: looking to the future. Lancet 2015; 385:398-399.
11. Liu L, Oza S, Hogan D, et al. Global, regional, and national causes of child mortality in 2000–13, with projections to inform post-2015 priorities: an updated systematic analysis. Lancet 2015; 385:430-440.
12. Norheim OF, Jha P, Admasu K, et al. Avoiding 40% of the premature deaths in each country, 2010–30: review of national mortality trends to help quantify the UN Sustainable Development Goal for health. Lancet 2015; 385:239-252.

CHAPTER 2.

Assembling the Global Health Epidemiology Reference Group: Could "academic crowd-sourcing" address gaps in global health estimates?

Rapid development of information technologies in the past two decades has brought about major improvements in the generation, sharing and analysis of information on the health status of the entire human population. This has facilitated the development of the field of *Global Health Metrics*", which has its champions in World Health Organization's Mortality and Burden of Disease Unit and University of Washington's Institute for Health Metrics and Evaluation (IHME). A number of other groups, initiatives and institutions also contribute substantially to this field and regularly publish population health estimates. These include national epidemiological services, population-specific (e.g. occupational, ethnic, age-and gender-defined) and disease-specific registries, academic research groups interested in specific health problems, professional societies that specialize in a particular disease(s), and initiatives by international organizations.

Examples of organizations specializing in population health surveillance that require health metrics as a starting point include the United States Centers for Disease Control and Prevention (USCDCP), European Centre for Disease Prevention and Control (ECDPC), Chinese Center for Disease Control and Prevention (CCDCP), International Agency for Research on Cancer (IARC) and the United Nation's Children Fund (UNICEF). All of these organizations regularly publish summaries of large amounts of information on population health that is collected through their services. Moreover, the Demographic and Health Surveys (DHS) Program, supported by USAID, continues to collect, analyze and disseminate representative data on population, health, HIV, and nutrition through more than 300 nationally-representative household surveys in over 90 countries. Similarly, UNICEF assists countries in collecting and analyzing data on health of women and children through its household survey program called Multiple Indicator Cluster Surveys (MICS).

Further to these efforts, professional societies such as the International Diabetes Federation (IDF) and Alzheimer's Disease International (ADI) work together with the World Health Organization to develop and regularly update the global, regional, and sometimes national estimates of type 2 diabetes and dementia, respectively. There are many other examples of successful collaborations between international agencies and academic research groups in order to develop accurate and transparent population health estimates. Some of the most notable examples are the United Nation's Inter-Agency Group for Child Mortality Estimation (IGME), and the Child Health Epidemiology Reference Group (CHERG), in which our group in Edinburgh has also been involved for the past decade. IGME regularly revises the overall child mortality estimates at the national level, while CHERG made major contributions to the understanding of the leading causes of child deaths globally, regionally and nationally. CHERG's work provided much needed evidence to inform and help direct policies towards achieving UN's Millennium Development Goal 4. CHERG developed into a collaboration between the WHO, UNICEF and a group of independent technical experts from leading academic institutions who worked together to assemble available information on the causes of child deaths in parts of the world where there was no adequate vital registration coverage. An important aspect of CHERG work was to critically review this information and to include only data which met stated quality criteria regarding validity and representativeness.

In addition to understanding the burden of disease in human populations, determinants of the burden – i.e., the underlying risk factor causes that make people ill – are also of interest to the field of global health metrics. Several countries or regions have set up large-scale biobanks in recent years to study determinants of population health on a very large scale, using a *"big data"* approach. Some of the most impressive examples are UK Biobank, the Kadoorie biobank in China, and the EPIC prospective study in Europe. Each one of these biobanks includes about 500,000 persons which should give them sufficient study power to tease out the effects of many different potential environmental, genetic and lifestyle contributors to human diseases. Likewise, there are academic groups that regularly review and assess the scientific literature to identify risk factors through large meta-analyses, such as the INTERHEART Study which evaluates risk factors for myocardial infarction (MI), or Environment and Global Health Research Group at the Imperial College London, which collaborates with the WHO to provide national-level updates on risk factors such as the prevalence of obesity, hypercholesterolemia, hypertension and hyperglycaemia.

The *"big data"* approach to global health metrics, currently championed by IHME and increasingly adopted by other groups, should work well over time. The application of sophisticated analytical methods to these massive datasets should be expected to yield population health estimates that would continuously improve over time. However, there are also problems with reliance on *"big data"* and the field of global health metrics is particularly prone to some of the most frequently highlighted concerns (1). The much larger amount of data under study will not necessarily make the estimates of disease burden more accurate if most of the data are systematically biased. Moreover, there is a false assumption that very large amount of data automatically implies that the collection will cover all parts of the world adequately and represent underlying populations well. Unfortunately, the global health data available in the public domain today suffers from both these problems. Despite the increasing availability of massive datasets of population-based data the field of global health metrics still faces a number of important challenges.

Firstly, a lot of population health data that is readily available in the public domain, or to organizations such as the WHO or IHME, are national-level estimates based on reporting to national epidemiological services. There is a possibility that these estimates suffer from systematic under-reporting, resulting in estimates that are much lower than the actual situation, even although they are based on very large amounts of data. Secondly, although the current global health estimates by both WHO and IHME for the year 2013 make a laudable attempt to model the estimates at the national level for each country in the world, this gives a false impression that there is relevant information available from all these countries. In reality, there are some parts of the world in which there is an abundance of information and the estimates are very precise. However, there are also other regions, and also certain diseases and risk factors, for which the amount of information is remarkably scarce. For some of these countries (or sub-national areas) and conditions the situation has not improved over the past 20-30 years, leading to very large degrees of uncertainty in disease burden estimates. The investment in and development of ever more sophisticated methods of computation and/or epidemiological modeling is less important to achieving valid disease burden estimates – which reflect the true burden in the world population – than investment in generating a sufficient amount of reliable information in those countries and conditions.

These inherent uncertainties are further compounded by the lack of complete transparency from the IHME over their input data that could allow other investigators to replicate their computations and assess the true amount of uncertainty in many of their estimates. In fairness to IHME, though, very few researchers outside the field of global health metrics can truly comprehend the scale of their effort and the size of their datasets, so it is perhaps not surprising that they may feel that they need to continue to refine their datasets and methods through further iterations before they are ready to fully expose them to the rest of the global health research community (2). However, as long as they do not open their input data and all their methods to a full independent replication by other legitimate academic groups, who do understand these issues – and there are several groups that could do this – it will continue to be difficult for the global health community to fully accept IHME's estimates. Consistent replication of any scientifically produced result by independent research groups has been a norm in other fields of science, making the key difference between an initial report and a broadly accepted new knowledge. In the end, IHME should benefit more than any other parties from opening their work to other groups – from getting an independent review and feedback on their work, to gaining scientific legitimacy and obtaining suggestions on where to focus further efforts to continue improving their estimates.

In recent months, the WHO and IHME have started to work together with a group of independent academic researchers from this field and senior staff from the *Lancet* and *PLoS Medicine* journals to improve the reporting of population health estimates and, through this, improve the accuracy and transparency of estimates. The new guidelines – likely to be named GATHER (which would stand as an acronym for the "*Guidelines for Accurate and Transparent Health Estimates Reporting*") – should improve practices of both those who generate and report primary information on health estimates and those who assemble the primary information and model it to develop global, regional and national health estimates for diseases and risk factors. Once adopted fully, the new reporting guidelines will represent a very helpful step forward that should benefit the field. Successful collaboration of the WHO and IHME teams and international academic experts (including from our Centre for Global Health Research in Edinburgh) on finalizing these guidelines would be a very welcome development, especially if adherence to such guidelines becomes a requirement for publication in all the leading medical journals (3).

We may conclude that, at this point, many positive developments are occurring in the field of global health metrics. The introduction of "*big data*" approaches, the development of more sophisticated and improved analytic methods, and improved use of new information technologies for data storage and visualization are all contributing to progress. The introduction of new guidelines should add to this progress and generate more papers with primary health data that would be of sufficient reporting quality to be useful for inclusion in different epidemiological models. They will also help to clarify which input data are being used in the models and how the models work.

However, as noted above, there is also a need to increasingly focus on how to generate a lot more information on disease burden and risk factors from *"gap"* areas of the world. This is particularly true for diseases and risks on which there is hardly any data or epidemiological research in recent decades, and where none of these elements of progress will be able to lead to trustworthy estimates. Possible approaches to address these gaps will need to include research capacity building in gap countries and regions in conducting and reporting epidemiological research. A network of international medical journals interested in global health – such as our *Journal of Global Health* – could play a substantial role in this capacity building. There is a need to educate both the researchers and the journal editors in less developed regions of the good practices and adherence to new guidelines in reporting their health estimates. It is possible that new technologies – such as mHealth and eHealth, i.e. the use of mobile phones and internet to gather information – may also enable forms of *"crowd-sourcing"* approaches to generate population health data in the areas of the world where no other approaches can guarantee success and to understand burden of health problems in real time.

In recent years, our Edinburgh-based group has *"specialized"* in finding useful health information and developing population health estimates for epidemiologically under-researched problems and areas (4). This led to the award of the status of the World Health Organization's Collaborating Centre for Population Research and Training. Our *"gap-filling"* efforts include trying to learn more about the emerging and alternative sources of medical literature and health information, such as recently digitalized Chinese medical databases CNKI, WanFang, VIP and others. This led to much improved estimates for several major health issues in transitioning China, such as a dramatic reduction of child mortality and its likely causes (5,6), a much finer resolution of the causes of mortality from childhood accidents (7), or the first comprehensive estimates of the burden of dementia (8) and schizophrenia (9) among the adult and elderly Chinese population. For the African continent, we have provided estimates of dementia, COPD, epilepsy, colorectal cancer and rheumatoid arthritis. Likewise, for South Asia, we have published estimates for type 2 diabetes (10-14). In this current journal issue, we are also publishing a study that estimated of the burden of rheumatoid arthritis in LMICs that was largely based on information from non-English databases and the so-called *"grey literature"* (15). We used similar approaches to develop global, regional and, national (wherever allowed by data) estimates for rather neglected and under-researched problems in global health such as childhood pneumonia (16,17), peripheral arterial disease (18) and sequelae from childhood meningitis (19).

Perhaps even more relevant to this *"gap-filling"* agenda, our group in Edinburgh also pioneered the approach of *"academic crowd-sourcing"* to address some health issues of specific interest, for which remarkably few data are available in the public domain. As an example, in our attempts to estimate the global, regional and national burden of RSV and influenza infections in children – both of which are important because of a possible opportunities for immunization – we gathered a group of well-minded independent experts who were in possession of either published or unpublished useful information on these under-researched topic, and who agreed to share these data for the purposes of developing global, regional and national estimates (20-22). Through this approach, we have found out that there is much more useful information available than could be concluded based on reviews of published sources. However, many of the most useful datasets were from studies established for other purposes such as data from control arms of randomized controlled trials which have a disease of interest as an outcome, or data from surveillance systems such as that set up to monitor the evolution of influenza and act as an alert mechanism for viruses with pandemic potential. Mobilizing these valuable sources of data have greatly improved that information available to burden of disease models compared to what was available solely through publically available sources (20-22).

This is precisely where we would like to position a new initiative – the *"Global Health Epidemiology Reference Group"* (GHERG). We would like to propose an informal and entirely voluntary international collaboration of academic groups willing to contribute to improving disease burden estimates to complement IHME activities and who agree to respect the principles of the new guidelines – a form of *"academic crowd-sourcing"*. Most importantly, all the input data, methods and work should be fully transparent and accessible to all other qualified researchers to verify and replicate them. Ideally, all GHERG papers should have more than one research group involved, and all of the collaborating groups would need to have full access to data. GHERG should, therefore, become an extension of Child Health Epidemiology Reference Group (CHERG), aiming to address global health issues in age groups beyond 0-4 years.

The overall goal of GHERG will be to develop and deploy new and improved evidence on the causes and determinants of morbidity and mortality among populations in all world regions, on the importance of a broad range of risk factors, and on the effectiveness of public health interventions, to inform and influence global priorities and programs. The main focus will continue to be on identifying the *"gap areas"* where not much information is available and where there is a lot of uncertainty present about the accuracy of the existing estimates. This approach should serve to complement the existing WHO and IHME estimates and to represent added value to both efforts.

The main purposes of the GHERG will be to publish papers, reports and reviews on global health epidemiology, with a special focus on identifying information of sufficient quality in low and middle-income countries and filling the gaps in information for regions where the data are very scarce and of insufficient quality. Also, we would like to advise WHO and other international organizations, institutions and initiatives on the most appropriate methods and assumptions for their global, regional and country level epidemiological estimates. We will aim to advise researchers and public health officials on the different issues involved in the estimation of cause-specific morbidity and mortality.

The core membership of GHERG will initially be offered to the editors and regional editors of the *Journal of Global Health,* who are all independent researchers working for the leading academic institutions. However, GHERG will be open to literally everyone to contribute their data, methods and estimates. It will aim to serve global health community by providing unrestricted open access to its datasets, methods and publications, and continuously revising and updating global health estimates for a targeted set of conditions.

Accurate global health estimates are extremely important because they expose the key issues, inform health policies, direct funding disbursements and eventually solve problems and save lives. In that sense, they could be viewed as a *"matter of life and death"*. Because of this, when it comes to global health estimates, we see value in both collaboration and competition. Two, three or even more estimates of the same problem, generated by independent research groups, are certainly more informative and helpful than only one – especially if all of them are fully transparent and their methods can be compared (2). If the principles of the new guidelines are respected by all research groups in the field, then all different estimates would eventually be expected to converge to the same, reliable set of estimates that we're hoping to deliver to the global health community for their unrestricted use.

Acknowledgement: *Originally published as: Igor Rudan, Harry Campbell, Ana Marušić, Devi Sridhar, Harish Nair, Evropi Theodoratou, Davies Adeloye and Kit Yee Chan: Assembling GHERG: Could "academic crowd-sourcing" address gaps in global health estimates? Reprinted with permission from Edinburgh University Global Health Society under Creative Commons Attribution License (Journal of Global Health 2015; 5:010101).*

References

1. Marcus G, Davis E. Eight (no, nine!) problems with big data. The New York Times. 6 Apr 2014. (Available from: http://www.nytimes.com/2014/04/07/opinion/eight-no-nine-problems-with-big-data.html?_r=0; Accessed: 5 Jun 2015)
2. Rudan I, Chan KY. Global health metrics needs collaboration and competition. Lancet 2015; 385:92-94.
3. Pan European Networks. WHO and IHME sign MoU. (Available from: http://www.paneuropeannetworks.com/health/who-and-ihme-sign-mou; Accessed: 5 Jun 2015)
4. Rudan I, Lawn J, Cousens S, Rowe AK, Boschi-Pinto C, Tomaskovic L, et al. Gaps in policy-relevant information on burden of disease in children: A systematic review. Lancet 2005; 365:2031-2040.
5. Rudan I, Chan KY, Zhang JS, Theodoratou E, Feng XL, Salomon JA, et al.; WHO/UNICEF's Child Health Epidemiology Reference Group (CHERG). Causes of deaths in children younger than 5 years in China in 2008. Lancet 2010; 375:1083-1089.
6. Feng XL, Theodoratou E, Liu L, Chan KY, Hipgrave D, Scherpbier R, et al. Social, economic, political and health system and program determinants of child mortality reduction in China between 1990 and 2006: A systematic analysis. J Glob Health 2012; 2:010405.
7. Chan KY, Yu X-W, Lu J-P, Demaio AR, Bowman K, Theodoratou E. Causes of accidental childhood deaths in China in 2010: A systematic review and analysis. J Glob Health 2015; 5:010412.
8. Chan KY, Wang W, Wu JJ, Liu L, Theodoratou E, Car J, et al.; Global Health Epidemiology Reference Group (GHERG). Epidemiology of Alzheimer's disease and other forms of dementia in China, 1990-2010: a systematic review and analysis. Lancet 2013; 381:2016-2023.
9. Chan KY, Zhao FF, Meng S, Demaio AR, Reed C, Theodoratou E, et al. Urbanization and the prevalence of schizophrenia in China between 1990 and 2010. World Psychiatry 2015; 14:251-252.
10. George-Carey R, Adeloye D, Chan KY, Paul A, Kolčić I, Campbell H, et al. An estimate of the prevalence of dementia in Africa: A systematic analysis. J Glob Health 2012; 2:020401.
11. Adeloye D, Basquill C, Papana A, Chan KY, Rudan I, Campbell H. An estimate of the prevalence of COPD in Africa: a systematic analysis. COPD 2015; 12:71-81.
12. Paul A, Adeloye D, George-Carey R, Kolčić I, Grant L, Chan KY. An estimate of the prevalence of epilepsy in Sub-Saharan Africa: A systematic analysis. J Glob Health 2012; 2:020405.
13. Dowman B, Campbell RM, Zgaga L, Adeloye D, Chan KY. Estimating the burden of rheumatoid arthritis in Africa: A systematic analysis. J Glob Health 2012; 2:020406.
14. Cheema A, Adeloye D, Sidhu S, Sridhar D, Chan KY. Urbanization and prevalence of type 2 diabetes in Southern Asia: A systematic analysis. J Glob Health 2014; 4:010404.
15. Rudan I, Sidhu S, Papana A, Meng SJ, Xin-Wei Y, Wang W, et al.; Global Health Epidemiology Reference Group (GHERG). Prevalence of rheumatoid arthritis in low and middle-income countries: A systematic review and analysis. J Glob Health 2015; 5:010409.
16. Walker CL, Rudan I, Liu L, Nair H, Theodoratou E, Bhutta ZA, et al. Global burden of childhood pneumonia and diarrhoea. Lancet 2013; 381:1405-1416.

17. Rudan I, O'Brien KL, Nair H, Liu L, Theodoratou E, Qazi S, et al; Child Health Epidemiology Reference Group (CHERG). Epidemiology and etiology of childhood pneumonia in 2010: estimates of incidence, severe morbidity, mortality, underlying risk factors and causative pathogens for 192 countries. J Glob Health 2013; 3:010401.

18. Fowkes FG, Rudan D, Rudan I, Aboyans V, Denenberg JO, McDermott MM, et al. Comparison of global estimates of prevalence and risk factors for peripheral artery disease in 2000 and 2010: a systematic review and analysis. Lancet 2013; 382:1329-1340.

19. Edmond K, Clark A, Korczak VS, Sanderson C, Griffiths UK, Rudan I. Global and regional risk of disabling sequelae from bacterial meningitis: a systematic review and meta-analysis. Lancet Infect Dis 2010; 10:317-328.

20. Nair H, Nokes DJ, Gessner BD, Dherani M, Madhi SA, Singleton RJ, et al. Global burden of acute lower respiratory infections due to respiratory syncytial virus in young children: a systematic review and meta-analysis. Lancet 2010; 375:1545-1555.

21. Nair H, Brooks WA, Katz M, Roca A, Berkley JA, Madhi SA, et al. Global burden of respiratory infections due to seasonal influenza in young children: a systematic review and meta-analysis. Lancet 2011; 378:1917-1930.

22. Nair H, Simões EA, Rudan I, Gessner BD, Azziz-Baumgartner E, Zhang JS, et al; Severe Acute Lower Respiratory Infections Working Group. Global and regional burden of hospital admissions for severe acute lower respiratory infections in young children in 2010: a systematic analysis. Lancet 2013; 381:1380-90.

CHAPTER 3.

Reducing mortality from childhood pneumonia and diarrhoea: The leading priority is also the greatest opportunity

Acute respiratory infections and diarrhoea have been the leading causes of global child mortality for many decades (1). Their relative importance in comparison to other causes of child deaths – e.g., malaria, preterm birth, birth asphyxia, accidents, neotanal infections, cancer and others – has become fully appreciated in 2003 through the work of the World Health Organization's and UNICEF's Child Health Epidemiology Reference Group (CHERG) (2). The *"Child Survival"* series, published by *The Lancet*, has been pivotal in raising awareness that the UN's Millennium Development Goal 4 cannot be achieved without increased focus on preventing and treating childhood infections – particularly pneumonia and diarrhoea – in low and middle-income countries (3). The next big step involved *"Global Action Plan for Pneumonia"* (GAPP), which summarized the evidence on the epidemiology of acute lower respiratory infections in children, the key etiological agents, the main determinants of the disease, the available and emerging solutions and the main obstacles to their implementation (4). GAPP's landmark publication in 2008 showed that there are about 156 million new cases of pneumonia each year, and that about one in ten results in a severe episode that requires hospitalization, and further 10% of severe episodes lead to deaths of affected children (5). The paper also proposed that Streptococcus pneumoniae (SP), Haemophilus influenzae type B (Hib), respiratory syncytial virus (RSV) and virus influenzae (flu) are the pathogens whose interplay is the most likely cause of the large majority of pneumonia deaths in children under five years of age (5). This led to increased attention to pneumonia prevention through available vaccines against PC, Hib and flu, instead of relying on treatments through community case management with antibiotics. The underdeveloped and weak health systems in low-resource settings, where most deaths occur, can not easily scale up antibiotic coverage to children who need them most, because of relatively low rates of access to health care (6). Another obstacle to progress is infrequent care-seeking among parents who did not receive adequate education on this important health issue (6).

Four papers that followed the GAPP initiative, all of them published by *The Lancet* journal, have estimated the global and regional burden of SP (7), Hib (8), RSV (9) and flu (10). In parallel to understanding the burden of specific pathogens, new financial mechanisms have been developed – such as *"advance market commitment"* (AMC) – to reduce the prices of available vaccines and deliver them in low and middle income countries, where they would otherwise remain unaffordable to local governments (11). Global Alliance for Vaccines and Immunization (now called GAVI Alliance) has been set up to raise funding to purchase these vaccines, and major contributions were seen from the Bill and Melinda Gates Foundation, who stood firmly behind the initiative to vaccinate children and prevent respiratory infections (12). Those efforts ensured that most children in low-resource settings have received Hib vaccination by 2010, and pneumococcal vaccination is also being scaled up (13).

The similar effort for diarrhoea has been lagging behind until recently, when an international collaboration of researchers launched a *"Diarrhoea Global Action Plan"* (DGAP) (14). Under co-ordination of UNICEF, the World Health Organization, and USAID, the initiative has been merged with GAPP into *"GAPPD"* – *"Global Action Plan for Pneumonia and Diarrhoea"* (15). This was a welcome move, because many risk factors are shared between the two diseases, and many approaches to control them could be delivered in parallel through integrated management of childhood illness (IMCI). Communities of researchers and policy-makers who are focused on diarrhoea control have also recently acquired the first vaccine effective in preventing an appreciable portion of the burden – rotavirus vaccine (16). This vaccine will be added to GAVI portfolio to supplement PC and Hib vaccines for pneumonia (17).

The GAPPD group has recently been invited by *The Lancet* to write a series of papers that address the epidemiology of childhood diarrhoea and pneumonia, the available cost-effective interventions, country-specific challenges and bottlenecks, and suggest policies that could accelerate progress in reduction of global mortality from the two diseases (15,18,19). The series proposed that scaling up of existing highly cost-effective interventions could prevent 95% of diarrhoea deaths and 67% of pneumonia deaths in children younger than 5 years by the year 2025, if delivered at scale. The cost of such effort was estimated at about US$ 6.7 billion (15,18,19). These activities, along with increased political stability in many low and middle-income countries, their economic development, improved sanitation and access to care, progress in empowering and educating women in the society and strengthening health systems, could all contribute to very substantial reduction of the global burden of child mortality attributable to pneumonia and diarrhoea (18,20,21). We should, therefore, conclude that addressing childhood pneumonia and diarrhoea is not only the leading priority, but also possibly the greatest opportunity in global health today.

There is a growing consensus that an improved understanding of the size of the burden, the leading risk factors and the relative contribution of the leading etiological causes; the available vaccines and other cost-effective interventions, such as community case management with antibiotics, oral re-hydration sachets and zinc supplementation; and the momentum that many low and middle-income countries have gathered in improving their economic outlook, have all provided the international health community with an un-precedented opportunity to substantially reduce the mortality from childhood pneumonia globally over the period of the next decade (15).

To support those ongoing initiatives, several leading medical journals published special issues, or series of articles, focused on childhood diarrhoea and pneumonia (and child survival in general) in the first half of 2013. We already mentioned *The Lancet*'s four-paper series on childhood diarrhoea, which is likely to have very large impact on the field (15,18,19). *PLoS Medicine* published a theme issue on improving intervention delivery progress track-ing and information systems in low-resource settings that could guide policy decisions. *BMC Public Health* is expected to publish a series of reviews that will provide meta-analysis of the effectiveness of several key interventions, such as breastfeeding and vaccination, which should further strengthen Lives Saved Tool (LiST) (22).

Acknowledgement: Originally published as: Igor Rudan, Harish Nair, Ana Marušić and Harry Campbell: Reducing mortality from childhood pneumonia and diarrhoea: The lead-ing priority is also the greatest opportunity. Reprinted with permission from Edinburgh University Global Health Society under Creative Commons Attribution License (Journal of Global Health 2013; 3:010101).

References

1. Rudan I, Theodoratou E, Zgaga L, Nair H, Chan KY, Tomlinson M, et al. Setting priorities for development of emerging interventions against childhood pneumonia, meningitis and influenza. J Glob Health 2012; 2:010304.
2. Black RE, Morris SS, Bryce J. Where and why are 10 million children dying every year? Lancet 2003; 361: 2226-2234.
3. Rudan I, Tomaskovic L, Boschi-Pinto C, Campbell H; WHO Child Health Epidemiol-ogy Reference Group. Global estimate of the incidence of clinical pneumonia among children under five years of age. Bull World Health Organ 2004; 82:895-903.
4. Greenwood B. A global action plan for the prevention and control of pneumonia. Bull World Health Organ 2008; 86:322-2A.
5. Rudan I, Boschi-Pinto C, Biloglav Z, Mulholland K, Campbell H. Epidemiology and etiology of childhood pneumonia. Bull World Health Organ 2008; 86:408-416.

6. Rudan I, El Arifeen S, Bhutta ZA, Black RE, Brooks A, Chan KY, et al.; WHO/CHNRI Expert Group on Childhood Pneumonia. Setting research priorities to reduce global mortality from childhood pneumonia by 2015. PLoS Med 2011; 8:e1001099.

7. O'Brien KL, Wolfson LJ, Watt JP, Henkle E, Deloria-Knoll M, McCall N; Hib and Pneumococcal Global Burden of Disease Study Team. Burden of disease caused by Streptococcus pneumoniae in children younger than 5 years: global estimates. Lancet 2009; 374:893-902.

8. Watt JP, Wolfson LJ, O'Brien KL, Henkle E, Deloria-Knoll M, McCall N, et al.; Hib and Pneumococcal Global Burden of Disease Study Team. Burden of disease caused by Haemophilus influenzae type b in children younger than 5 years: global estimates. Lancet 2009; 374:903-911.

9. Nair H, Nokes DJ, Gessner BD, Dherani M, Madhi SA, Singleton RJ, et al. Global burden of acute lower respiratory infections due to respiratory syncytial virus in young children: a systematic review and meta-analysis. Lancet 2010; 375:1545-1555.

10. Nair H, Brooks WA, Katz M, Roca A, Berkley JA, Madhi SA, et al. Global burden of respiratory infections due to seasonal influenza in young children: a systematic review and meta-analysis. Lancet 2011; 378:1917-1930.

11. Cernuschi T, Furrer E, Schwalbe N, Jones A, Berndt ER, McAdams S. Advance market commitment for pneumococcal vaccines: putting theory into practice. Bull World Health Organ 2011; 89:913-918.

12. Nossal GJ. Gates, GAVI, the glorious global funds and more: all you ever wanted to know. Immunol Cell Biol 2003; 81:20-22.

13. Countdown Coverage Writing Group; Countdown to 2015 Core Group, Bryce J, Daelmans B, Dwivedi A, Fauveau V, Lawn JE, Mason E, et al. Countdown to 2015 for maternal, newborn, and child survival: the 2008 report on tracking coverage of interventions. Lancet 2008; 371:1247-1258.

14. Zipursky A, Wazny K, Black RE, Keenan W, Duggan C, Olness K, et al. Global action plan for childhood diarrhea: developing research priorities. J Glob Health 2013; 3: 010406.

15. Chopra M, Mason E, Borrazzo J, Campbell H, Rudan I, Liu L, Black RE, Bhutta ZA. Ending of preventable deaths from pneumonia and diarrhoea: an achievable goal. Lancet 2013; 381:1499-1506.

16. Madhi SA, Cunliffe NA, Steele D, Witte D, Kirsten M, Louw C, et al. Effect of human rotavirus vaccine on severe diarrhea in African infants. N Engl J Med 2010; 362:289-298.

17. Bhan A, Green SK. Balancing safety, efficacy and cost: Improving rotavirus vaccine adoption in low and middle-income countries. J Glob Health 2011; 1:148-153.

18. Fischer Walker CL, Rudan I, Liu L, Nair H, Theodoratou E, Bhutta ZA, O'Brien KL, Campbell H, Black RE. Global burden of childhood diarrhoea and pneumonia. Lancet 2013; 381:1405-1416.

19. Bhutta ZA, Das JK, Walker N, Rizvi A, Campbell H, Rudan I, et al. Interventions to address deaths from childhood diarrhoea and pneumonia equitably: what works and at what cost? Lancet 2013; 381:1417-1429.

20. Feng XL, Theodoratou E, Liu L, Chan KY, Hipgrave D, Scherpbier R, et al. Social, economic, political and health system and program determinants of child mortality reduction in China between 1990 and 2006: A systematic analysis. J Glob Health 2012; 2:010405.

21.   Liu L, Johnson HL, Cousens S, Perin J, Scott S, Lawn JE, et al.; Child Health Epidemiology Reference Group of WHO and UNICEF. Global, regional, and national causes of
child mortality: an updated systematic analysis for 2010 with time trends since 2000.
Lancet 2012; 379:2151-2161.
22.   Fischer Walker CL, Friberg IK, Binkin N, Young M, Walker N, Fontaine O, et al. Scaling up diarrhea prevention and treatment interventions: a Lives Saved Tool analysis.
PLoS Med 2011; 8:e1000428.

CHAPTER 4.

Reducing the burden of maternal and neonatal infections in low income settings

Millennium Development Goals 4 and 5 require a substantial reduction in child and maternal mortality, respectively, between 1990 and 2015 (1). Infectious diseases are still the major cause of mortality in both population groups. Maternal and neonatal infections remain responsible for more than 1 million deaths each year (2-6), i.e. between 10-15% of all maternal and child deaths globally. The large majority of these deaths occur in low-income settings, among mothers and children that do not have access to the (underdeveloped) health systems of their countries (2-5). Maternal deaths are clustered around labour, delivery and the immediate postpartum period. HIV/AIDS is a leading cause of death where HIV-related mortality rates are high, and a number of other infectious agents also play a significant role (3). Newborn infections can be divided into early (within the first week of life) and late infections (during weeks 2-4). The former are frequently related to labour and childbirth and are caused by an entirely different spectrum of pathogens than the late neonatal infections (7-9).

Current approaches to prevention, early diagnosis and appropriate management of maternal and neonatal infections globally are limited by difficulties in developing vaccines against the leading prevalent pathogens, or alternatively diagnosing them accurately and managing them appropriately in low-resource settings (4-9). Implementation of existing diagnostic tests and treatments from industrialized countries is challenging in low-resource settings due to their high cost, complexity, infrastructure requirements, inadequately trained end users, low acceptability among health personnel, affected mothers and newborns' parents, risk of obtaining blood samples for diagnostic testing in unhygienic settings and lack of appropriate quality control measures (5-7).

The information on causal infectious agents in low income settings is available mainly from hospital-based studies, which are not always representative of hospital care at a national level, and may also have limited relevance to settings where most children are born at home (6-8). It is likely that the etiological spectrum also varies significantly across geographic regions (7-9). However, the information on geographic differences in low-income countries is at present very limited. Maternal infections can be caused by a number of bacterial, viral and parasitic agents (2). In neonates, the available data indicate that Gram-negative rods are the major cause in early neonates (the first week of life), where they may cause up to three in every four infections (7,8). *Klebsiella spp.*, *Staphylococcus aureus*, *Escherichia coli* and *group B Streptococci* are thought to be the leading causes in the early neonatal period, when most of the deaths occur (7,8). Many of those infections may be environmentally acquired because of unhygienic delivery practices in resource-poor settings rather than being passed on by mothers, which may also explain the predominance of Gram-negative infections among home-born infants (7,8). Their importance decreases in the late neonatal and post-neonatal periods when Gram-positive cocci (primarily *Streptococcus*) cause about 2 in every 3 infections (6-9).

Several studies in resource-poor settings have investigated the effectiveness of interventions to prevent and treat maternal and neonatal infections at both community and facility level. It has been reported that skin application of sunflower seed oil provides cheap, safe and effective protection against nosocomial infections in hospitalized preterm neonates and infants (10). Once the infection has developed, the standard treatment approach is oral (for mothers) or parenteral (for newborns) antibiotic treatment. However, a number of very complex and context-specific issues must be considered when selecting the appropriate antimicrobial regimens in the resource-poor settings where most deaths occur. The challenge is to choose a regimen that is effective against the causative pathogen yet affordable in that context, safe for the mothers, foetuses and newborns, and feasible to deliver reliably in the hospital or community setting, as appropriate (11).

Parenteral (intramuscular) regimens for newborns that are currently recommended by the World Health Organization and national paediatric associations comprise a combination of procaine penicillin G (or ampicillin) and gentamicin, or third generation cephalosporins given alone, which are safe and retain efficacy when administered at extended intervals (11). Attempts to estimate the effect of antibiotic use on the reduction of maternal and neonatal mortality in community settings in low income countries have encountered large methodological limitations, but have concluded that all available data suggest a substantial benefit associated with these case management approaches (12). However, recent reports based on hospital-based data suggest alarming rates of laboratory antimicrobial resistance to ampicillin and gentamicin, the first-line antimicrobial agents recommended for the treatment of serious infections in young infants. Significant in-vitro resistance to cotrimoxazole among all the major pathogens and to gentamicin and third generation cephalosporins among *Klebsiella spp.* and emerging resistance in E. coli are a cause for increasing concern (13).

The strategy promoted by the GAVI Alliance is to save children's lives and protect their health by increasing access to immunisation in the world's poorest countries, particularly through acceleration of the uptake and use of underused and new vaccines (14). The successful outcome of this approach is less sensitive to obstacles in accessing health care system throughout the childhood than some other proposed approaches, so it is continuously gaining support and improving child health worldwide. Passive transfer of antibodies from the mother coupled with the immature immune system of neonates acts to reduce the effectiveness of a vaccination strategy in this age period, although this is not true in all cases (e.g., maternal tetanus and influenza immunization). Prevention of microbial infection is a priority, because globally, a majority of neonates still die at home, and many of the deaths are thought to be due to infection (2). Maternal immunization probably offers the most promising means of achieving this objective in the longer term. However, vaccines against key pathogens involved in neonatal sepsis are still a long way from final phases of product development and licensing (15,16). It is likely that improving the diagnosis and treatment of neonatal infections will be a central approach to reducing deaths from neonatal infections in the medium term. Therefore, the slow and difficult route through improving local health systems and attention to specific contexts will be required to tackle neonatal infections globally (15,16).

Implementation of existing diagnostic tests and treatments from industrialized countries is challenging in low-resource settings due to their high cost, complexity, infrastructure requirements, inadequately trained end users, low acceptability among health personnel, affected mothers and newborns' parents, risks associated with obtaining blood samples for diagnostic testing in unhygienic settings, and lack of quality control. We propose that short-term priorities should focus on promotion of cost-effective home-based care practices to prevent maternal and newborn infections, with increased coverage and improved quality of maternal and neonatal care. Longer-term strategic priorities will ultimately need to focus on the development of vaccines and point-of-care diagnostic tests for maternal and neonatal infections. Diagnostic tests should help establish the aetiological diagnosis and inform treatment decisions. They will also need to be deliverable, affordable, sustainable and acceptable in low-resource settings. Cost-effectiveness of maternal immunization in protection of neonates will also need to be established (15,16).

The latter strategy may have different stages. In an earlier stage, tests that could separate viral and bacterial infections, and identify children who need treatment, could be considered a priority for development and implementation. In the longer term, tests that could identify a specific causal pathogen and predict antibiotic resistance may become a focus of interest. The development of such tests should maximize the effectiveness of the chosen treatment, whilst minimizing the emerging problem of antibiotic resistance. Biomarkers are very rarely used in low resource settings, because most of the cases and deaths occur at home and medical laboratories do not even have the most basic facility for blood culture. At this point there is no specific guideline for the use of biomarkers for maternal or neonatal infections. Even if they became available in high-income countries, the biomarkers will not be easily transferable to low resource settings due their high cost and complexity. A new generation of diagnostic tests will be needed at the point-of-care in low resource settings to diagnose neonatal infections, identify responsible pathogens, guide the choice of an appropriate treatment regimen, monitor effectiveness of interventions and determine drug resistance. One of the anticipated uses of the test is also for identifying those neonates that are severely ill and need to be immediately referred to the hospital for intensive care treatment. But in spite of the severe shortage of effective new diagnostics suitable for low-resource settings, there are very few research initiatives to address this problem. This may be due in part to a scarcity of information on the potential health impact and performance of essential diagnostics, and to the low return on investment in diagnostics perceived by the industry (15,16).

Considerable uncertainty still surrounds our current understanding of the epidemiology, aetiology, and effectiveness of available interventions, investment priorities, appropriateness of health policies, and true potential of new preventive interventions and diagnostic tools to address the burden of maternal and neonatal infections globally (2-9). The potential health impact of new diagnostic tools for neonatal infections is uncertain and needs to be modelled based on available information.

Acknowledgement: Originally published as: Igor Rudan, Evropi Theodoratou, Harish Nair, Ana Marušić and Harry Campbell: Reducing the burden of maternal and neonatal infections in low income settings. Reprinted with permission from Edinburgh University Global Health Society under Creative Commons Attribution License (Journal of Global Health 2011; 1:106-109).

References

1. Millenium Development Goals. Millenium Development Goals for 2015. (Available from: http://milleniumdevelopmentgoals.org/; Accessed: 21 Oct 2011).
2. Ronsmans C, Graham WJ, Lancet Maternal Survival Series steering group. Maternal mortality: who, when, where, and why? Lancet 2006; 368:1189–1200.

3. Hill K, Thomas K, AbouZahr C, Walker N, Say L, Inoue M, et al. Estimates of maternal mortality worldwide between 1990 and 2005: an assessment of available data. Lancet 2007; 370:1311–1319.

4. Black RE, Cousens S, Johnson HL, Lawn JE, Rudan I, Bassani DG, et al. Global, regional, and national causes of child mortality in 2008: a systematic analysis. Lancet 2010; 375:1969–1987.

5. Lawn JE, Cousens S, Zupan J, Lancet Neonatal Survival Steering Team. 4 million neonatal deaths: When? Where? Why? Lancet 2005; 365:891–900.

6. Lawn JE, Wilczynska-Ketende K, Cousens SN. Estimating the causes of 4 million neonatal deaths in the year 2000. Int J Epidemiol 2006; 35:706–718.

7. Thaver D, Zaidi AK. Burden of neonatal infections in developing countries: a review of evidence from community-based studies. Pediatr Infect Dis J 2009; 28(1 Suppl):S3–S9.

8. Zaidi AK, Thaver D, Ali SA, Khan TA. Pathogens associated with sepsis in newborns and young infants in developing countries. Pediatr Infect Dis J 2009; 28(1 Suppl):S10–S18.

9. Zaidi AK, Huskins WC, Thaver D, Bhutta ZA, Abbas Z, Goldmann DA. Hospital-acquired neonatal infections in developing countries. Lancet 2005; 365:1175–1188.

10. Darmstadt GL, Saha SK, Ahmed AS, Chowdhury MA, Law PA, Ahmed S, et al. Effect of topical treatment with skin barrier-enhancing emollients on nosocomial infections in preterm infants in Bangladesh: a randomised controlled trial. Lancet 2005; 365:1039–1045.

11. Darmstadt GL, Batra M, Zaidi AK. Parenteral antibiotics for the treatment of serious neonatal bacterial infections in developing country settings. Pediatr Infect Dis J 2009; 28(1 Suppl):S37–S42.

12. Bhutta ZA, Zaidi AK, Thaver D, Humayun Q, Ali S, Darmstadt GL. Management of newborn infections in primary care settings: a review of the evidence and implications for policy? Pediatr Infect Dis J 2009; 28(1 Suppl):S22–S30.

13. Thaver D, Ali SA, Zaidi AK. Antimicrobial resistance among neonatal pathogens in developing countries. Pediatr Infect Dis J 2009; 28(1 Suppl):S19–S21.

14. GAVI Alliance: GAVI's strategy. (Available from: http://www.gavialliance.org/about/strategy; Accessed: 21 Oct 2011).

15. Bahl R, Martines J, Ali N, Bhan MK, Carlo W, Chan KY, et al. Research priorities to reduce global mortality from newborn infections by 2015. Pediatr Infect Dis J 2009; 28(1 Suppl):S43–S48.

16. Lawn JE, Rudan I, Rubens C. Four million newborn deaths: is the global research agenda evidence-based? Early Hum Dev 2008; 84:809–814.

CHAPTER 5.

The deadly toll of *S. pneumoniae* and *H. influenzae* type b

Before 2000, the world of global child health was a very different place than it is today. The links between health information from the field in low-income countries and global child-health policies were weak (1). The agenda was driven by panels of experts with decisive influence on donors and policy makers, but there was little consensus among them on key issues (2). Over the years, this reliance on expert opinion has led to snowballing support for some issues over others and striking inequities between investments in research and development across different diseases (3). The legacy of relying on expert opinion rather than a critical review of the evidence has recently been exposed. In 2007, HIV/AIDS, malaria, and tuberculosis—diseases for which advocacy has been more successful—have each received between ten and 50 times more research and development funding for a given global disease burden than for bacterial pneumonia, meningitis, or diarrhoea—diseases that have attracted less international attention and support (4).

But Katherine O'Brien (5), James Watt (6) and their colleagues recently revealed for the first time that *Streptococcus pneumoniae* (pneumococcus) and *Haemophilus influenzae* type b (Hib)—the pathogens responsible for most child deaths from bacterial pneumonia and meningitis—are directly responsible for just as many child deaths as HIV/AIDS, malaria, and tuberculosis combined. This finding is shocking because vaccines against both pathogens are readily available and have been consistently safe and effective in trials in developing countries (7).

Since 2000, the link between evidence and global child-health policies has been steadily improving. First, the UN has set an overarching goal (Millennium Development Goal 4 (MDG 4)), which called on all stakeholders to reduce global child mortality by two-thirds between 1990 and 2015 (8). This noble aim has gained widespread support among key stakeholders—national governments, donors, and researchers alike. It helped to focus efforts and investments related to child survival and to garner political support. It also created a pressure for the available health information from developing countries to be critically evaluated and then used for policy development to promote progress towards achievement of MDG 4.

Several important initiatives were supported in parallel to improve the link between health information and investment policies – e.g., Global Burden of Disease (GBD) work, Health Metrics Network (HMN), Demographic Health Surveys (DHS), and others. An independent group of technical experts—the Child Health Epidemiology Reference Group (CHERG)—was sponsored by the Bill & Melinda Gates Foundation, WHO, and later UNICEF to define the key causes of child deaths with use of the best available evidence from low-income countries (9). The Lancet has played a key role in providing a high-profile platform for CHERG's results, which ensured that the evidence from developing countries reached wide audiences and influenced policy makers. Since 2003, the partnership between CHERG and The Lancet had a major effect in promoting an evidence-based approach that identifies the real priorities in global child health. It has highlighted the relatively neglected conditions, pneumonia and diarrhoea, as the major causes of child death and has also drawn attention to the importance of neonatal deaths (9). The leaders of G8 countries have just recognised and committed support to these efforts in a recent declaration (10).

O'Brien, Watt, and colleagues delivered the first global estimates of morbidity and mortality from diseases caused by the *S. pneumoniae* and *H. influenzae type b* in children aged 1 month to 5 years. These studies showed that pneumococcus (causing pneumonia, meningitis, and sepsis) is the leading bacterial cause of death in young children worldwide. An estimated 14.5 million episodes of serious pneumococcal disease occurred in 2000 in children aged 1–59 months and caused 826,000 deaths (uncertainty range: 582,000–926,000). Additionally, Hib caused 8.13 million serious illnesses and 371,000 deaths (247,000–527,000). 91,000 deaths due to pneumococcus and 8,100 deaths due to Hib occurred in HIV-positive children.

To produce these estimates at the global and national level, a partnership between PneumoADIP and the Hib Initiative (of the GAVI Alliance) and WHO was formed. A systematic review identified and critically reviewed over 15,000 articles in many languages. Although the final estimates are based on a disappointingly small evidence base, this exercise was thorough and the estimates can be considered the most authoritative available.

Nevertheless, several important areas of uncertainty remain. There are several countries with very large child populations but with very few country-specific data. The pneumococcal-specific and Hib-specific pneumonia incidence and mortality estimates are indirect and based on inferences from only a few vaccine-probe studies and published estimates of overall pneumonia mortality (themselves based on limited data). The varying approaches to the estimation of pneumonia, meningitis, and invasive disease make comparability of estimates across syndromes problematic (11). And these estimates do not take into account the disease burden in the neonatal period or important interactions with other key pathogens in causing child deaths (12).

Effective pneumococcal and Hib vaccines exist and can be successfully integrated into national immunisation programmes (7,13). Today's new estimates suggest that achieving high coverage with these vaccines could prevent a substantial proportion of child mortality globally. Current immunisation coverage with these vaccines is a striking example of global inequity: children in countries that do not yet use the vaccines have about a 40-fold greater risk of dying from pneumococcus or Hib than children in countries that include them in their routine immunisation programmes (14). The two studies by O'Brien et al. and Watt et al. (5,6) are an important international health-policy contribution to strengthen the case for action to counter this shameful inequity.

Acknowledgement: Originally published as: Igor Rudan and Harry Campbell: The deadly toll of S. pneumoniae and H. influenzae type b. Reprinted with permission from Elsevier (Lancet 2009; 374:854-856).

References

1. Rudan I, Lawn J, Cousens S, et al. Gaps in policy-relevant information on burden of disease in children: a systematic review. Lancet 2005; 365:2031–2040.
2. Rudan I, El Arifeen S, Black RE, Campbell H. Childhood pneumonia and diarrhoea: setting our priorities right. Lancet Infect Dis 2007; 7:56–61.
3. Enserink M. Some neglected diseases are more neglected than others. Science 2009; 323:700.
4. Moran M, Guzman J, Ropars A-L, et al. Neglected disease research and development: how much are we really spending? PLoS Med 2009; 6:e30.
5. O'Brien KL, Wolfson LJ, Watt JP, et al, for the Hib and Pneumococcal Global Burden of Disease Study Team. Burden of disease caused by Streptococcus pneumoniae in children younger than 5 years: global estimates. Lancet 2009; 374:893–902.
6. Watt JP, Wolfson LJ, O'Brien KL, et al, for the Hib and Pneumococcal Global Burden of Disease Study Team. Burden of disease caused by Haemophilus influenzae type b in children younger than 5 years: global estimates. Lancet 2009; 374:903–911.
7. Madhi SA, Levine OS, Hajjeh R, Mansoor OD, Cherian T. Vaccines to prevent pneumonia and improve child survival. Bull World Health Organ 2008; 86:365–372.
8. Murray CJ, Laakso T, Shibuya K, Hill K, Lopez AD. Can we achieve Millennium Development Goal 4? New analysis of country trends and forecasts of under-5 mortality to 2015. Lancet 2007; 370:1040–1054.
9. Bryce J, Boschi-Pinto C, Shibuya K, Black RE, WHO Child Health Epidemiology Reference Group. WHO estimates of the causes of death in children. Lancet 2005; 365:1147–1152.
10. G8 Leaders Declaration. Responsible leadership for a sustainable future. July 8, 2009. (Available from: http://www.g8italia2009.it/static/G8_Allegato/G8_ Declaration_08_07_09_final,0.pdf; Accessed: 15 Jul 2009).

11. Lanata CF, Rudan I, Boschi-Pinto C, et al. Methodological and quality issues in epidemiological studies of acute lower respiratory infections in children in developing countries. Int J Epidemiol 2004; 33:1362–1372.
12. Bahl R, Martines J, Ali N, et al. Research priorities to reduce global mortality from newborn infections by 2015. Pediatr Inf Dis J 2009; 28(suppl 1):S43–48.
13. Simoes EAF, Cherian T, Chow J, et al. Acute respiratory infections in children. 2006. (Available from: http://files.dcp2.org/pdf/DCP/DCP25.pdf; Accessed: 15 Jul 2009).
14. Bryce J, Terreri N, Victora CG, et al. Countdown to 2015: tracking intervention coverage for child survival. Lancet 2006; 368:1067–1076.

CHAPTER 6.

How big is the "next big thing"? Estimating the burden of non-communicable diseases in low and middle-income countries

Over the past year the pandemic of non–communicable diseases (NCDs) has become a key focus of the global political agenda. At the United Nations' high–level meeting on the prevention and control of NCDs in September 2011, a general consensus has been reached that NCDs were already the leading causes of death in all world regions and that their burden is increasing rapidly (1). The rate of this increase is particularly striking in low– and middle–income countries (LMICs), where life expectancy is increasing as a result of improved socio–economic conditions (2). It is expected that by the year 2030, NCDs could become responsible for 52 million deaths (3). In LMICs, health systems will face considerable challenge in adjusting to the rapidly growing demand for services, and this could in turn become an additional significant barrier to achieving the Millennium Development Goals (2). As a result of this evidence, many parallel advocacy efforts for tackling NCDs are taking place, with a particular focus on heart disease, cancer, respiratory diseases, diabetes and stroke (4). A number of interventions have been outlined that could have immediate preventive effect and slow down the pandemic, such as tobacco control, improved diet, exercise and decreased alcohol intake (4).

The release of the new global burden of disease (GBD) estimates, by the Institute for Health Metrics and Evaluation (IHME) at the University of Washington in Seattle, is anticipated with great interest (5). The new revision is expected to show substantial progress in the reduction of maternal and child mortality in the LMICs over the past two decades. However, many fear that there will be hardly any measurable progress in improving health and survival of adult populations in those countries. The UN conference in 2011 and the publication of the new GBD estimates could therefore mark the beginning of the era in which non–communicable causes of death and disability will dominate global health agenda for the foreseeable future. The progress in addressing their burden and achieving measurable reduction in LMICs will likely require similar steps that were effective in reducing maternal and child mortality globally: (i) defining the size of the burden and the main causes responsible for the majority of this burden; (ii) understanding the most important risk factors and their importance in different contexts; (iii) systematically assessing the effectiveness and cost of the interventions that are feasible and available within the contexts of different LMICs; and (iv) formulating evidence–based health policies that will define appropriate health care priorities and health research priorities to tackle the burden in the most cost–effective way.

The first step in this process is to measure the burden of NCDs in LMICs. This is a challenging task given the scarcity of available data, inconsistency in case definitions of the measured diseases, differences in reporting of the results (e.g. age groups) used by different investigators, lack of funding, research infrastructure and capacity for community–based studies in LMICs, changing definitions of diseases over time, low trans–cultural adaptability of screening instruments, and many others (6-8). Methodological approaches that could take into account all this diversity and scarcity in the available information and produce acceptable regional estimates using transparent and sound methodological approaches are urgently needed. Furthermore, the international research community could benefit from clear guidelines on conducting epidemiological studies in LMICs that could inform burden of disease analyses, so that their results are comparable and lead to more reliable estimates.

Future estimation of the burden of non-communicable diseases in low and middle-income countries will inevitably need to focus on prevalence, rather than incidence and/or mortality. Given that most NCDs are chronic conditions, the key question for both national governments and pharmaceutical industry will be the how many people are suffering from NCDs on a daily basis and require health services and specific treatments. Health systems in LMICs were not developed to provide care for chronic, long-term conditions, but rather for acute threats from infectious diseases. With growing life expectancy in many developing regions of the world, the prevalence of NCDs is expected to grow rather dramatically in very large populations, with health systems being unprepared for dealing with this burden and health workforce not being properly trained. This could lead to the problem of such magnitude, that it could seriously interfere with the current economic growth in many of the LMICs over time, with China and India being prime examples. A rethink will be needed on the strategies to control the NCD pandemic in many regions, with efforts placed on prevention and early diagnosis, rather than treatment at secondary or tertiary-level facilities.

Focus on mortality from NCDs will not be nearly as helpful to policymakers as the focus on prevalence. This is because many people will suffer from multiple NCDs for a long time, burdening health systems and requiring effective treatments, but their causes of death may eventually be a sudden manifestation of a previously unregistered problem, such as stroke, traffic accident or high-lethality cancer. Focus on incidence in addition to prevalence would be useful, though, in light of many dramatic changes in risk factor profile across LMICs. Incidence studies of NCDs in LMICs could provide valuable insights and confirmation of the role of risk factors which were characterised in high-income countries in relation to NCDs during the 20th century and further refine our understanding of the role of different genetic backgrounds, environments and lifestyles. However, we see the most important forthcoming task in assessing the point prevalence and lifetime prevalence for most NCDs in LMICs, as many gaps presently exist and good-quality primary studies are much needed and should be encouraged.

Acknowledgement: *Originally published as: Kit Yee Chan, Davies Adeloye, Liz Grant, Ivana Kolčić and Ana Marušić: How big is the "next big thing"? Estimating the burden of non-communicable diseases in low and middle-income countries. The original article was reviewed and modified by Igor Rudan with permission from the authors. Reprinted with permission from Edinburgh University Global Health Society under Creative Commons Attribution License (Journal of Global Health 2012; 2:020101).*

References

1. World Health Organization. UN High-level Meeting on NCDs: Summary report of the discussions at the round tables. Geneva: WHO, 2011. (Available from: http://www.who.int/nmh/events/moscow_ncds_2011/round_tables_summary.pdf; Accessed: 8 Dec 2012).
2. Alwan A, MacLean DR, Riley LM, d'Espaignet ET, Mathers CD, Stevens GA, et al. Monitoring and surveillance of chronic non-communicable diseases: progress and capacity in high-burden countries. Lancet. 2010; 376:1861-1868.
3. United Nations. Prevention and control of non-communicable diseases: Report of the Secretary-General- A/66/83. New York: UN, 2011. (Available from: http://www.un.org/ga/search/view_doc.asp?symbol=A/66/83&referer=/english/&Lang=E; Accessed: 8 Feb 2012).
4. Beaglehole R, Bonita R, Horton R, Adams C, Alleyne G, Asaria P, et al. Priority actions for the non-communicable disease crisis. Lancet. 2011; 377:1438-1447.
5. Murray CJL, Lopez AD. Evidence-based health policy: Lessons from the Global Burden of Disease study. Science. 1996; 274:740-743.
6. Boutayeb A, Boutayeb S. The burden of non-communicable diseases in developing countries. Int J Equity Health. 2005; 4:2.
7. Raban MZ, Dandona R, Dandona L. Availability of data for monitoring non-communicable disease risk factors in India. Bull World Health Organ. 2012; 90:20-29.
8. World Health Organization. Global status report on non-communicable diseases 2010. Geneva: WHO, 2011. (Available from: http://www.who.int/nmh/publications/ncd_report_full_en.pdf; Accessed: 8 Dec 2012).

CHAPTER 7.

Developing biobanks
in developing countries

The sequencing of the human genome, completed and reported a decade ago, increased the potential of what could be described as a *"data-driven"* or *"hypothesis-free"* approach to biomedical research (1,2). The rise of powerful new technologies for high-throughput analysis of human genetic material resulted in an avalanche of genome-wide association studies (GWAS), which currently contribute to an unprecedented progress in assigning *"biomedical"* functions to human genes (3). With massively increased capacity for studying human genetic material, which grew by several orders of magnitude over the past decade, while falling dramatically in price (4,5), we can now measure human genetic make-up more precisely than other human traits or environmental exposures that were traditionally studied in biomedical research – such as dietary habits, blood pressure or biochemical studies of the levels of proteins in the blood (4). Thus far, companies such as *Illumina* and *Affymetrix* have managed to provide tools in a form of chip-based technology, which are helping to understand common human genetic variation. Soon it will be possible to sequence the entire human genome, letter-by-letter, at a price under US$ 5000, and the key limit to further biomedical discoveries may be imposed by the limited capacity of contemporary computers to handle this massive amount of information (5).

In addition to this progress, great advances were made in the high-throughput analysis of so-called "*-omics*" traits – thousands of circulating molecules and metabolites that were jointly named the *"metabolome"*, *"proteome"*, *"lipidome"*, or *"glycome"* (6-8). An explosion of information that can now be collected and analysed for each individual led to the development of large *"human biobanks"*, the largest of which are catalogued by the Public Population Project in Genomics (or P3G) (9). These are repositories of human DNA material and plasma samples collected from large number of individuals and stored anonymously along with other information on their lifestyle, diet, anthropometric and physiological measurements, genealogies and psychological well-being. These biobanks all have several things in common. Firstly, they share the principle of adherence to rigorous ethical principles for recruiting participants and for using and handling the collected information. Secondly, they are very large and store information on many (tens of) thousands of individuals. Thirdly, they provide researchers with an opportunity to maximise the research and clinical and public health translation potential from the new high-throughput research technologies, which require such biobanks to generate important new health knowledge.

Biomedical research that relies on the application of high-throughput technologies in human biobanks can be described as *"data driven"*, *"hypothesis-free"* science. Traditionally, the advancement of science relied on the accumulated, existing knowledge, which was then used by the researchers to generate and test further hypotheses, thus advancing their field further. This alternate paradigm of biomedical research that relies on human biobanks is not dependent on *"a priori"* hypotheses, because it can simply apply rigorous statistical methods to search for apparent associations between thousands or millions of variables that were measured simultaneously in a very large sample of participants, using exceptionally precise (and increasingly inexpensive) measurement tools, while correcting for and discarding false positive results expected due to multiple testing (10).

What is so appealing about this *"hypothesis-free science"*? Firstly, it is virtually free of human bias, opinion, or imbalanced interpretation. It is typically based on extremely accurate measurements, often using very large sample sizes generated through international collaboration of many centres that applied the same measurement methods and a common analysis plan, so that the results are directly comparable, relatively free from bias and confounding and not subject to sampling variations due to small sample sizes. Many recent successes of this *"hypothesis free"* approach have also exposed that the science of the 20th century – where many small research groups were working in isolation from each other, using small sample sizes and publishing their results independently of each other – was much more likely to report false positive results (11). It was quite an embarrassment to the field to realize that the vast majority (more than 95%) of the reported results on associations between genes and human traits and diseases in the period before 2007, when the rise of genome-wide association studies begun, were not replicable in much larger and better designed studies (11). Secondly, and equally importantly – *"hypothesis-free"* studies do not depend on previous knowledge, thus allowing large leaps forward in scientific discovery, and unexpected and exciting new breakthroughs in understanding (12). However, there is still an important place for hypothesis-driven experiments in following up these findings to understand their full significance in terms of improved knowledge of underlying patho-physiological mechanisms or their health impact if translated into clinical guidelines or public health action.

However, the current state of *"hypothesis-free"* science that relies on human biobanks is not free from concern. A quick look at the biobanks listed in the P3G observatory shows that nearly all of them have been developed to address the health problems relevant to the minority of people living in wealthy countries, mostly the complex chronic non-communicable diseases of late onset. This reflects the disease burden in these countries and also the potential for research commercialization to address these problems. Ten years after the human genome has been sequenced there are still hardly any biobanks in low and middle-income countries. Even among those that exist, only a few seem to address the problems of the poor, which contribute to the majority of global burden of disease. A recent study showed that that nearly all the progress made by the powerful new high-throughput research technologies was currently confined to wealthy countries and their health needs (13).

The human genome has been shaped through continuing struggle of humanity to survive among many other species and in challenging environmental conditions. The strongest effect of human genes should therefore be expected to ensure successful conception and intrauterine growth and development, safe and full-term delivery and resistance to infectious diseases of childhood and early adulthood. These were historically the main selective pressures that could significantly shape the human genome. They are also still the main contributors to the burden of disease in many developing countries today, but they have not yet been the main focus of interest of human biobanks. The diseases that are currently being studied by the wealthy nations would have been almost entirely *"invisible"* to selection pressures. This may be one of the reasons why the results of genome-wide association studies have not yet found strong genetic effects that could be easily translatable into clinical practice and commercialized (14). Because of this, some opinion leaders are beginning to question this approach (14,15).

We believe that research into health problems of low-income countries and the poor may be a better-placed endeavour for human biobanks, and it may result in more obvious successes. Some experts have already proposed this, too, based on other considerations, such as needs, feasibility and equity (16-18). We call for the development of human biobanks in developing countries, and praise several examples from low-income countries which are already building their own biobanks (19,20). However, this will require strengthening of the research capacity in many low-income countries to enable them to use the new technologies. It will also require a shift in research investment priorities in order to reduce the inequity in international research that currently exists. Finally, a responsible approach from low-income countries to ethical issues will be another pre-requisite to the success of the *"hypothesis-free"* research that will target the needs of the world's poor.

Acknowledgement: *Originally published as: Igor Rudan, Ana Marušić and Harry Campbell: Developing biobanks in developing countries. Reprinted with permission from Edinburgh University Global Health Society under Creative Commons Attribution License (Journal of Global Health 2011; 1:2-4).*

References

1. Lander ES, Linton LM, Birren B, Nusbaum C, Zody MC, Baldwin J, Devon K, et al.; International Human Genome Sequencing Consortium. Initial sequencing and analysis of the human genome. Nature 2001; 409:860-921.
2. Venter JC, Adams MD, Myers EW, Li PW, Mural RJ, Sutton GG, Smith HO, et al. The sequence of the human genome. Science 2001; 291:1304-1351.
3. Singleton AB, Hardy J, Traynor BJ, Houlden H. Towards a complete resolution of the genetic architecture of disease. Trends Genet 2010; 26:438-442.
4. Maresso K, Broeckel U. Genotyping platforms for mass-throughput genotyping with SNPs, including human genome-wide scans. Adv Genet 2008; 60:107-139.
5. Venter JC: The human genome at 10: Successes and challenges. Science 2011; 331: 546-547.
6. Illig T, Gieger C, Zhai G, Römisch-Margl W, Wang-Sattler R, Prehn C, Altmaier E, Kastenmüller G, Kato BS, Mewes HW, Meitinger T, de Angelis MH, Kronenberg F, Soranzo N, Wichmann HE, Spector TD, Adamski J, Suhre K. A genome-wide perspective of genetic variation in human metabolism. Nat Genet 2010; 42:137-141.
7. Hicks AA, Pramstaller PP, Johansson A, Vitart V, Rudan I, Ugocsai P, Aulchenko Y, et al. Genetic determinants of circulating sphingolipid concentrations in European populations. PLoS Genet 2009; 5:e1000672.
8. Lauc G, Essafi A, Huffman JE, Hayward C, Knežević A, Kattla JJ, et al. Genomics meets glycomics – the first GWAS study of human N-Glycome identifies HNF1α as a master regulator of plasma protein fucosylation. PLoS Genet 2010; 6:e1001256.
9. http://www.p3gobservatory.org/ (Accessed: 21 Apr 2011)
10. de Bakker PIW, Yelensky R, Pe'er I, Gabriel SB, Daly MJ, Altshuler D. Efficiency and power in genetic association studies. Nat Genet 2005; 37:1217-1223.
11. Ioannidis JPA, Ntzani EE, Trikalinos TA, Contopoulos-Ioannidis DG. Replication validity of genetic association studies. Nat Genet 2001; 29:306-309.
12. Hunter DJ, Kraft P. Drinking from the fire hose: Statistical issues in genomewide association studies. N Engl J Med 2007; 357:436-437.
13. Rosenberg NA, Huang L, Jewett EM, Szpiech ZA, Jankovic I, Boehnke M. Genome-wide association studies in diverse populations. Nat Rev Genet 2010; 11:356-366.
14. Becker F, van El CG, Ibarreta D, Zika E, Hogarth S, Borry P, Cambon-Thomsen A, et al. Genetic testing and common disorders in a public health framework: how to assess relevance and possibilities. Background Document to the ESHG recommendations on genetic testing and common disorders. Eur J Hum Genet 2011; 19(Suppl 1):S6-S44.
15. Rudan I, Rudan P. From genomic advances to public health benefits: the unbearable lightness of being stuck. Coll Antropol 2004; 28:483-507.

16. Sgaier SK, Jha P, Mony P et al. Biobanks in developing countries: needs and feasibility. Science 2007; 318:1074-1075.

17. Singer PA, Daar AS. Harnessing genomics and biotechnology to improve global health equity. Science 2001; 294:87.

18. Daar AS et al. Top ten biotechnologies for improving health in developing countries. Nat Genet 2002; 32:229–232.

19. Sirugo G, Schim van der L, Sam O et al: A national DNA bank in the Gambia, West Africa, and genomic research in developing countries. Nat Genet 2004; 36:785–786.

20. Matimba A, Oluka MN, Ebeshi BU, Sayi J, Bolaji OO, Guantai AN, Masimirembwa CM. Establishment of a biobank and pharmacogenetics database of African populations. Eur J Hum Genet 2008; 16:780-783.

CHAPTER 8.

The case for the launch of an international DNA-based birth cohort study

Progress towards the reduction in child mortality target in Millennium Development Goal (MDG) 4 is being made in many low and middle-income countries (1). This is mainly a result of notable efforts of national governments and the international community to improve the prevention and treatment of the main causes of child death and to expand access to health care. The exact causes of the sharp declines in child mortality have not been identified definitively but successful countries have significantly increased coverage of basic public health interventions and increased access to quality health services (1). The *"advance market commitment"* (AMC) programmes, which are heavily supported by The Gates Foundation, Global Alliance for Vaccines and Immunization and national governments of the developed countries, will try to sustain and enhance the development and implementation of vaccination against major pathogens throughout the developing world (2).

Many low and middle-income countries are now experiencing a markedly different pattern of early mortality, with more than half of child deaths attributable to causes directly related to birth and very early infections and complications – such as preterm birth complications, birth asphyxia, congenital anomalies, sudden infant death syndrome and accidents (3). At the same time, attention is shifting from not only ensuring survival, but also attaining optimal development. A growing body of evidence suggests that social and environmental influences, especially during pregnancy and in early childhood, can have important long-term health and development implications (4). Another important trend that accompanies the epidemiological and demographic transitions is increasing inequities in child health outcomes within countries.

The global child health agenda for 2015 and beyond will inevitably need to broaden its focus from mortality reduction to also addressing the social determinants of deaths, growing inequities among children and mothers, and ensuring the sustainability of the progress made against the infectious diseases. With continued reduction in child mortality, the focus of international efforts will also need to shift from merely averting deaths to promoting better health, development, social functioning and education of children in the poorest countries and reduce the effects of inequity. The research needed to address those challenges will require conceptually different studies than those used in the past to address infectious causes.

The past decade has witnessed remarkable progress in the development of more reliable, replicable and standardized methods that have improved the quality of research in all areas of human health and development. This is true across a wide range of disciplines, from qualitative research and indicators of quality of life or inequity, to cutting-edge basic research. In parallel to global child mortality reduction, we have witnessed a particular revolution in biomedical research which was brought about by the progress in genetic technology as a result of the Human Genome Project (5).

Genome-wide association studies and whole-genome sequencing have led to an unprecedented level of discovery with novel insights into human biology and the genetic determinants of many common and rare human diseases. However, common human diseases of late onset – such as cardiovascular diseases, most types of cancer, or type 2 diabetes, which are typical of the industrialized countries, have a complex aetiology, including large numbers of strong environmental, social and behavioural determinants and non-genetic risk factors. For most traits studied, the contribution of genetic factors associated with those diseases is due to many common genetic variants, each with very small effects (6). More importantly, the research into genetic determinants of common human diseases has been very largely confined to industrialized countries and focused on their health needs, which form a relatively minor part of the global burden of disease (6). Several researchers in the field have expressed concern that genetic research into common diseases of late onset conducted to date has mainly been serving to increase the gap between the health needs of the global poor and the rich (7).

In the past 2 million years of human evolution, diseases of the late onset had little impact on the natural selection processes that shaped the human genome. They occur in a post-reproductive period and are therefore almost invisible to selection. Thus their genetic architecture is likely to be mostly defined by so-called *"neutral evolution"*. Diseases and conditions that had a much greater power to shape human genetic make-up – the problems related to birth, early child survival and maternal mortality – are still present in low-income countries. Those are mainly the problems occurring during labour and persisting infectious causes of mortality of children and young people. They have been shaping the human genome through natural selection. Applying new genetic technologies to study the genetic variants protecting from the major causes of maternal and child deaths would likely yield significant insights into pathogenesis of those diseases and mechanisms of evolved host resistance. Moreover, some of these traits are likely to be subject to balancing and shifting selection, and may reveal larger genetic effects.

Another impact of the human genome project was the development of technologies for fast and relatively cheap sequencing of genomes. Currently, a polymerase chain reaction (PCR) test for a specific infectious agent can be developed in the course of few days through re-sequencing of the genome of an infectious agent, as demonstrated by a recent example during the H1N1 (*"swine"*) flu outbreak in 2009.

The progress made recently through the application of novel genetic technologies in large population cohorts has also exposed the importance of very large and well-designed studies with adequate power to test study hypotheses. Comparison of small candidate gene studies (which were routinely performed in 1990s and in the beginning of 2000s) with large multi-centre collaborative genome-wide association studies (which became very popular from about 2007) shows that conducting many small studies with insufficient power and without the standardized methodology is an inefficient use of resources and leads to inconsistent and false positive reports in an overwhelming majority of cases. Conversely, large multi-centre studies using rigorous statistical approach lead to reproducible and consistent results.

The need for large-scale collaborative research programmes is even more important as research turns to the study of the interaction of genes and environment in causing disease (8). This problem is not limited to genetic research. Information on morbidity and mortality from the diseases of the poor, which form the large majority of global burden of disease and death, is often based on data from relatively few studies conducted in different low-income contexts without standardized methods. They often provide very inconsistent estimates that are not comparable. The recent progress made by genome-wide association studies and, more generally, in the field of genetic epidemiology, has highlighted the importance of *"biobanks"*. These are large collections of biological material and extensive associated epidemiological data from large population cohorts assembled in a standardized way. They are designed and developed with close attention to quality assurance, so that emerging technologies can be applied to generate high quality reproducible data on very large numbers of well-characterised individuals. One of the main reasons why the developing world is not enjoying potential benefits from the application of novel epidemiological and genetic research technologies is because there are very few biobanks and large population cohort studies in low and middle-income countries available for systematic study (9,10). Such cohorts are becoming a pre-requisite for reliable research into biological, environmental, genetic, behavioural and social determinants of diseases relevant to their population.

The development of a very large dataset ("*biobank*") that would include or contain directly comparable data on epidemiological, biological and social factors and samples representative of a large number of human populations would allow researchers to study the determinants of diseases which have made major contributions to the global burden of disease, thus reducing the large inequity in research effort on different causes of morbidity and mortality globally. An international biobank would allow researchers in low and middle-income countries to gain access to emerging research technologies and use them to study diseases that affect their populations. It would also serve to build and enhance the research capacity in developing countries, to create a large collaborating network of interested researchers globally, and to enable comparisons between their results using the same methodology. The results of biomedical research that would be generated from such a biobank would make a substantial contribution to improving the available information on the morbidity, mortality and the main risk factors for the diseases relevant to the developing world and provide the opportunity to study interactions between genes and a wide range of levels of environmental exposures in causing diseases in different contexts. (8). The longitudinal nature of the study could provide valuable information on long-term (life-course) effects of biological, environmental, genetic, social and other factors and their interplay in the modern age.

The development of a global birth cohort would hold out the promise of understanding genetic, environmental and social determinants of health, development and survival of pre-school children. It would also enhance our understanding of the interactions of context-specific social, economic and environmental factors and the human genetic make-up. Ultimately, what will start as a cohort of newborns and children will eventually, over the course of the 21st century, develop into a longitudinal cohort study of adolescents, and then adults with multiple data points through a time series. This will allow testing many current hypotheses on the causal role of different major risk factors – social, environmental, behavioural and genetic – in human disease and provide answers relevant to all human populations, rather than being limited to high-income countries. It would create a reliable information base that could assist in understanding the burden of health problems in mothers and children globally. There would also be a role for this resource to help understand the genetic and other factors that make children prone to poor response or adverse effects of medicines or vaccines. The conduct of this coordinated study in a consistent way across many sites from low and middle-income countries, starting with several "*core*" sites and expanding through addition of other sites interested in following the same methodological approach, and including up to one million newborns, would maximise the power to address many high priority research and health care system questions. Results would also be generalisable globally, rather than confined to specific ethnic, social or economic groups. Through parallel recruitment and involvement of mothers, it would serve to integrate research into inter-linked maternal and child health problems.

Building up an all-inclusive international biobank based on best research practice would, over time, develop into a resource that could serve the research needs of many diverse groups of researchers from developed and developing countries alike. The principle that would underlie this cohort is adherence to the highest ethical standards, which have now been developed through the setting up of large biobanks in developed countries, and also the principles of open access to anonymised data (consistent with adherence to ethical principles and local approvals) to interested researchers with legitimate research ideas. This is in line with the emerging *"open science"* framework, which enabled open discussion and reanalysis of existing data. Stringent adherence to the highest ethical standards needs to be emphasized throughout each study as one of the goals of the larger project. The development of an international biobank would involve the human and technological capacity of developing countries to work on this project and to assist in building their research capacity and competitiveness.

In many countries there will be a strong sensitivity towards allowing foreign institutions to access genetic material. Most poor countries will rightly fear that any commercial interests from this type of research will only benefit rich countries. Some of them already have laws in place which restrict sending any biological materials outside their borders, particularly those that may have commercial implications. This is why planning an international birth cohort based on DNA will require developing of local capacity. Local researchers will need to be trained to obtain biological materials in the same way across many field sites, store them properly, and generate data locally, while the analysis of the data could then be standardized and centralized. Preserving commercial interests from any patents and sharing them fairly with all the participants from low and middle income countries will represent an important challenge.

We need a vision beyond the MDG4 timeframe of 2015. It is time to move beyond focusing on simply averting child deaths and to start planning for this resource. We now have standard operating procedures developed specifically for setting up biobanks and validated genetic technologies and analytical methods for replicable and reliable genetic analyses. (11,12). We also have standard ethics principles that are applicable to biobanks and large experience in setting up biobanks in high-income countries (13). Greatly improved communication globally, through internet and mobile phones, and cheaper international travel, has enabled a new kind of research. It is based on massive collaborations of scientists, big projects and large sample sizes, and it generates more reliable results. We propose that globalization of the lifestyle, industry, and many other segments of human activity should be followed by globalization of research into human health and development. There is increasingly a technological capacity in developing countries that could support this kind of vision. For example, several large international organizations, multilateral agencies and even donor foundations have both the legitimacy and organisational infrastructure to provide parallel access to many field sites in low-income countries. They also represent a well-known *"brands"* in the international community that could ensure wide participation and commitment from all those taking part in this study. Some organizations and agencies maintain programmes of regular and repeated contacts with a high proportion of children in low resource settings, which could provide a highly cost-efficient framework for recruitment and longitudinal follow up throughout early childhood.

In addition, the incredibly fast progress in development of supporting genetic research technologies, which led to many recent genetic breakthroughs through genome-wide association studies, is beginning to make this vision increasingly realistic. In fact, technological advances are now the main driver of the research progress. It can already be assumed that the appropriate research technologies will become affordable in several years to perform large-scale whole-genome sequencing projects. The costs of genotyping and sequencing of the human genome have been falling rapidly since the year 2000 – from about US\$ 3 billion, which was spent to sequence the first human genome, to only about US\$ 4000 in early 2011 (14,15). The time required to sequence the entire human genome has also fallen from 11 years to only a few hours (14,15).

We need to anticipate the possibility of affordable mass-sequencing several years from now. With this vision, the remaining time would be well spent developing and assembling the datasets from many countries and designing studies which will be the most informative, assuming the availability of genomic information (16). The study sample should be large and represent many of the world's populations. In each country, a local academic expert in paediatrics / neonatology or obstetrics would be identified and would be responsible for obtaining ethics approval from the nationally relevant body to conduct the study. This person should also be a key / committed member of the study team and should own and drive the process at the country level.

The study would typically involve one large urban teaching hospital and 3-4 health facilities in less developed and rural regions. In each country, a proportional number of newborns and mothers would be recruited to achieve a global sample size of up to one million newborns and as many of their mothers and fathers. A sample size of this magnitude is required to ensure sufficient number of cases with different social, economic, behavioural, health and development outcomes in different contexts for an adequate, globally representative study. Each pregnant woman would be informed about the goals of the study and she would be asked to give informed consent for herself and the newborn. In some countries, the signature of the father will also be required. At birth, a baseline questionnaire with the basic information would be filled out for each mother and child, and a blood sample would be obtained from each participant. Any complications during birth would be recorded, as well as the basic anthropometric, clinical and psychomotor assessment of the child.

In the first phase, several *"core"* sites would be chosen in low and middle-income countries, in which the approach would be piloted. The sites would fall in one of two categories: (i) they would be set up in each one of the BRICS countries – Brazil, Russia, India, China and South Africa – i.e., the five very large and rapidly developing economies. Those five countries are front-runners among the developing nations and their economic potential and research capacity are both on a remarkable increase. These countries should have most interest in, and ability to, harbour study sites in which DNA-based birth cohorts could be developed, as a logical next step necessary to acquire competitiveness in genomic research at an international level; (ii) they would be set up in several rare sites in low-income countries in which high-quality research was being conducted for many years, and study populations are used to research of effectiveness of different interventions. These study sites were set up by driven individuals from low-income countries, frequently through bilateral collaboration with a western institution. Because of randomized controlled trials that are being conducted at such sites, the studies have availability of *"cold chains"* required for vaccine delivery, appropriate ethics approvals, and a motivated team of researchers and study populations. They represent rare and relatively unique sites where a proper DNA-based biobank could be set up.

The pilot studies in those several selected sites would improve our knowledge and understanding of the challenges with developing biobanks in low and middle-income countries. We would aim to develop standardized study protocols based on those early experiences, and then invite groups from many more low and middle-income countries to join this Generation 2015 with

Table 8-1. *Likely research outcomes of the proposed biobank.*

Likely short term research outcomes of *Generation 2015* for children would be:

- Description of the morbidity and mortality associated with major child diseases, pre-term birth and pregnancy complications;
- Description of normal and abnormal growth and development; and of health and disease from foetal life until early adulthood;
- Identification of biological, environmental, genetic, and social risk factors and their interactions for major child diseases and pregnancy complications in different contexts (including those associated with low birth weight, preterm birth and congenital anomalies; eclampsia, antepartum haemorrhage, placental abruption, thromboembolism and postpartum sepsis);
- Identification of biological, environmental, genetic, and social determinants of host resistance against the major neonatal and childhood infections (such as neonatal sepsis, pneumonia, diarrhoea) and determinants of immune system development;
- Identification of biological, environmental, genetic, and social determinants of malnutrition and stunting (including micronutrient deficiencies);
- Identification of biological, environmental, genetic, and social determinants of child development (including motor, behavioural, cognitive and psychomotor development);
- Understanding of genetic and environmental determinants of host-pathogen interactions, carriage of microorganisms, immune response to vaccination, and antibiotic resistance;
- Linking the whole genome studies to similar studies that are starting on global pathogens (17);

For mothers, short-term research outcome could include:

- Description of the mortality and morbidity associated with the major maternal diseases and pregnancy complications;
- Identification of biological, environmental, genetic, and social risk factors for these conditions and their complications (including eclampsia, placenta previa, lactation duration, postpartum haemorrhage, twinning, obstructed delivery, and puerperal sepsis) in different contexts;

Research outcome for participating countries could be:

- Training of local staff and development of local research capacity, establishing local biobanks and international competitiveness in biobanking;
- Possibility to participate in research on high international level through large collaborations and to compare its capacity and progress in maternal and child health research with other countries;

Likely indirect research opportunities afforded by *Generation 2015* would be:

- Identification of genes, gene-environment and gene-social interactions;
- Identification of biomarkers for birth related and early childhood disease outcomes or adverse events;
- Establishing global standards for the frequency of gene variants in different populations;
- Defining the content of a genotyping array containing the major disease associated variants across all global population groups;
- Studying the effects of urbanization on genetic structure of populations and impact of admixture on disease traits;
- Studying of the migrations of historical human populations;
- Looking for 'signatures' of natural selection in the genome;

---

their data collections assembled in a standardized way. Through this *"snow-balling"* development, we would hope to achieve sufficiently large numbers to develop a true international DNA-based birth cohort, which would allow studying of genetic determinants of health and disease in children across the world, but also try to document the effects of inequity and socio-economic differences on children's biology and development potential.

Acknowledgement: Originally published as: Igor Rudan, Mickey Chopra, Yurii Aulchenko, Abdullah H. Baqui, Zulfiqar A. Bhutta, Karen Edmond, Bernardo L. Horta, Keith P. Klugman, Claudio F. Lanata, Shabir A. Madhi, Harish Nair, Zeshan Qureshi, Craig Rubens, Evropi Theodoratou, Cesar G. Victora, Wei Wang, Martin W. Weber, James F. Wilson, Lina Zgaga and Harry Campbell: The case for launch of an international DNA-based birth cohort study. Reprinted with permission from Edinburgh University Global Health Society under Creative Commons Attribution License (Journal of Global Health 2011;1:39-45).

Disclaimers and Copyright Statement: The views expressed in this article are those of the authors and do not necessarily reflect the official policy or position of the Department of the Navy, Department of Defense, nor the U.S. Government. Author Claudio F. Lanata is an employee of the U.S. Government. This work was prepared as part of his official duties. Title 17 U.S.C. § 105 provides that 'Copyright protection under this title is not available for any work of the United States Government'. Title 17 U.S.C. § 101 defines a U.S. Government work as a work prepared by a military service members or employees of the U.S. Government as part of those persons' official duties.

References

1. Bhutta ZA, Chopra M, Axelson H, Berman P, Boerma T, Bryce J, et al. Countdown to 2015 decade report (2000-10): taking stock of maternal, newborn, and child survival. Lancet 2010; 375:2032-2044.
2. Levine MM, Robins-Browne R. Vaccines, global health and social equity. Immunol Cell Biol 2009; 87:274-278.
3. Black RE, Cousens S, Johnson HL, Lawn JE, Rudan I, Bassani DG, et al. Global, regional, and national causes of child mortality in 2008: a systematic analysis. Lancet 2010; 375:1969-1987.
4. Engle PL, Black MM, Behrman JR, Cabral de Mello M, Gertler PJ, Kapiriri L, et al. Strategies to avoid the loss of developmental potential in more than 200 million children in the developing world. Lancet 2007; 369:229-242.
5. Manolio TA, Collins FS. The HapMap and genome-wide association studies in diagnosis and therapy. Annu Rev Med 2009; 60:4434-4456.
6. McCarthy MI, Abecasis GR, Cardon LR, Goldstein DB, Little J, Ioannidis JP, et al. Genome-wide association studies for complex traits: consensus, uncertainty and challenges. Nat Rev Genet 2008; 9:356-369.

7. Wonkam A, Muna W, Ramesar R, Rotimi CN, Newport MJ. Capacity-building in human genetics for developing countries: initiatives and perspectives in sub-Saharan Africa. Public Health Genomics 2010; 13:492-494.

8. Cornelis MC, Agrawal A, Cole JW, Hansel NN, Barnes KC, Beaty TH, et al. The Gene, Environment Association Studies consortium (GENEVA): maximizing the knowledge obtained from GWAS by collaboration across studies of multiple conditions. Genet Epidemiol 2010; 34:364-372.

9. Campbell A, Rudan I. Systematic review of birth cohort studies in Africa. J Glob Health 2011; 1:46-58.

10. McKinnon R, Campbell H. Systematic review of birth cohort studies in South East Asia and Eastern Mediterranean regions. J Glob Health; 2011; 1:59-71.

11. Betsou F, Barnes R, Burke T, Coppola D, Desouza Y, Eliason J, et al. Human biospecimen research: experimental protocol and quality control tools. Cancer Epidemiol Biomarkers Prev 2009; 1818:1017-1025.

12. Public Population Project in Genomics. P3G Observatory. (Available from: http://www.p3gobservatory.org/; Accessed: 21 Mar 2011).

13. Gurwitz D, Fortier I, Lunshof JE, Knoppers BM. Research ethics. Children and population biobanks. Science 2009; 325:818-819.

14. Mardis ER. A decade's perspective on DNA sequencing technology. Nature 2011; 470:198-203.

15. Marshall E. Human genome 10th anniversary. Waiting for the revolution. Science 2011; 331:526-529.

16. Butler D. Human genome at ten: Science after the sequence. Nature 2010; 465:1000-1001.

17. Croucher NJ, Harris SR, Fraser C, Quail MA, Burton J, van der Linden M, et al. Rapid pneumococcal evolution in response to clinical interventions. Science 2011; 331:430-434.

PART 2.

Improving policy formulation

CHAPTER 9.

Millennium Development Goals: Caring about health

The health community has been arguing over whether one health area is more deserving than another. Various initiatives have been competing for a limited pot of funds based on debates about how their cause will contribute to progress on the Millennium Development Goals (MDGs).

We need to take a step back and start asking a different set of questions that look at priorities beyond health. Money is central to improving health. The World Health Organization estimates that basic health services cost around US$ 40 per person per year, and about one third of the world's people live in places with low national incomes where this cannot be provided, even with proper taxation. Until countries can finance their own efforts, the funds need to come from the international community as part of its responsibility for improving global health.

How does health compare to other world priorities? While the estimated US$ 22 billion devoted to international development assistance for health is extremely welcome, this level of funding is a small fraction of what high-income countries spend outside the health sector. For example, the international community allocates US$ 1.5 trillion annually to military expenditure – 2.43% of global gross domestic product (GDP) – and US$ 300 billion for agricultural subsides. High-income countries spent US$ 11 trillion on bank bailouts, and over US$ 1 trillion on the wars in Iraq and Afghanistan. South Africa, a transitional economy, devoted US$ 1.7 billion to World Cup football.

Global priorities are reflected at the national level. India is the largest recipient of external health funding, having received over US$ 1.6 billion from the World Bank and another US$ 500 million from the Global Fund. While this can be justified given the huge burden of death and disability, a closer look at the government's budget reveals that it spent over US$ 40 billion on defence last year.

A similar story can be told for China, the tenth largest recipient of external health funding which spends, officially, US$ 80 billion on defence; and for Brazil, the fifteenth largest recipient, which allocates US$ 20 billion to defence.

1. Success is possible. Critics allege that money makes little difference to improving health. Two countries identified as better performers in health are Rwanda and Mexico. What lies behind their success?

Rwanda, despite being one of the poorest countries in the world, has provided national health insurance for an estimated 92% of the population. The New York Times reports that the scheme, known as "*health mutuals*", includes a premium of two dollars a year which includes basic healthcare and treatment for the major causes of morbidity and mortality: diarrhea, pneumonia, malaria, malnutrition and infected cuts (1).

In addition, local health centers usually have all the medicines on the WHO's list of essential drugs and laboratories that can do routine blood and urine analyses, along with tuberculosis and malaria tests. Since introducing the national health insurance, life expectancy has risen – despite HIV/AIDS – and maternal and child mortality fallen.

Who pays for the healthcare? The two-dollar premium does not cover the cost, which is around US$ 10-20 per head. The Rwandan government has relied on external donors, primarily the US and the Global Fund to Fight HIV/AIDS, Tuberculosis and Malaria, to cover 53% of health spending. When asked by the New York Times about the rationale for the scheme, Dr Agnes Binagwaho of the Ministry of Health said: "*Solidarity – you cannot feel happy as a society if you don't organize yourself so that people won't die of poverty*" (1).

Mexico, in contrast, has relied on a social protection scheme to improve health using a conditional cash transfer programme, initially called "*Progresa*" and now known as "*Oportunidades*". Its main goal is to increase the basic capabilities of extremely poor people in rural areas. To do this, it provides monetary incentives direct to families to help overcome financial barriers to health service use and schooling. But this is conditional: mothers only receive the funds if their children attend health clinics and schools.

The mastermind behind the programme, Santiago Levy, noted: "*Compared with giving a kilo of tortillas or a litre of milk as we used to in the past, Progresa delivers purchasing power. But even poor parents must invest in their children's futures, that's why the strings are attached*" (2).

Since it was introduced in 1997, the scheme has reduced morbidity and stunting and increased school enrollment. The Mexican government initially paid, but as it rolled-out to cover five million families, it has had to take loans to cover the budget which was around US$ 1 billion in 2000. In 2008 costs reached US$ 3.8 billion, or 0.2% of GDP and 20% of the federal budget.

Of course, donors give health funding strategically, to influence governments by promoting democracy, or for geostrategic advantage, for example. But this raises questions regarding donor motivation behind providing foreign aid for health, despite altruistic rhetoric.

For example, while the US government has launched the President's new Global Health Initiative (GHI) which provides US$ 63 billion over six years focused around fifteen countries – *GHI-plus* – selected for good governance and results, the budget for the next financial year shows that only US$ 100 million has been given to the GHI-plus countries, while Afghanistan, Pakistan and Iraq receive 64% of the foreign assistance budget, a total of US$ 7.8 billion.

2. Crucial components. What are the five crucial components of success? The government, with major partners and international assistance, must ensure adequate resources; the public sector must assume leadership for providing and coordinating services; the host country, down to the local level, must be responsible for policies, programmes, and services; and health must be integrated across all sectors. Most importantly, success can be achieved only through an effective social contract within society that redistributes wealth from the richest to the poorest, as in Mexico, and provides health security for all, as in the case of Rwanda.

3. Basic rights. Ultimately, improving health and reaching the MDGs comes down to a social contract within countries, between the rich and the poor, and among nations. To mean something in practice, this contract needs to be institutionalised at the domestic level, through schemes such as universal health insurance or conditional cash transfers, and at the global level in a common agreement on roles and responsibilities in global health, such as a Framework Convention on Global Health (1). This is why governments legislate domestically and the WHO governs internationally.

The global health system is currently organised in a fragmented, uncoordinated, and inefficient way with initiatives arranged around diseases. We need to move towards an integrated approach focused around basic rights, such as a Framework Convention on Global Health (3). This kind of agreement would empower Ministries of Health and guide governments on how to improve health. It would focus on three areas:

(i) *Health systems and services*: the WHO sets out six essential building blocks of a well-functioning health system: health services; the health workforce; health information; medical products, vaccines, and technologies; a financing system that raises sufficient funds for health and ensures access; and leadership and governance. Health systems provide basic health care – primary, emergency, specialised care for acute and chronic diseases and injuries – and public health services look after surveillance, laboratories, and response for all citizens.

(ii) *Essential drugs, vaccines and technologies*: the WHO's Model List of Essential Medicines, includes *"the most efficacious, safe and cost-effective medicines for priority conditions"*. They are *"selected on the basis of current and estimated future public health relevance and potential for safe and cost effective treatment"*. Vaccines and medicines can be highly cost effective in treating common infections and chronic diseases. Other essential technologies, including medical devices and procedures, may also offer good value.

(iii) *Basic survival needs*: reframing the approach to global health requires a shift in national and international health funding and activities in the direction of basic survival needs, a traditional public health strategy essential to maintaining and restoring human capability and functioning. These needs include sanitation and sewage, pest control, clean air, potable water, diet and nutrition – neither under- nor over-nutrition – and tobacco and alcohol reduction.

This type of agreement, similar to other international agreements would institutionalise the social contract, a type of global social health insurance in which all states work together towards a common goal.

A treaty such as a Framework Convention on Global Health requires a broad global consensus. We are embarking on a Joint Learning Initiative for National and Global Responsibilities for Health to seek international consensus around broad health arrangements to meet the needs of the world's least healthy people and close health gaps between rich and poor (4). It will lead to an overarching, coherent, framework for shared national and global responsibilities for health, and concrete strategies for global health beyond the MDGs.

Acknowledgement: Originally published as: Devi Sridhar and Lawrence Gostin: Millennium Development Goals – Health: Caring about health. Reprinted from: Chatnam House World Today, 2010.

References

1. McNeil DG. A poor nation, with a health plan. New York Times, 14 Jun 2010;
2. Egan J. Mexico's welfare revolution. BBC News, 15 Oct 1999.
3. Gostin LO, Friedman EA, Buse K, Waris A, Mulumba M, Joel M, Dare L, Dhai A, Sridhar D. Towards a framework convention on global health. Bull World Health Organ. 2013; 91:790-793.
4. http://www.acslaw.org/node/16479. (Accessed: 3 Jun 2015)

CHAPTER 10.

Are there simple conclusions on how to channel health funding?

Chunling Lu and colleagues (1) present an important study in the Lancet journal, identifying the key determinants of government spending on health in developing countries. These researchers present a nuanced and careful discussion of their findings. We worry that others will draw two rather crude conclusions. The first is that development assistance given directly to governments has a negative effect on government spending on health, and therefore funding for health should not be routed through governments. The second is that assistance given to non-governmental organisations (NGOs) has a positive effect on government spending, and therefore funding should be routed through NGOs. There are at least three reasons not to draw these conclusions. We urge you to pay attention to the caveats and suggestions for further research made by the authors themselves.

First, there are major problems with the data both on government spending on health as well as on development assistance for health, which make it difficult to draw firm conclusions. Lu and colleagues have accomplished a herculean task in generating a dataset on health spending in developing countries, yet questions remain on the validity of these data. For government health spending, the authors rely on data from WHO (if 90% of the spending was obtained from country reports) and from the International Monetary Fund (IMF), and then impute missing values (41% for WHO low-income countries, 25% for IMF). Even for the non-missing data there are serious questions about quality. For example, the IMF and WHO data do not match up; the correlation between the two datasets is only 0.65.

For development assistance for health, Lu and colleagues rely on a published dataset (2) on development assistance which, when used for this analysis, leads to four sources of bias. First, the database relies on donors' disbursements, not how much is received by the country. The gap between what is disbursed by donors and what is actually received by governments is not insignificant (3). Second, official sources of development assistance, which the previous database draws on (2), do not fully capture the financial flows going to NGOs. These two issues would result in overestimates of the development assistance governments receive. This is offset by two additional sources of bias: a substantial amount of development assistance for health, US$ 13.3 billion in 2006, cannot be traced to developing countries and thus is not linked to particular governments. Finally, the database does not capture donors that are not members of the Development Assistance Committee of the Organisation for Economic Co-operation and Development, such as China, India, Saudi Arabia, and Venezuela, that make large aid contributions to developing countries although it is debatable how significant these contributions are to health (4). In view of the considerable uncertainty about the data for both government spending and development assistance, the conclusions should be carefully considered.

A second reason to be wary of simple conclusions is touched on by Lu and colleagues in their call for a careful assessment of the risks and benefits of expanded development assistance to NGOs – a hugely important point. NGOs might be an efficient mechanism to deliver vertical funds but, as Lu and colleagues note, this point has more often been hypothesised about than proved. One risk to this approach is that funding through off-budget channels bypasses the domestic systems, processes, and institutions that are meant to improve governance and sustain the effect of aid in the long term (5). The irony is that, in weak states, donors tend to give money to NGOs, which further detracts from the government's capability and results in a perpetually weak government. The Millions Saved study by the Center for Global Development is telling: strong public-sector involvement is a key feature in all the cases examined of clear success in global health assistance (6).

Collier (7) highlights another risk of funding NGOs directly by describing the severe coordination problems among NGOs that responded to Haiti's crisis. He calls for donors to stop donating to NGOs and to stream funding into a common pool which would be overseen by the government. The coordination problem is one which health ministers know well because they often have no way of knowing where NGOs are working in their country, how much funding these groups are receiving, and what health services they are providing (8). As the Health Minister of Tanzania noted, *"If they say, we have sent US$ 100 million dollars, you would expect government to be accountable. But the funding is not recorded. We do not know where it goes. Much goes to civil society, and much remains in donor countries"* (8). In short, off-budget funding might seem tempting, especially in view of Lu and colleagues' findings, but it is not a panacea.

Finally, we should be careful of the proposal Lu and colleagues make for the establishment of collaborative targets between donors and recipients on health spending. Their goal is appealing – to make governments spend more on health and, within their health budget, to spend more on specific priorities. But consider for a moment whether this is how a government's health budget (or, indeed, its overall budget) should be set. Should a government's budget follow the priorities of those international partnerships and campaigns that are most successful in mobilising funding? What if maternal mortality (still lamentably lagging among the Millennium Development Goals) is not the most successful global campaign—should antiretroviral treatments take priority over maternal health because donors have more successfully mobilised funding for HIV/AIDS? Should ministry of health budgets be increased at the expense of, say, prevention of road-traffic accidents (a serious cause of premature mortality), which might fall within the ministry of transport (9)? More profoundly, who should decide and who takes responsibility for setting priorities? Beware of the assumption that the international community does this well: donors neither set nor fund priorities in a rational way. Messing up good intentions are vested interests, pressures to disburse funds, a prioritising of efforts most likely to show measurable results in a short-time scale, and political incentives to announce new initiatives even if that means abandoning successful policies.

For all the above reasons, after years of negotiations, donors have agreed that national governments offer the closest approximation we have to an acceptable process for setting a country's priorities; hence the Paris Declaration on Aid Effectiveness and its follow-up, the Accra Agenda for Action (10). In these agreements, more than 100 signatories—from donor and developing country governments, multilateral donor agencies, regional development banks, and international agencies—have accepted the importance of country ownership and committed themselves not only to greater harmonisation and coherence in their own policies, but also to aligning their goals and policies more closely with those of developing-country governments. Donors have also accepted that they need to provide more predictable support, as discussed by Gorik Ooms and colleagues (11) in The Lancet, and that they should rely more on recipient governments' systems, for example, by giving budget support to governments with good management systems for public expenditure.

The Paris Declaration has been signed but the problem now lies in getting donors to practise what they preach. Bilateral donors are clinging to funding disease-specific programmes, and skewing health financing towards their interests not only in donor-dependent countries in sub-Saharan Africa but also in more independent countries such as Brazil and India (12). Countries that have improved their management systems for public expenditure are still not receiving more budget support. In Ghana, for example, an increase in the quality of such management systems has been accompanied by an 11% decrease in the use of these systems (13).

In the debate about how to channel health aid, the behaviour of donors has to be taken into account. So too does the difficult question of who should decide about, and take responsibility for, how public funding is allocated within a country. We commend Lu and colleagues for presenting an important paper on fungibility and development assistance. Their evidence provokes profound questions about who, in practice, is the most accountable and effective recipient of health funding. We underscore their calls for more research into this vital question.

Acknowledgement: Originally published as: Devi Sridhar and Ngaire Woods: Are there simple conclusions on how to channel health funding? Reprinted with permission from Elsevier (Lancet 2010; 375:1326-1328).

References

1. Lu C, Schneider MT, Gubbins P, Leach-Kemon K, Jamison D, Murray CJL. Public financing of health in developing countries: a cross-national systematic analysis. Lancet 2010; 375:1375-1387.
2. Ravishankar N, Gubbins P, Cooley RJ, et al. Financing of global health: tracking development assistance for health from 1990 to 2007. Lancet 2009; 373:2113–2124.
3. McCoy D, Chand S, Sridhar D. Global health funding: how much, where it comes from and where it goes. Health Policy Plan 2009; 24:407–417.
4. OECD. Managing aid: practices of DAC member countries. June, 2009. (Available from: http://www.oecd.org/dataoecd/58/29/42903202.pdf; Accessed: 8 Mar 2010).
5. De Renzio P. Aid effectiveness and absorptive capacity. May, 2007. (Available from: http://www.odi.org.uk/events/G8_07/opinions/de%20renzio.pdf; Accessed 3 Mar 2010).
6. Levine R. Millions saved: proven successes in global health. Washington, DC: Center for Global Development, 2004.
7. Collier P. How to fix Haiti's fixers. Foreign Policy 2010. (Available from: http://www.foreignpolicy.com/articles/2010/02/18/how_to_fix_haitis_fixers?page=0,0; Accessed: 5 Mar 2010).
8. Global Economic Governance Programme. Setting a developing country agenda for global health. May, 2008. (Available from: http://www.globaleconomic governance. org/wp-content/uploads/Working%20Group%20Report% 20May%202008.pdf; Accessed: 9 Mar 2010).
9. Robertson G. What kills more children than AIDS? Roads. Times Online, 2 Mar 2010. (Available from: http://www.timesonline.co.uk/tol/comment/columnists/ guest_contributors/article7045941.ece; Accessed: 9 Mar 2010).

10. OECD. The Paris declaration on aid effectiveness and the Accra agenda for action. March, 2005. (Available from: http://www.oecd.org/dataoecd/11/41/34428351.pdf; Accessed: 3 Mar 2010).

11. Ooms G, Decoster K, Miti K, et al. Crowding out: are relations between international health aid and government health funding too complex to be captured in averages only? Lancet 2010; 375:1403-1405.

12. Sridhar D, Gómez E. Comparative assessment of health financing in Brazil, Russia, and India: unpacking budgetary allocations in health. December, 2009. (Available from: http://www.globaleconomicgovernance.org/wp-content/uploads/ GEG-Working-Paper-Sridhar-Final.pdf; Accessed: 9 Mar 2010).

13. OECD. Managing development resources: the use of country systems in public financial management. Paris: OECD Publishing, 2009.

CHAPTER 11.

Balancing investments in existing and emerging approaches to address global health priorities

One of the common themes in contemporary global health is finding an optimal balance between investments in existing and emerging approaches to fight global health priorities (1). Existing interventions that have been proven to be effective can be scaled up at a certain cost to provide additional health gains, but they usually have limitations. Supporting the development of novel (emerging) interventions could potentially bring greater gains at a lower cost, but health gains are usually uncertain and take much more time to achieve. There are no simple solutions on how to balance funding support to these two competing approaches in order to achieve greatest gains at the lowest cost within a defined period of time (2). However, some components of successful strategies are beginning to seem increasingly apparent.

As a starting point, we could pose this question: why should anyone choose to invest in either scaling up existing health interventions, or developing new ones? Any investment can typically be linked to an expectation of the investor for some return on the investment. What can be seen as the return on investment in this case? This probably depends on who the investors are. Governments and international agencies are expected to use taxpayer's money to reduce the overall disease burden in a cost-effective way. Industry, however, may be primarily interested in generating patents on discoveries that could secure financial profit from future sales of both existing and emerging interventions. Not-for-profit organizations and private donors may have their own specific priorities that do not necessarily need to be either rational or transparent (3,4).

When balancing investments in existing and emerging health interventions, investors need to carefully consider the style of investing they wish to adopt. Among an incredibly broad set of options, investors can choose to support only one, or a subset of them; and can adopt a predominantly risk-neutral, risk-averting or risk-seeking approach. Governments are typically expected to adopt a risk-neutral approach and diversify their support across a set of proven existing interventions, while also identifying a few promising emerging approaches which they would like to introduce in the future. Industry would be more likely to adopt a risk-averting strategy by minimizing support to complex downstream research and focusing on improvements to existing interventions, while carefully selecting the most promising emerging ones that are already in the pipeline for investment. Private donors may adopt a risk-seeking strategy by focusing on a very specific target within a set time frame. They may be in a position to invite the most original ideas and out-of-the-box thinking that could revolutionize global health and eradicate the problem entirely, while accepting the risk that most of the funding will ultimately fail to result in any progress at all (5).

The time-frame within which investors expect a return on their investment is another critically important factor to consider. When the investment context is one of perceived urgency or of a short time horizon for action to achieve returns on investment, the balance will be heavily skewed towards support for implementing and upgrading existing interventions. If the investment context is one with a much longer-term horizon then the balance will shift towards more uncertain, higher risk options, which hold the promise of considerably greater benefits per unit of cost (6,7).

Acknowledgement: Originally published as: Igor Rudan, Ana Marušić and Harry Campbell: Addressing global health priorities: Balancing investments in existing and emerging approaches. Reprinted with permission from Edinburgh University Global Health Society under Creative Commons Attribution License (Journal of Global Health 2012; 2:010101).

References

1. Rudan I. Global health research priorities: mobilizing the developing world. Public Health 2012; 126:237-240.
2. Rudan I. The complex challenge of setting priorities in health research investments. Indian J Med Res 2009; 129:351-353.
3. Moran M, Guzman J, Ropars A-L, McDonald A, Jameson N, Omune B, et al. Neglected disease research and development: how much are we really spending? PLoS Med 2009; 6:e30.
4. Enserink M. Some neglected diseases are more neglected than others. Science 2009; 323:700.
5. Tomlinson M, Chopra M, Hoosain N, Rudan I. A review of selected research priority setting processes at national level in low and middle income countries: towards fair and legitimate priority setting. Health Res Policy Syst 2011; 9:19.
6. Rudan I, Chopra M, Kapiriri L, Gibson J, Lansang MA, Carneiro I, Ameratunga S, Tsai AC, Chan KY, Tomlinson M, Hess SY, Campbell H, El Arifeen S, Black RE. Setting priorities in global child health research investments: Universal challenges and conceptual framework. Croat Med J 2008; 49:398-408.
7. Viergever RF, Olifson S, Ghaffar A, Terry RF. A checklist for health research priority setting: nine common themes of good practice. Health Res Policy Syst 2010; 8:36.

CHAPTER 12.

Evidence-based priority setting for health care and research: tools to support policy in maternal, neonatal, and child health in Africa

Priority setting is required in every health care system. It guides investments in health care and health research, and respects resource constraints. It happens continuously, with or without appropriate tools or processes. Although priority-setting decisions have been described as difficult, value laden, and political, only a few research groups are focused on advancing the theory of priority setting and the development and validation of priority setting tools (1–4). These groups advocate the use of their tools, but their work is often not widely recognized, especially among the policy makers in developing countries, where these tools would be most helpful (2). Our primary objective in this essay is to present the available tools for priority setting that could be used by policy makers in low-resource settings. We also provide an assessment of the applicability and strengths of different tools in the context of maternal and child health in sub-Saharan Africa.

The analyses of investments in neglected diseases showed that they lack transparent priority-setting processes (2). This persisting situation results in remarkable levels of inequity between investments in different health priorities (1–6). Therefore, our secondary objective is to advocate the use of the tools that could lead to more rational priority setting in sub-Saharan Africa. An optimal tool should be able to draw on the best local evidence and guide policy makers and governments to identify, prioritize, and implement evidence-based health interventions for scale-up and delivery.

Although there is currently insufficient evidence that the use of priority-setting tools improves health outcomes and reverses existing inequities, we have ample evidence that the lack of a rational and transparent process generates inequity and stagnation in mortality levels (5,6). Recently, Youngkong et al. conducted a systematic review of empirical studies on health care priority setting in low-income countries (**Table 12-1**) (7). The review found that policy makers in developing countries rarely consider using the available priority-setting tools, but also that the available tools lack credibility for priority setting in low-resource settings (7,8). This is mainly because it is not easy to validate the tools or to link their output with concrete follow-up actions and policy development (9). Indeed, it is difficult to prove beyond all doubt that investments in health care or health research are valuable to society when compared to alternative investments such as infrastructure or the economy.

However, there are many examples of countries that have reduced their maternal and child disease burden substantially from very high starting levels, and of others that keep failing to achieve progress (10). We also have strong evidence on the key determinants of those successes, which has been incorporated into various priority-setting tools (1,4–9). The few studies that have evaluated processes in low-resource settings not using priority-setting tools found that most of them fell short on all four conditions of the "*accountability for reasonableness*" framework that assessed their basic legitimacy and fairness (11,12).

Moreover, there is evidence on the interventions and health research needed to improve maternal and child survival in low-resource settings. The key challenge is how to motivate and educate policy makers in sub-Saharan Africa to use the available priority-setting tools to direct the limited available resources into the most effective interventions and health research. We believe that addressing this challenge is critical, because it has been repeatedly shown that the scarcity of resources for health in sub-Saharan Africa is only part of the larger problem; the other part is that the scarce available resources are not being used efficiently by any standard, leading to tragic consequences for the population (2,4,6).

Several tools and processes are beginning to emerge as useful for priority setting in low-resource settings. In **Table 12-1** we classify different methodologies by the context (national/global level) and scope (health care/health research prioritization). We also provided some essential information on the use of each method: (i) the setting; (ii) participants included in the process; (iii) the specific topic addressed; (iv) the criteria that were used for prioritization; (v) the process that was used; and (vi) the nature of the outcome. An in-depth comparative analysis of all these tools is beyond the scope of this essay, but in **Table 12-1** we provide references to the key papers from which further information about those methods can be obtained ((13–37); Lawn et al., manuscript in preparation).

Table 12-1 shows that the "*burden of disease/cost effectiveness analysis*", promoted by the Disease Control Priorities Project (DCPP) (13), is an essential component of several tools that have been used for health care (interventions) prioritization: for example, the Marginal Budgeting for Bottlenecks (MBB) tool developed by UNICEF and The World Bank (14); WHO-CHOICE (Choosing

Interventions that are Cost-Effective) developed by the World Health Organization (14,15); and Lives Saved Tool (LiST) developed by Johns Hopkins University scientists and the Futures Institute (16). The DCPP approach for developing countries uses information on the burden of major diseases to assist decisions about the potential of affordable and effective interventions. The DCPP analysis identifies the *"best buys"*, i.e., the most cost-effective interventions in terms of DALYs saved per unit cost, that should compose a country's essential health care package (EHCP) (17). The EHCP should then influence program design and resource reallocation to help governments achieve the goal of reducing morbidity and mortality.

However, the DCPP authors note that factors other than cost-effectiveness influence priority setting in the real world, so the available evidence has to be considered in the context of local realities (13,17). Both MBB and WHO-CHOICE provide appropriate contextualization tools. However, the LiST software goes much further than any other tool in several dimensions. LiST contains an expansive evidence base of context-specific intervention effectiveness, generated by researchers from the WHO/UNICEF's Child Health Epidemiology Reference Group (CHERG) (33). It is a user-friendly decision-making computer software available in the public domain. It enables estimation of intervention impact on child mortality at national, regional, and global levels (16). Further important advantages of LiST include its validation in both African and South Asian contexts (34,35), an ability to perform very specific comparisons between alternative investment strategies over a specified time frame in terms of child survival outcomes (33–35), its application of an equity lens (36), and easy translation of outcomes into program planning with convincing country-level examples (37).

Policy makers in low-resource settings also need to set priorities for health research. **Table 12-1** shows that the CHNRI methodology has recently been used by several different groups to set health research priorities at the highest international level ((23–29), Lawn et al., manuscript in preparation). However, there are several other tools for setting research priorities at the national level, which were reviewed and evaluated by Tomlinson et al. (30). Whereas CHNRI method had its first national-level implementation in South Africa only recently (31), other tools and processes have been dominant at the national level. The Council on Health Research for Development's approach (COHRED) has been implemented in Brazil, Cameroon, Peru, and Philippines; the Essential National Health Research (ENHR) approach in Cameroon and South Africa; and the Combined Approach Matrix (CAM) in Malaysia, Pakistan, and Argentina (30).

COHRED, ENHR, and CAM all were developed by committees set up by international agencies. All these methods are very specific about context, and they are excellent for organizing all the available information. However, they do little to provide an algorithm, based on a transparent set of criteria, that can distinguish among many competing research investment options (4,29). This does not, however, diminish their utility in most situations where the development of an evidence base is required. That phase can then be followed by Delphi-type consultation processes among a designated set of experts. For example, CAM does exceptionally well in addressing the two dimensions of the context that it finds the most important: the *"public health"* dimension and the *"institutional"* dimension. Having only two dimensions limits CAM's flexibility, though, and it is difficult to see how additional dimensions – e.g., uncertainty over the outcome (inherent to all health research); accounting for investment styles; accounting for the risk exposure and benefit potential of each research option; or the likelihood of obtaining funding support from donors—could be added (33). The same limitation is also true for COHRED and ENHR.

Table 12-1. *Priority setting exercises for health care or health research in low resource settings (Abbreviations: PM – policy-makers; HM – health managers; HW – health workers; TE – technical experts; HP – health professionals; NGO – non-governmental organization; GP – general population; PA – patients; PS – private sector; OS – other stakeholders; DCPP – Disease Control Priorities Project; CHNRI – Child Health and Nutrition Research Initiative; CAM – Combined Approach Matrix; ENHR – Essential National Health Research; COHRED – Council on Health Research for Development).*

HEALTH CARE / HEALTH INTERVENTIONS – ALL LOW-RESOURCE COUNTRIES (REFS. 9,14,15)					
Setting	**Participants**	**Topic**	**Criteria**	**Process**	**Outcome**
Low-resource globally	TE	All major diseases	DCPP project consensus	Systematic reviews	Cost-effectiveness analysis
Low-resource globally	TE, PM, OS	Primary health care	Yes, modified CHNRI	CHNRI	Specific list with scores & ranks
Low-resource globally	TE, PM, OS	Stillbirth prevention	Yes, modified CHNRI	CHNRI	Specific list with scores & ranks
HEALTH CARE / HEALTH INTERVENTIONS – NATIONAL OR SUB-NATIONAL LEVEL (REF. 5)					
Setting	**Participants**	**Topic**	**Criteria**	**Process**	**Outcome**
Thailand	PM, HM, HW, TE	Several diseases	Yes, through lit. review	Semi-structured Interview	Table with choice frequency
Chile	None	Health system	Yes, through lit. review	Secondary data analysis	List with ranks for 56 choices

South Africa	PM, NGO, TE	HIV/AIDS	Yes, through lit. review	Group discus-sion & interview	List with ranks by 3 chosen criteria
Tanzania	PM	Health system	Yes, through group discuss.	Group discus-sion & question.	Ranking of criteria by importance
Tanzania	PM, HP, GP, PA	Health system	Not transparent	Group discussion	Description of different views
Tanzania	PM, HP, GP, PA	Several diseases	Yes, through lit. review	Deliberative process	List with ranks for 9 interventions
Argentina	PM (at all levels)	Health system	Yes, focus group and interviews	Focus group and interviews	List of criteria
Nepal	PM, HP	Several diseases	Yes, lit. review & group discus.	Individual rating	List with ranks for 33 interventions
Pakistan	PM	HIV/AIDS	Yes, in-depth interview	Interview	Description of po-licy maker's views
Burkina Faso, Ghana, Indon.	PM, HM, HW	Safe mother-hood program	Yes, self-admi-nistered quest.	Deliberative pr-ocess & quest.	Identifying 3 most important priorities
Uganda	PM, HW	Health system	Yes, interviews	Semi-structured interview	Description of criteria used
Uganda	PM, HW	Health system	Yes, one-on-one interviews	Interview & do-cument analysis	Description of criteria used
Ghana	PM, HW	Several diseases	Yes, group discussion	Individual rating	List with ranks for interventions
Uganda	PM, HW, GP	Health system	Yes, lit. & self-admin. quest.	Questionnaire with rating scale	List of criteria and their weights
Uganda	PM, HW, GP	Health system	Yes, group disc. & interviews	"Brainstorming" & questionnaire	List with ranks for criteria & choices
Ghana	PM, HM, TE, NGO	Reproductive health	Yes, lit. review and interview	Interview and secondary data	Demonstration of impact on priorities
Bosnia and Herzegovina	None	Health system	Not transparent	Secondary data analysis	Description of criteria used
South Africa	None	Health system	Yes, literature review	Secondary data analysis	List with ranks for interventions

HEALTH RESEARCH – ALL LOW-RESOURCE COUNTRIES (REFS. 16-23)					
Setting	**Participants**	**Topic**	**Criteria**	**Process**	**Outcome**
Low-resource globally	TE, PM, HP, OS	Mental health	Yes, standard CHNRI	CHNRI	Specific list with scores & ranks
Low-resource globally	TE, HP	Maternal and child survival	None – collec-tive opinion	Delphi	Specific list of priorities with ranks

Low-resource globally	TE, PM, HP, OS	Neonatal Infections	Yes, standard CHNRI	CHNRI	Specific list with scores & ranks
Low-resource globally	TE, PM, HP, OS	Childhood diarrhoea	Yes, standard CHNRI	CHNRI	Specific list with scores & ranks
Low-resource globally	TE, PM, HP, OS	Birth asphyxia	Yes, standard CHNRI	CHNRI	Specific list with scores & ranks
Low-resource globally	TE, PM, HP, OS	Childhood pneumonia	Yes, standard CHNRI	CHNRI	Specific list with scores & ranks
Low-resource globally	TE, PM, HP, OS	Zinc supple-mentation	Yes, standard CHNRI	CHNRI	Specific list with scores & ranks
Low-resource globally	TE, PM, HP, OS	Research into disabilities	Yes, modified CHNRI	CHNRI	Specific list with scores & ranks

HEALTH RESEARCH – NATIONAL OR SUB-NATIONAL LEVEL (REFS. 24,25)					
Setting	**Participants**	**Topic**	**Criteria**	**Process**	**Outcome**
Malaysia	TE, PM, OS	Health research	Yes, trans-parent list	CAM	General recom-mendations
Cameroon	Government officials	Health research	Not trans-parent	ENHR & COHRED	General objectives
Peru	TE	Health research	Not trans-parent	COHRED	General recom-mendations
South Africa	Government officials	Health research	Yes, trans-parent	ENHR	General recom-mendations
South Africa	TE, OS	Child health research	Yes, standard CHNRI	CHNRI	Specific list with scores & ranks
Brazil	PM, TE, HP, multiple OS	Health research	Yes, trans-parent	COHRED	General recom-mendations
Philippines	PM, TE, HP, OS	Health research	Not fully transparent	COHRED	General recom-mendations
Pakistan	PM, TE, HP, NGO, PS	Health research	Yes, transparent	CAM	General recom-mendations
Argentina	PM, TE, HP	Health research	Yes, transparent	CAM	General recom-mendations

An emerging tool that is rapidly gaining popularity in the area of health research prioritization is the CHNRI methodology. It was developed over four years (2005– 2008) with support from The World Bank for a transdisciplinary exercise of 15 experts. The experts assessed principles and practice of priority setting (4), reviewed universal challenges (18), developed a novel and robust conceptual framework (18), and provided guidance for stakeholder involvement (19) and for implementation of the method (20). Currently, they are in the process of development of user-friendly software that would enable simple, cheap, and effective conducting of CHNRI exercise via the internet.

The CHNRI methodology insists on transparency about the context in which priority setting takes place and the criteria used. It was initially developed for health research, but it has recently also been successfully used for health care and health interventions (**Table 12-1**) (21,22). Like the DCPP approach, it uses both cost-effectiveness and potential impact on disease burden as criteria. However, within a set of *"standard"* criteria, CHNRI also uses criteria relevant to the context—answerability, deliverability, affordability, sustainability, local capacity, likelihood of support, feasibility, equity, and others. The process is usually designed by policy makers or donors, conducted by technical experts in a transparent way (e.g., each vote counts equally), with a mechanism of stakeholder involvement. Stakeholders can assign different weights to the criteria used in the CHNRI exercise. The outcome is a comprehensive list with competing priorities ranked according to the combined scores they received in the process (18– 20). Such a list is helpful to policy makers because it provides an overview of strengths and weaknesses of competing investment options against many criteria, based on the collective input of technical experts. The list can also be adjusted by taking the values of many stakeholders into account.

The key challenges that need to be overcome in sub-Saharan Africa to improve the processes of prioritization in health care and health research include the following: increased acceptability and popularity with local policy makers, appreciation of the local context, clarity about the criteria used, transparency in the input from the stakeholders, and more specific guidance on translation into policy. Many papers that analyze the strategies for improving maternal and child survival conclude with highlighting the challenges such as integration, requirements for selection of community health workers, operational research into systems, among others. These are all admirable and important future areas of research. However, they are not exactly new, ground-breaking, or very specific, and the qualitative nature of the process frequently does not provide sufficient guidance to policy makers on the specific next steps. Tools such as LiST (for health care/interventions) and CHNRI (for health research) involve local experts and incorporate issues of local context into priority determination in a transparent, user-friendly, replicable, quantifiable and specific, algorithm-like manner. Both of these tools were primarily developed to address child health problems and should be considered by policy makers in the area of maternal and child health in sub-Saharan Africa.

The use of scientific evidence and principles in setting health priorities has an enormous potential to lead to more rational decision making, especially in low-resource settings where decision-making has long lacked formal tools, processes, or an evidence base. We believe one cannot overstate the value of building and supporting the capacity of local experts and policy makers in sub-Saharan Africa to initiate and assist their own national government's policy formation process in maternal and child health, and of government's being able to generate rigorous credible *"home grown"* advice (4,27,32). Regardless of the limitations of the available tools, we strongly recommend their use in development of sound maternal and child health policies in sub-Saharan Africa over the alternative of not using any method. The use of such tools would promote attention to objective evidence in public policy debates, often leading to decisions that are made are more clearly and in the public interest (27,32).

Acknowledgement: Originally published as: Igor Rudan, Lydia Kapiriri, Mark Tomlinson, Manuela Balliet, Barney Cohen and Mickey Chopra: Evidence-based priority setting for health care and research: tools to support policy in maternal, neonatal, and child health in Africa. Reprinted with permission from Public Library of Science (PLoS) under Creative Commons Attribution License (PLoS Medicine 2010; 7:e1000308).

References

1. World Health Organization. Report of the World Health Organization Expert Working Group on Research and Development Financing 2010. (Available from: http://www.who.int/phi/documents/ RDFinancingwithISBN.pdf; Accessed: 10 Mar 2010).
2. Kapiriri L, Norheim OF, Martin DK. Fairness and accountability for reasonableness. Do the views of priority setting decision makers differ across health systems and levels of decision making? Soc Sci Med 2009; 68:766–773.
3. Klein R. Puzzling out priorities. Why we must acknowledge that rationing is a political process. Br Med J 1998; 317:959–960.
4. Rudan I, Gibson J, Kapiriri L, Lansang MA, Hyder AA, et al. Setting priorities in global child health research investments: Assessment of principles and practice. Croat Med J 2007; 48:595–604.
5. Moran M, Guzman J, Ropars A-L, McDonald A, Jameson N, Omune B, Ryan S, Wu L. Neglected disease research and development: how much are we really spending? PLoS Med 2009; 6:e30.
6. Enserink M. Some neglected diseases are more neglected than others. Science 2009; 323:700.
7. Youngkong S, Kapiriri L, Baltussen R. Setting priorities for health interventions in developing countries: a review of empirical studies. Trop Med Int Health 2009; 14:930–939.
8. Kapiriri L, Arnesen T, Norheim OF. Is cost-effectiveness analysis preferred to severity of disease as the main guiding principle in priority setting in resource poor settings? The case of Uganda. Cost Effect Resource Allocat 2004; 2:1–11.
9. Allen L. The art of evaluating the impact of medical science. Bull WHO 2010; 88:4.
10. Rudan I, Chan KY, Zhang JSF, Theodoratou E, Feng XL, Salomon J, Lawn JE, Cousens S, Black RE, Guo Y, Campbell H. Causes of deaths in children younger than 5 years in China in 2008. Lancet 2010; 375:1083–1089.

11. Kapiriri L, Martin DK. Priority setting in developing countries health care institutions: the case of a Ugandan hospital. BMC Health Serv Res 2006; 6:127.
12. Mshana S, Shemilu H, Ndawi B. What do district health planners in Tanzania think about improving priority setting using "Accountability for Reasonableness"? BMC Health Serv Res 2007; 7:180.
13. Laxminarayan R, Mills AJ, Breman JG, Measham AR, Alleyne G, et al. Advancement of global health: key messages from the Disease Control Priorities Project. Lancet 2006; 367:1193.
14. UNICEF/The World Bank. Marginal Budgeting for Bottlenecks. (Available from: http:// www.who.int/ pmnch/topics/economics/costingtools_resources/en/index.html; Accessed: 10 March 2010).
15. Adam T, Lim SS, Mehta S, Bhutta ZA, Fogstad H, et al. Cost effectiveness analysis of strategies for maternal and neonatal health in developing countries. BMJ 2005; 331:1107.
16. Victora CG. LiST: using epidemiology to guide child survival policymaking and programming. Int J Epidemiol 2010; 39(Suppl 1):i1–2.
17. Bobadilla JL, Cowley P, Musgrove P, Saxenian H. Design, content and financing of an essential national package of health services. Bull World Health Organ 1992; 72:653–662.
18. Rudan I, Chopra M, Kapiriri L, Gibson J, Lansang MA, et al. Setting priorities in global child health research investments: universal challenges and conceptual framework. Croat Med J 2008; 49:307–317.
19. Kapiriri L, Tomlinson M, Gibson J, Chopra M, El Arifeen S, et al. Setting priorities in global child health research investments: Addressing the values of the stakeholders. Croat Med J 2007; 48:618–627.
20. Rudan I, Gibson JL, Ameratunga S, El Arifeen S, Bhutta ZA, et al. Setting priorities in global child health research investments: Guidelines for implementation of the CHNRI method. Croat Med J 2008; 49:720–733.
21. Walley J, Lawn JE, Tinker A, De Francisco A, Chopra M, et al. Primary Health Care: making Alma Ata a reality. Lancet 2008; 372:1001–1007.
22. Pattinson R, Lawn JE, Darmstadt G, Rubens C, Flenady V, et al. Priority interventions to reduce the global burden of stillbirths. Lancet, 2010; (in preparation)
23. Tomlinson M, Rudan I, Saxena S, Swartz L, Tsai AC, Patel V. Setting investment priorities for research in global mental health. Bull World Health Organ 2009; 87:438–446.
24. Costello A, Filippi V, Kubba T, Horton R. Research challenges to improve maternal and child survival. Lancet 2007; 369:1240–1243.
25. Bahl R, Martines J, Ali N, Bhan MK, Carlo W, et al. Research priorities to reduce global mortality from newborn infections by 2015. Pediatr Inf Dis J 2009; 28(Suppl 1):S43–S48.
26. Fontaine O, Kosek M, Bhatnagar S, Boschi-Pinto C, Chan KY, et al. Setting research priorities to reduce global mortality from childhood diarrhoea by 2015. PLoS Med 2009; 6:e41.
27. Rudan I, El Arifeen S, Black RE, Campbell H. Childhood pneumonia and diarrhoea: Setting our priorities right. Lancet Inf Dis 2007; 7:56–61.
28. Brown KH, Hess SY, Boy E, Gibson RS, Horton S, et al. Setting priorities for zinc-related health research to reduce children's disease burden worldwide: An application of the Child Health and Nutrition Research Initiative's research priority-setting method. Public Health Nutr 2009; 12:389–396.

29. Tomlinson M, Swartz L, Officer A, Chan KY, Rudan I, Saxena S. Research priorities for health of people with disabilities: an expert opinion exercise. Lancet 2009; 374:1857–1862.

30. Tomlinson M, Chopra M, Hoosein N, Rudan I. Research priority setting processes at national level: Good practices for health research. Health Syst Res Policy 2011; 9:19.

31. Tomlinson M, Chopra M, Sanders D, Bradshaw D, Hendricks M, et al. Setting priorities in child health research investments for South Africa. PLoS Med 2007; 4: e259.

32. Rudan I. The complex challenge of setting priorities in health research investments. Indian J Med Res 2009; 129:351–353.

33. Walker N, Fischer-Walker C, Bryce J, Bahl R, Cousens S. CHERG Review Groups on Intervention Effects Standards for CHERG reviews of intervention effects on child survival. Int J Epidemiol 2010; 39(Suppl 1):i21–31.

34. Friberg IK, Bhutta ZA, Darmstadt GL, Bang A, Cousens S, et al. Comparing modelled predictions of neonatal mortality impacts using LiST with observed results of community-based intervention trials in South Asia. Int J Epidemiol 2010; 39(Suppl 1):i11–20.

35. Hazel E, Gilroy K, Friberg I, Black RE, Bryce J, et al. Comparing modelled to measured mortality reductions: applying the Lives Saved Tool to evaluation data from the Accelerated Child Survival Programme in West Africa. Int J Epidemiol 2010; 39(Suppl 1):i32–9.

36. Amouzou A, Richard SA, Friberg IK, Bryce J, Baqui AH, et al. How well does LiST capture mortality by wealth quintile? A comparison of measured versus modelled mortality rates among children under-five in Bangladesh. Int J Epidemiol 2010; 39(Suppl 1):i186–92.

37. Bryce J, Friberg IK, Kraushaar D, Nsona H, Afenyadu GY, et al. LiST as a catalyst in program planning: experiences from Burkina Faso, Ghana and Malawi. Int J Epidemiol 2010; 39(Suppl 1):i40–7.

CHAPTER 13.

Population: Better lives, not just contraceptives

Last month's London Summit on Family Planning, hosted by the Bill & Melinda Gates Foundation and the UK government's Department for International Development, has been hailed as a resounding success. A total of US$ 2.6 billion was pledged to provide 120 million women and girls in developing countries with access to family-planning services by 2020. In measuring the success of this welcome campaign, the delivery of social change should also be taken into account.

The hosts emphasize that results will be rapid and quantifiable, for example in terms of the number of contraceptives supplied. But reducing unwanted pregnancies requires other improvements in women's lives, such as better education for girls and reduced child mortality (1), outreach by community-health workers and women's empowerment (see, for example, ref. 2), and quality family-planning programmes. Such factors are harder to quantify.

Focusing simply on what can be measured encourages short-term, narrow interventions rather than broader, longer-term strategies. For instance, value-for-money criteria make it tempting to sidestep national health-care systems, when supporting these is crucial to the delivery of appropriate technologies in developing countries.

Acknowledgement: Originally published as: Devi Sridhar and Karen Grépin: Population: Better lives, not just contraceptives. Reprinted with permission from MacMillan Publishers / Nature Publishing Group (Nature 2012; 488:32).

References

1. Dreze J, Murthi M. Popul Dev Rev 2001; 27:33–63.
2. Available from: go.nature.com/bpjgma

CHAPTER 14.

Childhood pneumonia deaths: A new role for health workers?

Pneumonia is the leading cause of child death worldwide, causing the deaths of more than 2 million children every year (1). Deaths from pneumonia, more than any other major childhood disease, affect mainly underprivileged and poor children who have limited or no access to health systems (2). Most of these deaths are potentially avoidable through application of existing interventions (3). However, highly cost-effective interventions are neither being adequately implemented in local settings, nor being implemented at a scale that reaches all children nationwide.

Historical evidence from developed countries suggests that the most effective way to fight mortality due to childhood pneumonia is through an overall improvement in living conditions along with improved nutrition (4). In the short term, strategies that offer most promise for the control of childhood pneumonia in developing countries include immunisation with new conjugate vaccines against *Streptococcus pneumoniae* and *Haemophilus influenzae type b*, improvement in the nutritional status of children (including good breastfeeding practices), reduction of environmental risks (such as exposure to indoor air pollution), and increased access to effective case management. Case management not only requires enhanced first-level care, but also needs promotion and development of community case management in areas with poor access to first-level facilities and investment to improve the quality of hospital care.

The Lancet study by Enayet Chowdhury and colleagues (5) shows the importance of implementation research. The investigators found that many sick children who were referred for hospital care by health workers in first-level facilities in Bangladesh never actually received treatment. They proposed a modification to WHO's Integrated Management of Childhood Illness (IMCI) guidelines (6) in response to this problem. Chowdhury evaluated an extension of the role of health workers from simple triage and hospital referral of very sick children to include treatment of children with severe pneumonia (IMCI classification) with oral amoxicillin at home. Allowing health workers to give antibiotic treatment was both safe and effective in this study setting, and the investigators recommended adoption of the modified guideline by IMCI national programmes.

This finding is consistent with results from controlled trials in other resource-poor settings, which showed that oral amoxicillin is as effective as intramuscular administration of benzylpenicillin or ampicillin for treatment of children with an IMCI classification of severe pneumonia (7,8). The modification also resulted in a greater than previous use of first-level health services, which the investigators interpret as a community response to the availability of improved care. This strategy seems to have been popular with users, and it significantly improved access to effective treatment for pneumonia.

The logical consequence of these findings would be to simplify the existing WHO guidelines by collapsing current IMCI classifications of pneumonia and severe pneumonia into one episode of pneumonia, and to treat all children with pneumonia at home with oral amoxicillin. Chowdhury and colleagues show that such a modification has the potential to substantially increase the proportion of patients in the community with pneumonia who will receive effective treatment. Additionally, restriction of hospital referrals to a more severely ill group of children with pneumonia could reduce overcrowding in referral hospitals, thus improving quality of care at the hospitals.

Health-systems research, as shown in Chowdhury and colleagues' study, is crucially important to help guide the development of effective, efficient, and locally relevant health systems. Although in theory the timely delivery of a cheap oral antibiotic to a child with pneumonia is the most cost-effective intervention to prevent pneumonia-related deaths, evaluations of IMCI programmes in The Gambia, Kenya, and Ethiopia have shown that in practice only a few patients ever get to hospital and receive correct management for pneumonia (9,10). Chowdhury shows how investment in implementation research can identify new solutions to existing difficulties and thus increase the effectiveness of case-management strategies. Their modification of the IMCI programme guidelines increased the coverage of correct treatment of children with severe pneumonia from 30–40% to as high as 90%. Although these findings should be replicated before adoption of this modification in high-mortality areas, we think that this approach can probably be applied widely. However, the exception will be areas in which HIV is a major public-health problem, because management of severe pneumonia differs in those settings.

We welcome a substantial increase in investment in controlled trials in developing countries to address crucial gaps in information (such as the correct case management of severe pneumonia in children with HIV infection), and in health-policy and systems research to identify effective ways to improve and scale up implementation of interventions against pneumonia (11,12).

Acknowledgement: *Originally published as: Igor Rudan and Harry Campbell: Childhood pneumonia deaths: A new role for health workers? Reprinted with permission from Elsevier (Lancet 2008; 372:781-782).*

References

1. Rudan I, Boschi-Pinto C, Biloglav Z, Mulholland K, Campbell H. Epidemiology and etiology of childhood pneumonia. Bull World Health Organ 2008; 86:408–416.
2. Mulholland K. Childhood pneumonia mortality—a permanent global emergency. Lancet 2007; 370:285–289.
3. Bryce J, el Arifeen S, Pariyo G, et al, and the Multi-Country Evaluation of IMCI Study Group. Reducing child mortality: can public health deliver? Lancet 2003; 362:159–164.
4. Greenwood BM, Weber MW, Mulholland K. Childhood pneumonia: preventing the world's biggest killer of children. Bull World Health Organ 2007; 85:502–503.
5. Chowdhury EK, El Arifeen S, Rahman M, et al. Care at first-level facilities for children with severe pneumonia in Bangladesh: a cohort study. Lancet 2008; 372:822-830.
6. Tulloch J. Integrated approach to child health in developing countries. Lancet 1999; 354 (suppl II): SII16–20.
7. Hazir T, Fox LM, Nisar YB, et al, for the New Outpatient Short-Course Home Oral Therapy for Severe Pneumonia (NO-SHOTS) Study Group. Ambulatory short-course high-dose oral amoxicillin for treatment of severe pneumonia in children: a randomised equivalency trial. Lancet 2008; 371:49–56.
8. Addo-Yobo E, Chisaka N, Hassan M, et al, for the Amoxicillin Penicillin Pneumonia International Study (APPIS) group. Oral amoxicillin versus injectable penicillin for severe pneumonia in children aged 3 to 59 months: a randomised multicentre equivalency study. Lancet 2004; 364:1141–1148.
9. WHO Division of Child Health and Development. Integrated management of childhood illness: conclusions. Bull World Health Organ 1997; 75 (suppl 1):119–128.
10. Bryce J, Terreri N, Victora CG, et al. Countdown to 2015: tracking intervention coverage for child survival. Lancet 2006; 368:1067–1076.
11. Rudan I, Lawn J, Cousens S, et al. Gaps in policy-relevant information on burden of disease in children: a systematic review. Lancet 2005; 365:2031–2040.
12. Rudan I, El Arifeen S, Black RE, Campbell H. Childhood pneumonia and diarrhoea: setting our priorities right. Lancet Infect Dis 2007; 7:56–61.

CHAPTER 15.

Ebola shows how our global health priorities need to be shaken up

Amnesia has set in across the world as the fear and global attention given to Ebola recedes. But this is not a new phenomenon. With SARS, avian flu, swine flu and MERS, there were repeated calls to fix the global health system to avoid previous mistakes. We cannot continue to be surprised when a health crisis emerges and we need to start to take a long-term, inclusive perspective to ensure health security across the world. Myopia was a key factor in the failure to respond to Ebola in a rapid and effective way. There are three immediate steps that should be taken:

1. We need a better definition of health security. This would focus on identifying the risks that challenge the health of individuals and populations across the world. Since the second world war, this concept has become increasingly narrowed to one in which health threats are perceived to be only those that affect rich countries' citizens and interests. Health security became part of national security, instead of its original definition as the health part of human security. However, as the Ebola crisis revealed, a national security lens is not always helpful in pandemic preparedness, given that it is difficult to predict which regions and countries will be affected, and how the disease might then spread across the world.

The self-interest of countries is exactly why the World Health Organisation was created: so that states would be willing to compromise their short-term interests for collaboration on long-term matters. Since then, rich countries, through the use of voluntary earmarked funds for specific short-term priorities, have increasingly eroded the core capacity of the WHO to deliver on this mandate. For example, its outbreak and crisis budget was cut in half from US$ 469 million in 2012-13 to US$ 241 million in 2014-15.

2. We need to listen to what governments are asking for assistance with. Throughout visits to health ministries across the world, including most recently in Liberia, what we have continually heard is that countries want support from the global community to build an infrastructure that is capable of both public health activities such as information-gathering and surveillance as well as delivering health services. Governments should be responsible for leading these efforts and the goal should be to have domestic sources of revenue fund recurrent expenditures such as health workforce salaries as well as the purchase of commodities.

Health ministers are weary of new initiatives and plans that jostle them from one disease priority to another. They want to build robust and flexible systems that can deal not only with outbreaks such as Ebola, but also with maternal health, diabetes, cancer and depression. On a basic level health facilities need to have running water, electricity, laundry facilities and good sanitation practices, including waste disposal, not to mention doctors, nurses, technicians and community health workers.

Citizens want to have the same democratic debates we have in the US and UK about what the health system should deliver, how it should be structured, who shoulders the financial burden and how to hold politicians to account for these promises. And it makes economic sense. As a recent *Save the Children* report noted, the gap in funding for comprehensive health services for the three Ebola-affected countries, was US$ 1.58 billion in 2012, only a third of the US$ 4.3 billion that international help to fight Ebola has pledged so far.

3. We need to invest in women and girls in a long-term way. This should focus not only on whether they complete primary school or have skilled attendants at birth, but also on broader economic, social and cultural empowerment. As the *No Ceilings Report*, a collaboration between the Clinton Foundation and the Gates Foundation, notes, a growing body of evidence clearly shows that investing in women and girls in education and more broadly has a true multiplier effect. One extra year of schooling beyond a country's average can increase a woman's wages by 10%. Those wages are good for a woman and her family – and provide more potential tax revenues to countries to invest in things like their health systems.

Higher female participation in legislatures has been found to correlate to higher perceptions among men and women of government legitimacy, a crucial dynamic when debating issues such as what a health system should look like and how it should be financed. As with health, many of the investments to get more girls in school and women in the workforce are longer-term, but unlike health, it requires shifts in mindsets and laws rather than only intensive investment.

On a final note, there is continual political pressure for novelty. The media has treated Ebola as if we have never had an infectious disease outbreak before and that we are surprised that it can spread across the world in a matter of weeks. The kneejerk response is to develop a disease-specific and narrow outbreak preparedness policy which neglects the two biggest risks to health security: weak to nonexistent public health infrastructure and the low status of women in society.

Let's start getting the politics behind the evidence and overcome the myopia when it comes to global health.

Acknowledgement: Originally published as: Chelsea Clinton and Devi Sridhar: Ebola shows how our global health priorities need to be shaken up. Reprinted with permission from The Guardian under open license terms and conditions (The Guardian, 2015).

CHAPTER 16.

Why no-one talks about non-communicable diseases

Infectious disease control was at the top of the agenda during the sixty-third session of the World Health Assembly, which took place in May 2010 in Geneva. With much attention given to progress towards achieving the health-related Millennium Development Goals, polio eradication, the implementation of the International Health Regulations, the regulation of counterfeit drugs, and influenza preparedness, there was little time to discuss one of the largest killers: non-communicable or chronic diseases.

Together, chronic diseases are responsible for about 60% of deaths worldwide. The big four – diabetes, cardiovascular disease, cancer, and chronic respiratory diseases – are caused by three common risk factors: tobacco use, unhealthy diet, and lack of exercise.

Contrary to popular perception, the poor are the worst affected. The All India Institute of Medical Sciences reported that 11% of men and almost 10% of women – living in urban slums in India had diabetes. Similarly, researchers from the Pan American Health Organization found that 47% of women and 44% of men in Peru had hypertension, with the poorest households in the study experiencing the highest burden of the chronic disease. Numerous studies demonstrate the strong link between poverty and chronic diseases.

What money is available to tackle this problem? It is estimated that less than 3% of total donor funding goes to addressing non-communicable diseases, and a Lancet study found that, in 2005, chronic disease funding from the four largest donors in health was estimated at US$ 3 per death annually, compared to US$ 1,030 for HIV/AIDS.

Research by the Center for Global Development has shown that major donors such as the United States Government, the World Bank, and the United Kingdom Department for International Development have been reluctant to provide grants and loans to tackle non-communicable disease. Why is there such miniscule funding on the table? Perhaps because chronic diseases are not seen as directly linked to poverty or development, but are superficially attributed to affluence and Westernization. Perhaps because these conditions do not evoke the same feelings of empathy and social justice as do the traditional diseases associated with poverty. Perhaps because we put the onus of responsibility on the individual rather than on society, on personal choice rather than socio-economic circumstance.

Since donors are not interested, financing and institution-building will need to come from national governments. Yet it is difficult for national governments to invest in preventing chronic disease. In low-income, aid-dependent countries, governments must orient health strategies towards the Millennium Development Goals (which exclude chronic disease) to receive external funding, which can constitute 50% or more of the health budget. Even self-reliant countries such as Brazil and India sing the same tune. Although both countries are overwhelmed by cardiovascular disease, mental health problems, unintentional injuries, and cancer, there is a tremendous mismatch between government spending priorities and priority needs for the people of these nations.

This is where regional forums in health become central, and can complement global discussion and activities. Recently, the Caribbean Community Secretariat pushed for a UN General Assembly resolution on non-communicable diseases and possibly a UN General Assembly Special Session. This suggests that issues of non-communicable disease might have more salience at the regional level, particularly in the Middle East and the Caribbean, which are being ravaged by these diseases, than at the global level where investment in infectious disease prevention and treatment still dominate.

The recent decision by the UN General Assembly to hold a High-Level Summit involving Heads of State on non-communicable diseases in September 2011 is a major step forward. The next year presents a huge opportunity to provide compelling evidence to key officials in governments and development agencies that non-communicable diseases are a development concern – a case which helped raise the profile of HIV/AIDS – and to persuade the public that non-communicable diseases are as deserving of financing and attention as infectious diseases.

Acknowledgement: Originally published as: Devi Sridhar: Why no-one talks about non-communicable diseases. From United Nations Chronicle, by Devi Sridhar, © 2010, United Nations. Reprinted with the permission of the United Nations.

CHAPTER 17.

Political priority in the global fight against non-communicable diseases

The prevalence of non–communicable diseases – such as cancer, diabetes, cardiovascular disease, and chronic respiratory diseases – is surging globally. In 2004 deaths due to NCDs accounted for three out of five deaths worldwide, with 80% of these deaths occurring in low– and middle– income countries (1). What is more, deaths due to NCDs are predicted to increase by 15% worldwide between 2010 and 2020 (2).

NCDs are no longer just the scourge of the rich. As the World Health Organization (WHO) recently observed: *"NCDs and poverty create a vicious cycle whereby poverty exposes people to behavioural risk factors for NCDs and, in turn, the resulting NCDs may become an important driver to the downward spiral that leads families towards poverty"* (3). A recent World Bank study in India found that treatment costs for an individual with diabetes typically consume between 15 to 25% of household earnings (4). Where families lack access to affordable health care – a reality that is especially commonplace in low and middle–income countries – they tend to forego care or fall into financial hardship; in both cases, the poor end up suffering the worst (5). Moreover, the main risk factors for NCDs are perpetuated through social norms and practices. According to the WHO, these risk factors include tobacco use and exposure to second–hand smoke, unhealthy diet, physical inactivity, and harmful use of alcohol (2). The impacts of these factors are not immediately detectable (as in the case of an infectious virus), but evolve over the course of one's lifetime. NCDs can thus be described as *"invisible"* diseases: their long–term nature makes it such that sufferers often go unnoticed.

NCDs are thus rooted in the social determinants of health and cannot be stopped through individual action alone. By way of example, current global marketing activities are driving the transition towards diets that are high in sugar and saturated fat, thus increasing the risk of developing one or more NCDs (6). Research has also demonstrated strong links between increased tobacco consumption, free trade, and foreign direct investment. For instance, in the 1980s bilateral trade agreements signed between the US and several countries in Asia resulted in a spike in demand for tobacco products, especially in the poorest Asian countries (7).

Recognising the need for a collective response, the WHO has responded with a shortlist of *"best buy"* policy interventions to prevent and treat NCDs. These policies include tax increases to curb tobacco use; restrictions on the marketing of alcohol; replacement of trans fats to promote healthier diets; hepatitis B immunisation to prevent liver cancer; and multi–drug therapy to prevent heart attacks and strokes (8). Most significantly, these *"best buys"* can be implemented at relatively low cost, ranging from US$ 1.50–2.00 per head in low and middle-income countries to US$ 3 per head in upper–middle income countries (8). The costs of inaction are much greater: the WHO estimates that each 10% rise in NCDs is associated with 0.5% lower rates of annual economic growth (3). Thus, in 2011 the World Economic Forum ranked NCDs among the major global threats to economic development (9). Yet despite the availability of cost–effective interventions, NCDs receive less than 3% of annual development assistance for health to low and middle income countries (10). The top donors in global health – including the Bill and Melinda Gates Foundation, the US Government, and the World Bank – commit less than 2% of their budgets to the prevention and control of NCDs (11). NCDs cause the highest burden of disease across the world, and yet the global response to this reality has been woefully inadequate.

Why is there such meagre funding on the table for the prevention and control of NCDs? Why has a global plan of action aimed at halting the spread of NCDs been so difficult to achieve? This paper aims to tackle these two inter-related questions by analysing NCDs through the lens of Jeremy Shiffman's (2009) political priority framework (12). We define global political priority as *"the degree to which international and national political leaders actively give attention to an issue, and back up that attention with the provision of financial, technical, and human resources that are commensurate with the severity of the issue"* (13). Grounded in social constructionism, this framework critically examines the relationship between agenda setting and technical factors in global health, such as the existence of cost–effective interventions and a high mortality burden. Shiffman calls into question the tendency on the part of many global health advocates to treat indicators of the burden of disease as self–evident. To this end, Shiffman argues that strategic communication surrounding the causes, effects, and implications of disease ought to be a central task of health advocates. Following this logic, we explore the ways in which the policy community surrounding NCDs – or the network of individuals and organisations concerned with the issue – have come to understand and portray the issue's importance. In this manner, we explain the neglect of NCDs on the global stage in terms of a lack of strategic communication.

We begin by outlining the theoretical approach and methodology to be followed throughout the paper. Next, we explore the various ideas and framing mechanisms that have been used to portray NCDs. Finally, we seek to address two weaknesses in the Shiffman framework. We conclude by reconciling the Shiffman framework's focus on strategic communication with the claim, advanced by several global health experts, that well–financed corporate and private agendas currently act to undermine the pursuit of health for all.

1. Social constructionism. This paper follows in the social constructionist tradition, whose most basic tenet holds that "*(our) socially shared interpretations mediate and form our perceptions of reality*" (12). While the social construction of reality is well established in social scientific research (14-16), this approach has been applied in only a handful of instances in the field of public health (17,18). This paper thus aims to show the rich insights to be gained from applying a social constructionist approach to the study of human disease. In order to attract attention for an issue, we argue that actors must engage in "*strategic social construction*". This is defined as the process whereby actors conduct means–ends calculations with a view to changing other actors' utility function in ways that reflect new normative commitments (19). Moreover, we operate from the assumption that a desire on the part of a group of actors to transform ideas into norms can be meaningfully translated into an effective plan of action; in other words, that "*we can think about the strategic activity of actors in an intersubjectively structured political universe*" (20).

Consequently, we use Shiffman's (2009) political priority framework as a tool for understanding the process of translating grievances into norms that demand action. Shiffman identifies three variables that are fundamental to raising the priority of a given issue area: (i) ideas, (ii) institutions, and (iii) policy communities (12). The framework to form the basis of the present analysis is a condensed version of an earlier framework proposed by Shiffman and Smith (2007). We use the 2009 version of the framework as it makes explicit its critique of materialist approaches that explain health priority–setting in terms of "*objective*" indicators (13).

From a methodological perspective, this paper fits within the category of discipline configurative case study (21). This type of study uses established theories to explain a case, whether for the purpose of highlighting important historical developments, improving pedagogy, or drawing attention to the need for new theory in neglected areas. One limitation of this approach is the temptation to make predictions about future events on the basis of theories that "*lack clarity and internal consistency*" (21). To date, the Shiffman framework has been applied to a limited number of cases, including maternal and child health, neonatal health, and oral health (13,22-24). Beyond these cases, the framework's theoretical implications remain unspecified. We endeavour to surmount this limitation by clarifying and refining the framework. A second limitation of this paper is its lack of interview data. However, wherever possible we incorporate primary source material, including direct statements from actors in the public sector, private industry, and civil society. Third, this paper does not focus on the institutional factors that have impeded the generation of priority for NCDs. While we acknowledge that well–financed institutions are crucial in terms of giving *"teeth"* to an issue, this paper aims to refine the framework's theoretical assumptions. If incorporated into future analyses, these refinements can be used to situate the role of institutions in the priority generation process.

2. The use of ideas in NCD advocacy. What ideas have been used to portray NCDs? What ideas have been ignored? This will be accomplished by analysing these ideas from three vantage points: issue framing, issue characteristics, and implementation. Framing refers to *"conscious strategic efforts by groups of people to fashion shared understandings of the world and of themselves that legitimate and motivate collective action"* (25). It follows from this definition that issues in global health do not automatically designate themselves as priority issues, but rather, that issues are selectively and consciously advanced by organised groups of people. Crucially, however, the frames that condition these strategic decisions often go unnoticed. As such, *"(we) do not see the frame directly, but infer its presence by its characteristic expressions and language. Each frame gives the advantage to certain ways of talking and thinking, while placing "other out of the picture"'* (26).

Why, then, do certain frames resonate with political leaders and the public at large and subsequently compel action, while others do not? Two characteristics that can be used to explain this variance in the efficacy of frames are *"credibility"* and *"salience"* (27). Credibility refers to *"how truthful people perceive the frame to be"*, whereas salience refers to *"how central (the frame) is to their lives"* (12). To zero in on how credibility and salience are portrayed, Shiffman (2009) identifies two types of claims generally used by activists in global health: problem claims, surrounding severity and neglect of their issue; and solution claims, surrounding a given problem's tractability and the benefits that would ensue from addressing it (12). An example of a problem claim from the literature on NCDs is as follows: *"An urgent and collective response is required because no country alone can address a threat of this magnitude"* (5). Conversely, in the aim of drawing attention to the need for concerted action on NCDs, other advocates have put forth the following solutions claim: *"The evidence is unequivocal: major and rapid health and economic gains are possible with only modest investments in prevention and control of chronic diseases"* (28).

The purpose of these claims is to convince others to *"buy into"* the interpretations that they advance. For instance, the notion of *"magnitude"* in the aforementioned problem claim is invoked in order to make a normative judgment. In this particular claim, magnitude is linked with the notion of a *"collective response"*, or the capacity of human beings to affect meaningful change. As such, the intended effect of this claim is to exclude interpretations that reduce the proliferation of NCDs to individual responsibility by framing the issue in terms of unrealised potential for collective action. Credible claims, therefore, are ones that align with previously held frames. But what role has framing played in contributing to the lack of priority for NCDs? What frames have been used to portray this issue, and how can we assess the effectiveness of these frames?

First, the issue of credibility has been dominated by calls to improve surveillance of these diseases, particularly in the developing world. The WHO's 2008–2013 *Global Strategy for the Prevention and Control of Noncommunicable Diseases* repeatedly identifies the elaboration of *"reliable population–based mortality statistics and standardized data"* as a key strategic objective (29). Indeed, for one well–versed in quantitative methods, the availability of credible facts demonstrating the effects of NCDs may be enough to motivate action. In response to enduring confusion about the causes of NCDs such as lack of personal control, the lead author of one of the papers in the first Lancet series on chronic diseases thus remarked: *"I thought we got rid of these myths. But they keep coming back"* (30).

However, for others in government and in industry, mere reliance on statistics may prove unconvincing. Indeed, a wide range of factors has served to reinforce the perception that NCDs are unworthy of attention. For instance, the very label of these diseases is a case study in poor branding: *"anything that begins with "non" may be considered a "non–issue" or a "non–starter""* (31). Moreover, it fails to convey the crucial point that NCDs are indeed communicable: not just through infectious modes of transmission, but also through social norms and practices. In China, for instance, 59% of Chinese men smoke, compared to only 4% of women (32). In the Chinese context, smoking – a key risk factor for NCDs – is therefore interwoven with gender roles and perceptions of social status. A label that at first glance excludes social processes as forms of disease communication thus represents a major impediment to the generation of priority.

The lack of a *"human face"* to portrayals of NCDs represents a second problem. In contrast to a disease such as polio, where the victim is immediately recognisable by virtue or his or her physical appearance, sufferers of diseases such as diabetes often go unnoticed. To suggest that evidence alone can compel action is to ignore the role of emotion and affect in shaping human reactions to external events (33). Yet NCDs have not been portrayed through the use of images and media clips that depict actual human sufferers (34). This serves to dehumanise the issue, limiting its emotional appeal, and ultimately, its salience.

These examples suggest that credibility, understood in terms of technical evidence, has dominated the debate surrounding NCDs. Crucially, this has happened at the expense of salience. The role of framing in conveying the implications of mortality statistics is often misunderstood (as evidenced by *The Lancet* lead author's above comment), or ignored entirely. The myths that, for some, evidently contradict convincing scientific evidence can seem irrelevant for others whose frames of reference do not consider such myths to be worthy of attention. As a result, intentionally shaping social norms and practices involves much more than outwardly projecting facts and figures and hoping that they *"stick"*. In the absence of context–sensitive communication strategies, claims surrounding the severity or tractability of NCDs may never make it off the page.

How, then, do certain technical aspects of NCDs interact with ideas in the priority generation process? We focus on three variables that mediate this relationship: (i) *"causes (that) can be assigned to the deliberate actions of identifiable individuals"*; (ii) *"issues involving bodily harm to vulnerable individuals, especially when there is a short and clear causal chain assigning responsibility"*; and (iii) *"issues involving legal equality of opportunity"* (35). In terms of the first and second factors, the fact that NCDs are caused by several risk factors and over the course of a long period of time makes it difficult to attribute their causes to the deliberate actions of identifiable individuals. Ultimately, the perceived uncertainty about NCDs, and about many public health problems in general, is a function of causality (17). As a result, the lack of attention for NCDs is at least partly attributable to a failure to engage with ideas of causality.

Similarly, the third factor identified above – legal equality of opportunity – represents another obstacle to the generation of priority for NCDs. To date, the WHO has not used its treaty–making power in order to articulate and enforce legally binding regulations surrounding NCDs. However, the WHO did exercise this power in 2005 in order to establish the *Framework Convention on Tobacco Control* (FCTC). The fact that cigarettes contain carcinogenic tar and other harmful agents – a material component of tobacco – provided sufficient rationale for the establishment of a legally binding treaty designed to curb tobacco use. The FCTC demonstrates that certain interpretations of the causes of disease are so widely shared that it is feasible to control them through the use of legal instruments. However, there has been little headway made towards a *Framework Convention on Alcohol Control* (36). From a legal standpoint, the lack of a short causal chain for the full range of risk factors for NCDs thus represents a core challenge for global health advocates.

Another example of the interplay between technical factors and ideas is captured by the role of consumer insights in food and beverage production. Private industry has actively called for further research "*to gain a better understanding of the biology of sweeteners in human sensory systems*" (37). This argument holds that in order to meaningfully halt the spread of NCDs, consumer taste preferences must be taken into account. *PepsiCo* has thus committed to remove 10,210 tonnes of salt from its products sold in the US by 2015 – and this, without compromising flavour (37).

However, it remains the case that these taste preferences are always mediated. For example, *PepsiCo*'s commitment to maintaining a wide range of product offerings reproduces ideas about the nature of consumption in a global marketplace. The very suggestion of responding implies that humans will continue to demand as many food and beverage options as possible in accordance with a free market mentality. Yet food is not seen as a symbol of free–market choice in all social contexts. Simply labelling certain foods "*bad*" in excess quantities assumes a common interpretation of the role these foods play in the lives of those who consume them. In developing world contexts, for instance, access to a variety of food options may be much more limited than in Western societies. In these contexts, acommoditised understanding of food may play little to no role in shaping local dynamics. A major gap thus lies in understanding the ways in which social meanings interact with potentially harmful foodstuffs, particularly in the informal sector and in home food preparation (37,38). In accordance with the Shiffman framework, disaggregating the different views attached to technical factors such as food, and examining the ideas and value systems upon which they are based, is crucial to devising effective strategies to elevate the importance of NCD prevention and control.

One could therefore ask: Is it necessary to have an elaborate base of evidence justifying a proposed intervention in order to generate support for that intervention? As previously mentioned, such a focus on expanding the evidence base is frequently invoked by public health experts. As a further example, one of the key problems identified at the *United Nations High–Level*

Meeting on the Prevention and Control of Non–communicable Diseases held in September 2011 was the lack of *"a proper evaluation on the differences between community and targeted initiatives"* with respect to minimum age regulations for youth (34).

Of course, we do not dispute that the availability of rigorous evidence is crucial to achieving better health outcomes. At the same time, the availability of evidence is merely one component that political leaders consider when deciding which issues to prioritise. Bull and Bauman (2011) echo this argument in reference to one of the key risk factors for NCDs, physical activity, calling *"inaccurate"* the perception that we do not have sufficient evidence to act. Instead, these authors assert that *"(much) better use of well–planned, coherent communication strategies are needed"* (39). In this vein, we argue that a useful way of understanding the generation of political priority for a given issue is to reflect on the ideas attached to proposed interventions related to that issue. If one accepts that the availability of evidence is one among many factors that motivate policy–making, understanding the underlying reasons that inspire the actions of policy–makers is crucial. In the case of NCDs, this would suggest that the availability of cost–effective interventions ought not to be ignored in the process of devising effective issue portrayals.

As an example in this regard, one can consider the many connotations of the term *"epidemic"*. One of the most salient debates in the lead–up to the UN High–Level Meeting on NCDs centred on the implications of labelling the spread of NCDs an *"epidemic"*. Applying this label to NCDs could allow countries to invoke flexibilities in World Trade Organization rules that allow drug manufacturers to make generic versions of patented drugs (40). These flexibilities find their origin in a provision in the Doha Declaration on the TRIPS Agreement and Public Health, which holds that *"public health crises, including those relating to HIV/AIDS, tuberculosis, malaria and other epidemics, can represent a national emergency or other circumstances of extreme urgency"* (41). In the end, the draft political declaration agreed by World Health Organization Member States referred to NCDs as a *"challenge of epidemic proportions"* (42). For many in public health, calling the global spread of NCDs an epidemic reflects the very real need for urgent action. This interpretation appeals to language traditionally used to refer to other diseases such as HIV/AIDS, on the basis that framing NCDs in a similar way will attract high levels of support. From this perspective, one could argue that to water down the impacts of NCDs by referring to them in any other way would be the equivalent of willfully ignoring sound evidence.

However, for others in government and in the business community, the term *"epidemic"* conjures up scenarios of stifled innovation and, its corollary, ineffective pharmaceutical products. For example, the director of the Office of Global Affairs at the US Department of Health and Human Services justified US opposition to eliminating all patent protections on drugs that treat NCDs as follows: "*(Doing away with patent protections), to our minds, was not the way you get a stream of ongoing research and development and the new and improved drugs that we continue to need*" (40). In terms of reconciling these conflicting positions, the Shiffman framework offers the following insight: Policies that may seem entirely rational in one social context may seem irrational in another. Just because an intervention can be understood by an audience does not mean that it will be understood in the way in which one intends. Thus, a strictly public health perspective on NCDs that ignores the broader economic implications of proposed interventions spread will have little appeal amongst these actors.

What is more, this particular understanding of the relationship between health and the economy is informed by socially constructed – or, in this case, free–market capitalist – ideas about the global economic order. This demonstrates that decisions on the part of political leaders regarding whether or not to implement policies aimed at the prevention of disease are inseparable from broader questions of ideology. Policies related to health are much more than just instrumental means of achieving a result of maximum "*utility*", but are inspired by value systems that cannot be explained by rational calculations alone (19). As a consequence, raising the political priority of a given issue is contingent upon engagement with the underlying rationales of policy proposals related to that issue. The full range of interpretations associated with proposed interventions must therefore be taken into account in the process of devising effective portrayals of NCDs and their effects.

3. Defining the NCD policy community. In this final section we reflect on what constitutes the policy community surrounding NCDs. We address this question by proposing two specific refinements to the Shiffman framework: first, to broaden the definition of policy community to include private industry; and second, to reconceptualise the structural determinants of NCDs in terms of ideas. Shiffman defines policy communities as "*networks of individuals (including researchers, advocates, policy–makers and technical officials) and organizations (including governments, non–governmental organizations, United Nations agencies, foundations and donor agencies) that share a concern for a particular issue*" (12). However, Shiffman does not specify what he means by "*sharing concern*" for an issue. From an analytical point of view, this generates significant uncertainty. The lack of clarity surrounding the notion of concern can lead one to focus too narrowly on the community of actors who actively proclaim to be in support of an issue, while failing to incorporate the influence of those "*outside*" this community. To this end, "*(an) analytic approach that offers policy community actors as the central creators and disseminators of ideational messages misses other possible sources of ideas that may prove persuasive in motivating action*" (24).

The desire on the part of many actors in the private sector to align profit objectives with broader social goals also represents a way of expressing concern, and one that has proven highly influential. As such, we seek to amend Shiffman's definition of policy community by explicitly including the private sector. We argue that an issue is concerning to an individual or set of actors when it is of interest, or of importance, to that individual or set of actors. This definition allows for concern to be expressed in many different ways, and not just through traditional methods, such as protest or lobbying. Under this definition, strategic communication is still essential to raising the priority of a given issue area, but the source of such communication is expanded to include a wider range of actors. In this manner, actors that have traditionally been excluded from the policy community and portrayed as forces to be resisted – such as multinational corporations in global health – are redefined as agents of change.

The funding trends are clear: private donors are increasingly driving the global health agenda. Furthermore, the role of private corporations in shaping public perceptions about the risk factors for disease extends well beyond the realm of aid for health. In the domain of advertising, for instance, 11 multinational companies – including such well–known companies as *General Mills, Nestlé, Mars,* and *PepsiCo* – account for approximately 80% of global advertising spending in the food and beverage industry (37). Much less clear, however, is the question of how to respond to these trends. One notable response is the adapted political process model (30). Among other factors, this model identifies vested corporate interests as a key obstacle to meaningful action on NCDs, claiming that such interests are often subversive, or, to use their words, "*diabolical*" in nature (30). These authors are also critical of the Shiffman framework. They argue that it "*(views) politics as a market, where the ultimate political outcomes are determined by a collision of forces involving people, interests groups, and ideas*". To those who would seek to advance the Shiffman framework, they present the following challenge: "*(does) it help to tell someone that their ideas about how to control diseases have not been influential, so they should come up with better ones?*" (30).

In our view this challenge is misguided in several respects. First, the act of strategic communication cannot be reduced to "*good*" vs "*bad*" ideas. This misses the crucial point that our frames paint certain ideas as unworthy of attention from our very first encounter with them. This does not mean that such ideas are intrinsically *"bad"*, but that they may not resonate with our target audience. In order to get past frames – the *"gatekeepers"* of ideas – the ideas that we employ must be salient in the lives of those whom we intend to influence. Second, this challenge overlooks the constructed nature of interests. The authors of the political process model do indeed acknowledge the need to identify corporate interests, concluding with the following recommendation: *"A challenge for global health is to identify these interests and bring them to the light of day, holding them to standards of transparency and public accountability"* (11). But this argument fails to recognise that *"they"* are also *"us"*. *"They"* – in this case, private corporations – respond to, influence, and are legitimated by, the ideas that *"we"* hold. Their very existence is contingent upon consent. To suggest that corporate interests must be resisted due to their *"diabolical"* nature is to depict these interests as irreconcilable with the interests of other (implicitly more benevolent) actors who operate within a given issue area. In short, it is to take the intentions, interests, and attitudes of these actors as granted. But more than that, it is to incite feelings of animosity towards private corporations whose interests may be much more complex than such feelings may lead one to believe. As a result, the adapted political process model may lead to oversimplifications that focus on dominant interpretations at the expense of alternative ones, and taken to the extreme, portray certain issues as polarised to the point of being beyond the reach of mutual dialogue.

This is not to suggest that corporations always act in the best interests of human health; indeed, history is replete with examples of corporate entities using ethically questionable marketing tactics and failing to internalise the environmental and social costs of their operations. In this regard, one can consider the *"Keep America Beautiful"* campaign in the United States that was aimed at reducing street litter and promoting environmental awareness. Funded by the tobacco conglomerate *Philip Morris*, this campaign targeted every kind of trash except tobacco waste, despite the fact that tobacco is estimated to make up 25% of all litter on US streets (30). This case clearly contradicts well–established evidence about the negative health effects of smoking.

Nevertheless, rather than categorically excluding corporations from the policy community, we contend that a more valuable approach is to focus on the contested ideas emerging within the modern–day economic system – even if these ideas are more incremental than alarmist in their assessment of the system's shortcomings. The concept of corporate social responsibility is most illustrative of this point. This concept holds that *"business models should marry performance and profitability with the deliberate purpose or goal of contributing to the solution of relevant social and environmental challenges"* (37). Under the leadership of CEO Indra Nooyi, *PepsiCo* has thus adopted the phrase *"Performance with Purpose"* to guide its operations. Similarly, the US Secretary of Health Kathleen Sibelius recently remarked: *"Healthy offering and healthy profits are not mutually exclusive"* (34).

In this regard, the success of the business community in attracting the support of US government and other high–level officials is due in no small part to the appeal of its overarching ethos: to *"(provide) consumers with the tools they need to maintain a healthy lifestyle"* (37). This consumer–centric focus is influential in two key respects. First of all, many Western states have reduced their foreign aid budgets in the wake of the 2008–2009 global financial crisis, thus limiting the funds available for global health initiatives. Second, governments must invariably confront other social and economic problems, including financial instability, terrorism, and climate change. While many of these problems can be addressed synergistically, the fact remains that global health advocates often compete with these issues for attention. As a result, strategies for improving health outcomes that are consumer–focused and that take the bulk of responsibility off the shoulders of government are, in many cases, more likely to gain traction. To be clear, we do not intend to argue in favour of greater private sector involvement in halting the spread of NCDs. We simply mean to highlight the power of the ideas employed by the private sector, and to suggest that any supposedly balanced analysis of NCDs must take them into account.

Finally, it is worthwhile to address relationship of social constructionism to notions of power. One major criticism of this approach holds that that simply identifying ideational constructs fails to address the powerful inequalities that restrict the ability of individuals to communicate ideas in the first place (43). It follows that *"(too) much emphasis on the message can draw our attention away from the carriers of frames and the complicated and uneven playing fields on which they compete"* (26). Similarly, engaging with power relations addresses the criticism that constructivists shy away from seemingly *"evil"* norms and ideas (44). Indeed, the dominant economic paradigm at present is one of free markets, trade liberalisation, and consumer choice. Particularly within the alternative globalisation movement, these free market forces are often considered predatory to the point of being evil – and it is clear that the private sector is a key driver of these forces (45).

A concrete example of an attempt to reorient the perception of the private sector as a structural force to be resisted is the *Pan American Health Organization Forum for Action on Chronic Disease*, also known as the *Partners Forum*. It has engaged the private sector by including business representatives in a reworked version of the CARMEN network, which is comprised of 32 countries in the region of the Americas that are committed to the prevention and control of NCDs and their risk factors. A key element of this Forum is the establishment of a *"clear definition on who the members should be, criteria for inclusion, admission, and rules for removal"* (46). In short, the *Partners Forum* represents a significant step forward in terms of reconciling the many ways in which that global health advocates – including private companies – express concern, but for reasons of fear, pride, or otherwise, fail to operationalise in the form of partnerships.

Moreover, it is clear from this example that the act of strategically communicating ideas about the social determinants of health is much more than just a one–way transfer of information. That some in global health see the private sector as a structural force to be resisted is the result of blaming a subset of actors that is not solely responsible for producing the current situation. Power is not something that actors automatically possess, the crucial point being that movements develop within communities, and not from the exploits of individual actors working in isolation (26). In this regard, social structures ought not be understood not as monolithic forces to be resisted (47). On the contrary, the process of advancing new normative commitments ought to be understood as a process of socialisation, through which boundaries between contested and shared ideas are debated, articulated, and redefined.

4. Conclusion. In conclusion, through the lens of Shiffman's political priority framework, we have sought to shed light on the factors that have relegated NCDs to the bottom of the agendas of governments and donors in global health. Our objective has not been to dictate what global health advocates should do in order to raise the priority of NCDs. Instead, we have attempted to elucidate the perceptions that have led to NCDs being ignored in the corridors of power. By deconstructing the attitudes, interests, and motivations of relevant national, international, and transnational actors in global health, we have sought to identify the ways in which these perceptions have been reproduced. This, in turn, enables advocates to communicate the causes and potential impacts of NCDs in a way that is sensitive to existing points of view.

We support Shiffman's claim that strategic communication – or ideas in the form of issue portrayals – ought to be a core activity of global health policy communities. But issue portrayals must be the products of a robust and inclusive debate. To this end, we also consider it essential to recognise that issue portrayals reach political leaders through a vast array of channels. This means acknowledging the role of actors, such as private entities whose intentions may not at first glance appear to be shared with the traditional members of a policy community, such as researchers, physicians, and NGOs.

Raising the political priority of NCDs means engaging with the diverse ways in which actors express concern for the global proliferation of these diseases. In the case of the private sector, this means recognising that companies often choose to pursue both economic and social goals in an integrated manner. As we have argued, portrayals of NCDs have been hampered by dissonance between the ideas espoused by actors in the public, private, and civil society sectors; a prominent example of this being the polarisation of the debate over whether to label the global spread of NCDs an epidemic. Promoting dialogue between these actors is a crucial first step in terms of devising communication strategies that are likely to resonate and compel action.

More broadly, we have endeavoured to show the value of social constructionism as an approach to the study of social and political change. The following insight is most instructive: *"Persuasion is the process by which agent action becomes social structure, ideas become norms, and the subjective becomes the intersubjective"* (19). Strategic portrayals of ideas thus constitute the practical equivalent of translating agent action into structure.

Indeed, this analysis opens up several avenues for further research. First, how have the frames used to portray NCDs varied over time? What criteria can we use to study the long–term success of issue portrayals, and how can we measure salience in the long–term? Second, this analysis also demonstrates the importance of studying unsuccessful attempts at attracting high–level attention for a given cause. In what ways have other neglected health problems been understood and portrayed? What commonalities do these portrayals share with those used by advocates for NCDs? Ultimately, our political interactions amount to struggles for influence, and determining which issues to champion in the midst of these struggles – and which to disregard – is informed by subjectively held notions of the right, the good, and the just. Indeed, the very act of choosing which issues to prioritise in our daily lives forces us to evaluate our values and aspirations as individual agents against the shared values that structure the societies in which we live.

Acknowledgement: Originally published as: Anthony Maher and Devi Sridhar: Political priority in the global fight against non-communicable diseases. Reprinted with permission from Edinburgh University Global Health Society under Creative Commons Attribution License (Journal of Global Health 2012; 2:020403).

References

1. Stuckler D, Basu S. Evaluating the health burden of chronic diseases. In: Stuckler D, Siegel K (eds). Sick societies. Oxford: Oxford University Press, 2011. pp. 1-26.
2. World Health Organization. Global status report on noncommunicable diseases 2010. (Available from: http://www. who.int/entity/nmh/publications/ncd_report_chapter1. pdf; Accessed: 25 Apr 2012).
3. World Health Organization. NCD Summary report 2011. (Available from: http://www. who.int/nmh/publications/ ncd_report_summary_en.pdf. Accessed: 24 Apr 2012).
4. Mahal A, Karan A, Engelau M. The economic implications of noncommunicable disease for India. Washington: World Bank, 2010.
5. Beaglehole R, Bonita R, Alleyne G, Horton R, Li L, Lincoln P, et al. UN High-Level Meeting on Non-Communicable Diseases: addressing four questions. Lancet 2011; 378:449-455.
6. Beaglehole R, Yach D. Globalisation and the prevention and control of non-communicable disease: the neglected chronic disease of adults. Lancet 2003; 362:903-908.
7. Taylor AL, Chaloupka F, Guindon GE, Corbett M. Trade policy and tobacco control. In: Jha P, Chaloupka F (eds). Tobacco control in developing countries. Oxford: Oxford University Press, 2000.
8. World Health Organization. From burden to "best buys": reducing the economic impact of non-communicable diseases in low and middle-income countries. (Available from: http://www.who.int/nmh/publications/best_buys_ summary.pdf; Accessed: 15 Apr 2012).
9. World Economic Forum. Global risks 2011. World Economic Forum Global Risks, 2011. (Available from: http:// www.riskreport.weforum.org/; Accessed: 8 May 2012).
10. Nugent R, Feigl A. Scarce donor funding for non-communicable diseases: will it contribute to a health crisis? Washington, DC: Center for Global Development, 2010.
11. Stuckler D, Basu S, King L, Steele S, McKee M. Political economy of chronic disease. In: Stuckler D and Siegel K (eds). Sick societies. Oxford: Oxford University Press, 2011. pp. 135-167.
12. Shiffman J. A social explanation for the rise and fall of global health issues. Bull World Health Organ 2009; 87:608-613.
13. Shiffman J, Smith S. Generation of political priority for global health initiatives: a framework and case study of maternal mortality. Lancet 2007; 370:1370-1379.
14. Hilgartner S, Bosk CL. The rise and fall of social problems: a public arenas model. Am J Sociol 1988; 94:53-78.
15. Kuhn TS. The structure of scientific revolutions. Chicago, IL: The University of Chicago Press, 1970.
16. Wendt A. Anarchy is what states make of it: The social construction of power politics. Int Organ 1992; 46:391-424.
17. Kunitz SJ. Explanations and ideologies of mortality patterns. Popul Dev Rev 1987; 13:379-408.
18. Nathanson CA. Disease prevention as social change: the state, society, and public health in the United States, France, Great Britain and Canada. New York, NY: Russell Sage Foundation, 2007.
19. Finnemore M, Sikkink K. International norm dynamics and political change. Int Organ 1998; 52:887-917.

20. Keck M, Sikkink K. Transnational advocacy networks in international and regional politics. Int Soc Sci J 1999; 51:89-101.
21. George AL, Bennett A. Case studies and theory development in the social sciences. Cambridge (Mass.): The MIT Press, 2005.
22. Benzian H, Holmgren C, Yee R, Monse B, Barnard JT, Van Palenstein Helderman W. Political priority of global oral health: an analysis of reasons for international neglect. Int Dent J 2011; 61:124-130.
23. Shiffman J. Issue attention in global health: The case of newborn survival. Lancet 2010; 375:2045-2049.
24. Smith SL, Neupane S. Factors in health initiative success: Learning from Nepal's newborn survival initiative. Soc Sci Med 2011; 72:568-575.
25. McAdam D, McCarthy JD, Zald MN (eds). Comparative perspectives on social movements: Political opportunities, mobilizing structures, and cultural framings. Cambridge: Cambridge University Press, 1996.
26. Ryan C, Gamson WW. The art of reframing political debates. Contexts 2006; 5:13-18.
27. Benford RD, Snow DA. Framing processes and social movements: an overview and assessment. Annu Rev Sociol 2000; 26:611-639.
28. Beaglehole R, Ebrahim S, Reddy S, Voute J, Leeder S. Prevention of chronic diseases: a call to action. Lancet 2007; 370:2152-2157.
29. World Health Organization. World Health Organization's 2008-2013 global strategy for the prevention and control of noncommunicable diseases. (Available from: http://whqlibdoc.who.int/publications/2009/9789241597418_eng.pdf; Accessed: 9 May 2012).
30. Stuckler D, Basu S, King L, Steele S, McKee M. Creating a social movement to raise the priority of global chronic disease. In: Stuckler D, Siegel K (eds). Sick societies. Oxford: Oxford University Press, 2011. pp. 168-186.
31. Sridhar D, Morrison JS, Piot P. Getting the politics right for the September 2011 UN High-Level Meeting on Noncommunicable Diseases. Washington: Center for Strategic & International Studies, 2011.
32. Martin-Moreno JM, Apfel F, Sanchez J, Galea G, Jakab Z. The social nature of chronic noncommunicable diseases and how to tackle them through communication technology, training, and outreach. J Health Commun 2011; 16:94-106.
33. Krause S. Civil passions: moral sentiment and democratic deliberation. Princeton: Princeton University Press, 2008.
34. Cooper K. The UN High-level Meeting on the Prevention and Control of NCDs (New York, 19-20 September 2011) and associated side events. C3 Collaborating for Health; 2011. (Available from: http://www.c3health.org/wp-content/uploads/2009/09/Complete-write-up-of-UN-HLM-and-side-events-v-2-20111108.pdf; Accessed: 22 May 2012).
35. Keck M, Sikkink K. Activists beyond borders: Advocacy networks in international politics. Ithaca, NY: Cornell University Press, 1998.
36. Sridhar D. Regulate alcohol for global health. Nature 2012; 482:302.
37. Acharya T, Fuller AC, Mensah GA, Yach D. The current and future role of the food industry in the prevention and control of chronic diseases: The case of PepsiCo. In: Stuckler D, Siegel K (eds). Sick Societies. Oxford: Oxford University Press, 2011. pp. 187–203.
38. Sridhar D. The Majaraja Mac. In: Unnithan-Kumar M, Tremayne S (eds). Fatness and the maternal body. Oxford: Berghahn Books, 2011.

39. Bull FC, Bauman AE. Physical inactivity: The "Cinderella" risk factor for noncommunicable disease prevention. J Health Commun 2011; 16:13-26.
40. Fink S, Rabinowitz R. The UN's Battle with NCDs. Foreign Affairs, 2012. (Available from: http://www.foreignaffairs.com/articles/68280/sheri-fink-and-rebecca-rabinowitz/the-uns-battle-with-ncds?page=show; Accessed: 5 Apr 2012).
41. World Trade Organization. Declaration on the TRIPS Agreement and Public Health. (Available from: http://www.wto.org/english/thewto_e/minist_e/min01_e/mindecl_trips_e.htm; Accessed: 4 Apr 2012).
42. United Nations. Draft political declaration of the High-level Meeting on the prevention and control of non-communicable diseases. United Nations General Assembly, 2011. (Available from: http://www.ghd-net.org/sites/ default/files/NCDs%20-%20Draft%20Political%20Declaration%20-%209%20September%202011(1).pdf; Accessed: 4 Apr 2012).
43. Clapham D, Clark W, Gibb K (eds). The SAGE Handbook of Housing Studies. London: Sage Publications Ltd., 2012.
44. Jervis R. Realism in the study of world politics. Int Organ 1998; 52:971-991.
45. Wiist WH. The corporate play book, health, and democracy: The snack food and beverage industry's tactics in context. In: Stuckler D, Siegel K (eds). Sick societies. Oxford: Oxford University Press, 2011. pp. 204–216.
46. Hospedales CJ, Jané-Llopis E. A multistakeholder platform to promote health and prevent noncommunicable diseases in the region of the Americas: The Pan American Health Organization Partners Forum for Action. J Health Commun 2011; 16:191-200.
47. Dessler D. What's at stake in the agent-structure debate? Int Organ 1989; 43:441-473.

CHAPTER 18.

Health policy: Regulate alcohol for global health

Unlike any other global-health body, the World Health Organization (WHO) can create legally binding conventions, and it only requires a two-thirds majority vote to do so. Yet this power is vastly underused. In more than 60 years, this United Nations agency has produced only two major treaties: the *International Health Regulations*, which require countries to report certain disease outbreaks and public-health events; and the *Framework Convention on Tobacco Control*, which commits governments to making legislative moves to reduce the demand for, and supply of, tobacco. The WHO has shown a reluctance to use hard legal instruments. Instead, it tries to influence societal norms through guidelines and recommendations (1). This is a major missed opportunity.

Now is the time for the WHO to take a bold step and move towards a third treaty to protect world health. There is an obvious target. About 2.5 million deaths a year, almost 4% of all deaths worldwide, are attributed to alcohol – more than the number of deaths caused by HIV/AIDS, tuberculosis or malaria (2). Alcohol consumption is the world's third-largest risk factor for health burden; in middle-income countries, which constitute almost half of the world's population, it is the greatest risk.

There are some good, evidence-based efforts for alcohol control already in place, such as the 2010 *WHO Global Strategy to Reduce Harmful Use of Alcohol*. This document lays out ten areas in which action can be taken, from raising awareness to preventing drink-driving and restricting the availability, marketing and pricing of alcohol. Its recommended policy interventions are general and sensible, including: banning unlimited drinks specials; enforcing a reasonable minimum age limit for purchase; and enacting graduated licensing for novice drivers with zero-tolerance for drink-driving. The strategy helpfully summarizes the cost-effectiveness of various strategies. But this is a portfolio of useful information and policy tips, not a binding document.

A WHO *Framework Convention on Alcohol Control* could and should turn those recommendations into legal requirements for member states. What difference would this make? Formally, countries would commit to applying the agreement through national legislation – which would require a ream of new policies for nations such as India where current regulation isn't so comprehensive. Nations would be required to report to the WHO on their progress. The international community would have a shared responsibility to support these efforts by providing financial and technical assistance as needed. Informally, ministries of health would have a stronger domestic negotiating position in prioritizing alcohol regulation above economic concerns. Non-governmental organizations would be able to pressure governments, and even bring issues to court.

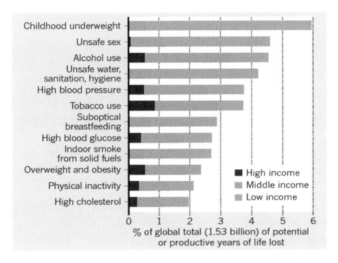

Figure 18-1. *Health burdens: Alcohol is the third-largest risk factor for loss of years to disease and disability. The effect is largest in middle-income countries (2004 data).*

The creation of a framework convention requires much political work and preparation. The WHO secretariat should, for example, map out the positions of countries on alcohol use, their links to industry, and how best to overcome opposition in each nation. Doing so will require donor funding for a special cabinet project, as was done for tobacco. The overarching goal would be to assemble a *"coalition of the willing and able"* to push this agenda forward in the World Health Assembly — the WHO's decision-making body.

We should not be overly idealistic about the effect of international health law on domestic public health. Despite a binding *Framework Convention on Tobacco Control*, tobacco use is increasing in many poor countries, and is still the second-largest cause of disease risk in middle-income countries. The problem is that oversight is minimal and no strong enforcement mechanisms exist, so compliance is weak.

To help overcome such problems, the WHO should endorse a commission on global health law, headed by an independent expert. Through analysis of other regimes, such as those of trade and finance, that have arguably been more successful in utilizing international law, this commission could provide recommendations on how to strengthen the WHO's normative power. The WHO's legal potential should not be focused solely on individual health hazards such as alcohol and tobacco, it should be used to create a broad framework convention on global health (3). This would identify a basic package of health services that governments ought to provide; identify who would be obliged to provide what; and examine how this could be achieved through reform of global health governance.

To flourish in an environment with numerous other better-financed and more-inclusive institutions, the WHO must take a hard look at itself and what makes it special. Other bodies can provide technical advice, give money, influence domestic health policy, assist in development and advocate for the importance of health in government policy. The WHO is the only body with the legitimacy and authority to proactively promote health through the use of international law. It needs to do so.

Acknowledgement: Originally published as: Devi Sridhar: Health policy: Regulate alcohol for global health. Reprinted with permission from MacMillan Publishers / Nature Publishing Group (Nature 2012; 482:302).

References

1. L'hirondel A, Yach D. World Health Stat Q. 1998; 51:79–87.
2. World Health Organization. Global Status Report on Alcohol and Health 2011. Geneva: WHO, 2011. (Available from: http://go.nature.com/ymav6z)
3. Gostin LO et al. The joint action and learning initiative. PLoS Med 2001; 8:e1001031.

CHAPTER 19

Understanding the determinants of the complex interplay between cost-effectiveness and equitable impact: EQUIST tool

In recent years, enormous efforts have been made to estimate the global burden of maternal and child mortality and identify the main causes, study the role of risk factors, assess the effectiveness of available interventions, and to track the coverage of those interventions in low and middle-income countries (1-10). However, this large body of evidence has not been followed by the development of sufficiently simple and accurate tools and approaches that effectively translate the evidence and information into health policy decisions where this is most needed – at the national and sub-national level in low-resource settings. In the absence of evidence-based planning, it is not surprising that unexpected outcomes can arise from efforts towards maternal and child mortality reduction. One of the most perplexing outcomes is that all too often the objective success in mortality reduction has been coupled with an increased health inequity in the population (12).

To understand the roots of this problem, we should appreciate that policy makers at the national and sub-national level have limited resources for scaling up cost-effective health interventions in their populations. When planning the *"best buys"* for committing their resources in maternal and child health, they are faced with a very complex task. They need to choose between at least several dozen interventions that target neonates, infants, children and mothers, most of which have been proven to be cost-effective in many contexts (4,5,8,9). They soon realize that it would take more than a simple calculation to decide on the most rational way to invest in health intervention scale up. Depending on the local and national context, the interplay between many important factors will affect both cost-effectiveness and the impact on equity for their chosen intervention scale-up programs. Neglect (or improper understanding) of these complexities can lead to decisions which result in maternal and child mortality reduction not being achieved in the most cost-effective way, or being associated with increases in health inequity within communities. The present set of tools does not sufficiently capture the full array of factors (11).

The aim of this study is to analyze the determinants of the complex interplay between cost-effectiveness and equity in maternal and child mortality reduction and suggest strategies that promote an impact on mortality that will reduce population child health inequities. To achieve this aim, we develop a transparent framework based on several key epidemiological concepts that can be used to support national-level decision making in health intervention prioritization. Using this framework, we try to expose the complex interplay among factors that influence both cost-effectiveness and equity in child and maternal mortality reduction and identify the key information needs for planning of equitable and cost-effective programs of health intervention scale-up.

1. The cost of intervention scale-up in different equity strata. The first important determinant to consider is *the cost of intervention scale-up in different equity strata*. In our framework, we will divide any population of interest into 5 equity strata (*"quintiles"*), each comprising 20% of the population, where Q1 denotes the wealthiest quintile, and Q5 the poorest. The cost of achieving complete coverage with any health intervention will clearly differ between the wealthiest (Q1) and the poorest (Q5) quintile, but there is remarkably little information available on the determinants of these costs in each quintile and the actual differences in cost of implementation. It is also clear that these differences between strata will be intervention-specific and also context-specific,

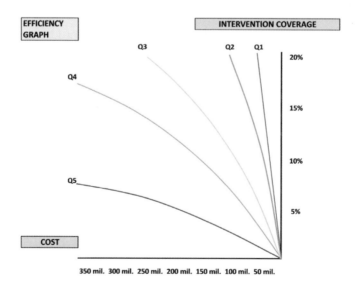

Figure 19-1. *The relationship between cost of the intervention scale-up and achieved intervention coverage, which determines the efficiency of intervention delivery, presented for each of the five equity strata in the population (Q1 – the wealthiest quintile; Q5 – the poorest quintile).*

rather than following any *"standard"*, predictable pattern. This means that, for some interventions, the costs may not increase dramatically (from the wealthiest to the poorest quintile) with increasing coverage. In fact, wherever the salary of health professionals is the main component of the cost, then it is possible to envisage circumstances in which, for some interventions, it may be even cheaper to cover the poorest quintile (e.g., when there is a well-developed network of village health workers who can administer cheap antibiotic treatment) than the wealthiest quintile (where this depends on skilled medical doctors who have access to both cheap and more expensive antibiotics). However, there will also be many examples where complete intervention coverage will be more readily achieved among the wealthy Q1 than in the poorest Q5, where it may be almost impossible or even unfeasible to achieve.

Figure 19-1 summarizes this relationship. The horizontal axis represents the increasing cost required for scaling up of an intervention, while the vertical axis measures the completeness of coverage in each equity quintile (ranging from 0% to 20% of the total population). Recently, substantial efforts have been made to track the coverage of interventions specifically by equity strata in many low and middle-income countries. This work has indicated that this is an important component that will be need to be included in planning the equitable delivery of interventions (13-15). However, we still need information on the actual cost components of intervention scale-up and how these differ across wealth quintiles in varying contexts and for each intervention. In reality, this cost can't be expressed as a fixed amount in US$ per person that is characteristic of each delivered intervention, nor does it increase linearly as the achieved population coverage increases (**Figure 19-1**). The cost of intervention scale-up includes more than just the market cost of an intervention (such as vaccine or a drug), because the successful delivery also requires everything else that is required to reach the targeted recipients, such as costs of health worker salaries, transport and storage, improved access and expanded outreach.

Those additional costs may be relatively small if the aim was to cover the most accessible 20% or 40% of mothers and children. In these circumstances the relationship between cost and achieved coverage may indeed be approximately linear. However, additional costs of intervention delivery will start increasing in complex and non-linear patterns when the coverage of the most deprived children and mothers is attempted, because many obstacles need to be overcome to reach them. Because of these additional costs, all too often we observe that the most accessible mothers and children are being covered with ever more interventions, while the marginalized are missing out on all of them. This approach would still be expected to reduce maternal and child mortality, but the progress would be very slow and inequitable. This is because most child and maternal deaths occur among the most inaccessible parts of the population and only a minor part of the mortality burden is being targeted with interventions. The progress that is being achieved benefits only those who are accessible, thus increasing inequity. Reducing the additional costs of intervention delivery when targeting the poor would involve challenges that are related to both supply and demand for the prioritized interventions.

One examples of this relationship between cost and achieved intervention scale-up by equity quintiles (Q1-Q5) is shown in **Figure 19-1.** This graph summarizes the *efficiency* of intervention delivery. In this hypothetical example, it is apparent that for the same intervention it is much cheaper, and therefore more efficient, to achieve full coverage in the most wealthy 20% of the population (Q1) than in the poorest quintile (Q5). In fact, in this example the difference in cost is so large that it poses a question whether the potential for mortality reduction in the poorest quintile (Q5) justifies such an inefficient delivery of a life-saving intervention at such a high cost? Sometimes, even when the equity argument is being respected, it may still be entirely unfeasible to attempt to reach the poorest Q5, because the infrastructure that would allow this in a cost-effective way simply does not exist. In such cases, investing in health system development may need to precede investing in intervention coverage. We will move through the rest of the framework to explore this further, because the answers will rarely be intuitive.

2. The effectiveness of an intervention in different equity strata. The second determinant of cost-effectiveness and equity to consider is *the effectiveness of an intervention in different equity strata*. The effectiveness of an intervention, or its *"potential impact fraction"*, indicates which proportion of the current mortality burden that is targeted by an intervention would be averted among those who receive the intervention, in comparison to those that do not receive it. In theory, the effectiveness of an intervention in relation to a specific cause of death – such as a specific antibiotic treatment against childhood pneumonia – should be relatively similar in all settings. This is because it should primarily be determined by the biology of disease and the interplay between the disease and the intervention. However, the experience from the field tells us that the effectiveness of the same intervention may differ substantially between Q1 and Q5. Some of the reasons may be, in the above example, that there is different spectrum of pathogens among the very poor (and less well nourished) (Q5), and /or higher levels of antibiotic resistance, and/ or later presentation with more severe symptoms because of barriers in access to care or differences in care-seeking behavior, all of which reduces the effectiveness of antibiotic treatment against pneumonia in comparison to Q1 children. In addition, and perhaps even more importantly, the quality of intervention delivery will not be the same in all socio-economic strata. Incomplete or inadequate delivery will be more likely among the poorest (Q5), which will decrease the effectiveness of the intervention against the same cause of death. Taking the example of pneumococcal and Hib vaccine against pneumonia, this may be because of more likely interruption of the cold chain when trying to reach the poorest, lower level of health workers' education and skills which may lead more often to inadequate administration of vaccines, and lower health awareness among the parents of the children leading to lower levels of full attendance for all immunization appointments.

We tried to capture this complex relationship between the achieved coverage by equity quintiles and the effectiveness in mortality reduction in **Figure 19-2**. In order to expose the continuum of relationships and effects that the important determinants in this framework have on mortality reduction and equity, the vertical axis is taken from **Figure 19-1**. It again shows the achieved coverage by each equity quintile, which can range from 0 to 20%. The horizontal axis shows the effectiveness of the intervention of interest in

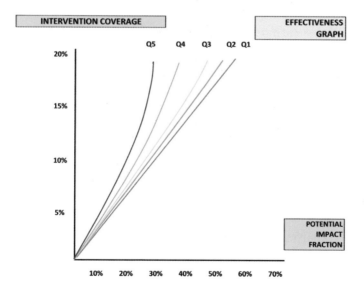

Figure 19-2. *The relationship between achieved intervention coverage and potential impact fraction, which determines the effectiveness of the intervention, presented for each of the five equity strata in the population (Q1 – the wealthiest quintile; Q5 – the poorest quintile; to expose the continuum of relationships and effects that the important determinants in this framework have on mortality reduction and equity, the vertical axis is taken from Figure 19-1, while the horizontal axis measures the effectiveness in different equity strata).*

terms of reduction in mortality in each equity stratum (expressed as a proportion of the total mortality in that stratum) that could be achieved for a given level of coverage shown on the vertical axis. The value on the horizontal axis where the coverage in Q1 becomes complete (in this case, between 50% and 60%) shows the maximum potential for the intervention to reduce mortality against a specific cause under ideal conditions. For example, if the cause of death of interest is pneumonia; if 50-60% of pneumonia deaths in this setting are caused by pneumococcus; and if pneumococcal vaccine is nearly 100% effective in preventing pneumococcal pneumonia deaths, then this is the maximum potential effectiveness of pneumococcal vaccine under ideal conditions. However, the adverse factors explained above (interruption of the cold chain, inadequate administration by health workers, failure to comply with full vaccination schedule by the parents) may act to reduce its effectiveness to only 20-30% among the poorest section of the population in Q5, even when the full coverage is achieved (**Figure 19-2**). Presently, there is remarkably little understanding or evidence about the nature and scale of differences in effectiveness of health interventions in different equity strata, although this is one of the most important determinants of overall cost-effectiveness and equitable impact.

3. The size and composition of the mortality burden in different equity strata. The third important determinant to consider is the *absolute size of the mortality burden in different equity strata and its composition*. The relationship between the burden of mortality and equity strata is rather predictable: the absolute number of deaths will always be much greater in the poorest (Q5) than in the wealthiest quintile (Q1), given that the quintiles are of the same size by definition (i.e. 20% of population), and that mortality rates are greater among the poor. However, the graph that captures this relationship (**Figure 19-3**) may still look very differently, depending of the level of inequity in the population. The lines representing the five equity strata in this graph may be relatively close to each other such as in a situation where the burden of mortality is, in absolute terms, only 2 times greater in Q5 compared to Q1. However, these lines could also be far apart such as when the burden of mortality is 10 times greater in Q5 than in Q1. In a sense, **Figure 19-3** is a visualization of the level of inequity in a society when expressed as bearing the burden of mortality. A substantial effort has been invested in recent years to understand and explore the differences in mortality rates between the equity strata in low and middle-income countries (9,14,16,17).

There is another factor that adds complexity to the relationship between intervention effectiveness and number of deaths averted by equity strata, as shown in **Figure 19-3**. The breakdown of the overall number of deaths by cause of death may differ quite substantially between equity quintiles. For example, causes of deaths among the wealthiest children will be dominated by congenital abnormalities, preterm birth complications and accidents – i.e., the problems that even well-functioning health system still can't easily tackle effectively. However, the poorest children will mainly be expected to die from infectious causes, such as pneumonia, diarrhea, malaria and neonatal sepsis. As an example, the proportional contribution of pneumonia to all child deaths observed in a developing country would typically be around 10% in the wealthiest quintile of children rising to up to 40% among the poorest children (18). This is why the *"potential impact fraction"* of an intervention that only targets pneumonia in reduction of the overall child mortality burden could be much larger in the poorest (Q5) than in the wealthiest quintile (Q1) despite lower quality of delivery in Q5 settings acting to reduce the intervention effectiveness.

The graph presented in **Figure 19-3** therefore exposes the *potential impact* of intervention delivery to reduce the burden of mortality in absolute terms. In the hypothetical case shown in **Figure 19-3**, it is apparent that for an intervention that targets e.g. infectious causes, it is usually more effective

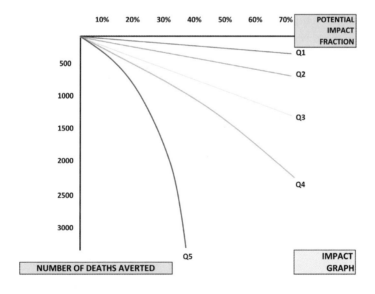

Figure 19-3. *The relationship between potential impact fraction and number of deaths averted, which determines the potential impact of the intervention in mortality reduction, presented for each of the five equity strata in the population (Q1 – the wealthiest quintile; Q5 – the poorest quintile; to expose the continuum of relationships and effects that the important determinants in this framework have on mortality reduction and equity, the horizontal axis is taken from Figure 19-2, while the vertical axis measures the number of deaths that could potentially be averted in different equity strata).*

to achieve full coverage in the poorest 20% of the population, regardless of the reduced effectiveness because of poorer quality of delivery. However, for interventions that target causes of deaths that are more prominent among the wealthiest, such as e.g. congenital abnormalities, these relationships would be inverse. Similarly, if a cause of death is equally important in all 5 strata, then the effectiveness of an intervention would usually be greater among the wealthy, because the lower quality of delivery and increased barriers to access and care-seeking would reduce it among the poor.

4. The cost-effectiveness of investing in different equity strata. The fourth determinant to consider is the one that usually drives policy decisions: *the number of deaths averted per cost of intervention scale-up in different equity strata.* Health investors usually like to know how many deaths could be averted with a fixed level of investment. The more deaths averted per fixed investment, the more cost-effective the scale up. Therefore, **Figure 19-4** exposes the *cost-effectiveness* of many competing investment options.

Figure 19-4 is drawn using the "*cost*" from **Figure 19-1** as a horizontal axis, and "*the number of deaths averted*" from **Figure 19-3** as the vertical axis. When the cost is low and the number of averted deaths high (i.e., the bottom-right corner of **Figure 19-4**), the intervention scale-up is highly cost-effective. When the cost is high and the number of averted deaths low (i.e., the top-left

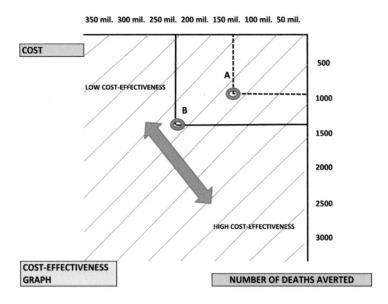

Figure 19-4. *The relationship between the cost of intervention scale-up and number of deaths averted, which determines the cost-effectiveness of the intervention in mortality reduction, presented for each of the five equity strata in the population (Q1 – the wealthiest quintile; Q5 – the poorest quintile).*

corner of **Figure 19-4**), the intervention scale-up is not cost-effective. In **Figure 19-4**, the hypothetical program that implemented intervention "*A*" proved to be more cost-effective than the program that implemented intervention "*B*". However, the cost-effectiveness of mortality reduction does not necessarily mean that it will also be "*equitable*", as these are two separate dimensions. Deaths can be reduced in a highly cost-effective way when investments are targeting the wealthiest quintiles, just as when they are targeting the poorest. In the former case, the mortality will be reduced, but the inequity will be increased. In the latter, both mortality and inequity will be reduced. We argue that this should be the goal whenever possible, and that a simple check using this framework can help highlight these important issues and enable decision-making that includes this goal. Scaling up health interventions in Q3 will be "*equity-neutral*", scaling up in Q4 and Q5 will always be "*equity-promoting*", while scaling up in Q1 and Q2 will be "*inequity-promoting*"; all three approaches, however, will result in reduction of mortality burden, and in some cases this reduction may even be more cost-effective when interventions are scaled in Q1 and/or Q2, rather than in Q4 an/or Q5.

5. The complex interplay among factors that influence equity and cost-effectiveness of mortality reduction. If we bring together the previous four graphs into a single decision-making framework, as shown in **Figure 19-5**, it becomes clear that the relationships between the four determinants (efficiency, effectiveness, impact on mortality and cost-effectiveness) and the impact on equity will not necessarily be intuitive in any setting. The final outcome will be governed by a series of complex and typically non-linear relationships between the determinants above. Anything that increases the efficiency of delivery (see arrow in the top left quadrant, **Figure 19-5**), the quality of delivery (see arrow in the top right quadrant, **Figure 19-5**), and acts upon the greater mortality burden (see arrow in the bottom right quadrant, **Figure 19-5**) will be more cost-effective (see arrows in the bottom left quadrant, **Figure 19-5**), and vice versa. Increased efficiency and quality of delivery will tend to make scaling up among the wealthier groups more cost-effective, while the increased size of the burden will tend to make scaling up among the poorer groups more cost-effective (**Figure 19-5**).

To further illustrate the nature of this complexity, **Figure 19-5** offers an illustrative example: a fixed sum of money (shown on the "*cost*" axis) is available to ensure delivery of an entirely new intervention to children in a country. Local policy makers have a choice: if they assume that children in Q1 would find ways to get this intervention anyway, while those in Q5 are arguably too hard to reach, they could invest the available funds to cover as

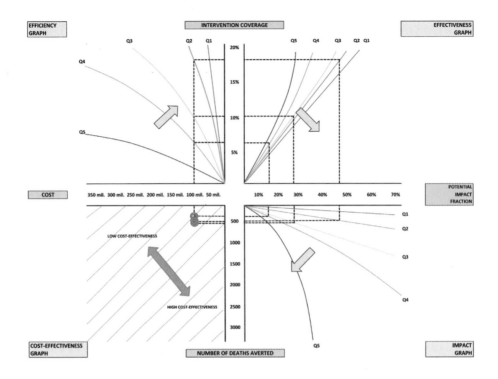

Figure 19-5. *A hypothetical case of planning the delivery of a new intervention to different equity strata in the population (Q2 vs. Q3 vs. Q4) with a fixed budget and assessing its cost-effectiveness under equity-neutral (Q3), equity-promoting (Q4) or inequitable (Q2) strategy (see the main text for further explanation).*

many children in Q2, Q3 or Q4 as possible. The difference is that covering Q2 would increase inequity, while covering Q4 would promote equity and Q3 would be equity-neutral. If similar cost-effectiveness between the three approaches could be demonstrated (in the bottom left quadrant of the proposed framework), then the equity-promoting approach (covering Q4) should be preferred. In this example, implementing the intervention to the children in Q3 is more cost-effective than the other two approaches (**Figure 19-5**), but the difference is not substantial and covering Q4 could be considered instead.

In the remainder of this paper, we will present and discuss a hypothetical case related to planning of the delivery of an intervention to different equity strata in the population and assessing its cost-effectiveness at different levels of investment.

We will consider a hypothetical case of framework implementation: planning of the delivery of a new intervention, such as vaccine, improved

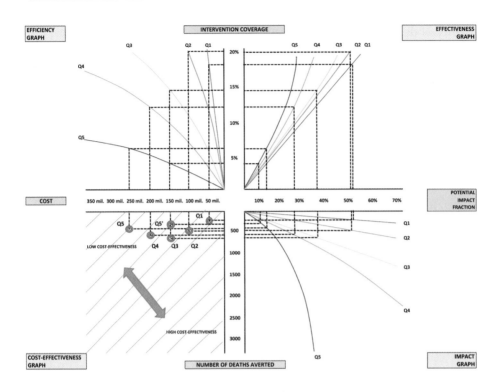

Figure 19-6. *Six hypothetical investment cases of different amounts of funding for scale-up of the same intervention in 5 different equity strata, and with different level of investment into the poorest quintile (Q5) (for explanation see text).*

sanitation, or maternal education program, to different social strata in the population and assessing its cost-effectiveness. The upper left quadrant graph in **Figure 19-6** shows how the level of investment translates to intervention coverage in different equity quintiles in the population of interest (Q1 being the wealthiest and Q5 the poorest). Clearly, in the population of interest an investment of US$ 50 million will ensure nearly complete coverage of all 20% children in Q1 quintile, while complete coverage can be achieved with US$ 100 million in Q2. US$ 150 million will cover about 7 out of 10 children in Q3, while US$ 200 million will cover two in three children in Q4. Reaching children in Q5 will be extremely difficult and expensive, and US$ 250 million will only cover about one third of the children in this quintile (**Figure 19-6**).

The upper right quadrant graph takes into account that the effectiveness of the same intervention will vary in different quintiles. This is because the quality of delivery usually decreases in the poorest equity strata, making the implementation in Q1-Q3 more effective than in Q4-Q5 (**Figure 19-6**).

The lower right quadrant graph takes into account that the burden of child deaths is not evenly distributed among the five quintiles and it quantifies the number of deaths averted. It is apparent that removing 50% of the mortality burden in Q1 or Q2 removes similar number of deaths (in absolute terms) as preventing 15% of deaths in Q5 (**see Figure 19-6c**).

Finally, the lower left quadrant graph brings the number averted deaths back to the relationship with the initial investment in US$. This allows us to compare many different scenarios and make informed predictions of cost-effectiveness of each scenario relative to alternative ones – all of which would be impossible to predict intuitively. Thanks to graphs in **Figure 19-6**, we can now conclude that an investment of US$ 50 million in coverage of children in Q1 will be more cost-effective than any of the other four scenarios, with investing US$ 250 million in covering children in Q5 being the least cost-effective. Still, an investment of US$ 150 million in Q5 (denoted as Q5', follow the parallel dotted lines in **Figure 19-6**) would be substantially more cost-effective than an investment of US$ 200 million in Q4 or 250 million in Q5. This means that it is, in fact, more cost-effective to invest $ 150 million into the coverage of children in the poorest quintile (Q5') than it would be to invest $ 250 million into the coverage of children in Q5.

The interplay between investments to increase intervention coverage and the "*returns*" in terms of the number of deaths averted is extremely complex and sometimes counter-intuitive. It is intervention-specific, context-specific, and it depends on several variables that show both linear and non-linear inter-relationships. All of this should be taken into account when planning investment policies and choosing between the many cost-effective interventions at the national and sub-national level. The lines in the "*efficiency*", "*effectiveness*" and "*impact*" graphs (**Figure 19-5, 19-6**) necessarily determine the resulting line in the "cost-effectiveness" graph. Any increase in efficiency and quality of intervention delivery, effectiveness of intervention, or burden of disease within any quintile will improve cost-effectiveness. Looking at **Figures 19-5 and 19-6**, shows that any rotation of the lines in the "*efficiency*", "*effectiveness*" and "*impact*" graphs in the clock-wise direction will lead to rotation of the corresponding line in the "*cost-effectiveness*" graph in the anti-clockwise direction, which is desirable.

Figures 19-5 and 19-6 also expose some unexpected and counter-intuitive properties of this framework. Firstly, when lines anywhere in the graph are located counter-clockwise from the line determined with an equation $x=y$, then the cost-effectiveness will decrease with increasing investment in the same population stratum. This means that smaller investments in the same quintiles may prove to be more cost-effective than larger investments. However, if it is possible to change the slope of the lines through improving contexts, then a scenario may be envisaged in which increasing investments in a population quintile also become increasingly cost-effective. This is particularly important for the poorest quintile, as shown in example in **Figure 19-6**. The scenario presented in both **Figure 19-5** and **Figure 19-6** has also shown that in some contexts the most equitable strategy (i.e., investing in the poorest quintiles) is not necessarily the most cost-effective. In this case, the decision-making process becomes really difficult, as it cannot be based on any rational framework, but it rather needs to include value choices. When faced with such interplay of the key determinants in their particular context, policy makers need to decide whether the majority of the society would value improved equity or cost-effective mortality burden reduction (i.e. more deaths averted per money invested, irrespective of the increasing inequity) as the more important goal.

Given the level of general interest in tools that could translate accumulated evidence and information into health policy at the national level, and also in improving equity within low and middle-income countries, there is remarkably little evidence on the differential cost of intervention scale-up, effectiveness of intervention, or the composition of mortality burden by equity strata to support even the most basic analysis. With recent progress in assembling information relevant for international child health policy (1-10), we believe that we will soon begin to have sufficient information to develop a model that could allow early comparative analysis, such as the one described above, at the national level in several representative countries. This model should enable the development of guidelines for prioritizing of interventions in different contexts to maximize the reduction in maternal and child mortality burden relative to the funding available, while taking into account the resulting impact on equity.

This model should not be considered in isolation from the other worthy and commendable efforts, all of which have *"burden of disease/cost effectiveness analysis"* as their essential component, such as those promoted by the *Disease Control Priorities Project (DCPP)* (19). For example, the *Marginal Budgeting for Bottlenecks* (MBB) tool was developed by UNICEF and The World Bank (20), WHO-CHOICE (*Choosing Interventions that are Cost-Effective*) was developed by the World Health Organization (21), and *Lives Saved Tool* (LiST) developed by Johns Hopkins University scientists and the Futures Institute (22). The DCPP authors correctly note that factors other than cost-effectiveness influence priority setting in the real world, so the available evidence has to be considered in the context of local realities (11,19). Both MBB and WHO-CHOICE provide appropriate contextualization tools. However, the LiST software goes further than other existing tools in several dimensions (11). LiST contains an expansive evidence base of context-specific intervention effectiveness, generated by researchers from the WHO/UNICEF's Child Health Epidemiology Reference Group (CHERG) (23). It enables estimation of intervention impact on child mortality at national, regional, and global levels (24,25). Further important advantages of LiST include its validation in both African and South Asian contexts (26), an ability to perform very specific comparisons between alternative investment strategies over a specified time frame in terms of child survival outcomes (24,25), and its attempt to apply an equity lens (27). However, due to the gap in information on the key determinants of the interplay between cost-effectiveness and equitable impact in maternal and child mortality reduction, none of the present versions of the available tools allow planning of an equitable strategy to reduce maternal and child mortality.

In order to assess cost-effectiveness at the national and local level, policy makers would need to know: (i) what is the differential cost of intervention delivery to achieve full coverage in Q1-Q5?; (ii) what is the difference in effectiveness of this new intervention in Q1-Q5?; (iii) what is the difference in mortality burden between Q1-Q5? The interplay among those key determinants needs to be understood, and relative trade-offs need to be quantified before investment decisions can be made. However, in most contexts and for most available interventions there is simply no information on differential cost of scale-up, differential effectiveness and differential mortality burden by equity strata.

We hereby propose a framework that exposes the most important determinants of cost-effectiveness and equitable impact in maternal and child mortality reduction and their interplay. One of the values of this framework is in suggesting how to make interventions delivered to the poorest in the population (Q5) more cost-effective, which is primarily by increasing the efficiency and the quality of intervention delivery, while improving access and promoting care-seeking behavior and infrastructure to support delivery mechanisms to Q5. The framework also exposes large gaps in information required to understand the interplay between the key determinants – above all, differential cost of intervention delivery by equity strata; differential effectiveness of intervention by equity strata; and differential size and cause composition of mortality burden by equity strata. Finally, the proposed framework should enable modeling of the "*thresholds of cost-effectiveness*" for the poorest in the population, by starting the analysis from the bottom-left quadrant ("*cost-effectiveness graph*") with setting the desired level of cost-effectiveness and, given the burden of mortality, finding the values of effectiveness and cost of scale up that would be required to make the implementation cost-effective while improving equity in the population.

Acknowledgement: Originally published as: Mickey Chopra, Harry Campbell and Igor Rudan: Understanding the determinants of the complex interplay between cost-effectiveness and equitable impact in maternal and child mortality reduction. Reprinted with permission from Edinburgh University Global Health Society under Creative Commons Attribution License (Journal of Global Health 2012; 2:010406). The idea for the development of this framework originated from MC, while IR received consultancy support from UNICEF to develop the initial version of the framework and perform several implementations with modelled and real data. MC and HC then contributed to improved versions of the framework. The views of the staff of the UNICEF (MC) represent his personal views and not the views of the organization.

References

1.   Black RE, Cousens S, Johnson HL, Lawn JE, Rudan I, Bassani DG, et al. Global, regional, and national causes of child mortality in 2008: a systematic analysis. Lancet 2010; 375:1969-1987.
2.   Liu L, Johnson HL, Cousens S, Perin J, Scott S, Lawn JE, et al. Global, regional, and national causes of child mortality: an updated systematic analysis for 2010 with time trends since 2000. Lancet 2012; 379:2151-2161.
3.   Ronsmans C, Graham WJ; Lancet Maternal Survival Series steering group. Maternal mortality: who, when, where, and why. Lancet 2006; 368:1189-1200.
4.   Bhutta ZA, Ahmed T, Black RE, Cousens S, Dewey K, Giugliani E, et al. What works? Interventions for maternal and child undernutrition and survival. Lancet 2008; 371:417-440.
5.   Black RE, Allen LH, Bhutta ZA, Caulfield LE, de Onis M, Ezzati M, et al. Maternal and child undernutrition: global and regional exposures and health consequences. Lancet 2008; 371:243-260.
6.   Bhutta ZA, Chopra M, Axelson H, Berman P, Boerma T, Bryce J, et al. Countdown to 2015 decade report (2000-10): taking stock of maternal, newborn, and child survival. Lancet 2010; 375:2032-2044.
7.   Rudan I, Lawn J, Cousens S, Rowe AK, Boschi-Pinto C, Tomasković L, et al. Gaps in policy-relevant information on burden of disease in children: a systematic review. Lancet 2005; 365:2031-2040.
8.   Lewin S, Lavis JN, Oxman AD, Bastías G, Chopra M, Ciapponi A, et al. Supporting the delivery of cost-effective interventions in primary health-care systems in low-income and middle-income countries: an overview of systematic reviews. Lancet 2008; 372:928-939.
9.   Chopra M, Munro S, Lavis JN, Vist G, Bennett S. Effects of policy options for human resources for health: an analysis of systematic reviews. Lancet 2008; 371:668-674.
10. Lawn JE, Blencowe H, Pattinson R, Cousens S, Kumar R, Ibiebele I, et al. Stillbirths: Where? When? Why? How to make the data count? Lancet 2011; 377:1448-1463.

11. Rudan I, Kapiriri L, Tomlinson M, Balliet M, Cohen B, Chopra M. Evidence-based priority setting for health care and research: Tools to support policy in maternal, neonatal, and child health in Africa. PLoS Med 2010; 7:e1000308.
12. You D, Jones G, Hill K, Wardlaw T, Chopra M. Levels and trends in child mortality, 1990–2009. Lancet 2010; 376:931-933.
13. Bryce J, Terreri N, Victora CG, Mason E, Daelmans B, Bhutta ZA, et al. Countdown to 2015: tracking intervention coverage for child survival. Lancet 2006; 368:1067–1076.
14. Gwatkin DR, Rutstein S, Johnson K, Suliman E, Wagstaff A, Amouzou A. Socio-economic differences in health, nutrition, and population within developing countries: An overview. Washington, DC: World Bank, 2007.
15. Countdown 2008 Equity Analysis Group. Mind the gap: equity and trends in coverage of maternal, newborn, and child health services in 54 Countdown countries. Lancet 2008; 371:1259–1267.
16. Victora CG, Wagstaff A, Schellenberg JA, Gwatkin D, Claeson M, Habicht JP. Applying an equity lens to child health and mortality: more of the same is not enough. Lancet 2003;362:233–241.
17. Reidpath DD, Morel CM, Mecaskey JW, Allotey P. The Millennium Development Goals fail poor children: The case for equity-adjusted measures. PLoS Med 2009;6:e1000062.
18. Rudan I, Chan KY, Zhang JS, Theodoratou E, Feng XL, Salomon JA, et al. Causes of deaths in children younger than 5 years in China in 2008. Lancet 2010; 375:1083-1089.
19. Laxminarayan R, Mills AJ, Breman JG, Measham AR, Alleyne G, Claeson M, et al. Advancement of global health: key messages from the Disease Control Priorities Project. Lancet 2006;367:1193.
20. UNICEF/The World Bank. Marginal Budgeting for Bottlenecks. New York/Washington, 2010. (Available from: http://www.who.int/pmnch/topics/economics/costing-tools_resources/en/index.html; Accessed: 12 Jun 2012).
21. Adam T, Lim SS, Mehta S, Bhutta ZA, Fogstad H, Mathai M, et al. Cost effectiveness analysis of strategies for maternal and neonatal health in developing countries. BMJ 2005; 331:1107.
22. Fox MJ, Martorell R, van den Broek N, Walker N. Assumptions and methods in the Lives Saved Tool (LiST). Introduction. BMC Public Health 2011; 11(Suppl 3):I1.
23. Walker N, Fischer-Walker C, Bryce J, Bahl R, Cousens S; CHERG Review Groups on Intervention Effects. Standards for CHERG reviews of intervention effects on child survival. Int J Epidemiol 2010; 39(Suppl 1):i21-31.
24. Fischer Walker CL, Friberg IK, Binkin N, Young M, Walker N, Fontaine O, et al. Scaling up diarrhea prevention and treatment interventions: a Lives Saved Tool analysis. PLoS Med 2011; 8:e1000428.
25. Bryce J, Friberg IK, Kraushaar D, Nsona H, Afenyadu GY, Nare N, et al. LiST as a catalyst in program planning: experiences from Burkina Faso, Ghana and Malawi. Int J Epidemiol 2010; 39(Suppl 1):i40-47.
26. Friberg IK, Bhutta ZA, Darmstadt GL, Bang A, Cousens S, Baqui AH, et al. Comparing modelled predictions of neonatal mortality impacts using LiST with observed results of community-based intervention trials in South Asia. Int J Epidemiol 2010; 39(Suppl 1):i11-20.
27. Amouzou A, Richard SA, Friberg IK, Bryce J, Baqui AH, El Arifeen S, et al. How well does LiST capture mortality by wealth quintile? A comparison of measured versus modelled mortality rates among children under-five in Bangladesh. Int J Epidemiol 2010; 39(Suppl 1):i186-92.

PART 3.

Improving development assistance for health

CHAPTER 20.

Analysing global health assistance: The reach for ethnographic, institutional and political economic scope

The big picture of global health assistance can be daunting, especially when viewed from the bottom up, and through an ethnographic lens which starts with local practice and outcome. However, the increasing scale and complexity of the situation offers unprecedented scope for a combination of ethnographic, sociological and institutional perspectives to be applied to the frameworks within which global health issues are addressed. Global health practice now works from global to local scales, often all within one project or programme. But the kinds of hybrid, ambidextrous perspectives that can capture or evaluate such a melding and upscaling are all too rare in contemporary international health and development analysis.

The scope and scale of the core issues in global health assistance are immense: global and local burden of disease, social determinants of health, health infrastructures, funding international programmes, access to core and emerging technologies; and the macro-complexions of these issues shift with the changing nature of international political economy: poverty, wealth, trade, work, migration. This macro-complexion remains grim in many aspects. Despite increasing prosperity, morbidity and mortality remain high in the developing world and are rising, especially in South Asia and Sub-Saharan Africa. An estimated 530,000 women die every year during or immediately following childbirth, while more than 4 million babies die in the first month of life. Annually almost 11 million children die before the age of five. The top four killers of children – diarrhoeal disease, malaria, TB, and upper respiratory infection – still exact appalling tolls. In the next 24 hours, diarrhoea caused by unclean water and poor sanitation will claim the lives of 4000 children. 6 billion people still have no access to even the most rudimentary latrine. Over one billion have no source of drinking water (1).

To address these disparities, a huge amount of activity takes place at the level of what we might call the global health system. Of course, not all of the health system is global in every way. But there are systemic interactions at every level, from basic water and sanitation (which is increasingly informed by global norms of programme and technical practice), to advanced medical and surgical interventions, which are governed globally in several dimensions, from systemic reviews of evidence to global technologies and refinements in basic medical science. The system – more and more complex by the day – also involves formal and informal institutions, modalities or common forms of service, practice and delivery, norms and processes which govern or directly influence both global health policy and local or household practices. Agencies involved at global or near global scale include a patchwork of donors, UN agencies, governments, civil society organisations, and the private sector, all working according to a sedimented, uneven, yet legible array of programme and institutional logics. As the scales at which these institutional logics are applied grow, so the significance of these logics becomes greater.

In the field of global health assistance, the kind of analysis we hope to see more of considers both the big picture (global programming, political economy) and everyday local practice, and the ways these two are linked by everyday institutional and programming logics and modalities (programme and project forms, modes of delivery and management/governance). Because these modalities span global and local programming, analysis tracking their workings and impact will need to comprehend both the context (population/ epidemiological and budget scale, political ecologies of health and illness) and too the logistic means through which scale is made manageable, and reaches into everyday lives (international global funding arrangements, delivery modalities and their impacts on outcomes).

It is the intersections between what we call emerging institutional logics, local health practice and wider health and social outcomes that this special issue scopes and exemplifies. Our argument in introducing these papers is that both the scope and the complexity of these interactions need to be embraced and analyzed, if the particular opportunities which exist in specific programme or disease contexts are to be practically framed. However, we note, and the papers demonstrate, this embrace holds considerable challenges. This, the papers exemplify, is by no means for want of imagination or innovative invention: rather, highly sophisticated but also highly aspectual modalities or forms of practice and analysis are being developed and applied in project and programme settings.

There is a great deal of innovation in international health programmes; but it is uneven between subsectors, and much of it happens within programme-specific contexts where its qualities remain buried in programme documents. Further, many of the modalities of practice and evaluation or analysis – the material buried in the programme documents – themselves struggle to comprehend especially the kinds of social and cultural dimensions we know heavily shape local practice. Emerging modalities of practice, be they *"New Institutional"* (see below) analyses – contracting processes or bottom up participatory approaches – get variously applied: but one is left with a sense that their scope and limits as modalities are only just being recognised. Seeing the whole becomes more difficult as the sums and interactions of its parts multiply.

As the papers here make clear, sophisticated and intensive processes of engaging health problems are also resource-intensive. Of course, no single programme or intervention needs to engage all the actors or activate all the potential mechanisms involved. Yet we think in the current ethos there remain basic questions of analytic and practical scope, wherein sharp modalities are applied, or enter into already complexly aggregated contexts. Here, they encounter properties of the entire system which emerge from its wider configuration, and which form crucial contexts for action. These *"whole of system"* properties, some of which are exampled below, nonetheless set such basic parameters as the numbers of actors which need to be engaged, the kinds of funding available over what terms, the kinds of programmes likely to be funded, and the kinds of roles health development professionals occupy.

1. Health and development: four important trends. In particular, we think four notable trends in the global health system demand consideration: new actors; new sectors; new money; new institutional modalities. The first trend is *the continuous expansion in the number as well as the type of actors involved*. Other than the formal multilateral institutions, there has been an exponential growth of civil society organisations and of transnational corporations, as well as increasing involvement in health by other UN organisations such as the World Bank, the World Trade Organisation, charitable foundations, research institutions, regional development banks, regional organisations such as the European Union, and various partnerships of these actors to address specific health topics. This kind of growth has been widely recognised across international development. There, in what might be argued to be a managerialist approach to emerging complexity, we have seen the emergence of such coordinative modalities as SWAps (Sector-Wide Approaches) (2). But as in wider Development contexts, these devices, which function on the ground as working and technical committees, have focussed on planned coordination at the expense of both renegotiating the politics of health aid, or the fragmentation tendencies inherent in aid modalities (3).

The politics can be most readily seen by paying special attention to the new philanthropists who are making a large impact. Large funders wield significant influence and the new philanthropic foundations, which rely on the experience and expertise of relatively limited numbers of advisors, and have largely inward accountability, today have far greater financial influence (hence power) than many government agencies. For example, the Bill & Melinda Gates Foundation has become a central provider of research funds to many universities across the world (4). Existing programmes develop vested interests, with a considerable throw forward in terms of budget commitments. As historical institutional analysis makes clear, the entry of new actors into the field has indeed brought new configurations of practice: but these too can quickly become path dependant, as interests re-coalesce around them.

Thus, and in a number of other important ways, the institutional ecology of health aid has shifted with the arrival of these new players. These players are by no means neutral actors in the field. They bring with them – and add great power and impetus to – orthodoxies about how health aid is to be organised. Their power means existing institutional arrangements which might work are set aside, as actors at all levels prioritise alignment with new modes of organisation. This can have a positive effect, as *"best practice"* models can rise to greater prominence. On the other hand, the balance of power and (human/ intellectual) resource shifts away from locally embedded actors and towards those oriented to the new money sources. And once a new orthodoxy emerges in this context the ripples and path dependencies it sets in place will take some time settle, and longer to be re-oriented. As will be explored in this special issue, we have some experience already of such programmes persisting in questionable approaches for internal institutional reasons which obscured alternate views. Here, ethnographers with institutional analysis skills, free and open access, and academic freedom, are needed to monitor and critique such emergences.

The second trend is *the continuous expansion of what we might call the sectorial territories of health*. The Declaration of Alma-Ata in 1978 made health a concern for development and focused on socio-economic determinants of health. Since then, health has become increasingly viewed as inter-sectoral, in which the health care provision sector is only one of many sectors (e.g. transportation, housing, education, environment) that both affect and are affected by health. Initially Ministries of Health and the World Health Organisation were largely staffed by medical professionals. Now these institutions are also staffed by social scientists and trade lawyers. This medicalisation of fields – and the concomitant socialisation of medicine – have a range of implications, not least in the ways it creates an overreach situation where health experts are involved in wider public policy. Health professional are adaptable and can learn quickly. But they could also do with more research focussed on the ways new public health logics can in fact translate and span into other sectorial contexts. Here too there is a need for a great deal of real and close observation, especially in relation to the inevitable trial and error approaches that will characterise these and ongoing attempts to translate social determinants and health inequalities approaches into wider policy. These questions are starting to be wrestled with especially in a range of OECD contexts (5). But their ability to reach across sectors in developing countries is much less well understood.

The third trend is *the incredible (but highly uneven) increase in the amount of money directed to global health*, rising from tens of millions of dollars in 2000 to today's global health contributions, coupled with increased domestic commitments and foreign debt forgiveness, reaching nearly US$ 20 billion (6). Much of this money has been used to target three diseases: HIV/ AIDS, tuberculosis and malaria. As the papers in this special issue demonstrate, this surge in monies adds to the overall flux and change possible in the system, as well as to the scope of institutional and ethnographic analysis which can be brought to the programme context. In terms of timing, however, this investment focus comes with an acute global crisis in human resources for health, both in wealthy and poor nations, forcing newly-funded health programmes (such as the *U.S. President's Emergency Plan for HIV/AIDS Relief* (PEPFAR) which only targets HIV/AIDS) to draw health talent from a limited pool, resulting in declining personnel directed to other public health and medical problems (7). Thus, while one set of targeted diseases show striking improvement, primary care has deteriorated and other less "*fashionable*" diseases, such as child diarrhoeal disease, go unnoticed. While this phenomenon might be critically addressed via approaches which measure burdens of disease, it might also be helpfully understood by the kinds of close study which monitors institutional shifts, changing incentives and professional priorities as they happen. Aid, it is widely recognised, distorts local priorities, and draws capabilities and incentives out of areas which are governed through older institutional means, and into those governed short term through projects, contracts, and technologies which produce readily countable "*outputs*". Research alert to these grounded tendencies might raise, perhaps in something close to real time, questions as to whether the path set out down is really in the public health interest, or whether it mostly enables development assistance to be channelled transparently and easily.

A fourth, closely related, involves *programming modalities* themselves. As health assistance has gone global, it has picked up many of international development's institutional modalities, which tend to be of a generic family type. Shaped by the need for both adaptation (policy experimentation) and international replicability (policy and programmatic transfer) (8), these approaches have also embodied both *New Institutional* and neoliberal (*New Public Management*) modes of organisation (a focus on transaction costs, efficient delivery, decentralisation, outsourcing, local participation and local values (3,9-11).

The age of multiple agencies produces enough fragmentation. But even when managerially harmonised, the actual delivery modalities around health programmes have intrinsic fragmenting qualities of their own, to which little analytic or critical attention has so far been drawn. Informed by *New Institutional Economics* (9,12), these vertically integrated programmes create accountabilities through narrow contracting means, which are often designed precisely to take government line managers and levels of bureaucratic management out of the equation. Programmes routinely reproduce these narrow logics in their own self-evaluation activities, focussed too on counting outputs. It is becoming increasingly clear is that these modalities have a range of unintended consequences, which remain little understood. They also weaken, for example, political accountability, in that services are paid for by others, often off-budget, and allocated technocratically rather than in response to voter demand. Staff on special salary supplements are drawn from the mainstream system, or services are contracted out into much narrower accountability regimes focussed on producing outputs. Policy is not deliberated locally, but written by consultants attached to central ministries, and signed off via the executive, often without debate in the legislature. Meanwhile, politicians focus the revenues they have on more direct patronage and election winning, instead of into reforming services. Thus health services like other areas become institutionally layered, with effective accountability firewalls between executive and political actors each retaining their own control structures, but leaving the mainstream of services impoverished.

Thus despite all this activity, including attempts at aid effectiveness improvement through sector wide approaches, disparities remain and in several countries are becoming even greater. Perhaps the paradox of our time is that despite all the activity and resources concentrated in this area, health is not improving as dramatically as it should in emerging and developing countries. We think that important explanations for this paradox lie in the institutionalised nature of health assistance, or more broadly, the efforts of global health institutions to address these disparities.

2. Developing institutional ethnographies for health? Alternatives to existing approaches. The primary services which global health institutions offer developing countries and their citizens are financial resources and/or technical expertise, what can be broadly referred to as *"aid"*. Worried by the scope of investment in aid, and the unevenness of results emerging, economists such as (13-15) have long debated whether and what kinds of aid work. Primarily this debate has been driven by quantitative analysis at the macro-scale level looking at growth rates and poverty headcount ratios across countries. In addition, the aid debate tends to focus on quantitative indicators of progress, as represented in the Millennium Development Goals, rather than actually seeing whether aid results in increasing household welfare as defined by the communities themselves. In health, global burden of disease models (16) have been important in assessing, on a macro scale, whether the right amounts of money are going to the right contexts. Few of these analyses, Easterly (14) aside, have questioned the internal institutional dynamics through which aid programmes are delivered, and the ways in which these can often set even well targeted funding and local realities at considerable odds with each other.

In contrast, we would like to see more studies building on the now classic work of (17), which worked to understand the aid process at the micro-scale level using rigorous qualitative analysis. What actually happens to the huge amounts of money being disbursed? Where does it go? And who benefits? Social science of health and development scholars have long recognized the need to analyse the way in which global actors and institutions affect the communities they study. As Cris Shore and Susan Wright have recognized, globalisation has resulted in an interdependent world in which understanding the plight of poor people requires an understanding of the way institutions such as banks, governments, multinational companies, and geopolitics operate (18,19). Important steps have been taken to document the aid policy process such as by Fergusson (20), Harper (21), Mosse and Lewis (22), Corbridge, Williams, Srivastava, and Véron (23), and Wedel (24). Our own work (3,25,26) aims to encompass both big and small pictures, and to locate explanations within the dispositions and routinised practices and habitus of organisations (27,28). But there is much more to study.

Both institutions and political development are well suited to the kinds of close study health social science researchers can bring to their work. Institutional theory, both its old and *"New"* varieties, provide a vast array of analytical framings and concepts, many of which can be relatively easily imported into ethnographic/sociological frames (see for example Thelen (29,30)). This is in part because institutions are like cultures: they involve the kinds of routinised practices and popular representations ethnographers are attuned to. But institutional analytic perspectives also investigate the historical and cultural sedimentation and layering of these practices over time (10,11) that a wider political and critical sociology can inform. Some analyse crucial turning points or junctures (10) in the orientations, cultures and practices of institutions, and form judgements as to why these happened, and their effects. Some can consider effects of deeply structured underlying factors, such as political economy, social and cultural values and mores, and particular *"layering"* patterns of institutionalised interactions between institutionally located actors (26,29,30). These factors need to be unearthed and subjected to analysis by ethnographic and social approaches linked to critical institutional awarenesses.

Historically, international development (though less so international health assistance) has benefited from such analyses from figures like Albert Hirschman (31), whom we now recognise as a seminal actor in the field. More recently, Mosse and Lewis (22) have proposed a model to study such processes. They note that any approach must account for the network of relationships, incentive structures, power dynamics and ideological constraints on how institutions work. In the current context, such an approach must pay special attention to the complexity of the policy process, the social life of organisations, the heterogeneity of interests behind policy models and the voices of the actors themselves. Their model can be taken forward to study the links between international organisations and local communities, tracing the ways in which power creates webs and relations between actors, institutions and discourses over time and space. This analytical innovation permits research to derive conclusions that relate not just to the researchers and universities to maintain their independence. The reflexive nature of anthropology becomes increasingly important in this environment to ensure that attention is paid to how research is funded such that academia retains some distance from the larger funding pressures at work that serve at best to direct the research agenda and at worse, to co-opt findings to fit a pre-established policy. Given the critical information that qualitative research can reveal regarding aid effectiveness, it is time for anthropologists to further engage with this arena and work to complement the quantitative debate.

3. The special issue on global health assistance. We now turn to the papers of the *Special Issue*. Much of the range of current institutional analysis is reflected in the group of papers which has emerged from our call for papers for the part *Special Issue*. The papers provide a rich and intriguing taste of current practice. All represent innovative and sophisticated programmes and evaluative analysis. All emerge in relation to larger well funded international programmes in particular sectoral / disease areas. And all in different ways at the same time point to struggles to engage wider complexities, especially in relation to the social contexts the programmes being analysed emerge in.

First, the papers here show some of the scope of innovative institutional and social context analysis that is possible: they include *New Institutional Economics* approaches to transaction costs, *New Public Management* approaches to outsourcing, and close descriptions of programme relations with World Bank programme modalities, including *Poverty Reduction Strategy Papers, Conditional Cash Transfers*, and more. They also include more diffuse ethnographic analyses, and new ways of measuring mobilization. All these add considerable dimensions of richness.

Second, all of the papers represent innovative attempts to graft often very sophisticated forms of *New Institutional* analysis onto existing or emerging programmatic practice. Perhaps we should not be surprised here: strong and substantive analysis demands a considerable investment of resources, and programme evaluation is one branch of applied research with the resources to attempt this kind of analysis. Here we see both strengths and weaknesses: as we argue above, extended institutional ethnographies – especially those with significant mixed methods aspects attached which can generate the kinds of quantified analyses funders require – demand a long term commitment and multiple skill sets, which seldom inhere in the same person. Multidisciplinary groups seem to be required in many contexts. But so too is support and access, for example, to a PhD student or an academic working outside a *"large grant team"* environment, able to innovate more freely and critically across complexities where larger programmatic approaches will often fear to tread.

What we also see emerging in the overall complexion of the papers is the sectorially asymmetric pattern of this innovation. Perhaps the most innovative technical analyses have emerged in areas associated with HIV/AIDS, and with wider socio-economic support targeted at families with high health needs (*Multilaterally supported Conditional Cash Transfers* and poverty-contextualised *Mother and Child Health programmes*). These are funded by the larger and/or newer funding bodies, often at national or at least regional scale, and have been developed from the outset with a sense that biomedicine is not necessarily the most significant contributor to health outcomes. Here we see innovation primarily in terms of analysis of programmes which reach into areas on the edge of traditional clinical health: attempts to reach out to communities, the poor, marginalised ethnic groups from within a health programme, using a range of participatory and empowering institutional modalities drawn from community practice into mainstream service delivery.

In this part Special Issue, both HIV and social assistance areas are exemplified. Here, barriers to the effectiveness of the extremely popular *Conditional Cash Transfer Systems* modality (CCTs) are described by Adato, Roopnaraine, and Becker (32). Their paper sums extensive ethnographic research on CCTs impact on health outcomes and practices over 10 years in Mexico, Nicaragua, El Salvador and Turkey. Pointing out the extent to which CCT programmes and their evaluation are still reliant on models wherein mothers are seen as rational utility maximisers, they demonstrate how the programme's modalities and assumptions are in fact subject to range of other crucial everyday contextualisations. These include *"beliefs around traditional and modern biomedical practices, sociocultural norms, gender relations, and the quotidian experience of poverty in many dimensions"* (32). These same areas of programme vulnerability, we note, recur in other papers in this issue, in relation to other other modalities and analyses. Adato, Roopnaraine & Becker's (32) engagement in four countries over ten years focussed on a particular modality is nonetheless exceptional, and it raises questions for other modes of analysis and practice: for all the sharp focus, how fully did these analyses capture the richness local context? Conversely, what are the risks of less extensive analyses constituting an imported add-on to a programme which also imported funding, genesis, and accountabilities?

What is however clear from all the papers is that the analytic modalities they reveal in action all show some cut through: new, focussed institutional analytic approaches both inform and demonstrate the plausible achievement of programmatic gains. This seems especially apparent where new and innovative analytic approaches beginning to engage and even hybridise approaches with ethno-graphic analysis of local institutions and practice. In both evaluation and programme practice, hybrid arrangements involving a range of innovative institutional modalities are clearly possible, as demonstrated in Jonathan Garcia's (33) account of enrolment of church groups into HIV. This largely ethnographic approach – which also deployed a particular variant of mobilisation theory – was able to demonstrate that *"...mobilization of resources from international donors, political opportunities (i.e., decentralization of the National AIDS Programme), and cultural framings enabled local Afro-Brazilian religious groups to forge a national network. On the micro-level, in Rio de Janeiro, we observed how macro-level structures led to the proliferation of capacity-building and peer educator projects among these religious groups"*, and that *"beyond funding assistance, the interrelation of religious ideologies, leadership, and networks linked to HIV can affect mobilization"* (33). We consider this analysis which casts both macro-level structures and particular local mobilisation capabilities in the same frame as demonstrating some of the scope of what is possible. Again, innovation came in an emerging area, with new actors, and researchers given remarkable innovative scope by a developing programme involving the World Bank, WHO and a national level aids programme.

Other papers' analyses reveal systemic difficulties in articulating programme gains into the wider system. Guinness (34) paper *"What can transaction costs tell us about governance in the scaling up of HIV prevention programmes in southern India?"* is able to demonstrate the programmatic effectiveness of out-contracting based reforms in a single area. The research deploys a *New Institutional* analytic of transaction costs (and associated corruption) involved with different contracting modalities in HIV service delivery. The hybrid relational contracting mode emerging from the involvement of an autonomous third party agency operating at one remove from direct state control. Acknowledging this success, the author remains sceptical about the possibility for achieving measurable change without this outsourcing, given the wider context, which is characterised as uncertain, corrupt and *"information weak"* (34). While we may well remain wary of outsourcing approaches based on assumptions state structures are relatively impervious to reform, the transaction costs analysis was able to shine a closer light on particular mechanisms and their effects. As it develops, this kind of analysis could inform a range of reform contexts, including those where outsourcing is less obviously desirable.

Ruger, Baird and Ma's (35) analysis of a World Bank maternal and child health programme operating in the complex context of other significant decentralisation and health system reforms in Indonesia is a sophisticated attempt to reach down into rapidly changing local contexts (in areas including gendered education and employment) to chart outcome shifts. Positive programmatic impact is measurable in under–five mortality, and recognisable in certain *"clinically relevant improvements"*. But it is not so trackable in *"infant mortality, total fertility rate, teenage pregnancy, unmet contraceptive need or percentage of deliveries overseen by trained health personnel"* (35). At the same time, neither of the companion programmes operating in the maternal child health (MCH) programme's context demonstrated independent effects either. Here, the research reveals the difficulty of measuring complementarity and redundancy in aid programmes. But it also might point to wider systemic and institutional under-reach for health focussed programmes, especially in difficult to reform areas such as the scope and reach of the Human Resource establishment (or salary) budget, which translates quite directly into such outcomes as the *"percentage of deliveries overseen by trained health personnel"*. We join the authors, then, in urging ongoing development of research in these complex contexts.

Ruger, Baird and Ma's paper (35) points to the fact that few of the current approaches are able to assist investigation of, for example, the structural or political economic base of power in existing systems: bases which in turn underpin resistance to institutional reform, more grounded in revenue flows and political responsiveness. Ruger's determination to explore these difficult contexts is we think exemplary. Ruger and Wachira's (36) paper on the Malawi HIV programme linked to the *Poverty Reduction Strategy Paper* (PRSP) programme signals further scope and limits for joined up health and wider contextual reform, as currently practised and modality-enabled. In this paper we see how a global institutional development initiative – the World Bank's PRSP programme – begins to impact on a particular health area, HIV aids programming, especially in terms of creating a context of partially *"shared health governance"* (36). The PRSP is just the kind of global initiative we see as altering (but not fully transforming) the global health context. To appear significant (and to attract necessary attention from government and donors), all development programmes need to adopt some kind of stance to what is effectively a broad ranging (but shallow reaching) planning modality, driven by international actors with limited local buy in. Yet questions as to how far shared health or other governance can go in promoting change on the ground either in health outcomes of poverty reduction terms are difficult indeed to scope in this context (3). The paper is able to identify points of progress in creating shared accountability. But this too proved aspectual and prone to under-reach, in that *"the process may have marginalized key stakeholders, potentially undercutting the implementation of HIV/AIDS Action Plans, while wider "Accountability for achieving results also fell short"."* (36).

We would expect falling short, or under-reach, to be generic to institutional reform practices which rely heavily on one aspect of *New Institutional* analysis, but underplay or perhaps under resource others. Under-reach in analytic or transformational power also take us back to the need modalities and approaches which are able to deal with both the big picture of political economy and historical patterns of institutional emergence, and are able to draw a sharper analytic focus to particular areas of rectifiable weakness. Currently, most institutional analysis is we suspect undermined by the lack of transformational potential (in other words, under-reach) in actual programmes. Programmes, then, no less than their analyses and evaluations, need to take us beyond what Adato et al. (32) describe as the limits of *"beliefs around traditional and modern biomedical practices, sociocultural norms, gender relations, and the quotidian experience of poverty in many dimensions"* (32), and out into factors including the wider political economic, social determinant and historical institutional will only make sense in terms of programmes and reforms which themselves have that sense of necessary scope.

Meantime, this part of the *Special Issue* shows that both the sharply focussed and the wider research are expanding their reach, and are we hope becoming better able to talk to each other. As the papers together demonstrate, ethnographic analysis joined to institutional logics and a wider sense of political and economic contexts can shine innovative light on how global health aid works in practice – from the top to the bottom and back up again.

In sum, there is plenty of room in analysis of *Global Health Assistance* for widening and deepening the scope of analyses, and moving them beyond the current field largely constituted by analyses joined to intervention modalities in a limited number of sectors. This will require not just a blend of current specialist analytic skills: it will need more resourcing, not least from programmes themselves willing to be open to a deeper embedding of their work. It will need further expansion of disciplinary boundaries, and greater reach into different institutional analyses, political sociologies, and across into critical understandings of wider international development. In this, as is the case in analyses of international development (20), it may well be that the extended case study- book length, grounded in history and extending over time and scale – will become the favoured mode of telling. Meantime, we hope this special issue itself makes a useful contribution to the scope and reach of *Global Health Assistance* analysis.

Acknowledgement: *Originally published as: Devi Sridhar and David Craig: Analysing global health assistance: The reach for ethnographic, institutional and political economic scope. Reprinted with permission from Elsevier (Social Science in Medicine 2011; 72:1915–1920).*

References

1. Sridhar D. Global health: WHO can lead? Chatham House World Today 2009; 65:25-26.
2. Hill P The rhetoric of sector-wide approaches for health development. Soc Sci Med 2002; 54:1725–1737.
3. Craig D, Porter D. Development beyond neo-liberalism: Governance, poverty reduction and political economy. London: Routledge, 2006.
4. McCoy D, Kembhavi G, Patel J, Luintel A. The Bill & Melinda Gates foundation's grant-making programme for global health. Lancet 2009; 373:1645–1653.
5. Bambra C, Gibson M, Sowden A, Wright K, Whitehead M, Petticrew M. Tackling the wider social determinants of health and health inequalities: evidence from systematic reviews. J Epidemiol Comm Health 2010; 64:284–291.
6. Garrett L. The challenge of global health. Foreign Affairs, 2007. pp. 14–38.
7. Sridhar D. Seven failings in international development assistance for health. J Law Med Ethics 2010; 38.
8. Brenner N, Peck J, Theodore N. After neoliberalization? Globalizations 2010; 7:327–345.
9. North DC. Institutions, institutional change and economic performance. Cambridge: Cambridge University Press, 1990.

10. Pierson P. Politics in time: History, institutions and social analysis. Princeton: Princeton University Press, 2004.
11. Peters G. Institutional theory in political Science: The new institutionalism. New York: Continuum Press, 2005.
12. Coase R. The nature of the firm. Economica 1937; 4:386–405.
13. Collier P. The bottom billion: Why the poorest countries are failing and what can be done about it. Oxford: OUP, 2007.
14. Easterly W. The white man's burden: Why the west's efforts to aid the rest have done so much ill and so little good. Harmondsworth: Penguin, 2006.
15. Sachs J. The end of poverty: Economic possibilities for our time. Harmondsworth: Penguin, 2006.
16. Murray C, Lopez A. Evidence-based health policy: lessons from the global burden of disease study. Science 1996; 274:740–743.
17. de Waal A. Famine that kills: Darfur, Sudan. Oxford: Clarendon Press, 1989.
18. Shore C, Wright S. British anthropology in policy and practice: a review of current work. Human Organization 1996; 55:475–480.
19. Shore C, Wright S. Anthropology of policy. In: Shore C, Wright S (eds). Anthropology of policy: Critical perspectives on governance and power. London: Routledge, 1997.
20. Fergusson J. The anti-politics machine: "Development", depoliticization, and bureaucratic power in Lesotho. Minneapolis: University of Minnesota Press, 1994.
21. Harper I. Interconnected and interinfected: DOTS and the stabilisation of the tuberculosis control programme in Nepal. In: Mosse D, Lewis D (eds). The aid effect: Giving and governing in international development. London: Pluto, (2005).
22. Mosse D, Lewis D. Theoretical approaches to brokerage and translation in development. In: Lewis D, Mosse D (eds). Development brokers and translators: Ethnography of aid and agencies. Bloomfield: Kumarian, 2006.
23. Corbridge S, Williams G, Srivastava M, Veron R. Seeing the state: Governance and governmentality in India. Cambridge: CUP, 2005.
24. Wedel J. Collision and collusion: The strange case of western aid to Eastern Europe. NYC: Palgrave, 2001.
25. Craig D. Familiar medicine: Everyday health knowledge and practice in today's Vietnam. Honolulu: University of Hawaii Press, 2002.
26. Craig D, Porter D. Winning the peace: New institutions and neopatrimonialism in post conflict Cambodia. Ann Arbor: University of Michigan Press, 2011.
27. Bourdieu P. Outline of a theory of practice. Cambridge: Cambridge University Press, 1977.
28. Meinert L. Resources for health in Uganda: bourdieu's concepts of capital and habitus. Anthrop Med 2004; 11:11–26.
29. Thelen K. Historical institutionalism and comparative politics. Ann Rev Polit Sci 1999; 2:369–404.
30. Thelen K. How institutions evolve: The political economy of skills in Germany, Britain, Japan and the United States. Cambridge: Cambridge University Press, 2004.
31. Hirschman A. Exit, voice and loyalty: Responses to decline in firms, organizations and states. Cambridge MA: Harvard University Press, 1970.
32. Adato MT, Roopnaraine T, Becker E. Understanding use of health services in conditional cash transfer programs: insights from qualitative research in Latin America and Turkey. Soc Sci Med 2011; 72:1921–1929.

33. Garcia J. Resource mobilization for health Advocacy: afro-Brazilian religious Organizations and HIV prevention and control. Soc Sci Med 2011; 72:1930–1938.

34. Guinness L. What can transaction costs tell us about governance in the scaling up of HIV prevention programmes in southern India? Soc Sci Med 2011; 72:1939–1947.

35. Ruger JP, Baird J, Ma R. Effects of the world bank's maternal and child health intervention on Indonesia's poor: evaluating the safe motherhood project. Soc Sci Med 2011; 72:1948–1955.

36. Ruger JP, Wachira C. National poverty reduction Strategies and HIV/AIDS governance in Malawi: a Preliminary study of shared health governance. Soc Sci Med 2011; 72:1956–1964.

CHAPTER 21.

Seven challenges in international development assistance for health and ways forward

Over the past 20 years, international development assistance for health has increased, albeit for some diseases more than others (1). However, the triple crises of food, fuel, and finance have raised questions regarding whether aid flows will continue to increase, or even be maintained in the coming future. Health and education are often the first victims of budget cuts in times of limited funding and competing priorities as they are viewed to be in the realm of "*low politics*" as opposed to security and military spending, which are seen as "*high politics*" (2). Cuts in overseas development aid will have a drastic impact on countries where external funding makes up a significant proportion of national health budgets. Although global health aid accounts for only 0.3% of total expenditures on health globally (6.5% in sub-Saharan Africa) (3), in some countries like the Solomon Islands and Mozambique, for example, 82% and 66% of the national health budgets respectively come from external resources (4). WHO estimates that 23 countries have over 30% of their total health expenditures funded by donors.

Given this situation, it is of utmost importance that a strong case continues to be made for development assistance to health and that in the context of a stable, or shrinking, pot, funds are used most effectively to improve the health of those living in low and middle-income countries. While the financial crisis has brought much attention to aid quantity and quality, the problems developing countries face are not new. As one former Sub-Saharan African Health Minister noted in 2008 at a workshop at the Harvard School of Public Health, "*Insecurity of funding has been something we have been facing for many years now. It is not a new phenomenon*". This paper outlines seven challenges in development assistance for health, which in the current financial context, have become even more important to address. The purpose of this paper is to provoke debate and discussion. It does not aim to be prescriptive. Only with scrutiny over the perceived or real failings of global health assistance can steps be made to not only make the system more effective, but also to make a stronger case to policy makers for increased overseas development aid.

Throughout the paper, the theme of country ownership is underlined. On September 4, 2008, the Accra Agenda for Action was agreed upon which emphasized that country ownership over health must be strengthened. While the Accra Agenda, which builds on the 2005 Paris Declaration on Aid Effectiveness, is a major step forward, this paper argues that there are still structural factors that impede country ownership in health.

1. Challenge 1: The proliferation of initiatives and the *"dream"* of coordination. At the international level, there has been a constant deluge of initiatives, focusing on specific diseases or issues, most recently the International Health Partnership (IHP+) and the Campaign for the Millennium Development Goals (MDGs). It is estimated that there are more than 40 bilateral donors, 26 UN agencies, 20 global and regional funds, and 90 global health initiatives active at the moment (5–7).

Despite the articulation of a set of principles for more effective and equitable aid delivery, in the form of the Paris Declaration and Accra Agenda, it is disconcerting to note that the current landscape is charing to build long-term national capacity. Many of these initiatives are narrowly focused on specific diseases (e.g., HIV/AIDS, malaria, and TB) rather than systems-wide strengthening, tend to be *"top-down"* in nature and are largely driven by donor agendas rather than the country's own needs and priorities. However ambitious or well intentioned the initiative might be, it becomes difficult in this environment for governments to develop and implement sound national plans for their country. As Francisco Songane, former Minister of Health from Mozambique has noted: *"We need to reach some sort of stabilisation, because what happens is that countries are being jostled from one initiative to another... We need to reverse the situation and reach the stage where donors can stay the course. It is the moral duty of international community to change their tune and support weak countries and accept developing country leadership. That is a crisis right now — the international community is not accepting developing country leadership"* (7).

In non-health sector aid, after many years of debate, there has been recognition of the importance of ownership, as demonstrated by the endorsement of the 2005 Paris Declaration and the 2008 Accra Agenda. Ownership was defined in the Declaration as developing countries exercising effective leadership over their development policies and strategies and coordinating development actions (8).

Small steps are being made in this direction in global health, but they must be examined critically. For example, the International Health Partnership (IHP+), launched in 2007 by Gordon Brown, aims to provide better coordination among donors; focus on improving health systems as a whole; and

develop and support countries' own health plans (9). The IHP+ is an attempt
to bring 35 donor and recipient countries, 12 organizations, and civil society to
work together in a partnership to improve health outcomes through a single,
harmonized in-country implementation strategy. At the centre of this strategy
is the "*country compact*" where development partners work in the context of
existing in-country mechanisms through a single, results-oriented national
health plan with the objective of scaling-up effective coverage as a means of
achieving the targets set by the health-related MDGs. To date 22 recipient countries, including Benin, Cambodia, Kenya, Nepal, and Vietnam, have signed
the country compact. However, as of today, there has been little progress.

The lack of progress with the IHP+ is an indication that the rhetoric of
coordination should be viewed skeptically. There are two main challenges in
focusing solely on coordination. First, there are concerns that coordination will
decrease the policy space of developing countries by shifting the balance of
power towards a "*consortium of donors acting in unison*", and thus there could
be an inherent contradiction in the partnership (10). In fact, it has been argued
that donor coordination to provide budgetary support has taken donors into
the "*heart of government*" and further reduced the space for countries to set
their own priorities (11). The assumption built into the rhetoric of coordination
is that an external body needs to coordinate donors or various institutions.
However, there is a real case to be made for coordination to be led by national
governments, not by external initiatives.

Second, although they might agree in rhetoric or on paper, there is little
incentive for various development partners/institutions to coordinate their activities. Even within the UN system, the case of UNAIDS, which was designed to be
a coordinating entity among the UN bodies, illustrates how difficult coordination is in practice. As one senior policymaker commented: "*No one wants to be
coordinated... the job of being coordinator is the most thankless and ungrateful job*" (12).

While the rhetoric is in place, and the principles are outlined in the
Paris Declaration and Accra Agenda, action lags far behind. Rather than put
countries in the driver's seat so that investment can be made in long-term
priority-setting and planning, donors focus on "*quick wins*" and measurable
returns through vertical programming. The focus on these quick results discourages investment in health systems and indicates the need for a country-led
process of priority-setting.

**2. Challenge 2: Overemphasis on "*new players*", rather than reforming
and strengthening existing institutions**. At present, the global health system
can be viewed as a patchwork of donors, UN agencies, governments, civil
society organizations, and the private sector.

(i) The first group of actors is the multilateral institutions such as the World Health Organization, UNICEF, UNDP, UNFPA, World Bank, and the indirect effects of the WTO and IMF. The two main multilaterals are the WHO and the World Bank. The WHO was established in 1948 with the objective to aid all peoples in the attainment of the highest possible level of health, broadly conceived. It was created to be the director and coordinator of international health work. It has focused on two activities: providing scientific and technical advice and setting international normative standards. However, the World Health Organization's limited core financial resources results in its dependence to external priorities achieved through extra-budgetary funds from member states and philanthropic organizations (6). The World Bank was not created to address health directly, but has a more broad poverty alleviation objective. Since 1980, it has played an increasingly important role in health primarily due to its financial power as a lender, its interaction with Ministries of Finance in developing countries, as well as its reputation for its intellectual prowess (13). Member countries can establish trust funds in the Bank with funds earmarked for specific diseases. These funds are essentially a bilateral form of aid channelled through a multi-lateral institution.

(ii) The second group consists of national aid agencies, or bilaterals, such as the U.K. Department for International Development (DFID), and the U.S. agency for international development (USAID). The biggest player here is the U.S. government through its HIV/AIDS, malaria, and child survival initiatives. Bilateral aid has increased relative to multilateral aid in the past ten years.

(iii) The third group consists of non-governmental organizations and networks, with key players including the People's Health Movement (grassroots network of developing country activists) and Oxfam GB (with field presence throughout the world). This kind of governance has been grouped under the broad category of civil society organizations, or CSOs.

(iv) The fourth group is private foundations (e.g., the Rockefeller Foundation) with the biggest player being the Bill & Melinda Gates Foundation.

(v) The fifth group is the private sector, and its engagement through public-private partnerships (e.g., Medicines for Malaria, Stop TB Alliance), the largest being the Global Fund to Fight HIV/AIDS, Tuberculosis and Malaria. The private sector brings expertise on technical norms and standards, injects financial resources, and has proved to be a crucial actor in global health (although some have criticized partnerships for allowing the private sector a seat at the table without sufficient checks on commercial interests).

As noted under the section on initiatives, there has been a continuous expansion in the number as well as the type of actors involved. Instead of creating new forums and initiatives, there is a real case to be made for reforming and strengthening the existing global health institutions, particularly the WHO and the World Bank. While the WHO was created to be the lead health agency, an increasing number of the initiatives referred to above are completely independent of the WHO. For example, UNAIDS was created from the WHO's Global Programme on HIV/AIDS. Why was HIV/AIDS first taken out of the WHO? As Michael Merson et al. note: *"There was growing concern about the senior leadership of the WHO among donor governments, who reacted to the re-election of Hiroshi Nakajima to a second term of Director-General by decreasing their overall support and voluntary contributions to WHO, calling for organizational reforms, and devising new health-related initiatives outside the agency's influence or control"* (14).

Thus the birth of UNAIDS is intricately linked to the real and perceived failures of the WHO. Even today, when the question is raised whether UNAIDS can become a special program of the WHO, or whether it can play a larger role in monitoring health financing, the shortcomings of WHO are listed as key reasons why new initiatives need to be created (15). These include that it is perceived to be bureaucratic and inefficient, is subject to political pressure from its more powerful Member States, and lacks clear priorities among a multitude of programs. There is also a perception that the organization has not been able to deal with the challenges posed by globalization and that, as a result, others have stepped into the void. Importantly, it suffers from inadequate resources, and the reality that nearly 80% of its budget now comes from external donors, rather than from assessed contributions of its Member States, has brought into question WHO's neutrality and independence.

However, as has been articulated by various academics, strong leadership is urgently needed and as the lead international public health agency representing 193 sovereign states, the WHO *"is uniquely positioned to provide this leadership by virtue of its role in setting evidence-based norms on technical and policy matters, highlighting best practices that improve health globally, and monitoring and coordinating action to address current and emerging global health threats"* (16). Instead of examining how the WHO should be reformed, new initiatives are launched that erode the WHO's authority as the leader in global health.

Similarly, the World Bank's role in health is often reduced to its role in structural adjustment program and user fees (17). However, in the context of the current financial crisis, there is an important role to be played by the Bank given its comparative advantage as *"the lender of last resort"*. The World Bank has a particular role to play in shaping health policies through its interaction with government, and in supporting country's efforts to strengthen health systems (18). In contrast to many of the *"new players"*, the World Bank must lend to governments, thus ensuring that the state plays the central role in driving health policy.

It is worth briefly mentioning the Gates Foundation, which is now one of the largest institutions in health. The Gates Foundation has received criticism due to its focus on funding scientific research focused on the development of new technologies for preventing infectious disease (19). Is this criticism justified? The Foundation's research investment has been characterized by grants for the creation and improvement of health interventions, particularly through technology development. This is in line with the Gates Foundation's desire to develop tools that can *"change global health for all time"* (20). The Foundation's ability to take risks and its freedom from short-term assessments of impact shape its comparative advantage: it is able to invest in long-term scientific research with the expectation that the results will take more time than the other donors can allow. However, despite its articulated objectives to focus on technological innovation, the Gates Foundation has become arguably a *"gap filler"*, funding research and services in global health that other donors cannot or will not fund ranging from advocacy initiatives to vaccine research to university centres to service provision. However, given that it is a private philanthropic foundation, the Gates Foundation should not be looked at to be *"everything to everyone"*, and in this situation, maybe more attention should be paid to reforming the main health multilaterals, the WHO, and World Bank rather than looking to new players to compensate for their shortcomings.

3. Challenge 3: Donor influence on priority-setting and their lack of accountability. The third major challenge is donor influence on priority-setting and their lack of accountability. As noted above, global health aid accounts for only 0.3% of total expenditures on health globally (6.5% in sub-Saharan Africa). Given this small percentage, why is the impact of donors so critical? Many Ministries of Health have become *"donor dependent"*, with Ministers from Tanzania, Kenya, and Uganda reporting that 40-60% of their budgets come from donors (21). Due to this donor dependence, the priorities and services established by national governments, even those operating on national funds, may be vulnerable to the magnified influence of donor priorities. This is true, not only of heavily dependent countries such as Uganda, but also of middle-income countries such as India (22) and Brazil (23).

Imrana Qadeer notes that although only roughly 1.6–2.0% of financing in the health sector in India comes from external funds, this small percentage is distorting national priorities (21). For example, she notes that from 1990–91 until 1998–99 investments only increased for selected programs for TB, leprosy and AIDS Control at the expense of the National Malaria Control and Diarrhoeal Diseases Control Programs. Similarly, Anil Deolalikar et al. note that external assistance constitutes a sizable share of national disease control programs for TB, HIV/AIDS, and malaria (24).

The proliferation of initiatives discussed in section one brings other challenges for recipient governments. These include lack of alignment of donors with the national approach, lack of harmonization among donors, and excessive transaction costs on recipient governments. Too often donors have their own ways of implementing initiatives in a country, thereby weakening national health strategies and systems. As one official from a developing country noted: "*Ideally assistance should be free from political pressures, it should not detract from national plans, it should be grants not loans, it should be properly aligned with national health systems, and donors should not be intrusive*" (7).

The example of the World Bank has been used to demonstrate why governments sometimes choose not to take assistance: "*The World Bank is offering loans, not grants, these are not aligned with national systems and priorities, and it is intrusive*", and as another official noted: "*From our assessment, it is only 40% of World Bank aid that has tangible benefit. The other 60% is in the form of technical assistance*" (7).

Donors tend to over-involve themselves even with assistance that is more broadly aimed at strengthening local capacity. They push "*technical assistance*" on recipient governments through consultants and training workshops. In terms of consultants, an advisor from Nepal noted: "*Now, there is a chronic problem of hiring highly paid consultants from outside, and a lot of money goes back to those consultants. So why not use our own consultants, who are national, who are equally competent, who know the country well*" (7). On the other hand, capacity-building projects can result in numerous workshops and training sessions, which draw key staff members away from ministries where they are most needed.

Much of the challenges outlined above, stem from the underlying lack of accountability of donors to recipient governments. Accountability is defined as the relationship "*in which an individual, group, or other entity makes demands on an agent to report on his/her activities, and has the ability to impose costs on the agent*" (25). Accountability can take a number of different forms ranging from supervisory to fiscal, and to peer and reputational (26).

For example, the U.S. government disbursements through USAID, PEPFAR, and the Malaria Initiative follow a bilateral aid model. The Executive Branch of the government, especially since USAID has been absorbed into the

State department, executes the initiatives. The funds are acquired from taxpayers with congressional approval of the budget. Ultimately, the initiatives, and the related agencies within the U.S. government, are accountable to Congress, which can be viewed as a distinct and regulatory agent within government that exerts supervisory power. Congress members in turn are accountable to their constituents ranging from individuals to large corporations. Thus, there is no direct accountability of U.S. government assistance to recipient governments.

In addition, donors seldom report on their activities, and while they monitor recipients according to good governance indicators, they themselves do not follow this. For example, there is a lack of transparency about the quantity of aid flowing into a country and how it has been used. Part of the difficulty is that recent funders, such as PEPFAR and the Gates Foundation, disburse funds directly to NGOs, thus making it difficult for Ministries to plan their efforts. The Health Minister of Tanzania noted: *"If they say, we have sent $100 million dollars you would expect government to be accountable. But the funding is not recorded. We don't know where it goes. Much goes to civil society, and much remains in donor countries"* (7).

Thus, recipient governments have difficulty knowing how much money is actually in their country, and where in the process funds are *"leaking"*. Adding to the difficulty in monitoring donors is that the same donors have adopted strategies that vary across countries.

4. Challenge 4: The rhetoric of *"health systems"*. Since the Declaration of Alma-Ata, attention to health systems has waxed and waned. Most recently, in the global health community there has been a shift back towards promoting health systems, or horizontal, interventions. Horizontal interventions are defined as those that strengthen the primary care system, improve health systems service and delivery, and address general non-disease specific problems such as health worker shortages and inadequate skilled birth attendants. However, there are pragmatic difficulties with realizing the rhetoric and financing horizontal interventions. For example, there is a lack of consensus over how financing should penetrate the system, through promoting specific targets that indicate the strength of a health system, such as maternal mortality (27), or through general approaches such as building clinics. In addition, it is difficult for donors to accurately monitor and evaluate horizontal interventions since the impact is not easily attributable.

Thus, the tension remains between the desire to fund horizontal activities with the reality of financing for vertical interventions such as through the U.S. government and Global Fund. Much of the increase in monies for global health has been directed to address HIV/AIDS, malaria, and TB. A recent study of the four major donors in global health noted that in 2005, funding per death varied widely by disease area, from US$ 1029 for HIV/AIDS to US$ 3 for non-communicable disease (3).

The focus on separate vertical initiatives rather than investing in capacity building at the national level partially arises from an underlying issue: the global health community does not have good estimates for non-disease-specific deaths. For example, information is not available on mortality caused directly or indirectly by lack of access to health systems. The insufficiency of current health metrics, particularly in determining community (as well as national and regional) needs has been widely recognized. It is worth noting the implications of the lack of measurement tools for assessing not only the impact of financing on health systems, but also the impact of financing for preventive public health measures. This leads to considerable uncertainty not only for researchers, but also for donors making decisions on where to invest their funds. With the current measurement system driven by disease-specific causes of death, investing in health systems is perceived as a *"bottomless"* pit since there is not yet a universally accepted proxy for the impact of health systems investment on mortality. Once funds are put into the *"health systems"* basket, it becomes difficult to track and measure their impact. The imperative for donors to fund programs that show measurable results in a short-time frame clearly demonstrates that there is little incentive to fund health systems (13). Only when the incentives are aligned towards funding health systems will real change in resource allocations take place.

5. Challenge 5: Going around government. In addition to distribution of funding by disease area, the question of whom donors fund is extremely important. As noted above, there has been a move towards funding non-state actors especially by the newer institutions. For example, the Global Fund's use of country-coordinating mechanism (CCMs) gives a larger voice to civil society as it is supposed to include a wide range of actors in a participatory process. The Global Fund reliance on CCMs indicates that the focus of donors has changed from a state-centric approach to financing to a process aimed at increasing the role of non-state actors. PEPFAR, the U.S. government initiative, also reduces the role of the state in the prevention, care and treatment of HIV/AIDS as it predominantly funds faith-based organizations and NGOs. Similarly, the Gates Foundation predominantly works through civil society and private research institutions and essentially bypasses government. This can be viewed as part of the Foundation's strategy to complement government, by engaging in high-risk activities that cannot be pursued by governments. The Avahan service initiative, although partnered with government agencies, is not financed through the Indian government.

Despite its push for increased private sector involvement, the World Bank is the only donor that exclusively funds recipient governments. This is a result of its historical mandate. While legally tied to government, the Bank has focused on creating a policy environment conducive to the private sector (28) through conditionality to strengthen the private sector, direct interaction with the private sector, and a reduction in funding to state-owned enterprises.

The marginal involvement of developing country governments in many global health initiatives raises questions about sustainability. In terms of process, it can be argued that in most cases, bypassing the state is an unsustainable approach. In fact, the civil society report to the WHO Commission on Social Determinants on Health notes that the state is the key actor in development and that government action is the key to collaborative and collective action because governments are ultimately responsible for health of populations: *"Public sector has played a major role in almost all situations where health outcomes have improved significantly"* (29). Although it might be more difficult in the short-term, strengthening health systems through government might be the most efficient in the long-term. In contrast, in terms of short-term outcome, bypassing government and going straight to communities can potentially result in more immediate impact. The poor quality and lack of capacity of public institutions can create enormous obstacles to delivering services, especially in countries with poor governance. In pressing situations, when lives could be saved through ARV provision, is there justification to prioritize short-term outcomes over long-term process?

The debate about the role of government is being fought, inconsistently and somewhat incoherently, in the health services of low-and middle-income countries. In this debate, the U.S. government and Gates Foundation are united in largely bypassing government health programs (despite PEPFAR's selection of countries based on good governance, and the discussion by the Gates Foundation of transitioning of programs to government), and the World Bank and Global Fund engage and financially support government programs, yet may shape them based on international priorities.

6. Challenge 6: Channelling funds through northern organizations. In addition to aid quantity, and what types of institutions should be funded, a third issue of importance is where, geographically, donors should be funding. As David McCoy et al. discuss, global health is a multi-billion dollar industry, and there are clearly competing interests amongst different actors to make use of this funding (30). The heavy reliance on certain northern-based organizations raises the question of whether global health financing is organised to suit the interests of particular actors. For example, pharmaceutical companies appear to benefit considerably from global health programs that emphasize the delivery of medical commodities and treatment (as well as from the positive image created by their participation in public-private partnerships). NGOs, global health research institutions, and UN bureaucracies also have an interest in increasing or maintaining their levels of income and thus tend to prefer that funding from major donors flows through them (as managers of funding), rather than directly to developing countries. Further scrutiny is needed on aid flows in global health to assess whether they are being *"captured"* by vested interests and used to support inappropriate spending on the private commercial sector or on a large and costly global health bureaucracy and technocracy based in the north. It is important to look at not just the volume of money raised, but also how it is spent and who it benefits so as to help ensure that the needs of recipient countries are kept at the forefront (30).

For example, while the World Bank and Global Fund directly fund developing country recipients, the Gates Foundation and PEPFAR have tended to fund northern organizations (3). However, even by the Bank and Global Fund there are certain *"leakages"* in the North such as the reliance on consultants, as well as on auditing firms such as *PricewaterhouseCoopers* that can assume relatively large parts of the budget. In global health research, there is no clear consensus among institutions and scholars about where the most effective investments should be made, suggesting that a plurality of approaches may be warranted.

Investing in health research based in North America and Western Europe has logical justification. These regions have, arguably, the best capacity to deliver results on a short-time scale, dedicate personnel to new projects, and absorb large financial flows. An alternative geographical distribution of investments, which would favor the global south, may lead to slower success given the dual process of building capacity and conducting research.

Concerns have been raised that research investment should be in institutions in developing rather than developed countries (7). Financial flows can enhance and develop the research capacity as well as provide incentives for talented young scientists to remain in-country. Perhaps most significantly, scholars and leaders in the global south are best placed to inform how delivery systems for health interventions can improve.

7. Challenge 7: Linking health to national security/foreign policy interests. The past four years have witnessed the linking of global health and foreign policy (2). In 2006, the Ministers of Foreign Affairs from Brazil, France, Indonesia, Norway, Senegal, South Africa, and Thailand issued a joint statement in Oslo highlighting the need to apply a health lens to foreign policy: *"We* *believe that health is one of the most important, yet still broadly neglected, long-term foreign policy issues of our time... We believe that health as a foreign policy issue needs a stronger strategic focus on the international agenda. We have therefore agreed to make "impact on health" a point of departure and a defining lens that each of our countries will use to examine key elements of foreign policy and development strategies, and to engage in a dialogue on how to deal with policy options from this perspective"* (31).

There are two unintended consequences of this linking that require further research. First, as Lawrence Gostin has noted: *"Do political leaders acknowledge, and act on, the evidence just presented that global health is in their national interest? The answer may be that States are beginning to understand that responding to health threats outside their borders serves their interests, but their engagement is relatively limited. And the sad truth is that the coincidence of interests is narrower than activists, and even scholars, have suggested"* (32).

Gostin makes an important point. While translating health into national security and foreign policy language might attract attention from high levels of government, it is only for a *"few high-profile problems: AIDS, pandemic influenza and the Indian Ocean tsunami"*. In fact, Gostin notes that national security assessments offer *"relatively narrow justifications for State action on global health"*. Thus, while health advocates might use the language of foreign policy as instrumental in gaining attention, this attention does not move into less glamorous areas such as health systems, malnutrition, and water and sanitation. A review of six country policies in health and foreign policy, Norway, U.K., Switzerland, France, Brazil, and Thailand, illustrates that many, but not all, strategies tend to be catalyzed and supported by concern with surveillance and control of infectious disease (33). It remains to be seen whether this concern extends to other areas, since as Gostin notes: *"In many respects, States may be correct that true global engagement does not serve their interests"* (32).

Second, while global health advocates have often emphasized the links between health and national security to place health issues on the agenda (34), it may be precisely this link to national security that leads states to favor a bilateral funding approach. The move towards bilateral aid has been noted in areas both within health, such as by the U.S. and German governments, and outside health by new donors such as China and India. While multilateral aid has the advantage of shielding allocations from direct foreign policy priorities, bilateral aid is often quicker to disburse.

8. Suggestion 1: Strengthen mechanisms to hold donors to account. What are suggestions to address these seven challenges? In the second part of the paper, three ideas are put forward that require further research and analysis. These draw on the suggestions made at a meeting in May 2008 of former and serving health ministers (7). First, the global health community must work to strengthen the mechanisms to hold donors to account through ensuring implementation and enforcement of the Paris and Accra agreements. The Paris Declaration, as noted above, focused on ownership through the three mechanisms of harmonization (donors adopting the same goals and policies), alignment (donors aligning their goals/policies with those of developing country governments), and coherence (ensuring goals in different issue areas are not contradictory, e.g., trade policy or intellectual property policy does not contract health goals). While the Paris Declaration outlines the necessary adjustments donors need to make, its implementation has lagged far behind its acceptance. A key obstacle is that many of those working in public health in middle and low-income countries are not aware of the contents of the Paris Declaration, and what donors have agreed to.

The larger issue is that there is basically no institution or forum to monitor donors either at the national and global level. While the WHO might be looked at to fulfil this function, given its dependence on extra-budgetary funding, it cannot be seen to be independent. As Srinath Reddy has noted, while the WHO carries the best imprimatur among international health organizations, its limited budget, lack of mandate for primary research, sparse technical capacity, and its need to derive its mandate from countries, indicate that the WHO could not take on such a political task (7). While academia could assume this role, even universities have become heavily dependent on donor funds and thus would not be perceived as objective by recipient governments. Perhaps what is needed is a partnership between donors and recipients to monitor progress, what has been referred to as a *"Donor Maximization Review"* (7).

9. Suggestion 2: Develop national plans and support national leadership in health. Second, countries require adequate policy space to develop national plans and cultivate national leadership in health. One minister recounted her approach to donors: *"The Ministry of Health was rather being run by our donors, saying what needed to be done. And until I said, "can we have a health sector strategic plan that we come up with that says who provides, who says exactly what should be done." We understand the problems better than our partners and also we understand the priorities — where we need to put the resources. We needed first of all to have a meeting with them and tell them where our priorities were and where we want to put resources – available resources. Of course, at that point there was a lot of resistance because that business had gone on for a long time. And they would not put money were we wanted to put money. Until at one point I said, "you may want to do your business but don't do it in the health sector" and then they came back, "what do you want us to do." And I said, let us work out a strategic plan first. And when we* *provided leadership, we have seen the Ministry of Health and the health sector change dramatically because we are looking at the problems facing the country"* (7). Similar to this, the Minister of Health of Tanzania has noted: *"We have a program. Whoever wants to help must swim with us in the program"* (7). As T.J. John and Franklin White note: *"Public health in South Asia should not be left to the international community to define; it is primarily the responsibility of the countries themselves to define their priorities. The global agenda should be viewed as complementary at best, and South Asian countries must build their systems more assertively in accordance with their public health needs and with their own resources"* (35).

At the national level, the difficulty arises from the need to engage with Ministries, such as Finance and Trade, whose primary concern is not necessarily health. For example, if the Ministry of Health approaches the Ministry of Water and Irrigation and requests assistance addressing diarrheal diseases, the latter Ministry needs to have incentive to allocate some of its budget to diarrheal diseases. These incentives seem to be currently lacking in most cases. Perhaps the paradox of health policy is that the policies that have the most impact in terms of preventing illness often lie outside the traditional health sector. Thus, Ministries of Health predominantly focus on treatment.

10. Suggestion 3: Study and learn from south-south collaboration. Perhaps one of the least explored areas by academics is south-south collaboration, both bilaterally between the emerging powers and low-income countries and pluri-laterally through clubs and coalitions. South-south collaboration can provide alternative forums for countries to approach for financial and technical assistance. Anecdotal evidence from Sub-Saharan Africa has noted the success of China's bilateral aid program in improving infrastructure and providing what governments' request. Similarly, positive news has been reported from the partnership between Brazil and Mozambique on HIV/AIDS (7).

In April 2008, India hosted the Africa-India Summit to explore furthering its relations in aid and trade, and to enhance partnership to achieve the MDGs. In February 2009, the Indian Foreign Minister Pranab Mukherjee launched a project to connect eleven African countries with India in providing medical education. The project provides virtual classes for medical staff, helping around 10,000 African students annually to receive specialized nursing degrees. It also provides online medical consultations where patients in parts of rural African can seek medical advice from Indian doctors via satellite. If the project is successful, it will be scaled up to all 53 African countries. Thus, there is considerable potential in south-south collaboration in both service provision and research.

In addition, low and middle-income countries can work together through coalitions to push forward their collective agenda. In the WTO, developing country coalitions have built and used coalitions to improve their bargaining power. As Mayur Patel describes, this pooling of bargaining resources has improved the technical and lobbying capacity by which developing countries engage in the WTO (36). These coalitions are highly visible, formalized and co-ordinated and focus on working within the WTO and existing trading structures to proactively engage in the negotiation process with the purpose of improv-ing outcomes for developing countries. These coalitions are bolstered by civil society. In health, coalitions can serve two purposes. First, they can increase negotiating power directly. Reflecting on the possibility, Francisco Songane has noted: "*What happens is there is an exploitation of weakness in countries. If the donors see that in country A there is strong leadership, and direction on what they should do, they are not going to mess around. They go to another country where they can do things differently, and that country will accept. We need to get a grouping of countries with one voice, that say, 'if you want to deal with us let us be together, and what we have to achieve is the country benefit, not for donors A, B or C*" (7).

Second, coalitions can serve as a forum for developing country coalitions to consult one another and coordinate before major meetings of donors and of international institutions. The increasing reliance on meetings at regional forums such as UNASUL (South America) and ASEAN (Southeast Asian) be-fore WHO negotiations indicates that while coalitions may be less developed or formalized as within the WTO, they are still being used by certain regions and like-minded countries to advance their agenda (33).

This paper has outlined seven challenges in international development assistance for health, and three possible ways forward. Underlying the paper has been the argument that we must get beyond rhetoric to ensure that neces-sary changes in the global health system are made so that developing countries can assume ownership in policy making. Attention must be paid to who gets what, when, and how. While there are no simple answers to the questions raised in this paper, space should be created for discussion and exploration of these issues. Only with open dialogue of the possibilities as well as the conse-quences of the current international development architecture for health can steps be taken to make the system more efficient and make a stronger case to policy makers to prioritize international development assistance to health in the context of limited funds.

Acknowledgement: Reprinted with permission from Wiley. Originally published as: Seven challenges in international development assistance for health and ways forward / Devi Sridhar / Journal of Law and Medical Ethics / 38:459-469. Copyright (c) 2010

Wiley. The author would like to acknowledge the comments received at a workshop hosted by Georgetown Law School on Global Health Governance, particularly the insights from Lawrence Gostin, Rajaie Batniji and Ngaire Woods also provided comments.

References

1. Shiffman J. Has donor prioritization of HIV/AIDS displaced aid for other health issues? Health Policy Plann 2008; 23:95–100.
2. Fidler D. Health and foreign policy: A conceptual overview; Harnessing globalization for health; Vital Signs. In (respectively): The Nuffield Trust, 2005; Health Promotion International, 2006; World Today, 2009.
3. Sridhar D, Batniji R. Misfinancing global health: A case for transparency in disbursements and decision making. Lancet 2008; 372:1185–1191.
4. World Health Organization: World Health Statistics. Geneva: WHO, 2008.
5. McColl K. Europe told to deliver more aid for health. Lancet 2008; 371:2072–2073.
6. Sridhar D. Global health: WHO can lead? Chatham House World Today 2009; 65:25–26.
7. Global Economic Governance Programme. Preliminary report of a High-Level Working Group. May 2008. (Available from: http://www.globaleconomicgovernance.org/wp-content/ uploads/Working%20Group%20Report%20May%202008. pdf ; Accessed: 20 Jun 2010).
8. The Paris Declaration on Aid Effectiveness and the Accra Agenda for Action. (Available from: http://www.oecd.org/dataoecd/11/41/34428351.pdf; Accessed: 24 Jun 2010).
9. Pang T et al. Are existing governance structures equipped to deal with today's global health challenges? – Towards systematic coherence. Global Health Governance 2009; (Special Issue)
10. Murray CJL, Frenk J, Evans T. The global campaign for the Health MDGs: Challenges, opportunities, and the imperative of shared learning. Lancet 2007; 370:1018–1020.
11. De Renzio P et al. Contested sovereignty in Mozambique: The dilemmas of aid dependence. Global Economic Governance Programme Working Paper, 2007; 2007/25.
12. Sridhar D et al. Background Report for UNAIDS Leadership Transition Working Group, 2008. (Available from: http://www.cgdev.org/doc/UNAIDS_Leadership_11_03_08.pdf; Accessed: 20 Jun 2010).
13. Sridhar D. The battle against hunger. Oxford: Oxford University Press, 2008.
14. Merson M. The history and challenge of HIV prevention. Lancet 2008; 372:475–488.
15. Lee K. World Health Organization. London: Routledge, 2009.
16. Institute of Medicine. The U.S. Commitment to Global Health: Recommendations for the New Administration. 2008.
17. People's Health Movement. Global Health Watch, 2005. (Available from: http://www.ghwatch.org/taxonomy/term/1; Accessed: 20 Jun 2010).
18. The World Bank. Healthy development: World Bank's strategy for health, nutrition and population. Washington, DC: The World Bank, 2007.
19. Birn A. Gates's grandest challenge: Transcending technology as public health ideology. Lancet 2005; 366:514–519.
20. Editorial. A conversation with the leaders of the Gates Foundation's Health Program: Gordon Perkins and William Foege. Lancet 2000; 356:153–155.
21. Qadeer I. Health care systems in transition III. India, Part I. The Indian Experience. J Publ Hlth Med 2000; 22:25–32.

22. Sridhar D, Gomez E. Health financing in Brazil, Russia, and India: What role does the International Community Play? Health Policy Plann 2011; 26:12–24.

23. Gomez E. Why Brazil responded to AIDS & not tuberculosis: International organizations and domestic institutions. Harvard Rev Latin Am, 2007. (Available from: http://www.drclas.harvard.edu/revista/articles/view/939; Accessed: 9 Jun 2010).

24. Deolalikar A et al. Financing health improvements in India. Health Affairs 2008; 27:978–990.

25. Keohane R. Global governance and democratic accountability. In: Held D, Koenig-Archibugi M (eds): Taming globalization: Frontiers of governance. Oxford: Polity Press, 2003.

26. Grant R, Keohane R. Accountability and abuses of power in world politics. Am Polit Sci Rev 2005; 99:29–43.

27. Garrett L. The challenge of Global Health. Foreign Affairs 2007; 86:14–38.

28. McCoy D. The World Bank's new health strategy: Reason for alarm? Lancet 2007; 369:1499–1501.

29. Civil Society's Report to the Commission on Social Determinants of Health. (Available from: http://www.who.int/social_ determinants/resources/cs_rep_sum_18_7.pdf; Accessed: 24 Jun 2010).

30. McCoy D et al. Global health funding: How much, where it comes from and where it goes. Health Policy Plann 2009; 24:407–417.

31. Oslo Ministerial Declaration. Global health: A pressing foreign policy issue of our time. Lancet 2007; 369:1373–1378.

32. Gostin L. Meeting basic survival needs of the World's least healthy people: Towards a framework convention on Global Health. Georgetown Law Journal 2008; 96:331.

33. Sridhar D, Smolina K. Altruism or self-interest: Country and regional strategies in health and foreign policy. Working Paper, 2010.

34. Donaldson L, Banatvala N. Health is global: Proposals for a UK Government-Wide strategy. Lancet 2007; 369:857–861. (and Institute of Medicine. America's vital interest in Global Health, 2007).

35. John T, White F. Public health in South Asia. In: Beaglehole R (ed): Global public health: A new era. Oxford: Oxford University Press, 2003.

36. Patel M. New faces in the Green Room: Developing country coalitions and decision-making in the WTO. Global Economic Governance Programme, 2007; Working Paper 2007/33.

CHAPTER 22.

Misfinancing global health: A case for transparency in disbursements and decision making

An unprecedented amount of money is being pledged and used to fund health research and services throughout the world. Although estimates are difficult to obtain, the 2004 estimate for international health funding was about US$ 14 billion, and is rapidly increasing, largely because of the emergence and growth of the Bill & Melinda Gates Foundation (BMGF) and the US Government's AIDS initiative (1). In parallel with increased financial commitment, the consensus for technical strategies for global health is increasing (2), an emerging though controversial, epidemiological evidence-base might provide information about the disbursement of the health funds (3). Clarification of technical and social strategies for disease prevention and treatment, though perhaps flawed, can facilitate cooperation and political commitment.

The absence of knowledge about the present investments by the major donors to global health might hinder cooperation among developing countries and international donors. The focus of previous efforts has been on tracking funding according to disease (e.g., HIV/AIDS), strategic approach (e.g., eradication vs. control), country (e.g., Organisation for Economic Cooperation and Development (OECD) and Development Assistance Committee), and within country (e.g., national health accounts) (4–11). The OECD creditor reporting system provides information about the individual aid activities of 23 member countries and several UN and multilateral agencies (4,8). However, this database does not contain information about the activities of the BMGF or detailed information about grants disbursed (e.g., primary recipient of funds) (12). As noted in the reports by the Center for Global Development and Research and Development (RAND), no information source exists to provide an overall idea of health resource flows, leading to an absence of credible estimates of donor commitments and actual funds (13,14). No systematic effort has been made to track all disbursements from the major global health donors because of the difficulties (14). In this paper we use the few available sources to analyse health disbursements with the aim of prompting further disclosure of resource flows from major global institutions. We assess the discrepancy between what needs to be done, according to public-health evidence, and the financial commitments by considering all disbursements made in 2005 by the major donors relative to the burden of disease. We create a baseline from which we can assess deviations in priority that might be due to other influences on the major donors by relating disbursements to mortality and burden of disease.

1. Global health donors. Although some consensus has been reached about what needs to be done for health, questions that remain are who is going to do what and how. Of the many different possible candidates (e.g., governments, non-governmental organisations, and WHO), four institutions have come to the fore as donors — i.e., the World Bank, US Government, BMGF, and Global Fund for HIV/AIDS, Tuberculosis and Malaria; see **Table 22-1**). These donors play the largest part in terms of financial contributions but they are estimated to contribute only about a third of all donor funding for global health (4).

All donors are estimated to account for about 0.3% of total expenditures on global health, 1.3% in non-OECD countries, and 6.5% in sub-Saharan Africa (14). Data for national health financing in developing countries is inadequate; individuals in the poorest countries often pay about 50% of health-care costs, and sometimes up to 80%, with private funds (14,15). The four donors account for about 0.1% of all health expenditures worldwide. Why is their effect so important? Many health ministries have become donor dependent, with ministers from Tanzania, Kenya, and Uganda reporting that 40–60% of their budgets come from donors (16). Because of this dependence, the priorities and services established by national governments, even those working with private funds, could be affected by the donor's priorities.

The specific mandate, capacity, and decision-making mechanisms of each donor can affect the funding priorities; thus of importance is to understand the structures of each institution.

Bank is governed by an executive board in which all member states are formally but not equally represented – i.e., large donor countries have more voting power (17). Similarly, an independent board is responsible for the overall governance of the Global Fund, including the approval of disbursements. The Global Fund is unique because it has a board that includes substantial developing-country and private-sector representation (18). The US Government undertakes initiatives that are supervised by the state department, which is ultimately responsible to the President of the USA and US Congress. The BMGF, a private initiative, has four co-chairs who oversee operations. Although the co-chairs do not authorise every grant (delegation of authority depends on the size of the grant), they do approve grant-making strategies in advance. Governance structures might explain the decision-making and priority-setting processes.

Table 22-1. *Stated priorities of worldwide health donors.*

World Bank
• Childhood mortality reduced (MDG 4, target 5, and MDG 7, target 10) • Childhood malnutrition improved (MDG 1, target 2) • Avoidable mortality and morbidity from chronic diseases and injuries reduced • Improved maternal, reproductive, and sexual health (MDG 5, target 6) • Reduced morbidity and mortality from HIV/AIDS, tuberculosis, malaria, and other priority pandemics (MDG 6, targets 7 and 8) • Improve financial protection (reduce the impoverishing effects of illness for the poor or near poor) • Improve funding sustainability in the public sector from both domestic and external sources • Improved governance and transparency in the health sector (MDG 8, target 12)
US Government
• PEPFAR: HIV/AIDS • President's Malaria Initiative • USAID: environment, health, family planning, health systems, HIV/AIDS, infectious disease, maternal and child health, nutrition
Gates Foundation
• Acute diarrhoeal disease • Acute lower respiratory infections • Child Health • HIV/AIDS • Malaria • Poor nutrition • Reproductive and maternal health • Tuberculosis • Vaccine-preventable diseases • Other infectious diseases
Global Fund
• HIV/AIDS • Tuberculosis • Malaria

Legend: MDG=millennium development goal; PEPFAR=President's Emergency Plan for AIDS Relief; USAID=United States Agency for International Development; For US Government commitment data see http:// www.usaid.gov/policy/budget/ cbj2005; For Global Fund disbursements see http://www.theglobalfund. org/en/files/disbursements indetail_raw.xls; For World Bank disbursements see http://web.worldbank.org/ WBSITE/EXTERNAL/PROJECTS/ 0,,menuPK:115635~pagePK: 64020917~piPK:64021009~ theSitePK:40941,00.html; For BMGF commitments see http://www. gatesfoundation. org/GlobalHealth/Grants/default.htm?showYear=2005.

With information gathered from the annual reports and budgets (**Table 22-2**), we created a database of disbursements classified by donor, type of disease, regional focus, type of investment, and type of receiving agency for 2005. The main health-financing goal of the four donors is the improvement of public health worldwide. Thus, we include funding for vaccines, clinical treatments, improvements in water and sanitation, improved quality and quantity of roads, emergency relief, and public health advocacy in this paper. Although this method provides a valuable idea of global health financing, we recognise that assessment of one year, which offers standardisation, does impose a constraint. The database is available on request from the corresponding author.

We considered a total of 1006 grants or loans made by the World Bank (n=65), US Government (n=115), Global Fund (n=543), and BMGF (n=283). We independently classified these grants or loans according to type of disease based on key words used in their descriptions, and then conferred with each other to reach a consensus. For multi-priority grants, we divided funding equally across the categories. To differentiate research from services, we grouped all funds specified for exploratory purposes as research (including large-scale trials), and all those for the provision of health services as service. All donors had classified funding according to type of disease, with inconsistency between the donors. Thus, we established categories to show the primary targets of donor funding and placed each grant or loan in a category based on project descriptions and existing categories.

For the US Government, we assessed commitments because of the absence of accessible data for disbursements. For the other three institutions, we assessed the disbursements. Comparison of the 2005 disbursements from the World Bank, BMGF, and Global Fund with commitments from the US Government in this analysis is problematic because of the time delay between commitments and disbursements (10). The commitments reported are for

Table 22-2. *Sources for commitment and disbursement data for four financiers.*

FINANCIER	SOURCE OF DATA
World Bank	*Commitment data:* Not Available *Disbursement data:* IBRD, IDA loan database, http://web.worldbank.org/WBSITE/EXTERNAL/PROJECTS/0,menuPK:115635~pagePK:64020917~piPK:64021009~theSitePK:40941,00.html
Global Fund	*Commitment data:* (http://www.theglobalfund.org/en/funds_raised/commitments/). *Disbursement data:* http://www.theglobalfund.org/en/files/disbursementsindetail_raw.xls
U.S. Government	*Commitment data:* Congressional Budget Allocation, PEPFAR, Global Health Council, (http://www.usaid.gov/policy/budget/cbj2005/, http://www.pepfar.gov/progress/76936.htm, http://www.globalhealth.org/public_policy/funding/ *Disbursement data:* not available
Bill & Melinda Gates Foundation	*Commitment data:* http://www.gatesfoundation.org/GlobalHealth/Grants/default.htm?showYear=2005 *Disbursement data:* made available by Gates Foundation

funding during one year, which is the same as for the disbursements. In a study of 2005 US disbursements for HIV, tuberculosis, and malaria – based on the creditor reporting system database, legislation records, and interviews with US staff – the total foreign payouts (excluding the Global Fund contributions of $348.0 million) were reported to be $ 1.942 billion (19). This amount is similar to the $ 2.0 billion estimated for commitments to HIV, tuberculosis, and malaria, and provides some validation for the comparison of the US data with that of other donors.

For each disease group, we included morbidity and mortality estimates in low-income and middle-income countries according to the global burden of disease project (3). This project, led by WHO, compiles estimates of incidence, prevalence, severity, and mortality for more than 100 causes, making use of a wide range of sources (20). Of note, mortality data from the global burden of disease study are for 2001, whereas disbursements are for 2005. To estimate child mortality, we used all-cause mortality for age less than 5 years, including deaths due to vaccine-preventable causes, and combined data for vaccine funding and child health. The justification for this grouping is that funding agencies specify child health as a target, rather than the treatment of specific diseases. Further, age-specific data are not fully available for individual diseases. Maternal morbidity and mortality include the burden of disability-adjusted life years and death related to conditions associated with poor maternal health and cervical cancer. The justification for this grouping of conditions associated with poor maternal health and cervical cancer is that they are combined for disbursements from donors.

The categories presented here are not mutually exclusive – e.g., a child death due to measles would be counted as child health (all-cause) and might be associated with undernutrition. Further, interactions between categories exist because many health interventions are mutually reinforcing. Improvement of the child's nutritional status would reduce the risk of death from measles and so would a vaccination campaign. The mutually reinforcing nature of health interventions has been widely recognised, and has led many public-health experts to call for health-systems support and for packages of interventions, as in the disease control priorities project. We controlled for double counting of financial commitments by excluding disbursements made by one donor to another. Thus, US contributions to the Global Fund were excluded from the US Government data.

2. Global health disbursements and donor priorities in financing. Surprisingly, little attention has been given to analysis of global health disbursements. Advocates for particular disease types or interventions often cite the abysmal funding for their disease, without the context of the overall global health funding allocations. In 2005, the World Bank disbursed $ 3.8 billion through both the International Bank for Reconstruction and Development, and the International Development Association for health (**Tables 22-3 and 22-4**). The main areas of investment – health systems, non-communicable disease and injury prevention, water and sanitation – are integrated into general support loans to low-income and middle-income countries. The focus of the World Bank's funding is on services for disease prevention, rather than research or treatment of disease (**Table 22-4**). Loans for injury prevention are specifically to improve road quality and quantity in countries. In 2005, 93.4% of the World Bank's total funding was disbursed directly through finance or health ministries. The remaining 6.6% was given to state-owned enterprises (e.g., Manila Water Company).

The US Government gave $3.5 billion through the United States Agency for International Development (USAID) bureau for worldwide health, President's Emergency Plan for AIDS Relief (PEPFAR), and the President's Malaria Initiative in 2005. It favoured vertical programmes to address HIV/ AIDS and malaria (**Table 22-3**). 8% of all funding was for abstinence-only programmes (21). Although complete information about the recipients of funding in developing countries is not available, the funds are shared with several partner organisations, which are a combination of civil-society organisations (e.g., faith-based non-government organisations), the private sector, and government ministries (21). Although these organisations are publicly listed, a breakdown of how much funding reaches each organisation is not publicly available.

In 2005, the BMGF disbursed about US$ 826.5 million through 283 grants (**Tables 22-3, 22-4**), mainly for vaccines and research done by organisations based in North America and western Europe. The foundation's focus was on basic and clinical science research in infectious diseases. No grants were disbursed for non-communicable diseases and injuries, and one grant was for health-systems research. 76% of the BMGF's disbursements were for prevention programmes and research.

In 2005, the Global Fund disbursed US$ 1.05 billion in 543 payments (**Table 22-3, 22-4**). The investments in HIV/AIDS and malaria accounted for 56% and 29% of disbursements, whereas the investment in tuberculosis was 14%. The Global Fund does not directly fund research initiatives and 100% of disbursements were for services, though many grants included provisions for monitoring and assessing programmes.

Table 22-3. *Disbursements (in millions US$), deaths (in millions) and disability-adjusted life-years (DALYs) (in millions) according to type of disease.*

Disease Group	World Bank (%)	U.S. Government (%)	Bill & Melinda Gates Foundation (%)	Global Fund (%)	Deaths* in Low and Middle Income	DALYs in Low and Middle Income	Total Funding per death, dollars
Child Health (excluding vaccines)	140.4 (3.6)	466.0 (13.4)	14.4 (1.7)	0	10.25 (21.2)	132.2	60.5
Child Health (including vaccines)	140.4 (3.6)	570.8 (16.4)	240.9 (29.1)	0	10.25 (21.2)	132.2	92.7
General ID	159.9 (4.1)	230 (6.59)	76.9 (9.3)	0	NA	NA	NA
Global Health Strategy, Partnerships and General Budget	0	96.1 (2.8)	62.5 (7.5)	0	NA	NA	NA
Health Systems	1287 (33.0)	0	0	8.2 (0.8)	NA	NA	NA
HIV/AIDS	202.8 (5.2)	1719 (49.3)	119.3 (14.4)	593.4 (56.3)	2.56 (5.3)	70.8	1029.1
Injury	705.1 (18.1)	0	0	0	4.71 (9.75)	155.9	149.7
Malaria	78.0 (2.0)	156.6 (4.5)	239.7 (28.9)	308.2 (29.2)	1.21 (2.5)	39.9	646.7
Maternal Health (including family planning)	187.2 (4.8)	406.1** (11.6)	29.6 (3.6)	0	0.73 (1.5)	26.4	853.28 / 295.9 excluding FP
NCD	83.5 (2.1)	0	0	0	26.03*** (53.8)	678.8	3.2
Nutrition	74.1 (1.9)	29.7 (0.9)	15.7 (1.9)	0	5.89 (12.2)	29.6	20.3
Polio	51.7 (1.4)	127.3 (3.6)	35.1 (4.2)	0	0****	0	>1 million
TB	3.9 (.1)	124.0 (3.5)	41.9 (5.0)	146.1 (13.8)	1.60 (3.3)	35.9	197.8
Vaccines (excluding specific disease areas above)	0	104.8 (3.0)	191.4 (23.1)	0	1.48 (3.1)	43.2	200.1
Water and Sanitation	854.1 (21.9)	0	0	0	1.78 (3.7)	58.7	479.8
Total	3823.9	3490.1	826.7	1055.9			

Data are number (%), unless otherwise indicated. n/a=not applicable; *Data are for low-income and middle-income countries, and are taken from reference 3; **Entire amount for family planning; ***Data are for all deaths due to child and maternal undernutrition as a risk factor, and are taken from reference 3; ****No reported deaths due to polio in low-income and middle-income countries, and one death in high-income countries in 2001, according to reference 3.

Table 22-4. *Key dimensions of the major worldwide health donors in 2005.*

KEY DIMEN-SIONS	WORLD BANK	U.S. GOVERN-MENT	BILL & MELINDA GATES FOUNDATION	GLOBAL FUND
Funding Source	IDA: Members capital subscriptions; IBRD: Private capital markets, members capital	U.S. Taxpayers	Bill and Melinda Gates (private assets), Warren Buffet	Donations from governments and private actors
Accountable to	Executive Board	Congress	Co-Chairs (Bill, Melinda and William Gates Sr.)	Board
Leadership Structure	President, Managing Director, Vice-Presidency of Human Development	Executive Branch (White House, State Dept., USAID)	Co-Chairs, CEO, a CFO, a CCO, a CAO, a Managing Director of Public Policy, a General Counsel and Secretary, Presidents for each Initiative (Global Health)	Executive Director, small Secretariat in Geneva
Funding Type	Loans (IBRD, IDA)	Grants	Grants	Grants
%of Funding to Service v. Research	Research: .26 Service: 99.5 Both: .21	Research: ~5, Service: ~95	Research: 60.6 Service: 33.5 Both: 3.5 NA: 2.3	Research: 0 Service: 100
% of Funding to Prevention v. Treatment	Prevention: 77 Treatment: .1 Both: 22.9	Not specified, but for PEPFAR ~30 for prevention and ~70 for treatment	Prevention: 75.5 Treatment: 5.9 Both: 16.2 NA: 21.3	Funding integrated; not specified
Region of Recipient Agency	SSA, SA, SEA, and L. America, Caribbean, Central Asia, Middle East, N. Africa	Sub-Saharan Africa	North America and Western Europe	Sub-Saharan Africa
Primary Recipients of Funds	Government	Civil-Society Organisations, Government	Private Research, Universities, Civil society, Public-Private Partnerships	Government/ Country Coordinating Mechanism (CCM)
Financier has major field staff presence	Yes	Yes	No	No, in-country CCMs
2005 Disbursement	US$ 3.8 billion	US$ 3.5 billion (Commitment)	US$ 827 million	US$ 1.05 billion

n/a=not applicable; BMGF=Bill & Melinda Gates Foundation; IDA=International Development Association; IBRD=International Bank for Reconstruction and Development; USAID=United States Agency for International Development; CEO=chief executive officer; CFO=chief financial officer; CAO=chief administrative officer; CCO=chief communications officer; COO=chief operating officer; CCM=country coordinating mechanism; *Pending transfer of Warren Buffet's pledge to BMGF.

Comparisons of aggregate spending with mortality (**Figure 22-1**) and disability (**Figure 22-2**) data show the discrepancy between burden of disease in low-income and middle-income countries, and the focus of disease-specific funding. When we assessed total disbursements from all four donors (**Figure 22-2**), three deviations in funding trends were noted: HIV/AIDS received more funding per death and disability-adjusted life years, whereas child health, and non-communicable disease and injury received less, than did other diseases.

3. Assessment of global health financing. Our approach has several limitations. Although data for disbursements are available from the major health donors, they are of poor quality and are not standardised. Of equal importance, mortality data are incomplete for many of the funded specialties, leading to potentially imprecise assessments of disease burden. We do not suggest that mortality and disbursements should be perfectly correlated because the cost per year of life saved is not equal for all causes of mortality, with differences in cost-effectiveness of essential interventions (22). Additionally, other dimensions to resource allocation are equally, if not more, important, than disease burden, and thus decisions should not solely focus on this measure. Justifiable, politically-guided deviations from even the best technical evidence in global health finance might exist. Our assessment of institutional mandates, process of priority setting, and governance of the global health donors suggests that each has selected priorities based on perceived comparative advantage. In the World Bank's new health, nutrition, and population strategy, the comparative advantage is in infrastructure (which explains the renewed focus on health systems) (23); for the Global Fund, the comparative advantage is rapid delivery of funds (however, PEPFAR has done better according to this measure) (24,25); and for BMGF, the comparative advantage is technology and innovation (26). Comparative disadvantages might affect funding too. Multilateral institutions, because of their inclusion of low-income and middle-income countries in their governance structures and their interaction with government, might be better placed than bilateral donors to lead efforts to support a country in developing a health system. Delivery and development of drugs and health technology, which have been the focus of the bilateral (e.g., US Government) and private (e.g., BMGF) institutions, are less likely and less politically complex than is long-term investment in infrastructure. In our analysis, a perfect match of disbursements to mortality was considered the baseline, rather than the ideal, from which deviations should be explained. We did not do a political economic analysis, which would be an important step to understanding the decision-making processes of the major global health donors, and would most likely reinforce our recommendation of continued attention to the development of country ownership, particularly planning and priority setting.

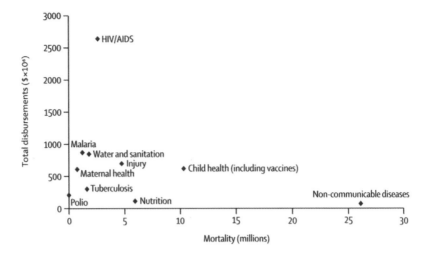

Figure 22-1. *2001 worldwide mortality versus 2005 disbursements of World Bank, US Government, Bill & Melinda Gates Foundation, Global Fund to fight HIV/AIDS, Tuberculosis and Malaria. (Health-systems funding cannot be represented as a graph because no reliable measure of mortality and disability due to the absence of a good health system exists. The omission of health-systems funding excludes about a third of all World Bank disbursements from this figure).*

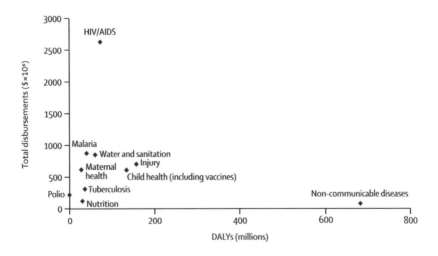

Figure 22-2. *2001 disability-adjusted life years (DALYs) versus 2005 disbursements of World Bank, US Government, Bill & Melinda Gates Foundation, Global Fund to fight HIV/AIDS, Tuberculosis and Malaria. (Health-systems funding cannot be represented as a graph because no reliable measure of mortality and disability due to the absence of a good health system exists. The omission of health-systems funding excludes about a third of all World Bank disbursements from this figure).*

4. Inadequate data for disbursements and disease burden. The task of tracking, then standardising, global health disbursements from the major donors is difficult. A two-year project to track resources in global health, done by the Center for Global Development, showed substantial information gaps, including absence of credible data for commitments and funds available to global health, and a gap between the rhetoric of transparency and account-ability, and the data systems to provide this information (14). The report, like a previous report by the RAND corporation (13), makes recommendations to improve standardisation and access to data for global health funding. Three inter-related problems exist.

First, data for the global burden of disease are imperfect and incom-plete. In our analysis, we used disability-adjusted life years and mortality to consider the match between technical evidence and allocations. As noted for the burden of disease estimates, roughly two-thirds of deaths are not recorded (27). Thus estimates rely not only on death registration systems, but also on epidemiological estimates, cause of death models, and expert opinion, thus leading to margins of error in calculations of mortality.

The second problem is that the global health community does not have good estimates for non-disease-specific deaths. For example, information is not available for mortality caused directly or indirectly by absence of access to health systems, and thus we are unable to consider health-system allocations on the same basis in which we consider those for HIV/AIDS. The insufficiency of current health measures, particularly in determination of community (and national and regional) needs has been widely recognised. The launch of the BMGF-funded Institute for Health Metrics and Evaluation at the University of Washington holds promise for further progress on the assessment of health investments (28). Of note, the absence of methods for assessment not only affects the financing of health-systems but also the financing of preventive public-health measures (29). This absence of a universally accepted measure-ment method leads to considerable uncertainty for researchers and donors making decisions about investment of their funds. With the present measure-ment system driven by disease-specific causes of death, investment in health systems is seen as a bottomless pit because we do not have a universally ac-cepted proxy for the effect of health-systems investment on mortality. Once funds are labelled as health systems, tracking and measurement of their effects become difficult.

Third, public access to data for the disbursements made by the major global health donors varies — e.g., the Global Fund and the World Bank have made all their data publicly available, whereas the US Government and the

BMGF have not. The Center for Public Integrity has documented the difficulty in accessing information about US Government disbursements for PEPFAR. It gained access to two grant databases by suing the US State Department, and reported many inconsistencies in reporting of disbursements. For example, the *"Center found more than 100 instances in which the total amount awarded to sub-partners was listed as being greater than the total amount received by their prime partners"* (30). Across the donors, the absence of standardisation in the organisation of funding data makes any analysis of global health funding difficult.

On the basis of this research, we suggest that all health donors provide data in a standardised format, which should include the date and amount (in US$) of the financial commitments and disbursements, the organisation to receive the funding, the purpose and function of the funding, and a notice of any irregularities, including withdrawal or reduction in the funding. These data could be similar to those provided by the OECD creditor reporting system but would need to build on this system to include the BMGF, provide further information about grants (such as what exactly the funds were given for within health and to whom), and to ensure that the information provided is consistent across the donors (12). The data could be managed through the OECD system or perhaps overseen by the new Institute for Health Metrics and Evaluation. Such standardisation and transparency could help facilitate the development of country input into health financing by reduction of the uncertainties and confusion about financing that have often stifled this input.

5. Development of country ownership in health. All four donors do not explicitly incorporate the demands of the governments or citizens of the developing country, or articulate the concept of ownership in setting the priorities but instead choose their priorities on the basis of what each organisation defines as important. Even those who point to the inclusive board of the Global Fund or its country-coordinating mechanism must acknowledge that the priorities of the Global Fund, namely HIV/AIDS, tuberculosis, and malaria, were included in the organisation's mandate.

In non-health sector aid, after many years of debate, the importance of ownership has been recognised, as shown by the endorsement of the 2005 Paris Declaration. Ownership was defined in the declaration as developing countries exercising *"effective leadership over their development policies, and strategies"* and coordinating development actions (31). Small steps are being taken in this direction in global health but they should be examined critically. For example, the International Health Partnership launched in 2007 by eight donor countries and 11 donor agencies aims to provide better coordination among donors; focus on improvement of health systems as a whole; and develop and support countries' own health plans (32). Yet, the concerns are that coordination will reduce the participation of developing countries in policy making by shifting the balance of power towards the *"consortium of donors acting in unison"* and thus could result in an inherent contradiction in the partnership (33). The International Health Partnership might be seen to create new strings without providing additional sources of funds to developing countries. Although the rhetoric is in place and the principles are outlined in the Paris Declaration, action lags far behind. Rather than countries taking ownership so that investment can be made in long-term priority setting and planning, donors focus on quick results and measurable returns through vertical programming. The focus on these quick results discourages investment in health systems and indicates the need for a country-led process of priority setting.

A high-level working group for setting a developing country agenda for global health reported widespread views that the inclination of donors to repeatedly create new initiatives, like the parallel priorities and delivery of care by donors, weakens national strategies (16). This difficulty was exacerbated by the absence of transparency among donors, and restricted awareness by health ministries about what donors were directing funds to. As one minister said about donors, *"they like to monitor activities, but they do not like to be monitored and evaluated"* (16).

The global health community should now move towards incorporating the concept of ownership into health assistance and realising the principles of the Paris Declaration. Without systematic attention to the articulated needs of developing countries through consultation and real partnership, donors for global health will not achieve informed and inclusive decision-making.

6. Toward more equitable global health financing. The billion-dollar health institutions vary in their distribution of funding by geographic focus, investment in service or research, and support of government or civil society and private groups. Global health governance can be viewed as a patchwork of donors, UN agencies, governments, civil-society organisations, and the private sector (34). In this paper, we have analysed the investments of the major global health donors — i.e., the World Bank, US Government, BMGF, and Global Fund. The pluralism of global health institutions and the informal alliances on which power in global health rests make a unified and fully coordinated health system highly unlikely (34,35). Our analysis shows first, a clear part to be played by donors in improvement of the information gap through reporting of their funding in a complete, standardised manner, fully accessible to the public, and adequately communicated to the governments of developing countries; and second, the need to move towards decision making based on the articulated needs of the developing countries in a manner consistent with the Paris Declaration.

Acknowledgement: Originally published as: Devi Sridhar and Rajaie Batniji: Misfinancing global health: A case for transparency in disbursements and decision making. Reprinted with permission from Elsevier (Lancet 2008; 372:1185-1191). We thank David Fidler, Harold Jaffe, Jennifer Kates, Kelley Lee, David McCoy, Jeff Mecaskey, Michael Merson, Jeremy Shiffman, Ngaire Woods, and Shunmay Yeung for their assistance.

References

1. Kates J, Morrison JS, Lief E. Global health funding: a glass half full? Lancet 2006; 368:187–188.
2. Jamison D. Disease control priorities project. Disease control priorities in developing countries, 2nd edition. New York: Oxford University Press, 2006.
3. Lopez AD. Disease Control Priorities Project. Global burden of disease and risk factors. New York: Oxford University Press, 2006.
4. Shiffman J. Donor funding priorities for communicable disease control in the developing world. Health Policy Plan 2006; 21:411–420.
5. OECD. OECD Development Assistance Committee. (Available from: http://www.oecd.org/dac; Accessed: 4 Jul 2008).
6. WHO. National health accounts. Geneva: World Health Organisation, 2007. (Available from: http://www.who.int/nha/en; Accessed: 4 Jul 2008).
7. Kates J, Lief E. International assistance for HIV/AIDS in the developing World: taking stock of the G8, other donor governments and the European commission. Washington, DC: Kaiser Family Foundation, 2006.
8. MacKellar L. Priorities in global assistance for health, AIDS, and population. Popul Dev Rev 2005; 31:293–312.
9. Lane C, Glassman A. Bigger and better? Scaling up and innovation in health aid. Health Aff 2007; 26:935–948.
10. Michaud C. Development Assistance for Health (DAH): Recent trends and resource allocation. Geneva: World Health Organization, 2003.
11. Barrett S. Eradication versus control: the economics of global infectious disease policies. Bull World Health Organ 2004; 82:683–688.
12. OECD. Creditor reporting system. (Available from: http://stats.oecd.org/WBOS/ Index.aspx?DatasetCode=CRSNEW-12; Accessed: 28 May 2008).
13. Eiseman E, Fossum D. The challenges of creating a global health resource tracking system. Rand Corporation, 2005.
14. Levine R, Blumer K. Following the money: toward better tracking of global health resources. Washington, DC: Center for Global Development, 2007.
15. Gottret P, Schieber G. Health financing revisited: a practitioner's guide. Washington, DC: World Bank, 2006.
16. Global Economic Governance. Preliminary report of a high-level working group, May 11–13, 2008. (Available from: http://www.globaleconomic-governance.org/health; Accessed: 15 Jul 2008).

17. Woods N. The challenge of good governance for the IMF and the World Bank themselves. World Dev 2000; 28:823–841.
18. Global Fund. Composition of the board of the Global Fund to Fight AIDS, Tuberculosis and Malaria. 2007 fifteenth board meeting. Geneva: Global Fund, 2007.
19. Salaam-Blyther T. US International HIV/AIDS, tuberculosis, and malaria spending: FY2004–FY2008. Washington, DC: Congressional Research Service, 2007.
20. WHO. About the Global Burden of Disease Project. Geneva: World Health Organisation, 2008. (Available from: http://www.who.int/healthinfo/bodabout/en/index.html; Accessed: 29 May 2008).
21. PEPFAR. Emergency plan for AIDS relief, fiscal year 2005 operational plan. Washington, DC: President's Emergency Plan for AIDS Relief, 2005.
22. Laxminarayan R, Mills AJ, Breman JG, et al. Advancement of global health: key messages from the Disease Control Priorities Project. Lancet 2006; 367:1193–1208.
23. World Bank. Healthy Development: The World Bank strategy for health, nutrition and population results. Washington, DC: World Bank, 2007.
24. Institute of Medicine (US). Committee for the evaluation of the President's Emergency Plan for AIDS Relief (PEPFAR) implementation. PEPFAR implementation: progress and promise. Washington, DC: National Academies, 2007.
25. Shakow A. Global Fund–World Bank HIV/AIDS programs: comparative advantage study. Global Fund and World Bank, 2006.
26. Birn AA. Gates's grandest challenge: transcending technology as public health ideology. Lancet 2005; 366: 514–519.
27. Lopez AD. Disease Control Priorities Project. The burden of disease and mortality by condition: data, methods, and results for 2001. New York: Oxford University Press, 2006.
28. Murray CJL, Frenk J. Health metrics and evaluation: strengthening the science. Lancet 2008; 371: 1191–1199.
29. Sridhar D. The battle against hunger. Oxford: Oxford University Press, 2008.
30. Center for Public Integrity. Divine intervention: about this data. (Available from: http://www.publicintegrity.org/aids/report.aspx?aid=816; Accessed: 29 May 2008).
31. OECD. Paris Declaration on Aid Effectiveness. (Available from: http://www.oecd.org/dataoecd/11/41/34428351.pdf; Accessed: 15 Jul 2008).
32. DFID. The International Health Partnership Launched Today. (Available from: http://www.dfid.gov.uk/news/files/ihp/default.asp; Accessed: 15 Jul 2008).
33. Murray CJL, Frenk J, Evans T. The global campaign for the health MDGs: challenges, opportunities, and the imperative of shared learning. Lancet 2007; 370:1018–1020.
34. Chen L, Evans T, Cash R. Health as a global public good. In: Kaul I, Grunberg I, Stern MA (eds). Global public goods: international cooperation in the 21st century. New York: Oxford University Press, 1999.
35. Fidler DP. Architecture amidst anarchy: Global Health's quest for governance. Glob Health Governance 2007; 1: 1–17.

CHAPTER 23.

Improving aid for maternal, newborn, and child health

Catherine Pitt and colleagues reported in the *Lancet* journal (1) on trends in official development assistance (ODA) for maternal, newborn, and child health (MNCH), from 2003 to 2008 as part of the Countdown to 2015 initiative. Their excellent paper presents a window of opportunity to examine how aid for MNCH can be improved. I highlight three findings that require further consideration.

First, Pitt and colleagues find that ODA for MNCH activities increased in real terms by 105% for all developing countries and 120% for the 68 Countdown countries between 2003 and 2008 (1). However, they also note that, because funding for global health as a whole has increased in real terms by 105% during the same period, these gains do not reflect increased prioritisation of MNCH relative to other health areas. Although this observation is important, we should not attribute normative judgment to this finding. Particularly over the past few years, as manifest by the AIDS backlash, the health community has been arguing over whether one health area is more deserving than another. Various initiatives have been competing for a limited pot of funds, drawing on links about how their cause will contribute to progress towards the Millennium Development Goals (MDGs) (2). The more important question is whether there is more money overall targeting the largest causes of morbidity and mortality and the social determinants of better health.

For example, last June, Canadian President Stephen Harper announced the US$7.3 billion Muskoka Initiative, which includes $5 billion from G8 countries and $2.3 billion from non-G8 sources: the Netherlands, Norway, New Zealand, South Korea, Spain, Switzerland, the Bill & Melinda Gates Foundation, and the UN Foundation (3). But for the G8 countries, is this just old wine in a new bottle? Oxfam noted: *"With total G8 aid flatlining, any "new" money for maternal health will have to be taken from vital areas such as education and food... Unless aid increases, African children will be paying for their mother's health care by sacrificing their education"* (4). Thus, while tracking financing for specific health issues is important, the danger is that narrow calls for more money for particular diseases or groups can detract from a larger mission of improving health outcomes through increased health aid.

Second, Pitt and colleagues find that the 68 Countdown countries received between 70.3% and 77.9% of all ODA for MNCH activities, with a clear correlation between mortality and ODA. Although mortality is a crucial dimension of resource allocation by donors, it is equally important to look at governmental capacity to address this problem. For example, three countries included in the Countdown initiative are India, China, and Brazil, which received $372 million, $55 million, and $5.7 million in 2008 for ODA for MNCH, respectively.

The elephant in the room is whether such middle-income countries should continue to receive aid (5). India is the largest recipient of external health funding, and although this level of support can be justified in view of the huge burden of death and disability there, a closer look at the government's budget reveals that it spent over $40 billion on national defence last year. A similar story can be told for China, the tenth largest recipient of external health funding, which spends, officially, $80 billion on defence and holds $2.5 trillion in foreign reserves; and for Brazil, the 15th largest recipient, which spends $20 billion on defence. In allocating limited donor funding, the ability of countries to respond should be considered, in addition to the extent of morbidity and mortality. To put it impolitely, why should aid dollars subsidise countries that can afford to independently provide health care?

Third, Pitt and colleagues found that more than 90% of funding for MNCH continued to be disbursed through project-based modalities from 2003 to 2008 for MNCH with sector-wide approaches, health-sector basket funding, and direct budget support to ministries of health accounting for only 7.2% of ODA in 2008. Although it is widely recognised that ministries of health play a crucial part in health-systems stewardship, it seems that very little is being done to strengthen these institutions. A study by the African Centre for Global Health and Social Transformation about supporting ministerial health leadership identified insufficient economic capacity as an explicit challenge for governments, resulting in inadequate funds for infrastructure development and poorly trained personnel (6). Although project-based aid might lead to short-term measurable results, without investments made in strong ministries of health (which are found in almost all countries independent of external aid), what is the long-term exit strategy for donors?

Pitt and colleagues present an important paper on financial flows for MNCH and should be commended for their careful and painstaking analysis, which included manual coding of OECD-CRS data. Their report leaves us with two further research steps that are central to better understand and improve the aid relationship. First, although Pitt and colleagues capture ODA, this does not encompass total development assistance for health (7). For example, the Bill & Melinda Gates Foundation is not included in this analysis, nor are emerging donor states such as Brazil and China. It is unclear what percentage of total aid flows are captured through ODA, which means we simply do not know how much of the picture we are seeing. Second, we do not know the effect of this aid on improving health. Although money is of course central, our main interest is whether health outcomes for mothers, newborns, and children are improving. This has yet to be answered.

Acknowledgement: Originally published as: Devi Sridhar: Improving aid for maternal, newborn, and child health. Reprinted with permission from Elsevier (Lancet 2010; 376:1444–1446).

References

1. Pitt C, Greco G, Powell-Jackson T, Mills A. Countdown to 2015: assessment of official development assistance to maternal, newborn, and child health, 2003–08. Lancet 2010; 376:1485–1496.
2. Sridhar D, Gostin L. Caring about health. Chatham House World Today 2010; 66: 26–28.
3. The Partnership for Maternal, Newborn & Child Health. G8 Communique 2010. (Available from: http://www.who.int/pmnch/media/g8watch_2010/en/index1.html; Accessed: 7 Sep 2010).
4. Oxfam GB. Minimal G8 Maternal Health Initiative sends disturbing message to women and girls. (Available from: http://www.oxfam.org/en/pressroom/ reactions/ minimal-g8-maternal-health-initiative-sends-disturbing- message-women; Accessed: 7 Sep 2010).
5. Sridhar D. China, Brazil and India's billion dollar aid appetite. July 22, 2010. (Available from: globalhealthpolicy.net http://www.globalhealthpolicy.net/?p=44; Accessed: 7 Sep 2010).
6. Omaswa F, Boufford JI. Report on strong ministries for strong health systems. January, 2010. (Available from: http://strongministries.org; Accessed: 7 Sep 2010).
7. Schaeferhoff M, Schrade C, Yamey G. Financing maternal and child health—what are the limitations in estimating donor flows and resource needs? PLoS Med 2010; 7:e1000305.

CHAPTER 24

Health financing in Brazil, Russia and India: what role does the international community play?

1. Introduction. In recent years, Shiffman (1,2) and others (3-5) have argued that global health financing has become increasingly skewed towards HIV/AIDS and to a lesser extent malaria and tuberculosis (TB). This pattern is reproduced at the national level in many countries. Studies of Mozambique, Uganda and Zambia have shown that a large proportion of health resources is being devoted to address HIV/AIDS in comparison with other disease areas (6). While some have argued that the spending on HIV/AIDS has been to the detriment of primary health care and has in fact weakened health systems, for example by taking away skilled staff from other sectors through higher salaries offered by donors (6,7), others have noted that HIV/AIDS has brought attention to the importance of strengthening health systems and made new monies available for global health (8). The allocations at the country level have been explained by the donor-dependency of low-income countries, resulting in considerable influence of donor countries and multilateral institutions over country priority-setting in health (9). Do we see the same effect of international influence on budgetary allocation for health in middle-income countries?

Three countries that represent the core of the middle-income group are Brazil, Russia and India, members of the well-known BRIC group (with China). In each of these countries, health funding has become primarily endogenous and independent of external aid (**Table 24-1; Figure 24-1**). Each of their health care systems straddles provision for diseases across the epidemiological transition: having to provide services for both acute infectious diseases and chronic diseases associated with affluence. They have all embarked on a process of decentralization and reform of the health care sector; they all face the constraints of having to work with several states and hundreds of municipalities, scattered throughout a large geographical area; and they have large populations with high levels of income inequality. However, their political systems show some diversity. Brazil and India are two of the largest democracies, while Russia is one of the largest less democratic states.

Given that these nations are mostly aid-independent, that is, not significantly relying on donor aid and predominantly financing health through

domestic sources, we test the assumption that there will be no biased response to any particular kind of disease and that health budgetary allocations will reflect the epidemiological burden of disease. This assumption is
based on the higher likelihood that countries that are less dependent on aid
are less constrained by donor aid assistance and are, consequently, much
more autonomous in how they allocate funding (10-15). Because they receive
far less funding for particular health sectors, such as AIDS, relatively compared with low-income countries, they are expected not to be as influenced
by international pressures and biased in broader funding patterns. In the
process of exploring the influence that global players have in setting health
care priorities in these countries, we ask the following: "*How do country-level
budgetary allocations compare with epidemiological estimates of burden of disease?*"
By relating disbursements to burden of disease, we create a baseline from
which we can assess deviations in priority that may be due to influences other
than epidemiological evidence. Underpinning the analysis is the question
of whether Brazil, Russia and India have similar health financing patterns
domestically to those observed globally. Analysing budgetary allocations in
health is the first step to understanding the power relationships among various stakeholders at global, national and local levels, as well as the relative
influence of power, ideas, institutions and culture in promoting investment
and policy in certain health areas and not others (16).

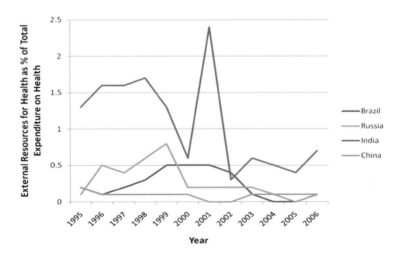

Figure 24-1. *External resources for health as a percentage of total expenditure on health (1995–2006).
(Source: WHO Statistical Information System (WHOSIS), ref. 83).*

Table 24-1. *External resources for health as a percentage of total expenditure on health, Brazil, Russia, India and China, 1995–2006 (Source: WHOSIS, ref. 83).*

	1995	1996	1997	1998	1999	2000	2001	2002	2003	2004	2005	2006
Brazil	0.2	0.1	0.2	0.3	0.5	0.5	0.5	0.4	0.1	0.0	0.0	0.1
Russia	0.1	0.5	0.4	0.6	0.8	0.2	0.2	0.2	0.2	0.1	0.0	0.1
India	1.3	1.6	1.6	1.7	1.3	0.6	2.4	0.3	0.6	0.5	0.4	0.7
China	0.2	0.1	0.1	0.1	0.1	0.1	0.0	0.0	0.1	0.1	0.1	0.1

We look in particular at the major causes of burden of disease in each country, as well as the contribution that HIV/AIDS, TB and malaria make to the total burden of disease estimates. We focus on these three diseases because of their centrality on the global stage (1,2,5), demonstrated by the establishment of multilateral bodies such as the Global Fund to Fight HIV/AIDS, TB and Malaria (Global Fund) and UNAIDS, major bilateral programmes such as the President's Emergency Plan for AIDS Relief (PEPFAR) and the President's Malaria Initiative, and Millennium Development Goal 6 which focuses exclusively on combating HIV/AIDS.

2. Methods. Our purpose for comparing Brazil, Russia and India is not to illustrate or test the effectiveness of a generalizable theory about the determinants of domestic spending for diseases (17), but rather to highlight each country's unique policy response (18,19). Our goal is then to propose several hypotheses accounting for differences in spending outcomes. Instead of generating a new theory from our findings, we saw this as an exercise for creating new ideas, hypothesis-building and providing suggestions for new areas of research; others have noted that this is a benefit of conducting comparative case study analysis (20,21).

With regard to empirical data, to assess whether health allocations are aligned with epidemiological estimates for burden of disease, we used central government budgetary allocations through the Ministry of Health or its equivalent, e.g. National HIV/AIDS or TB programme. Information on health funding – that is, the amount of money allocated from the federal budget for a particular disease – was sourced primarily from country-specific departments of finance and health, and when primary data were not available, from secondary sources. For Brazil and India, we used actual health budgets from the ministries of health and finance, respectively. As primary data were not available for Russia, we used World Bank summary data. Despite it being a key member of the BRIC group, China has been excluded from analysis and discussion in this paper. This is due to the absence of primary and secondary data for spending on each type of disease in China. We reviewed several prominent journal publications, such as The Lancet Special Series on China, as well as consulted senior academics and a consultant for the Ministry of Finance in China, but were not able to obtain the data on allocations.

Financial information is provided in standardized US$ dollar equivalents. To support the budgetary data, we also reviewed reports published by national governments, multilateral organizations and established academics to better understand the structure and flow of finances within each country's health system. In addition, for the Brazil and Indian case studies, we have drawn on interviews conducted with health officials and members of civil society by the authors of this paper. These interviews were conducted in July–August 2006 and August 2008 in Brasilia, and in August–September 2007 and July 2008 in New Delhi.

Burden of disease data were taken from the Global Burden of Disease and Risk Factors (for 2001) project published by the World Health Organization (WHO). Burden of disease data are presented as disability-adjusted life year (DALY) rates. While the calculation of DALYs has been criticized by Anand and Hanson (1997), the use of DALYs is in line with previous analyses similar to our paper by Shiffman (1), Sridhar and Batniji (4) and Ravishankar et al. (5). Age-standardized rates facilitate cross-country comparisons by adjusting for the differences in population structure between countries. It should be noted that while the most recent DALY data are from the Global Burden of Disease study of 2001, health funding data are from 2001 to 2006.

3. Resource allocation versus burden of disease. The primary task undertaken in this paper is the comparison of financial allocations between those diseases that cause the greatest burden of disease and the *"Big three"* within the three countries.

In **Brazil**, total government spending for health, as a percentage of total government spending, equalled 3.9% in 2001, dipping to 3.2% in 2005, then increasing to 3.7% in 2007 (22). In 2001, total expenditure for the control of communicable diseases equalled 0.001% of the total federal budget, remaining at this level in 2003. Funding for improving the quality and efficiency of SUS (*Sistema Unico de Saude*), the decentralized health systems programme, was 0.0015% of the total federal budget, increasing to 7.8% of the total health budget in 2003 and remaining at this level in 2005 (22). This surge reflects the federal government's increased commitment to helping municipalities fund crucial diseases, such as AIDS and more recently TB.

If measured using age-standardized DALY rates, several diseases emerge as the most burdensome in Brazil. The first is neuropsychiatric disorders, receiving a measure of 4337, per 100000 in a population, followed by cardiovascular disease at 2537, then respiratory conditions and fourth unintentional injury at 1542 (**Table 24-2; Figure 24-2**). HIV/AIDS received a score of 229, followed by TB 164, and malaria 22. The burden of disease by HIV/AIDS, TB and malaria is much less when compared with other disease areas when measured in terms of DALYs.

Table 24-2. *Burden of disease (in disability-adjusted life years, DALYs) (84) in Brazil, Russia and India (Source: World Health Organisation, ref. 85).*

BRAZIL		RUSSIA		INDIA	
Neuropsychiatric disease (1)	4337	Cardiovascular disease (1)	5551	Cardiovascular disease (1)	3284
Cardiovascular disease (2)	2537	Unintentional Injury (2)	4043	Neuropsychiatric disease (2)	3044
Unintentional injury (4)*	1542	Neuropsychiatric disease (3)	3701	Unintentional injury (4)	2913
HIV/AIDS	229	HIV/AIDS	361	HIV/AIDS	1011
Tuberculosis	164	Tuberculosis	444	Tuberculosis	869
Malaria	22	Malaria	1	Malaria	69

*Respiratory conditions, non-infectious, rank number 3 in terms of age-standardized DALY rates in Brazil.

Yet this does not seem to be reflected in the financing allocated to various disease areas. As **Table 24-3** and **Figure 24-3** demonstrate, the health conditions that are the most burdensome do not receive nearly as much funding from the federal government as HIV/AIDS. Even funding for TB was only US$ 10.8 million in 2002, climbing to US$ 26 million in 2006. Despite evidence of a co-infection problem with HIV as well as the emergence of multi-drug resistant TB (MDR-TB), these findings confirm the fact that TB has not been a priority for the government when compared with AIDS (23). Since 2006, allocations for TB have gradually increased, and new programmes have been jointly sponsored with the national HIV/AIDS programme (24-26). However, data on budgetary allocations for recent years are not available.

Table 24-3. *Brazil's budgetary allocation for health (US$ million) from 2001 to 2006 vs burden of disease (in disability-adjusted life years, DALYs (84); Source: Brazilian Ministry of Health, ref. 27).*

	2001	2002	2003	2004	2005	2006	DALY
Cardiovascular disease	23.0	22.3	61.5	N/A	N/A	N/A	2537
Neuropsychiatric disease	0.9	14.4	19.7	0.5	0.2	0.1	4337
Unintentional injury	7.0	7.1	7.7	8.9	9.6	N/A	1542
HIV/AIDS	353.7	433.5	372.2	475.5	508.6	705.9	229
TB	N/A	10.8	9.5	16.2	24.3	26.0	164
Malaria	42.2	21.4	40.7	37.5	36.8	35.4	22

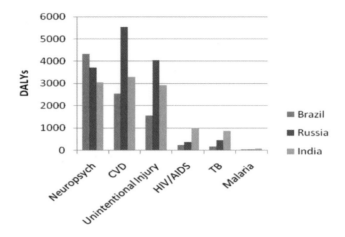

Figure 24-2. *Burden of disease (in disability-adjusted life years, DALYs) (84) in Brazil, Russia and India. (Source: World Health Organisation, ref. 85).*

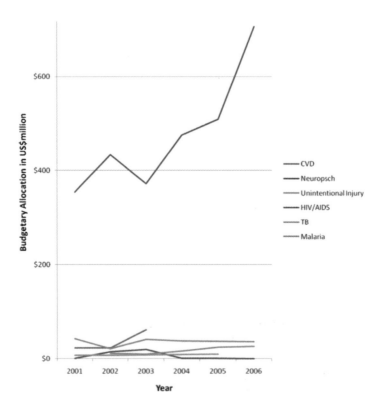

Figure 24-3. *Brazil's budgetary allocation for health (US$ million) from 2001 to 2006. (Source: Brazilian Ministry of Health, ref. 27).*

With regard to the Ministry of Health's dependence on donor aid assistance, again the outcomes for each sector vary. When it comes to HIV/ AIDS, the government has become less dependent on the World Bank and other creditors. In fact, congressional outlays for the AIDS programme have continued to increase and now far surpass the amount given by the World Bank: US$ 353.7 million from the government in 2001 versus a World Bank loan of US$ 28 million (which was that year's portion of a total loan package worth US$ 100 million signed in 1998); and US$ 741 million in 2008 versus a World Bank loan of only US$ 13.8 million that year (that year's disbursement of a total US$ 100 million loan signed in 2003) (27). Nevertheless, the Ministry of Health is still dependent on donor aid for other diseases, such as TB and malaria (23,28). In 2005, Brazil received a US$ 11 million dollar grant from the Global Fund for TB and US$ 2 million in 2008 for malaria.

In sum, despite Brazil's progressive universal health care system, it is clear that the burden of disease does not explain funding allocations. While HIV/AIDS is not even close to being as burdensome as neuropsychiatric disorders and chronic disease, it still receives much more domestic funding. Moreover, while Brazil is no longer dependent on donor aid for HIV/ AIDS – in fact, it is now starting to become a foreign aid donor, as evident through its recent contributions to the Global Fund (26,29) – it is still dependent on aid assistance for other diseases.

In **Russia**, total central government spending on health is estimated to be 5.3% of GDP, while as a percentage of total health spending (including both government and private), it equalled 60.4% in 2001, rising to 64.3% in 2005 (30). Total spending for public health nevertheless declined during the 1990s and has not increased since then (31). Most spending for public health occurs at the oblast (regional) level, which reflects the government's commitment to health policy decentralization, which started in 1993.

As **Table 24-2** and **Figure 24-2** demonstrate, when measured in terms of DALY rates, cardiovascular disease, neuropsychiatric disorders and unintentional injury are the most burdensome disease categories. Marquez (32) notes that the government has allocated an estimated US$ 2.9 billion, or 20.8% of total federal health spending for hypertension, ischaemic heart disease and cerebrovascular disease. When combined, spending for cardiovascular, unintentional injuries and neuropsychiatric disorders assume more than 50% of the country's total health spending (32).

This is much higher than spending for other types of disease, such as HIV/AIDS, TB and malaria. Although new HIV cases did not begin to increase sharply until after 1998, there was nevertheless a sizeable increase in newly reported cases from 1995 until that period, increasing from 1090 in 1995 to 3971 in 1998, jumping radically to 19.758 in 1999 (33). However, no domestic funding for prevention or treatment emerged prior to 1998, which indicates an initial weak government response to the epidemic. Nevertheless, in 1998 federal funding commenced with an allocation of US$ 0.09 million, followed by US$ 1.3 million in 2000, and US$ 3.7 million in 2001, and it stayed at this level through to 2004. There was also a disparity in funding by each level of government. Finally, it has been noted that the lack of transparency about the HIV/ AIDS budget has led to the diversion of HIV/AIDS funding for other purposes (34). While in recent years, essentially beginning in 2005, the government has publically announced its commitment to increase its funding for HIV prevention and treatment, it remains to be seen if it can follow through with its commitments (35). The Associated Press (36) recently noted that since 2006, Russia has increased by 33 times its spending on AIDS programmes, but we are unable to verify this claim empirically.

With regard to TB, funding is minimal and new. Prior to 1999, there was no federal funding for TB (34). Thereafter, approximately 90% of all funding for the production of drugs was provided at the "*oblast*" level. Federal spending for TB has gradually increased, but the bulk of all funding still comes from the state level. With regard to malaria, federal spending is essentially non-existent. This is due to the rapid decline in the number of cases since World War II. From 2001 to 2005, the total number of malaria cases dropped from 984 to 34 (37). Funding allocations and commitment seem to reflect the low number of cases.

Government receptivity to donor assistance is minimal but has started to gradually increase. In 1996, US$ 18.3 million in aid was provided by all sources of foreign aid, increasing to US$ 65.8 million in 1999, yet this declined to US$ 30.9 million in 2001 (38). In 1999, the World Bank began to work closely with the Ministry of Health for the implementation of a new TB programme, with HIV/AIDS being added later that year. In the same year, the World Bank offered a loan package of US$ 150 million, with US$ 100 million going towards TB and US$ 50 million to HIV/AIDS. After a long delay due to the Russian Ministry of Health's negotiations with the World Bank over the implementation of WHO DOTS (*Directly Observed Treatment, Short-course*) standards (34), agreements were finally reached and the loan was provided in 2003. Before the World Bank, other donors, such as WHO, the UK Department for International Development (DFID), the Canadian International Development Agency (CIDA) and the Open Society Institute / George Soros Foundation, provided assistance, though this has been limited in amount and overall effectiveness.

Since 2001, the government has been more receptive to donor aid. The receipt of several grants to combat HIV/AIDS and TB since 2003 from the

Global Fund provides a good example. Nevertheless, while this has helped to strengthen the TB and HIV/AIDS programme and kindled greater political commitment to combating these diseases, it is not clear that donor aid has shaped the historic evolution of Russia's AIDS and TB programme, or any other health programme for that matter. In fact, in 2006, Russia pledged that it would reimburse the Global Fund by 2010 for the US$ 270 million the country had received for HIV prevention and treatment programmes (39,40).

In sum, it seems that central government spending for disease reflects domestic need, rather than global priorities. This is evident through the secondary data which shows that more funding is allocated for the most burdensome diseases, such as cardiovascular diseases, neuropsychiatric disorders and unintentional injury, and not HIV/AIDS or TB. This, in turn, could reflect Russia's ongoing decision to implement policies that do not reflect international pressures to conform to global priorities.

In **India**, total government spending for health, as a percentage of total government spending, equalled 3.6% in 2004, with household expenditure forming 73.5%. Central government expenditure formed 23% of government health spending, with state government expenditure being 77% (41). While health is constitutionally a state responsibility, it has been noted that despite only controlling 23% of the funds, central government sets the priorities in health which are executed by state governments (42). In addition, the central government dominates financing of public health and family welfare activities as well as centrally sponsored communicable disease programmes for HIV/AIDS, TB and malaria (43). Thus central government priorities in public health provide an important indicator of state priorities in public health.

If measured using age-standardized DALY rates, several disease areas emerge as the most burdensome in India. The first is cardiovascular disease at 3284, followed by neuropsychiatric disease at 3044, then respiratory conditions and then unintentional injury at 2913 (**Table 24-2; Figure 24-2**). In contrast the DALY rates for HIV/AIDS, TB and malaria are 1011, 869 and 69, respectively.

How financing compares with the burden of disease is shown in **Table 24-4**. HIV/AIDS receives a significantly higher allocation than all the other health areas, with a huge increase since 2004 (**Figure 24-4**). HIV/AIDS has been addressed through the National AIDS Control Organisation (NACO) within the Ministry of Health and Family Welfare. External donors have played a significant role in funding NACO's National AIDS Control Projects (NACP) as well as providing technical assistance (**Table 24-5; Figure 24-5**). In the second phase of NACO (1999–2006), the government only contributed 9.5% to the total budget, although by the third phase (2006–11) the percentage had increased to 40.8%. The total budget for the third phase is US$ 1484.96 million, which divided by 5 years equals roughly US$ 297 million per year. In contrast, the National TB programme was allocated only US$ 39.02 million for 2006–07. From 2001 to 2006, malaria was addressed through the *National Anti-Malaria Programme*. The programme was then integrated into the National Vector-Borne Disease Control Programme (malaria, kala-azar, Japanese encephalitis, filaria, dengue) in 2006. This programme is predominantly funded externally through the World Bank's US$ 520.75 million *National Vector Borne Disease Control and Polio Eradication Support Project* (44).

Table 24-4. *India's budgetary allocation for health (US$ million) from 2001 to 2007 vs. burden of disease (DALYs, disability-adjusted life years, 2001) (Source: India Ministry of Finance, ref. 86).*

	2001–2002	2002–2003	2003–2004	2004–2005	2005–2006	2006–2007	DALY
Cardiovascular disease	15.2	30.7	30.8	34.1	42.7	65.6	3284
Neuropsychiatric disease	0.93	5.6	5.8	6.3	7.5	9.5	3044
Unintentional injury	N/A	N/A	N/A	N/A	6.7	8.9	2913
HIV/AIDS	37.5	41.3	42.7	48.4	99.3	134.9	1011
Tuberculosis	25.4	22.9	22.5	24.0	34.7	39.0	869
Malaria	36.1	40.0	37.2	40.1	58.1	73.1	69

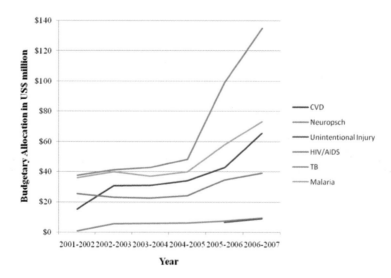

Figure 24-4. *India's budgetary allocation for health (US$ million) from 2001 to 2007. (Source: India Ministry of Finance, ref. 86).*

The findings for 2001–2007 seem to be in line with what earlier research-ers have noted: that although only roughly 1.6–2.0% of financing in the health sector in India comes from external funds, this small percentage is distorting national priorities. For example, Qadeer (45) notes that from 1990–91 until 1998–99 investments only increased for selected programmes for TB, leprosy and AIDS control at the expense of the National Malaria Control and Diar-rhoeal Diseases Control Programmes. Similarly, Deolalikar et al. (43) note that external assistance constitutes a sizeable share of national disease control programmes for TB, HIV/AIDS and malaria.

4. Discussion. This comparative case study design illuminates some key similarities and differences in government response to various disease areas.

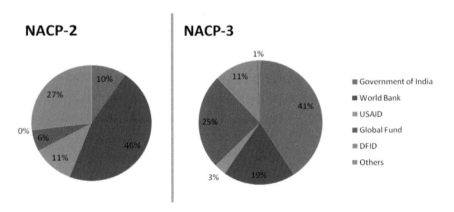

Figure 24-5. *Funding breakdown (percentage of total funding) of India's National AIDS Control Project-2 (NACP-2) (1999–2006) and National AIDS Control Project-3 (NACP-3) (2006–2011). (Source: National AIDS Control Organisation, ref. 87).*

Table 24-5. *Funding of India's National AIDS Control Project-2 (NACP-2) (1999–2006) and National AIDS Control Project-3 (NACP-3) (2006–2011) (Source: National AIDS control orga-nization, ref. 87).*

	NACP-2 (US$ million)	NACP-3 (US$ million)
Government of India	41.53 (9.5%)	606.14 (40.8%)
World Bank	203.18	281.36
USAID	48.85	47.67
Global Fund	26.00	367.60
DFID	N/A	171.19
Total	437.43	1484.96

It is important to note that there are several limitations to our work. The first is in terms of data availability. While two of the countries, Brazil and India, provide solid primary data on budgetary allocations for 2001–06, the other case, Russia, did not; this, in turn, reflects differences in government transparency. For Russia, secondary data provided by the World Bank allowed us to examine financing patterns; however, we are unable to verify how comparable this data is to that provided by the Brazilian and Indian governments. The second limitation relates to our focus on central government expenditure. This is in line with other analysts' work (46). Despite their lower share in financing compared with state/local expenditure, across the countries studied, central government expenditure provides a solid indication of priority-setting in health (43). The third limitation relates to comparing the burden of disease and disbursements, as the cost per DALY gained is not equal for all diseases, with differences in cost-effectiveness of essential interventions. Additionally, other dimensions to resource allocation are equally, if not more, important than disease burden, and thus decisions should not focus solely on this measure. Finally, as noted in the methods section, we have relied on burden of disease data for 2001, which is the most recent data available, while budgetary allocations are for 2001–06.

By tracking the resources that Brazil, Russia and India have devoted to various disease areas, we can see that in Brazil and India there has been a bias in the level of investment in various health areas and convergence with global patterns of financing. HIV/AIDS, for example, seemed to obtain the most assistance from the federal government. And this occurred despite the fact that AIDS and other related disease, such as TB, were not the most burdensome. In contrast, Russia shows divergence from global patterns of financing, although with increased spending for HIV/AIDS and TB, this might be shifting slowly towards convergence.

We would like to put forth several factors that could explain the current bias in Brazil and India, but not yet in Russia. We build on Reich's framework of examining the state *"from above, from within, and from below"*. Reich proposes a complex political ecology, where health policy emerges from the interaction of *"top-down"* pressures from international actors, *"bottom-up"* pressures from civil society and domestic government politics. We find his approach extremely useful in proposing what factors might be important in resource allocation other than disease burden. It is important to note that we are not testing the relative explanatory impact of each variable, as our goal is not to create and test a generalizable theory. Rather, we primarily draw on evidence from published sources as well as supporting data from primary interviews to describe what factors deserve further attention in understanding this puzzle (**Figure 24-6**).

The first group of factors relates to those from *"top-down"* pressures. The first factor we propose that might be important is the availability of external funding from multilateral banks, bilateral donors, philanthropists and public–private partnerships. Here, the World Bank and the Global Fund seem particularly important (**Table 24-6, 24-7**). Funding from the Bank for HIV/AIDS has acted, in certain country contexts, as a catalyst for increased domestic spending and policy commitment to HIV/AIDS, and more recently to TB. In Brazil, World Bank loans in 1994 instigated domestic institution-building, such as the creation/strengthening of national AIDS programmes/councils (47-49). Similarly, although the first case of HIV was detected in India in 1986, it was only with a World Bank loan of US$ 84 million in 1991 that India's first National AIDS Control Project (1992–1999) was launched with the objective of preventing new infections, raising awareness and increasing surveillance (50,51).

External funding seems to be a crucial factor in explaining the relatively earlier convergence in Brazil and India. In both countries it seems that although external funding constitutes a fraction of the total health budget, it is being allowed to distort national priorities. As the former Director of NACO in India, K. Sujatha Rao, and colleagues note: *"Instead of the health system being strengthened by external funding, priorities get skewed and distortions created, as non-funded programmes, which could be equally if not more important, get lower funding priority"* (52). This shift in priorities has been expressed not only by the WHO (53), but also by several Indian non-governmental organizations

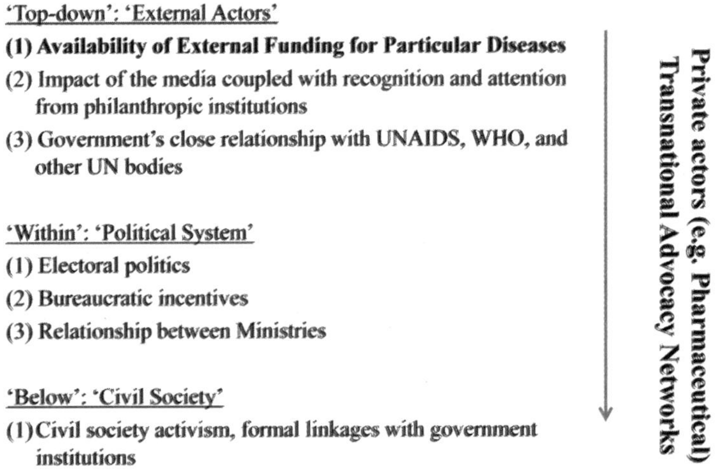

'Top-down': 'External Actors'

(1) Availability of External Funding for Particular Diseases

(2) Impact of the media coupled with recognition and attention from philanthropic institutions

(3) Government's close relationship with UNAIDS, WHO, and other UN bodies

'Within': 'Political System'

(1) Electoral politics

(2) Bureaucratic incentives

(3) Relationship between Ministries

'Below': 'Civil Society'

(1) Civil society activism, formal linkages with government institutions

Private actors (e.g. Pharmaceutical) Transnational Advocacy Networks

Figure 24-6. *Possible explanatory factors for budgetary allocations in health.*

Table 24-6. *World Bank loans (in US$ million) primarily for HIV/AIDS, TB and Malaria to Brazil, Russia and India. (Source: World Bank Project Portfolio, ref. 88).*

Brazil		Total	768
	March 1988	Northeast Endemic Disease Control Project	109
	May 1989	Amazon Basin Malaria Control Project	99
	November 1993	AIDS and STD Control Project	160
	September 1998	AIDS and STD Control Project – II	100
	September 1998	Disease Surveillance and Control Project	100
	June 2003	AIDS and STD Control Project – III	100
	May 2004	Disease Surveillance and Control Project – II	100
Russia		Total	150
	April 2003	Tuberculosis and AIDS Control Project	150
India		Total	1591
	March 1992	National AIDS Control Project	84
	January 1997	Tuberculosis Control Project	142
	June 1997	Malaria Control Project	164
	June 1999	Second National HIV/AIDS Control Project	191
	June 2004	Integrated Disease Surveillance Project	68
	August 2006	Second National Tuberculosis Control Project	170
	April 2007	Third National HIV/AIDS Control Project	250
	July 2008	National Vectorborne Disease Control and Polio Eradication Support Project	521

(NGOs) and health experts who have argued that the emphasis on HIV/AIDS is detrimental to primary care and other communicable diseases (54). In Russia, a similar concern emerged during the 1990s with donor assistance from the WHO, DFID, CIDA and the World Bank in 2003. However, this concern was temporary and quickly subsided as donor assistance did not skew domestic priority funding towards AIDS.

In contrast to Brazil and India, the World Bank played a more limited role in Russia in the 1990s (38). Despite discussions with the World Bank during the latter part of the decade, the first World Bank loan to Russia for HIV/AIDS and TB was only made in 2003 in parallel with grants from the Global Fund (**Table 24-7**). But as recent scholars note (55), this funding has not motivated the government to increase domestic funding commitments to strengthen the Ministry of Health's AIDS Control Program, whether in the area of infrastructural capacity, coordination or resources for the states. Thus, even if World Bank funding had arrived earlier, this by no means suggests that AIDS programme expansion would have occurred at an earlier point in time. It remains to be seen whether external funding will have a future effect for HIV and TB. Yet Russia's response so far corroborates our point that while

Table 24-7. *Global Fund to Fight HIV/AIDS, TB and Malaria grants (in US$ millions) to Brazil, Russia and India. (Note: Principle recipients in parentheses; Source: Global Fund Grant Portfolio, ref. 39).*

	Round 1	Round 2	Round 3	Round 4	Round 5	Round 6	Round 7	Round 8	Round 9	Total
HIV / AIDS										
India		106 (DEA)		81 (DEA, PFI)		76 (DEA, PFI, IAA)	14 (DEA, INC, TISS)		21 N/A	299
Russia			89 (OHI)	115 (RHCF)	8 (RHRN)					213
AIDS/TB										
India			13 (DEA)							13
Tuberculosis										
India	8 (DEA)	41 (DEA)		19 (DEA)		9 (DEA)			69 N/A	146
Brazil					11 (FAP, FSTD)					11
Russia			11 (PIH)	86 (RHCF)						97
Malaria										
India				48 (DEA)					38 NA	86
Brazil							2 (FTMA)			2

Legend and abbreviations: Principle Recipients; DEA = Department of Economic Affairs; PFI = Population Foundation of India; IAA = India AIDS Alliance; INC = India Nursing Council; TISS = Tata Institute of Social Sciences; OHI = Open Health Institute; RHCF = Russian Health Care Foundation; RHRN = Russian Harm Reduction Network; PIH = Partners in Health; FAP = Foundation Ataulpho Paiva; FSTD = Foundation for Science and Technological Development; FTMA = Foundation for Tropical Medicine of the Amazons; Source: http://www.theglobalfund.org/programs/

external funding is important, its positive and enduring consequences are not guaranteed and may only occur within certain historical and political contexts. We therefore consider other factors motivating government response.

A secondary factor related to external forces is the impact of the media coupled with recognition and attention from philanthropic institutions. This creates incentives for countries to focus on certain diseases at the expense of others. For example, in a recent *Financial Times* news article, the Executive-Director of the Global Fund, Michel Kazatchkine, called on emerging countries to fund HIV/AIDS activities using their own resources and to stop relying on external financiers (56). Similarly, the head of UNAIDS, Michel Sidibe, visited India in October 2009 and pushed the government to expand access to HIV treatment, to continue to expand its response to the HIV/ AIDS epidemic, as well as to start becoming a donor to UNAIDS (57). Russia has also been pushed to expand its response to HIV/AIDS both in terms of quantity of financing and its HIV/AIDS prevention policy (36,58). Our findings suggest that all three countries are responsive to this type of 'soft pressure'. As noted above, **Table 24-5** demonstrates how the National AIDS Control Project-3 is being funded largely by the Indian government (40.8%), from only 9.5% funding in the previous project. Similarly in Brazil, the Congress has started to finance most of the AIDS programme, leading to a substantial and continued decline in World Bank assistance to the programme, as noted above. Recently, Russia was praised by HIV/AIDS experts for expanding antiretroviral treatment drastically for AIDS patients as it has increased coverage of antiretroviral therapy to those at advanced stages of HIV from 4% in 2004 to 16% in 2007 (36,59). This praise has been accompanied by criticism for the neglect in HIV/AIDS programming injection drug users and the need for opioid drug substitution, such as methadone and buprenorphine (60).

Adding to this, constant media reporting of *"successful"* responses to HIV/AIDS may generate incentives for thriving middle-income nations to use this as a way to increase their international popularity and influence, as has been the case in Brazil (49,61). Recognition from leading philanthropists, such as the Bill & Melinda Gates Foundation's granting of a formal prize to Brazil for having the best response to HIV/AIDS in 2003, creates ongoing incentives for the President, Congress and the Ministry of Health to invest more in HIV/ AIDS policy at the expense of other diseases (24,49). Similarly, in 2003, the Gates Foundation entered India and established the US$ 258 million Avahan initiative, which is the largest HIV/ AIDS prevention programme in the world. Those close to the negotiations with the Indian government mention the key role the Gates Foundation played in lobbying for increased domestic attention to HIV/AIDS (59); as one respondent noted: *"Bill pressed the government hard to allow a completely parallel programme – he had the clout from his relationships in the private sector with Microsoft"*. Avahan is currently working closely with the NACO to transition the programme from the Gates Foundation to the government. Ashok Alexander, the head of Avahan, noted: *"We are not perpetual funders. We try to be catalytic"* (62). However, asking the government to assume the full cost of Avahan will result in an even higher proportion of funding being allocated to HIV/AIDS, and even the former head of the NACO, Sujatha

Rao, remarked: *"We told them you can't create a huge number of assets and then just leave and expect the government to take over everything"* (62). To address the government's concern, the Gates Foundation donated an additional US$ 80 million for HIV/AIDS prevention, as well as praised the Indian government for their stellar response to the epidemic (63). In Russia, the Gates Foundation has not directly set up operations or engaged with government, but rather made a US$ 44.7 million grant to Partners in Health to implement programmes to address TB.

A third top-down factor that might be important is a government's close relationship with UNAIDS, WHO and other UN bodies. Functions provided by UN bodies, such as surveillance, policy guidance and technical support for country planning for certain diseases, provide the necessary resources for domestic policy to follow global priorities (23).

A particularly important in-country body is UNAIDS, which was created to advocate for increased institutional and financial commitment to HIV/AIDS, based on the premise that the disease is exceptional and thus deserves an exceptional response (64). In addition, as will be discussed below, strong partnerships between domestic health officials and officials in these agencies can lead to biased commitments to certain disease areas (24). This does not seem to be as significant a factor as external financing.

We now turn to look at factors within the state, particularly the political and bureaucratic incentives for reform and relationships between ministries. In some instances, biased attention to AIDS may reflect politicians' interest in using the popularity of AIDS as a platform for election (65). In other instances, politicians may wish to use AIDS policy in order to garner more political support, or use AIDS as a successful platform in order to increase their international influence through donor aid assistance. Since the mid-1990s, this was certainly the case in Brazil (66,67), and has started to emerge in India (68). The absence of electoral accountability and competition in Russia has not yielded such a response (69).

Similarly, increased international attention and resources for AIDS in the 1980s compared with other diseases has increased the legitimacy and influence of AIDS bureaucrats. The AIDS epidemic first emerged on the international agenda in 1985 with the creation of the WHO's Global Programme on AIDS, which was directed by the late Dr Jonathan Mann. In contrast, TB was not declared by the WHO as a *"global emergency"* until 1993, while the WHO's Stop TB Partnership was only created in 1998. Similarly, international attention to malaria arguably did not begin until 1997 with the first International

Conference on Malaria in Dakar, Senegal, and was further reinforced by the Abuja declaration in 2000, where African leaders affirmed their commitment to cutting malaria mortality by half by 2010 (70). In this situation where AIDS received earlier international recognition, domestic AIDS bureaucrats have had incentives to use their popularity and influence with the President or Prime Minister, who is supportive of international partnerships for AIDS policy, to obtain more support from the Congress or Parliament. This has certainly been the case in Brazil (23) and seems to also be true in India (51). On the other hand, in Russia various factors have all contributed to AIDS officials' lack of popularity and influence. These include: Russia's more isolationist approach and tenuous partnerships with donors (38,69), plus politicians' ongoing discrimination towards drug users and the gay community (71), with the parliament being consistently influenced by the communist party and its close alignment with the Russian orthodox church, which is always adamantly opposed to sex education in schools and condemns HIV victims for behaving immorally (72). This has not increased AIDS officials' ability to secure Presidential and Congressional support for more funding.

The third group of factors are "*bottom-up*" pressures emanating from civil society activism. While there are civil society groups representing a host of disease areas ranging from diarrhoeal disease to malnutrition, HIV/AIDS activists tend to be better organized and financed (73). HIV/AIDS groups have relatively more access to governments through national AIDS councils and legislative hearings (74), while having the ability to influence the global policy process through UNAIDS, the World Bank and the Global Fund, which all facilitate civil society–government engagements. While this is true in Brazil (28,75,76) and India (77), in Russia, the NGO movement is weak and based mainly at the state ("*oblast*") level (78). In Russia, in contrast to Brazil and India, there are no direct institutional linkages between national AIDS agencies and NGOs (69). This might account for differences in effective lobbying pressures and budgetary allocations for HIV/AIDS between Brazil and India versus Russia.

Two additional factors explaining our findings cross-cutting all three levels are the strength of the private sector in health, specifically the pharmaceutical industry, and the influence of transnational advocacy movements for particular diseases. The pharmaceutical industry is expanding rapidly in all three countries. As of 2009, India's pharmaceutical market size is US$ 10.4 billion with annual growth of 8.4%, Brazil's is US$ 13.6 billion with growth of 5%, and Russia's is US$ 8.3 billion with 15.9% growth (79). The pharmaceutical industry has an incentive to lobby government towards treatment programmes, specifically in acquiring antiretrovirals for HIV/AIDS treatment programmes, rather than for prevention, or to address health issues, such as unintentional injury, where drugs are not the direct solution. This push for treatment is evident in Brazil, which provides free first and second-line antiretrovirals, in India, which provides free first-line antiretrovirals, and in Russia, which has rapidly expanded treatment to those affected by HIV/AIDS. The private sector exerts influence not only within these three countries, but also in donor countries, as explored by Reich (80). It should be noted that it is not only the private sector that pushes for treatment, but also key multilaterals such as UNAIDS (e.g. by holding governments accountable for commitments to universal access to antiretrovirals) and WHO (e.g. through its 3 by 5 initiative), for both patented and generic drugs (81).

The second major cross-cutting factor is the influence of transnational advocacy movements, specifically AIDS activist organizations. These organizations, largely based in the USA and Western Europe, have pushed donor governments to finance programmes for HIV/AIDS in low and middle-income countries (82), as well as provided financial and technical support to those local civil society organizations in line with their normative agenda (51). The combination of pressure from donors through financing of particular diseases, from the pharmaceutical industry and from transnational advocacy movements across the three levels seems to be the key to understanding the convergence in Brazil and India with global priorities in health, namely HIV/AIDS, TB and malaria.

5. Conclusion. The findings in this paper raise issues for future research on the interactions between global, governmental and civic actors. Although the results in this paper are preliminary, they indicate the need for further investigation into priority setting mechanisms at the national level instead of relying on the traditional explanation that the financial dependence of recipient countries on donors results in national budgetary allocations towards global priorities, such as HIV/AIDS. In particular more attention needs to be paid to the role that the international community plays in shaping domestic policy through identifying the various stakeholders and better understanding how they negotiate and interact. Our paper also indicates the need for further disclosure and transparency on budgetary allocations by the Russian government. While the findings in this paper should be relevant for those interested broadly in global health, they should be of particular interest to those working for key donors, multilaterals such as the UNDP, UNODC, WHO and UNAIDS, the Brazilian, Russian and Indian governments, and academics examining global health financing.

Acknowledgement: Originally published as: Devi Sridhar and Eduardo J Gomez: Health financing in Brazil, Russia and India: what role does the international community play? Health Policy and Planning 2011; 26: 12–24, reprinted by permission of Oxford University Press.

References

1. Shiffman J. Has donor prioritization of HIV/AIDS displaced aid for other health issues? Health Policy Plann 2008; 23:95–100.
2. Shiffman J, Berlan D, Hafner T. Has aid for AIDS raised all health funding boats? J AIDS 2009; 52:S45–8.
3. OECD. Measuring aid to health. Paris: Organization for Economic Cooperation and Development, 2007. (Available from: http://www.oecd.org/dataoecd/20/46/41453717.pdf).
4. Sridhar D, Batniji R. Mis-financing global health: case for transparency in disbursements and decision-making. Lancet 2008; 372:1185–1191.
5. Ravishankar N, Gubbins P, Cooley RJ, et al. Financing of global health: tracking development assistance for health from 1990 to 2007. Lancet 2009; 373:2113–2124.
6. Oomman N, Bernstein M, Rosenzweig S. Seizing the opportunity on AIDS and health systems. Washington, DC: Center for Global Development, 2008.
7. England R. Are we spending too much on HIV? Br Med J 2007; 334:344.
8. Horton R. Venice statement: global health initiatives and health systems. Lancet 2009; 374:10–12.
9. Global Economic Governance Programme. Preliminary Report of a High-Level Working Group, 11–13 May 2008. Oxford: Oxford University Press, 2008. (Available from: http://www.globaleconomicgovernance.org/wp-content/uploads/Working%20Group%20Report%20May%202008 .pdf).
10. Buse K, Walt G. An unruly m´elange? Coordinating external resources to the health sector: a review. Soc Sci Med 1997; 45:449–463.
11. Brautigam D. Aid dependence and governance. Stockholm: Almqvist & Wiksell, 2000.
12. Brautigam D, Knack S. Foreign aid, institutions, and governance in sub-Saharan Africa. Econ Dev Cult Change 2004; 52:255–286.
13. Van de Walle N. Overcoming stagnation in aid-dependent countries. Washington, DC: Center for Global Development, 2005.
14. Moss T, Pettersson G, van de Walle N. An aid-institutions paradox? A review essay on aid dependency and state-building in Sub-Saharan Africa. Washington, DC: Center for Global Development, 2006.
15. Whitfield L. The politics of aid: African strategies for dealing with donors. Oxford: Oxford University Press, 2009.
16. Gilson L, Buse K, Murray S, Dickinson C. Future directions for health policy analysis: a tribute to the work of Professor Gill Walt. Health Policy Plann 2008; 23:291–293.
17. Przeworski A, Tuene H. The logic of comparative social inquiry. Hoboken, NJ: Wiley-Interscience Press, 1970.
18. Skocpol T, Somers M. The uses of comparative history in macro-social inquiry. Comp Stud Soc Hist 1980; 22:174–197.
19. Katznelson I. Configurative analytical analysis. In: Zuckerman A, Lichbach M (eds). Comparative Politics. New York: Cambridge University Press, 1997.

20. Eckstein H. Case study in theory in political science. In: Greenstein F, Polsby N (eds). Handbook of Political Science. Reading: Addison-Wesley Press, 1975.

21. Abbot A. What do cases do? In: Ragin C, Becker H (eds). What is a Case? Exploring the foundations of social inquiry. New York: Cambridge University Press, 1992.

22. Brazil Federal Senate. 2008. Official Budget. (Available from: http://www9.senado. gov.br/portal/page/portal/orcamento_senado).

23. Gomez E. Responding to contested epidemics: democracy, international pressure, and the civic sources of institutional change. PhD dissertation, Department of Political Science, Brown University, 2008.

24. Gomez E. How Brazil outpaced the United States when it came to HIV/AIDS: international politics and domestic policy reform. Working Paper. Camden, NJ: Rutgers University, 2009.

25. Delcalmo 2006, personal communication;

26. Moherdai 2006, personal communication;

27. Brazil Ministry of Health. National AIDS Programme. Brasilia, 2008.

28. Filho 2006, personal communication;

29. Kaiser Family Foundation. Donor contributions to the Global Fund to Fight AIDS, TB, and Malaria. Global Facts. 2009. (Available from: http://www.globalhealthfacts. org/topic.jsp?i1/459).

30. WHO. National health accounts. Russian Federation: national expenditure on health. 2007. (Available from: http://www.who.int/nha/country/RUS.pdf).

31. Marquez P. Dying too young: Addressing premature mortality and ill health due to non-communicable diseases and injuries in the Russian Federation. Washington, DC: World Bank, 2005.

32. Marquez P. Public spending in Russia for health care: issues and options. Washington, DC: World Bank, 2008.

33. World Bank. Officially registered HIV cases in the Russian federation. 2009. (Available from: http://web.worldbank.org/WBSITE/ EXTERNAL/NEWS/0,contentMDK:21034 565pagePK:34370piPK: 34424theSitePK:4607,00.html).

34. Vinokur A, Godinho J, Dye C, Nagelkerke N. The TB and HIV/ AIDS Epidemics in the Russian Federation. Technical Working Paper, No. 510. Washington, DC: World Bank, 2001.

35. Kaiser Family Foundation. Leading public figures thank President Putin for increased commitment to fight against HIV/AIDS. News Release, 2005. (Available from: http:// www.kff.org/hivaids/phip 113005nr.cfm).

36. Associated Press. 2009. Russia urged to switch its approach to curbing HIV/AIDS. (Available from: http://www.nytimes.com/2009/10/29/health/ policy/29russia.html).

37. WHO. Russian federation: overview of the malaria situation. 2009. (Available from: http://www.euro.who.int/malaria/ctrinfo/affected/ 20020722_14).

38. Twigg J, Skolnik R. 2004. Evaluation of the World Bank's assistance in responding to the AIDS epidemic: Russia case study. OED Working Paper. Washington, DC: World Bank.

39. Global Fund to Fight AIDS, TB, and Malaria. Grant portfolio. (Available from: http:// www.theglobalfund.org/en/portfolio/?lang1/4en).

40. Global AIDS Alliance. Report card shows many donors failing on AIDS, TB, and malaria. 2009. (Available from: http://www.globalaidsalliance .org/newsroom/press_re-leases/press081406/).

41. WHO. India fact sheet: Country Cooperation Strategy. 2006. (Available from: http://www.who.int/countryfocus/cooperation_strategy/ccsbrief_ind_en.pdf)
42. Berman P, Ahuja R. Government health spending in India. Econ Polit Weekly 2008; 46:26–27.
43. Deolalikar A, Jamison D, Prabhat J, Laxminarayan R. Financing health improvements in India. Health Affairs 2008; 27:978–990.
44. World Bank. National Vector Borne Disease Control and Polio Eradication Support Project. 2008. (Available from: http://web.worldbank.org/ external/projects/main?pagePK1/464283627&piPK1/473230&theSitePK 1/440941&menuPK1/4 228424&Projectid1/4P094360)
45. Qadeer I. Health care systems in transition III. India, Part I. The Indian Experience. J Publ Hlth Med 2000; 22:25–32.
46. WHO. Mental health atlas 2005. (Available from: http://www.who.int/ mental_health/evidence/mhatlas05/en/index.html).
47. Gauri V, Lieberman E. Boundary politics and HIV/AIDS policy in Brazil and Africa. Studies in Comparative International Development, 2006; 38:3. (Available from: www.princeton.edu/esl/Gauri-Lieberman_Final.pdf).
48. Barbosa 2008, personal communication;
49. Teixeira 2008, personal communication;
50. Beck E, Mays N. Health care systems in transition III: the Indian subcontinent. J Publ Hlth Med 2000; 22:3–4.
51. Sridhar D. Why did India respond to HIV/AIDS? GEG Working paper. Global Economic Governance Programme. Oxford: University College Oxford, 2009.
52. National Commission on Macroeconomics and Health. 2005. Financing and Delivery of Health Care Services in India. NCMH Background Paper. New Delhi: Ministry of Health and Family Welfare. (Available from: http://mohfw.nic.in/reports/reports/Report_on_NCMH/ BackgroundPapersreport.pdf).
53. WHO. WHO Country Cooperation Strategy 2006–2011: India. 2009. (Available from: http://www.who.int/countryfocus/cooperation_strategy/ ccs_ind_en.pdf).
54. Chinai R. Donors are distorting India's health priorities, say protestors. Bull World Health Organ 2003; 81:152–153.
55. Ancker S. Demographic impact of HIV/AIDS in Russia: projections, analysis, and policy implications. China Eurasia Forum Quart 2008; 6:49–79.
56. Jack A. Emerging nations urged to foot bill on Aids bill. Financial Times, 2008. (Available from: http://us.ft.com/ftgateway/superpage.ft?news_id1/4 fto080720082110514511.Expenditures/).
57. UNAIDS. Michel Sidibe argues India to continue AIDS effort. Press release, 2009. (Available from: http://www.unaids.org/en/KnowledgeCentre/ Resources/Feature-Stories/archive/2009/20091007_EXD_India.asp/).
58. International AIDS Society (IAS). IAS expresses concern over future of HIV prevention efforts in Russia. 2009. (Available from: http:// www.iasociety.org/Web/WebContent/File/IAS%20Statement%20on %20HIV%20Prev%20in%20Russia%20(8%20Oct%20 09%20FINAL_ ENG).pdf).
59. WHO/UNAIDS/UNICEF. Epidemiological Fact Sheet on HIV and AIDS: Russian Federation: 2008 update. (Available from: http://apps .who.int/globalatlas/predefinedReports/EFS2008/full/EFS2008_ RU.pdf).

60. WHO. Injecting drug users and harm reduction. 2009. (Available from: http:// www. who.it/aids/prevention/20040325_1).

61. Passerelli 2009, personal communication;

62. Flock E. How Bill Gates blew $259 million in India's HIV corridor. Forbes India Magazine, 2009. (Available from: http://business.in.com/article/cross-border/how-bill-gates-blew-$258-million-in-indias-hiv-corridor/ 852/1).

63. Gates Foundation. Avahan AIDS Initiative commitment increased to $338 million. 2009. (Available from: http://www.gatesfoundation.org/press-releases/Pages/foundation-and-health-minister-azad-reaffirm-commitment-to-hiv-prevention-090723.aspx).

64. Sridhar D, Kuczynski D, Latulippe K. Background report for UNAIDS Leadership Transition Working Group. Washington, DC: Center for Global Development, 2008.

65. Whiteside A. The threat of HIV/AIDS to Democracy and Governance. Unpublished USAID briefing paper. 1999.

66. Gomez E. Brazil's blessing in disguise: how Lula turned an HIV crisis into a geopolitical opportunity. Foreign Policy, 2009. (Available from: http://www.foreignpolicy.com/articles/2009/07/22/brazils_blessing_ in_disguise)

67. Passerelli 2009, personal communication;

68. Lieberman E. Boundaries of contagion: How ethnic politics have shaped government response to AIDS. Princeton, NJ: Princeton University Press, 2009.

69. Wallander C. The politics of Russian AIDS policy. PONARS Policy Memo, No. 389, 2005.

70. Roll Back Malaria. Global burden and coverage today. 2009. (Available from: http:// www.rollbackmalaria.org/gmap/1-3.html).

71. Tkatchenko-Schmidt E, Renton A, Gevorgyan R, Davydenko L, Atun R. Prevention of HIV/AIDS among injection drug users in Russia: Opportunities and barriers to scaling-up of harm reduction programmes. Health Policy 2008; 85:162–171.

72. Chervyakov V, Kon I. Sex education and HIV prevention in the context of Russian politics. In: Rosenbrock R (ed.). Politics Behind AIDS Policies: Case Studies from India, Russia, and South Africa. Berlin: Wissenschaftszentrum Berlin fur Sozialforschung Press, 1998.

73. Barnett T, Whiteside A. HIV/AIDS and development: case studies and a conceptual framework. Eur J Develop Res 1999; 11:200–234.

74. Loewenson R. Civil society–state interactions in national health systems. Working Paper, Civil Society Initiative. Geneva: World Health Organization, 2003.

75. Teixeira P. 1997. Politicas publicas em Aids. In: Parker R (ed). Politicas, Instituicones e Aids: Enfrentando a Epidemia no Brasil. Rio de Janiero: ABIA Publications, 1997.

76. Terto 2006, personal communication;

77. UNGASS. India Country Progress Report. New Delhi: Ministry of Health and Family Welfare, 2009.

78. McCullaugh M. NGOs and HIV/AIDS in Russia. Paper presented at the conference on public health and demography in the former Soviet Union, Davis Center for Russian and Eurasian Studies, Harvard University, March 22, 2005.

79. Espicom. The market for pharmaceuticals in Brazil, Russia, India and China 2009. (Available from: https://www.espicom.com/Prodcat.nsf/ Search/00000939?OpenDocument).

80. Reich M. Reshaping the state from above, from within and from below: implications for public health. Soc Sci Med 2002; 54:1669–1675.

81. UNAIDS. Fast facts about HIV treatment. 2009. (Available from: http:// data.unaids. org/pub/FactSheet/2009/20090903_fastfacts_ treatment_en.pdf).

82. Behrman G. The invisible people: How the U.S. has slept through the global AIDS pandemic: the greatest humanitarian catastrophe of our time. Northampton, MA: Free Press, 2004.

83. WHOSIS. WHO Statistical Information System. 2009. (Available from: http:// www. who.int/whosis/en/, accessed 7 August 2009).

84. Anand S, Hanson K. Disability-adjusted life years: a critical review. J Health Econ 1997; 16:685–702.

85. WHO. Global burden of disease estimates. 2002. (Available from: http:// www.who. int/healthinfo/bodestimates/en/).

86. India Ministry of Finance. Union Budget and Economic Survey. New Delhi, 2008. (Available from: http://indiabudget.nic.in).

87. National AIDS Control Organization, India. Funds and expenditures. New Delhi: Ministry of Health and Family Welfare. 2007. (Available from: http://www.nacoonline. org/About_NACO/Funds).

88. World Bank, undated. Project portfolio. (Available from: http://web.worldbank.org/ WBSITE/EXTERNAL/PROJECTS)

CHAPTER 25.

Improving health aid for a better planet: the Planning, Monitoring and Evaluation Tool (PLANET)

The last two decades have brought revolutionary changes in global health, driven by popular concern over AIDS, re-emergence of tuberculosis, novel pandemics of infectious diseases (such as SARS, H1N1pdm09 influenza and MERS CoV), the rising burden of non-communicable diseases and falling but still unacceptably high maternal and child mortality (1). International development assistance for health (DAH) quadrupled between 1990 and 2012, from US\$ 5.6 billion to US\$ 28.1 billion, with the private and voluntary sectors taking on an increasing share of the commitment (2). Influential philanthropic organizations (e.g., Bill and Melinda Gates Foundation) and disease-specific public-private partnerships (e.g., Global Fund to Fight AIDS, Tuberculosis and Malaria) have reformed the architecture of global health funding (3). This generates an increasing need for transparent, fair, replicable and coordinated processes and tools that could be used to direct global health funding. The key challenges are setting investment priorities, monitoring the distribution of funding in real time, and evaluating the impact of these investments.

Currently, policy-makers have access to two types of information to assist with these three tasks. The first type is rooted in epidemiology and focuses on understanding the present burden of disease and the reduction in that burden (i.e. morbidity and mortality) that a project or policy could achieve. Most recently, the *"lives saved"* terminology has been adopted by agencies such as the Global Fund and used to drive evidence-based health policy (4). To support this, resources have been invested (e.g. by the UN agencies and the Institute for Health Metrics and Evaluation (IHME) at the University of Washington-Seattle) in generating more comprehensive and detailed estimates of global, regional and national disease burden and in getting this information into the hands of decision-makers (5). While successful at identifying the major causes of morbidity and mortality, the focus on the burden of disease as the dominant criterion for priority setting has been criticized (6).

The second type of available information is economic and focuses largely on cost-effectiveness. Policy makers at the national and sub-national level have limited resources for scaling up cost-effective health interventions in their populations (7). When planning the *"best buys"* for committing their resources in maternal and child health, they are faced with a complex task. They need to choose among at least several dozen interventions that target various diseases and vulnerable populations and decide on the most rational way to invest in the scale up of selected health interventions. Health investors usually like to know how many deaths (or episodes of disease) could be averted for a fixed level of investment. The more deaths averted per fixed investment, the more cost-effective the scale up. When the cost is low and the number of averted deaths high the intervention scale-up is highly cost-effective. When the cost is high and the number of averted deaths low then the intervention scale-up is not cost-effective. This type of analysis has been promoted by the World Bank, the Commission on Macroeconomics and Health and the recent report *"Global Health 2035"* (8–10).

However, this approach also has several limitations. For example, cost-effectiveness of mortality reduction does not necessarily mean that it will also be *"equitable"*, as these are two separate dimensions (7). Deaths can be reduced in a highly cost-effective way when investments are targeting the wealthiest quintiles in a population, just as when they are targeting the poorest. For example, there will be instances when an equity-promoting approach, i.e., trying to reach the poorest and most excluded sectors of a population with health interventions, will also be the most cost-effective approach. However, there will be instances in which this will be entirely unfeasible, and where equity-neutral or even inequity-promoting approaches may be substantially more cost-effective. In those cases, investments into health system development among the poorest that increase the quality and reduce the cost of intervention delivery may be required before intervention scale-up is planned.

While the above epidemiological and health economic approaches should, in theory, result in better-informed decisions, there may be a large gap between theory and practice. In some circumstances, sound epidemiological and health economic arguments may not result in successful project outcomes due to problems related to the mechanisms of delivery. For example, most DAH projects fail to align with the principles of the *Paris Declaration* and the *Accra Agenda for Action*, which outline best practice approaches to aid effectiveness (11).

The complexity and technocratic nature of both burden of disease and cost effectiveness exercises have often led to these being conducted in an opaque manner and not in line with these best practice principles. These types of analyses are often unstandardized, subjective (given the huge variation in quality and type of data), time-intensive, costly and not replicable. In this article we attempt to overcome these problems by proposing a novel approach to planning, monitoring and evaluation of development assistance for health.

1. Proposing the PLANET tool. We present a new methodology called PLANET (PLANning, monitoring and Evaluation Tool) that could be used to improve information on the delivery and implementation of DAH. Fundamentally, PLANET is based on a combination of two useful procedures: (i) the reduction of the multi-dimensional space of a complex system to a smaller number of core variables that capture most of the variation (e.g. using a statistical procedure known as *"principal component analysis"*); and (ii) the use of collective knowledge for decision-making (12,13). Our approach brings transparency, inclusiveness, fairness and replicability to the process.

Principal component analysis is a statistical technique which reduces a very complex system of large number of variables to a small number of relatively independent *"principal components"* which still capture a sizeable proportion of variation in the system (13); by defining a set of 15 *"criteria"*. Through this the PLANET process effectively reduces a notoriously complex and multi-dimensional task, which could be approached through an almost infinite number of *"lenses"*, into an exercise in which 15 of the most important (and reasonably independent) criteria for priority setting are clearly defined. If necessary these can later be weighted according to their relative importance to the users.

Collective knowledge has been increasingly recognized as a way to address these types of challenges (12). Collective knowledge and crowdsourcing refer to the process of taking into account the collective input of a group of individuals rather than of a single expert (or small number of experts) to answer a question (12). This is based on the observation that the average of collective judgments is closer to the truth than any single expert judgment in most circumstances (12). The pre-requisites for this process to work are: (i) *diversity of opinion* (each person should have private information even if it is just an eccentric interpretation of the known facts); (ii) *independence* (people's opinions are not determined by the opinions of those around them); (iii) *decentralization* (people are able to specialize and draw on local knowledge); and (iv) *aggregation* (some mechanism exists for turning private judgments into a collective decision – in this case, the PLANET method) (12). Once each individual is given an opportunity to express their opinion in a way that is treated equally with respect to the opinion of any other individual, then the personal biases that those individuals bring into the process tend to cancel and dilute each other regardless of who the participants are. What is left is information based on the accumulated knowledge, lifetime experience and common sense of those who took part. This collective knowledge illustrates that disagreement and contest, rather than consensus and compromise, among independent minds can lead to the best decisions (12).

2. Conceptual framework. We conceptualize DAH as a process in which multiple stakeholders invest a finite sum of money each year into improving health and development in low and middle-income countries. In theory, if the total sum was known, if it was all coordinated centrally, and if appropriate evidence on the *"architecture"* of missed development potential was available globally, then there would be one optimal way to invest these resources with the maximum possible impact, while all other approaches would achieve a lesser improvement in global development. In this process, the funding can be thought of the *"energy"* or *"resource"* required to fill the gaps in development, while all steps through which these funds need to be taken during this process can be seen as potentially retarding forces which may cause deviations from the most effective approach. These forces do not disappear even if more money is injected into the system. A problem is that, in reality, we neither have the detailed evidence nor the information required for the optimization of the process of DAH, nor can we monitor and centrally coordinate the flows of funding.

However, regardless of that, we can develop a conceptual framework that can systematically define all the fundamentally important retarding forces that are at work through this process, and try to assess, for each initiative (based on the collective knowledge of the persons most closely informed about each step in the process), how likely it is to complete its mission, and how vulnerable it is to retarding forces (see **Figure 25-1**).

Building on McCoy et al 2009 (14), we identify three functions associated with DAH and the associated stakeholders. The first function is labeled *"providing"* and is concerned with the need to raise or generate funds (the funders of DAH) to improve global health through development. The second function is *"managing"* and is concerned with the management or pooling of those funds, as well as with mechanisms for channeling funds to recipients (the managers of DAH). The third function is *"spending"* and is concerned with expenditure and consumption of those funds (the recipients of DAH). It is worth noting that while this schematic establishes a clear time sequence of the key events in the DAH process, several actors work across all three levels simultaneously. Nevertheless, similar to McCoy et al. 2009 (14), we believe that these categories provide a useful framework for studying the DAH process.

3. Funders of development assistance for health. The first level of stakeholders of interest are the funders of DAH, referred to here as donors, which could include philanthropists, government or international organizations,

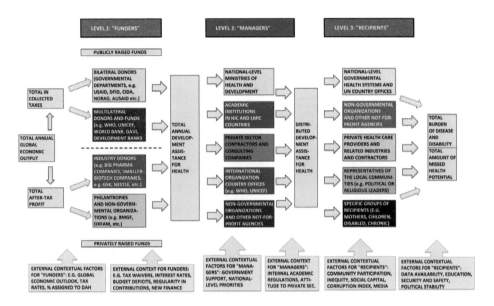

Figure 25-1. *A summarized overview of the structure and some key determinants of function of the global development assistance system.*

and the investors from the private sector and industry. Donors have become increasingly aware of the importance of measuring success in terms of political sustainability but have not been in possession of a clear framework or technology to help them undertake this task effectively. Often their priority is on disbursing resources according to internal interests, or they find delivery data too difficult to collect accurately, or too politically sensitive (see **Figure 25-2**).

At the level of donors, several factors could hinder the effectiveness of investments. Firstly, donors could misalign the size of their support (financial commitment) with the size of the problem (burden of disease). An unprecedented amount of money is being pledged and used to fund health services throughout the world. However, several studies have shown that funding does not correspond closely to burden (2). For example, Shiffman (2006) demonstrates that within communicable diseases for the years 1996 to 2003, there were several neglected topics such as acute respiratory infections and malaria (15). Similarly, Sridhar & Batniji (2008) noted that in 2005, funding per death varied widely by disease area from US$ 1029.10 for HIV/AIDS to US$ 3.21 for non-communicable disease (16). The reasons for this misalignment could be due to the social construction of the problem (17), lobbying by vested interests (18) or the personal interests of donors (19). *Thus, the risk that the donors are*

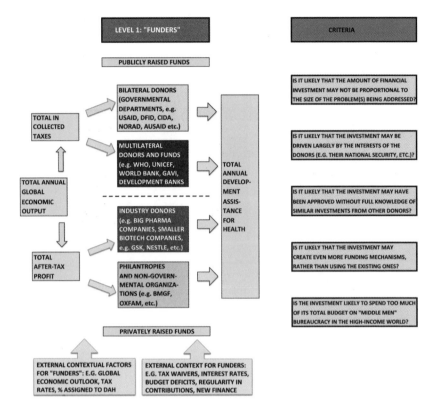

Figure 25-2. *The level of funders and key performance risks at this level.*

misaligning their financial commitment to a disease area with the burden it causes needs to be assessed.

Second, donors could prioritize initiatives that focus on their national self-interest rather than those that support improved health in the recipient country. For example, since the *Oslo Declaration* in 2006, health and foreign policy have become increasingly linked (20). While translating health into national security language might attract attention from high levels of government, this focus has been limited to a few high-profile problems such as AIDS, pandemic influenza and humanitarian assistance and not expanded to less glamorous areas such as health systems, malnutrition or water and sanitation (21). In fact a review of six countries' policies illustrates that most strategies tend to be catalyzed and supported by concern with surveillance and control of infectious disease (22). *Thus, the risk that a development project serves national self-interests, such as economic, geopolitical or security, rather than improved health outcomes in the recipient country needs to be established.*

Third, donors could fail to coordinate their activities. The current architecture of funding of global health and development is characterized by fragmentation, lack of coordination and even confusion as a diverse array of well-funded and well-meaning initiatives which descend with good intentions on countries in the developing world (23). However ambitious or well-intentioned these initiatives might be, it becomes difficult in this environment for recipient governments to develop and implement sound national plans for their country. While there is, in general, little incentive for various development partners to coordinate their activities, some development projects work better through a joint strategy. *Thus, the risk that development partners will fail to coordinate their activities for a specific project needs to be established.*

Fourth, donors could invest in new players and models rather than strengthening and building on the existing institutional infrastructure. As noted above, there has been a continuous expansion in the number as well as type of actors involved in DAH. Instead of examining how the existing institutional infrastructure – specifically the WHO and World Bank – can be reformed to deliver on projects, new initiatives are launched that attempt to compensate for their shortcomings (24). For example, the World Bank has an important role to play in DAH given its long history working in countries through governments, as well as in its knowledge-bank role. Similarly the WHO is unique in being governed by 193 member states and its role in setting evidence-based norms on technical and policy matters, highlighting best practices that improve health globally and monitoring and coordinating action. *Thus, the risk that a development project will result in a new institution rather than working through the existing institutional infrastructure needs to be established.*

Finally, donors could fund their initiatives in a way that results in too much funding going to more costly institutions. As McCoy et al. (2009) discuss, global health is a multi-billion dollar industry, and there are clearly competing interests amongst different actors to make use of this funding (14). For example, pharmaceutical companies appear to benefit considerably from global health programs that emphasize the delivery of medical commodities and treatments. NGOs, global health research institutions and UN bureaucracies also have an interest in increasing or maintaining their level of income and thus tend to prefer that funding from major donors flows through them (as managers of funding), rather than directly to developing countries. Further scrutiny is needed on aid flows in global health to assess whether they are being captured by vested interests and used to support inappropriate spending on the private commercial sector or on a large and costly global health bureaucracy and technocracy. *Thus, the risk that a development project will be designed in a way that results in too much funding going to costly organizations needs to be established.*

4. Managers of development assistance for health. The second level of stakeholders in DAH consists of the managers of DAH grants. These could be national government ministries, NGOs, academic institutions in donor or recipient countries, private sector (with pharmaceutical companies and bio-tech industries), various private or not-for-profit independent consultants and country offices of international organizations. Managers are often torn between global priorities, specifically the priorities of donors, and being accountable to local communities and the ultimate recipients of aid (see **Figure 25-3**).

At the middle level, several factors can hinder the effectiveness of investments. First, managers could deliberately steal resources from the investment for their own benefit, i.e. the risk of corruption. The need to identify and address corruption and weak governance is often lost in the commitment to raise funds and expand services (25). *Thus, the risk that funding from the project will be stolen needs to be assessed.*

Second, managers could inadvertently channel resources to purposes other than project objectives because of miscommunication, lack of competence, or lack of capacity (26). For example, those managing the project may not have the necessary technical or administrative skills to meet key objectives. *Thus, the risk that managers inadvertently channel resources to purposes other than project objectives due to lack of competence needs to be assessed.*

Third, managers could lack credible information and evidence to maximize the cost-effectiveness of investments. The basis of cost-effectiveness is that interventions should not only have established effectiveness in reducing disease burden but also represent an effective use of resources. For a certain budget, population health would then be maximized through choosing interventions that show the best value for money. Most information about cost-effectiveness, such as that generated through the WHO-CHOICE project, are available at the regional level (27). This creates challenges when applying these estimates to country and district level projects. *Thus, the risk that managers lack good information on the cost-effectiveness of investments needs to be assessed.*

Fourth, managers could route funding through non-governmental organizations or private sector bodies rather than working through governments. In the past two decades there has been a move towards funding non-state actors, especially by the newer funding institutions (23). For example, the Global Fund's use of country-coordinating mechanisms gives a larger voice to civil society as it is supposed to include a wide range of actors in a participatory process. The US government, particularly through its HIV/AIDS funding,

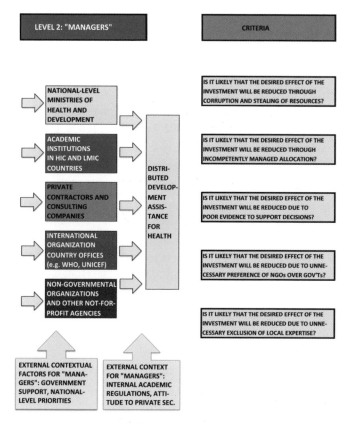

Figure 25-3. *The level of managers and key performance risks at this level.*

predominantly funds faith-based organizations and NGOs. The marginal involvement of developing country governments in many DAH projects raises questions about long-term sustainability (28). However, in some situations funding through NGOs or private sector bodies rather than through governments can work better but this should be carefully considered over a long term time horizon. *Therefore, the risk that a project routes funding through nongovernmental organizations or private sector bodies rather than through government needs to be assessed.*

Fifth, managers could exclude the participation of local experts and the inclusion of local evidence in the processes of priority setting. Managers face strong incentives to orient 'upwards' towards the donors that are funding the project (29). They have little incentive to include local experts and local knowledge. *Thus the risk that local experts and local evidence are excluded in the processes of priority setting needs to be assessed.*

The above are the first ten PLANET criteria to evaluate an initiative on DAH. The informants for these aspects would include policy-makers in various global health institutions as well as health economic, governance and health systems experts (see **Box 1**).

5. Recipients of development assistance for health. The third level of stakeholders includes all those involved in the final stage of DAH of reaching the recipients (i.e. government health systems, NGOs, private healthcare providers, local community representatives, and recipient groups (e.g. mothers and children) themselves, including the operational workforce. At this level, several factors could hinder the effectiveness of investments (see **Figure 25-4**).

First, the primary recipient could deliberately steal funding or commodities from this process for his/her own benefit. Numerous studies have documented such problems, for example, in the procurement of health supplies, in under-the-table payments for services, and in nurses and doctors who fail to show up at their clinics but nonetheless collect their salaries (30). *Thus, the risk that funding from the project will be stolen needs to be assessed.*

Second, the recipient could set up unnecessary parallel structures to deliver on the project rather than working through government or "*horizontally*". Horizontal interventions are defined as those that strengthen the heath care system, improve health systems service and delivery, and address general non-disease specific problems such as health worker shortages and stock outs of medicines and supplies (31). Despite the consensus that DAH should be funded horizontally, most financing is channeled vertically (defined as setting up separate systems to deliver on the objectives often related to specific diseases). In recent years much of the funding has been directed to address HIV/AIDS, malaria and TB (2). The imperative to show measurable results in a short-time frame results in setting in place short-term fixes that deliver on the project with the problem that relatively little funding may go towards capacity-building or working through government. *Thus the risk that a project will result in unjustified parallel local implementation structures rather than work through the existing health system needs to be assessed.*

Third, the project may not be aligned with local priorities or promote community involvement. The choice of a DAH priority directly affects recipients' health, meaning that these individuals should also have the right to participate in deciding on the priorities and implementation of the project (32). If this participation is to be meaningful nationally (or locally), then the results of the participation must have the possibility of having an impact, in this case, of affecting the nature of the project. *Thus the risk that the project will not be aligned with local priorities or promote community involvement needs to be assessed.*

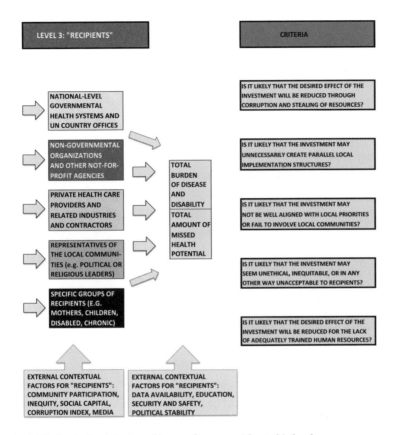

Figure 25-4. *The level of recipients and key performance risks at this level.*

Fourth, the project could be seen as unethical, inequitable or unacceptable to the final recipients. In recent years policy-makers have increasingly become aware of the disparities in health status between different groups in society and the distributional impact of interventions (33). In particular, concern focuses on the extent to which interventions reach and benefit disadvantaged groups, such as the poor, women or certain ethnicities or otherwise marginalized populations. *Thus, the risk that the project is not ethical, equitable or acceptable to the final beneficiaries needs to be assessed.*

Finally, the project may not be sustainable, defined in terms of ensuring required human resource capacity to deliver on targets and objectives. It is increasingly recognized that the success of local implementation is highly dependent on a strong health workforce (26). Despite this awareness, much of the focus of DAH is on commodities such as vaccines and drugs. While these are of course necessary, it is people who prevent disease and administer cures.

Thus the risk that the project will lack the requisite human resources, such as trained health workers, needs to be assessed.

The informants reporting of these final 5 criteria could be representatives of operations workforce and / or the ultimate recipients. The above factors can be used as the 15 criteria to plan an initiative on DAH at the inception stage, to monitor its implementation in real-time, and/or to evaluate previously conducted efforts. The resulting questions that could be asked of key informants are provided in **Table 25-1**.

6. Three applications of PLANET. The PLANET approach, as defined above, has three major applications in the field of development assistance. First is in *planning* of new initiatives in development. Donors in particular might be considering different investment options and project possibilities to address problems in development. While the overarching concern is justifiably a reduction in burden of disease, running a PLANET exercise will look at other equally important dimensions that would impact on the success of the project in reducing burden of disease as well as aligning with best practice in development.

How could the framework be used? Based on this conceptual framework we have developed a questionnaire (see **Table 25-1**) that can be used to engage three groups of respondents. These would include those with knowledge of health governance, economics and health systems as well as policy-makers intimately involved with the execution of the project. It would also include those at the local level who are likely to be involved with the delivery of the project as well as the actual beneficiaries. All relevant stakeholders would be given this questionnaire and asked to respond independently and anonymously based on their knowledge of the project. The process could be conducted by technical experts in a transparent way (e.g. each vote counts equally). The outcome would be a comprehensive list of the strengths and weaknesses of particular projects against many criteria, based on the collective input of technical experts. Additional criterion or questions can be added or substituted in to ensure covering all aspects relevant to that specific project. Analysis of the respondent data would, taken together, provide a complete picture of the strengths and weaknesses of the project that would be made available publicly.

Given that donors would be running this exercise using the expertise and accumulated knowledge of respondents, an additional step is necessary. Donors would need to define the context of the exercise based on their anticipated outcomes, the population they are targeting, the time-frame they are working under as well as stating how much risk they are willing to take to reach certain outcomes. For example, the Bill & Melinda Gates Foundation

Table 25-1. *Questionnaire for implementation of PLANET tool.*

	PLANNING	MONITORING	EVALUATING
Level 1: Donors	1. Is it likely that the amount of financial investment may not be proportional to the size of the problem(s) being addressed?	1. Is the amount of financial investment disproportional to the size of the problem(s) being addressed?	1. Was the amount of financial investment disproportional to the size of the problem(s) being addressed?
	2. Is it likely that the investment may be driven largely by the interests of the donors?	2. Is the investment driven largely by the interests of the donors?	2. Was the investment driven largely by the interests of the donors?
	3. Is it likely that the investment may have been approved without full recognition of similar investments from other donors?	3. Is the investment being implemented without full recognition of similar investments from other donors?	3. Was the investment approved without full recognition of similar investments from other donors?
	4. Is it likely that investment may create even more funding mechanisms rather than using existing ones?	4. Is the investment creating even more funding mechanisms rather than using existing ones?	4. Did the investment create even more funding mechanisms rather than using existing ones?
	5. Is the investment likely to spend too much of its total budget on costly "middle men" organizations?	5. Is the investment spending too much of its total budget on costly "middle men" organizations?	5. Did the investment spend too much of its total budget on costly "middle men" organizations?
Level 2: Managers	1. Is it likely that the desired effect of the investment will be reduced through corruption and stealing of resources?	1. Is the desired effect of the investment being reduced through corruption and stealing of resources?	1. Was the desired effect of the investment reduced through corruption and stealing of resources?
	2. Is it likely that the desired effect of the investment will be reduced through incompetently managed allocation?	2. Is the desired effect of the investment being reduced through incompetently managed allocation?	2. Was the desired effect of the investment reduced through incompetently managed allocation?
	3. Is it likely that the desired effect of the investment will be reduced due to poor evidence to support decisions?	3. Is the desired effect of the investment being reduced due to poor evidence to support decisions?	3. Was the desired effect of the investment reduced due to poor evidence to support decisions?
	4. Is it likely that the desired effect of the investment will be reduced due to unnecessary preference for NGOs over government?	4. Is the desired effect of the investment being reduced due to unnecessary preference for NGOs over government?	4. Was the desired effect of the investment reduced due to unnecessary preference for NGOs over government?
	5. Is it likely that the desired effect of the investment will be reduced due to unnecessary exclusion of local expertise?	5. Is the desired effect of the investment being reduced due to unnecessary exclusion of local expertise?	5. Was the desired effect of the investment reduced due to unnecessary exclusion of local expertise?

Table 25-1. *Continued.*

	PLANNING	MONITORING	EVALUATING
Level 3: Recipients	1. Is it likely that the desired effect of the investment will be reduced through corruption and stealing of resources?	1. Is the desired effect of the investment being reduced through corruption and stealing of resources?	1. Was the desired effect of the investment reduced through corruption and stealing of resources?
	2. Is it likely that the investment may unnecessarily create parallel local implementation structures?	2. Is the investment unnecessarily creating parallel local implementation structures?	2. Did the investment unnecessarily create parallel local implementation structures?
	3. Is it likely that the investment may not be well aligned with local priorities or fail to involve local communities?	3. Is the investment not well aligned with local priorities or failing to involve local communities?	3. Was the investment misaligned with local priorities or did it fail to involve local communities?
	4. Is it likely that the investment may seem unethical, inequitable, or in any other way unacceptable to recipients?	4. Is the investment unethical, inequitable, or in any other way unacceptable to recipients?	4. Was the investment unethical, inequitable, or in any other way unacceptable to recipients?
	5. Is it likely that the desired effect of the investment will be reduced due to lack of adequately trained human resources?	5. Is the desired effect of the investment being reduced due to lack of adequately trained human resources?	5. Was the desired effect of the investment reduced due to lack of adequately trained human resources?

might be willing to take a major risk for a high-payoff while public donors such as the UK government might be looking to minimize risk and under those conditions to maximize health outcomes. The outcome would be a comprehensive list with competing priorities ranked according to the combined scores they received in the process. Such a list would be helpful because it provides an overview of the strengths and weaknesses of competing DAH options against many criteria, based on the collective input of technical experts. The list can also be adjusted by taking the values of many stakeholders into account such as occurred during the extensive experience with the implementation of CHNRI in health research prioritization (34).

Second, PLANET can be used to *monitor* ongoing initiatives and receive real-time feedback on their implementation. Third, PLANET could also be used to *evaluate* the success of previous initiatives. Evaluation is often woefully neglected in development and efforts such as by the Center for Global Development to fill this gap have focused on the creation of new institutions with the capacity to undertake this kind of work (35). However, no standardized methodology exists to evaluate projects across multiple criteria capturing the essence of whether or not it was successful. Furthermore, this approach is not only concerned with considerations of disease burden reductions or change in health outcomes but with the actual process of implementation of the project, its strengths and weaknesses and whether it aligns with *"best practice"*. The implementation would be similar to that described above using a modified questionnaire (see **Table 25-1**).

7. Strategies for data collection. Exploitation of collective knowledge is now possible and moreover easier and cheaper than ever before. Information / communication technology becoming a digital utility enables us now to seek input from hundreds or thousands of independent individuals at little higher cost than asking one person. We can now, in real-time, in almost every country or setting collect feedback or opinions from an estimated 6.8 billion people who actively use mobile phones (with the proportion of smartphones rapidly growing) (36). This can be done through text-message (37,38), automated phone calls, dedicated apps, email or the internet in a device or platform agnostic manner. It is certain that this is redefining not just the norms of who provides a feedback or communication of their assessment of a programme and how and when this is done, but also how DAH and indeed healthcare is delivered or consumed. The PLANET questionnaire is currently being developed into an app that would be freely available to all governments, international institutions and individuals looking for a simple, tech-friendly tool to plan, monitor and evaluate DAH.

The PLANET tool has several major advantages over existing efforts in planning, monitoring and evaluation. First, it presents a standardized methodology that can be used for planning, monitoring and evaluation of any type of DAH project, but it also has sufficient flexibility to be tailored to the context of specific projects or initiatives. PLANET would be an additional tool available to policy-makers, along with LiST (for health care/interventions) (39) and CHNRI (for health research) (13) which will involve local experts and incorporate issues of local context in the process of determining priorities in a transparent, user-friendly, replicable, quantifiable and specific, algorithm-like manner. Second, it is simple to implement and with the development of mobile-phone software, should be able to be run anywhere in the world at low-cost. The low-cost of input means it can be run multiple times resulting in real-time monitoring of DAH. Third, while respondents are protected through anonymity in feedback, the results are provided transparently. Finally, the exercise gives equal voice to all those involved in the process of development from the donor (e.g. in London, Seoul or Seattle) to a manager and to a recipient (in rural Uganda, Dhaka or Antigua). The voice of local stakeholders, including operations teams and beneficiaries, is included in every exercise.

The use of these types of novel methodologies can lead to more rational planning, higher quality evaluation as well as more knowledgeable future decision-making, especially given that DAH has traditionally lacked formal tools to examine delivery and implementation. The use of such tools would promote attention to objective evidence on planning, monitoring and evaluation leading to more effective aid and ultimately better evidence on reduction in the burden of disease across the world and how this relates or could relate to specific development efforts.

Acknowledgement: Originally published as: Devi Sridhar, Josip Car, Mickey Chopra, Harry Campbell, Ngaire Woods and Igor Rudan: Improving health aid for a better planet: the planning, monitoring and evaluation Tool (PLANET). Reprinted with permission from Edinburgh University Global Health Society under Creative Commons Attribution License (Journal of Global Health 2015; 2:020404).

References

1. Fidler, DP. After the revolution: global health politics in a time of economic crisis and threatening future trends. Maurer School of Law, Indiana University Faculty Publication 145, 2009. (Available from: http://www.repository.law.indiana.edu/facpub/145; Accessed: 1 Mar 2014).
2. Institute for Health Metrics and Evaluation. Financing global health 2012: the end of the golden age? Seattle: Institute for Health Metrics and Evaluation, 2012. (Available from: http://www.healthmetricsandevaluation.org/publications/policy-report/financing-global-health-2012-end-golden-age; Accessed: 1 Mar 2014).
3. Sridhar D. Who sets the global health research agenda? The challenge of multi-bi financing. PLoS Med 2012; 9:e1001312.
4. Low-Beer D, Komatsu R, Kunii O. Saving lives in health: global estimates and country measurement. PLoS Med 2013; 10:e1001523.
5. Murray CJL, Ezzati M, Flaxman AD, Lim S, Lozano R, Michaud C, et al. GBD 2010: design, definitions, and metrics. Lancet 2012; 380:2063–2066.
6. Baltussen R, Niessen L. Priority setting of health interventions: the need for multi-criteria decision analysis. Cost Eff Resour Alloc 2006; 4:14.
7. Chopra M, Campbell H, Rudan I. Understanding the determinants of the complex interplay between cost-effectiveness and equitable impact in maternal and child mortality reduction. J Glob Health 2012; 2:010406.
8. World Bank. World Development Report 1993: Investing in health. New York: Oxford University Press, 1993. (Available from: http://wdronline.worldbank.org/worldbank/a/c.html/world_development_report_1993/abstract/WB.0-1952-0890-0.abstract1; Accessed: 1 Mar 2014).
9. Commission on Macroeconomics and Health. Macroeconomics and health: Investing in health for economic development. Canada: World Health Organization, 2001. (Available from: http://whqlibdoc.who.int/publications/2001/924154550x.pdf; Accessed: 1 Mar 2014).
10. Jamison DT, Summers LH, Alleyne G, Arrow KJ, Berkley S, Binagwaho A, et al. Global health 2035: a world converging within a generation. Lancet 2013; 382:1898-1955.

11. The Organisation for Economic Co-operation and Development (OECD). Evaluation of the implementation of the Paris Declaration. 2012. (Available from: http://www. oecd.org/dac/evaluation/evaluationoftheimplementationoftheparisdeclaration.htm; Accessed: 2 Mar 2014).

12. Surowiecki J. The wisdom of crowds: why the many are smarter than the few and how collective wisdom shapes business, economics, societies, and nations. New York: Doubleday, 2004.

13. Rudan I, Chopra M, Kapiriri L, Gibson J, Ann Lansang M, Carneiro I, et al. Setting priorities in global child health research investments: Universal challenges and conceptual framework. Croat Med J 2008; 49:307–317.

14. McCoy D, Chand S, Sridhar D. Global health funding: how much, where it comes from and where it goes. Health Policy Plan 2009; 24: 407-417.

15. Shiffman J. Donor funding priorities for communicable disease control in the developing world. Health Policy Plan 2006; 21:411-420.

16. Sridhar S, Batniji R. Misfinancing global health: a case for transparency in disbursements and decision making. Lancet 2008; 372:1185-1191.

17. Shiffman J. A social explanation for the rise and fall of global health issues. Bull World Health Organ 2009; 87:608-613.

18. Buse K, Hawkes S. Health post-2015: evidence and power. Lancet 2014; 383:678-679.

19. Sandberg KI, Andresen S, Bjune G. A new approach to global health institutions? A case study of new vaccine introduction and the formation of the GAVI Alliance. Soc Sci Med 2010; 71:1349-1356.

20. Ministers of Foreign Affairs of Brazil, France, Indonesia, Norway, Senegal, South Africa, and Thailand. Oslo Ministerial Declaration – global health: a pressing foreign policy issue of our time. Lancet 2007; 369:1373-1378.

21. Gostin, LO. Meeting basic survival needs of the world's least healthy people: Toward a framework convention on global health. Georgetown Law J 2008; 96:331-392.

22. Sridhar D, Smolina K. Motives behind national and regional approaches to health and foreign policy. The global economic governance programme (GEG) working paper 68. 2012. (Available from: http://www.globaleconomicgovernance.org/geg-wp-201268-motives-behind-national-and-regional-approaches-health-and-foreign-policy; Accessed: 2 Mar 2014).

23. Gostin L, Mok EA. Grand challenges in global health governance. Br Med Bull 2009; 90:7–18.

24. Garrett L. The challenge of global health. Foreign Affairs 2007; 86:14-38.

25. Lewis M. Governance and corruption in public health care systems. Center for Global Development Working Paper 78. 2006. (Available from: http://boetig.net/documents/adjunct%20faculty/Lyons,%20Scott/Corruption%20in%20Public%20Health%20Care%20Systems%20-%20Lewis%20-%202006.pdf; Accessed: 2 Mar 2014).

26. Chen L, Evans T, Anand S. Human resources for health: overcoming the crisis. Lancet 2004; 364:1984-1990.

27. World Health Organization. CHOosing Interventions that are Cost-Effective (WHO-CHOICE). (Available from: http://www.who.int/choice/en/; Accessed: 2 Mar 2014).

28. World Health Organization. Civil society report on commission of social determinants of health. 2007. (Available from: http://www.who.int/social_determinants/resources/cs_rep_sum_18_7.pdf; Accessed: 2 Mar 2014).

29. Sridhar D. Seven challenges in international development assistance for health and ways forward. J Law Med Ethics 2010; 38:459-469.

30. Lewis M. Tackling healthcare corruption and governance woes in developing countries. Washington, DC: Center for Global Development, 2006. (Available from: http://www.cgdev.org/sites/default/files/7732_file_GovernanceCorruption.pdf; Accessed: 2 Mar 2014).

31. World Health Organization Maximizing Positive Synergies Collaborative Group. An assessment of interactions between global health initiatives and country health systems. Lancet 2009; 373:2137-2169.

32. GO 4 Health. Realizing the right to health for everyone: the health goal for humanity. Copenhagen: Goals and governance for health, 2013. (Available from: http://www.go4health.eu/wp-content/uploads/Go4Health-interim-report-September-2013.pdf; Accessed: 3 Mar 2014).

33. Commission on Social Determinants of Health. Closing the gap in a generation: health equity through action on the social determinants of health. Final report of the commission on social determinants of health. Geneva: World Health Organization, 2008. (Available from: http://www.who.int/social_determinants/thecommission/finalreport/en/; Accessed: 3 Mar 2014).

34. Rudan I, Gibson JL, Ameratunga S, El Arifeen S, Bhutta ZA, Black M, et al.; for Child Health Nutrition Research Initiative (CHNRI). Setting priorities in global health research investments: Guidelines for implementation of the CHNRI method. Croat Med J 2008; 49:720-733.

35. Centre for Global Development. Closing the evaluation gap. (Available from: http://www.cgdev.org/initiative/closing-evaluation-gap; Accessed: 3 Mar 2014).

36. International Telecommunication Union. ICT Facts and Figures, 2013. (Available from: http://www.itu.int/en/ITU-D/Statistics/Documents/facts/ICTFactsFigures2013-e.pdf; Accessed: 3 Mar 2014).

37. Li Y, Wang W, van Velthoven M, Chen L, Car J, Rudan I, et al. Text messaging data collection for monitoring an infant feeding intervention program in rural china: Feasibility study. J Med Internet Res 2013; 15:e269.

38. van Velthoven M, Li Y, Wang W, Du X, Chen L, Wu Q, et al. mHealth Series: Factors influencing sample size calculations for mHealth–based studies – A mixed methods study in rural China. J Glob Health 2013; 3:020404.

39. Steinglass R, Cherian T, Vandelaer J, Klemm JD, Sequeira J. Development and use of the Lives Saved Tool: a model to estimate the impact of scaling up proven interventions on maternal, neonatal and child mortality. Int J Epidemiol 2011; 40:519-520.

PART 4.

Improving governance and legislation

CHAPTER 26.

Overseeing global health

The recent outbreak in West Africa of the highly infectious and often fatal Ebola virus highlights the need for global cooperation in health. The current Ebola crisis – along with the outbreak of Middle East respiratory syndrome (MERS) and the resurgence of polio in the Middle East and Africa – is simply the latest example of governments' inability to control the spread of infectious diseases when they act in isolation: global rules negotiated among governments are crucial to protecting the health of citizens.

The Ebola outbreak is precisely the type of crisis world governments had in mind when they founded the World Health Organization (WHO) in 1948 and placed it at the center of global health governance. The fight against Ebola, which the WHO declared an international emergency in August 2014, requires careful reporting of the spread of the disease to allow authorities to track it, concerted international efforts to contain it, and resources to treat those infected. These needs pertain to global health governance – the rules and related formal and informal institutions, norms, and processes that govern or directly influence global health policy. The essential functions of health governance, which are generally within the purview of the WHO and its governing board, include convening key stakeholders, defining shared values, establishing standards and regulatory frameworks, setting priorities, mobilizing and aligning resources, and promoting research.

Global governance requires governments to forgo aspects of their sovereignty by delegating certain prerogatives and authority to an international agency such as the WHO. Rules such as the International Health Regulations, which direct countries' response to international health risks, are a clear example of such delegation of authority. But in recent years new organizations have begun to crowd the global health stage. Specific concerns – about, say, HIV/AIDS or maternal mortality – have brought more money into the global health system. But those additional funds are often channeled through the new institutions. Some work within the WHO, some outside it, and others do both. In contrast to the wide, integrated mandate of the WHO, the focus of most of these new organizations is vertical, concentrated on narrow goals, such as a particular disease or condition.

Protecting the health of citizens across the world requires long-term investment in the WHO and its broad mandate. But donors with focused, short-term objectives are driving much WHO activity, and new partnerships aimed at specific diseases and issues are gaining prominence. Yet there is growing awareness of the need to strengthen health systems – the people, organizations, and resources at the center of health care delivery – to complement disease-specific efforts. Moreover, the recent efforts of Latin American, Asian, and African nations to play a larger role in global institutions is affecting global health governance.

1. A growing crowd. The original purpose of the World Health Organization was, among other things, to ensure that governments would collaborate on health matters with a long-term perspective. To that end it was given more authority and resources than its predecessor organization under the League of Nations. Virtually every government in the world is a member of the one-country, one-vote World Health Assembly, which governs the WHO. However, the WHO is no longer the only global health institution and today faces stiff competition in some areas from new actors, such as the Global Fund to Fight AIDS, Tuberculosis and Malaria (the Global Fund); GAVI, The Vaccine Alliance; and the Bill & Melinda Gates Foundation, the world's largest private foundation whose core focus is global health.

Over the past half century, the World Bank too has become increasingly influential in global health care, with considerable resources, access to senior decision makers in ministries of finance, and in-house technical expertise. The bank has lent billions of dollars to governments to help them improve their health services. As a result of this changing environment, the WHO faces both financing and governance difficulties. Although total resources have not diminished, they have not grown much in recent years either. The organization's 2012–13 budget was US$ 3.95 billion; its 2014–15 budget is US$ 3.97 billion (1). But the real challenge is the constraints on the way much of that money can be spent. About 80% of the WHO budget is *"voluntary"* funding from donors with specific mandates and cannot usually be spent for general purposes. A shortage of unrestricted funds was one of the factors that hindered the WHO response to the recent Ebola outbreak.

The World Health Organization (WHO) has been criticized for a slow and weak initial response to containing the Ebola virus outbreak in west Africa. The agency cites a lack of in-house technical expertise and staff. Because so much of its budget is decided by donors who earmark funds for their short-term priorities, the WHO's core strength in emergency and epidemic and pandemic response has atrophied over the past decade. Its outbreak and crisis budget was cut in half, from US$ 469 million in 2012–13 to US$ 241 million in 2014–15 (1), and its epidemic and pandemic response department was dissolved and its duties split among other departments (2). In September 2014, donors such as the Bill & Melinda Gates Foundation pledged funds to the WHO, but there is a need for long-term sustainable financing for the organization that is at the center of global health governance.

What has been largely criticized as a slow initial reaction to the epidemic has sparked some calls for creation of a new global fund to respond to infectious disease outbreaks. Voluntary funding – which comes from government donors such as the United States and Japan and from private sources – can be earmarked for specific diseases or initiatives, such as the Stop TB Partnership, or specific regions, such as the Americas. Over the past 12 years, voluntary contributions have increased 183%, while assessed core contributions from member countries have increased only 13% (3). During 2012–13, the WHO had discretion over the use of only 7.6% of voluntary funds. Moreover, administrative costs for management of the more than 200 voluntary contributors approached US$ 250 million, more than 5% of its budget. Still, without voluntary funding it is likely that the total WHO budget would be much smaller.

Governments overall remain the WHO's primary source of funds (assessed and voluntary), but nongovernmental organizations (NGOs) are increasingly influential. The US$ 300 million the Gates Foundation donated in 2013, for example, made it the WHO's single largest contributor. In some cases NGOs help implement WHO programs – *The Stop TB Partnership*, for example, which seeks to eradicate tuberculosis. NGOs are seeking power and voice in global health governance through board membership and voting rights in international institutions, but they have only observer status at the WHO – governments direct policy. The challenge is for the WHO to engage meaningfully with this wider range of stakeholders while maintaining its status as an impartial intergovernmental body that benefits all its members equally.

The WHO has had to deal with some discontent on that issue. For example, in 2007, the Indonesian health minister refused to supply H5N1 virus samples to the WHO for analysis and vaccine preparation, despite global concern about an outbreak of avian flu (4). The minister argued that vaccines and drugs derived from its viral samples were unlikely to become available to developing countries and invoked the principle of viral sovereignty to withhold samples until a more equitable system for access to vaccines in a pandemic was established. After tense negotiations, member states agreed in 2011 to the *Pandemic Influenza Preparedness Framework* for the sharing of influenza viruses and access to vaccines and other benefits. The agreement seeks to balance improved and strengthened sharing of influenza viruses with efforts to increase developing countries' access to vaccines and other pandemic-related supplies.

As the Indonesian incident demonstrates, international institutions must balance buy-in by the powerful (who often have a special degree of influence) against the need to assure all members, including the least powerful, that their interests are best served by belonging to and participating in the organization. Countries must trust an international agency to report infectious threats and use the health information it gathers for the general benefit, without stigmatizing or denigrating the countries where threats arise. The revised 2005 *International Health Regulations* require its nearly 200 signatory countries to report to the WHO certain public health events of international concern (such as Ebola outbreaks) and establish procedures that the WHO and its members must follow to uphold global public health security. The regulations seek to balance sovereign rights with a shared commitment to preventing the international spread of disease.

The flip side of the emergence of new actors on a stage once occupied by the WHO alone is that countries seeking the best way to achieve their health goals have more options. For example, countries can apply to the Global Fund or the Gates Foundation for money to fight TB and bypass the WHO, forcing the long-time leading player to examine its role and arguably operate more strategically. The WHO was never meant to undertake every global health function, partly because when it was founded there were already regional public health agencies (such as the Pan American Health Organization). Its main strength is as a forum that brings together various stakeholders but permits only member governments to negotiate global health rules and determine the support countries receive from the WHO to disseminate and implement those rules.

2. Partnership. The still relatively new story in global health cooperation is the emergence of public-private partnerships such as the Global Fund and GAVI. The governance structures of these vertical funds differ in important ways from those of the WHO and the World Bank (5). Vertical funds have narrowly defined goals, unlike the broad mandates of the WHO (*"the attainment by all people of the highest possible level of health"*) and the World Bank (*"to alleviate poverty and improve quality of life"*). The Global Fund's mandate is to attract and disburse resources to prevent and treat HIV/AIDS, tuberculosis, and malaria; GAVI's is to save children's lives and protect health more broadly by increasing access to childhood immunizations in poor countries. Critics claim that these new global health resources go to pet concerns of donors and often would be better deployed by a multilateral body like the WHO. But it seems unlikely that the resources, which represent a net increase in global health funding, would otherwise be available to serve the broader WHO mandate. The Gates Foundation provided the initial impetus for GAVI with a US$ 750 million pledge, and the Group of Eight governments (Canada, France, Germany, Italy, Japan, Russia, United Kingdom, United States) specifically bypassed the United Nations in launching the Global Fund in 2002.

Vertical funds empower diverse stakeholders, unlike the WHO, which invests only governments with the authority to coordinate policies and, at times, collective actions. The Global Fund's board includes voting members from civil society, the private sector, and the Gates Foundation – as well as representatives from developing and donor countries. It also includes as nonvoting members such partners such as the WHO and the World Bank. GAVI also has a multistake-holder board, which includes as permanent voting members the Gates Foundation, UNICEF, the WHO, the World Bank, and 18 rotating members from developing and donor country governments, vaccine makers, and civil society. Enfranchising nongovernment actors has engendered greater legitimacy for GAVI and the Global Fund among those groups (6).

These initiatives are funded entirely by voluntary contributions, whereas the WHO and the World Bank financial models are based on assessed contributions, despite the growing number of voluntary donations to the WHO. The Global Fund receives voluntary contributions from governments, individuals, businesses, and private foundations. GAVI relies on donor contributions to support the development and manufacture of vaccines. Governments are the more significant source of funding, but solely through voluntary mechanisms. GAVI and the Global Fund do not work directly in recipient countries, unlike the WHO and the World Bank, which work through government agencies and have offices and personnel in recipient countries.

The Global Fund relies on country coordinating mechanisms to develop and submit grant proposals and choose organizations to implement them. These mechanisms usually include representatives from the applicant country's government, local and international NGOs, interested donors and private sector representatives, and people who have the targeted disease. GAVI funds national governments, which use the resources to increase vaccine coverage. The Global Fund and GAVI derive legitimacy from their effectiveness in improving specifically defined health outputs and outcomes, unlike the WHO and World Bank, which stand on their status as inclusive, participatory intergovernmental bodies.

3. Moving toward health systems. Vertical funds continue to proliferate, and targeted contributions are still the bulk of WHO donor funding. But advanced and developing countries are increasingly focusing on the need for robust primary care and strong hospital systems – a horizontal approach.

Ebola's spread across West Africa shows the need for stronger health systems, not only to provide maternal and child health care and confront noncommunicable diseases such as cancer and heart ailments, but also to detect and treat infectious diseases. Ethiopia, for example, established programs to build comprehensive health systems funded by increased domestic investment and donor support.

Vertical funds, though, have stayed out of efforts to strengthen health systems or ensure health care for all members of society (universal health coverage). For the most part these donors believe domestic resources are growing fast enough to enable recipient countries to strengthen their health systems and provide universal health coverage. They also worry that governments would use new funds as an excuse to reduce their health investment. National programs must be country led, these donors believe, and designed domestically because of differences among health systems (for instance, whether a country already has a domestic private care delivery system), domestic insurance markets, and government approaches to prevention of noncommunicable diseases. Many donors are also wary of further fragmenting global health governance. But the rapid spread of the Ebola virus in West Africa highlighted the difficulties that poorly funded health systems had in identifying, then containing the disease. The United States has pledged more than US$ 250 million and the United Kingdom more than US$ 200 to support the response to the outbreak, some which is destined to improving health systems. Whether the Ebola crisis will elicit more sustained contributions from vertical funders to improve health systems is unclear.

4. Rise of emerging markets. In recent years, emerging market economies have demanded a greater role in multilateral institutions – from the IMF to the United Nations. That new assertiveness has spilled over into global health, where the major emerging market economies are playing a role that reflects both their domestic needs and their constraints. When the most economically advanced emerging market economies – Brazil, Russia, India and China (BRICs) – have engaged in the area of global health, it has generally been in issue-specific areas, such as access to essential medicines or technological cooperation, such as in TB treatment.

Regional concerns also appear to drive engagement in international cooperation and have given rise to regional health-related bodies in Africa, Asia, and Latin America. Since its launch in 2002, for example, the African Union has involved member states' health ministers in such regional health issues as infectious diseases, health financing, food security, and nutrition. Brazil, India, and South Africa have agreed to work together to coordinate international outreach on health and medicine. Whether these developments will strengthen the WHO – with regional bodies acting largely as WHO adjuncts – or chip away at its authority is unclear.

Notably, global health takes a backseat to other international issues, such as financial policies and national security, in China, India, and Russia. Brazil has embraced health issues as central to its foreign policy agenda, but – as measured by its participation in the Global Fund at least – has not stepped up financially. The Global Fund directors continually call on emerging market economies to shoulder some of the financial burden of fighting HIV/AIDS, TB, and malaria, but Brazil, which has received US$ 45 million in grants, has contributed only US$ 200,000. The story is similar with other BRICs. India has received US$ 1.1 billion and donated only US$ 10 million; China has received US$ 2 billion but donated only US$ 16 million. Russia's record is better: US$ 354 million received and US$ 254 million donated. During the global financial crisis, hard-hit advanced economies scaled back or even eliminated their commitments to the Global Fund. The BRICs weathered the crisis better than many advanced economies. Their failure to step up commitments to the Global Fund (or to GAVI) since the crisis raises questions about their long-term commitment to global health leadership.

How long should the BRICs, the four largest emerging market economies, continue to receive development assistance for health? India is the largest recipient of external health funding, China the 10th largest, and Brazil the 15th largest. At issue is whether aid should continue to subsidize countries that can arguably afford to provide at least basic health care and that have an increasing economic interest in halting infectious diseases, whether old scourges like TB or newer concerns like the avian flu virus. But despite their middle-income status, Brazil, China, and India remain relatively poor in *per capita* terms and must focus on economic growth. Because they also face massive health problems, donors still believe that continued health assistance is justified. But multilateral institutions and bilateral donors must continually examine whether middle-income countries should continue to receive aid that might better be used in poorer countries.

A key lesson from the Ebola crisis is the need for a strong, organized global response and an authoritative, well-funded WHO to lead it. to lead it. Whether the outbreak impels member states and other powerful stakeholders to strengthen the WHO's resources and authority or to set up another institution to fight disease outbreaks will be the critical global governance issue of the next few years.

Acknowledgement: *Originally published as: Devi Sridhar and Chelsea Clinton: Overseeing global health. Reprinted from the magazine of the International Monetary Fund (Finance & Development 2014; 51: 26-29).*

References:

1. World Health Organization (WHO). Proposed Programme Budget 2014–2015. Geneva: WHO, 2013.
2. New York Times. Cuts at WHO hurt response to Ebola crisis. 3 Sept 2014.
3. Clift C. What's the World Health Organization for? Final Report from the Centre on Global Health Security Working Group on Health Governance. London: Royal Institute of International Affairs, Chatham House, 2014.
4. Gostin LO. Global health law. Cambridge, Massachusetts: Harvard University Press, 2014.
5. Sridhar D. Who sets the global health research agenda? The challenge of multi-bi financing. PLoS Med 2012; 9:e1001312.
6. Wallace Brown G. Safeguarding deliberative global governance: The case of the Global Fund to Fight AIDS, Tuberculosis and Malaria. Rev Int Studies 2010; 36:511–530.

CHAPTER 27.

Recent shifts in global governance

As the 2010 Global Burden of Disease study confirmed, non-communicable diseases (NCDs) (primarily cardiovascular disease, cancer, chronic respiratory disease, and diabetes) are now the major cause of death and disability across the world (1). In 1990, 47% of disability-adjusted life years worldwide were attributable to communicable, maternal, neonatal, and nutritional deficits, 43% to NCDs, and 10% to injuries. By 2010, this had shifted to 35%, 54%, and 11%, respectively. Over 80% of NCD-related deaths occur in low and middle-income countries, with lower socio-economic groups the worst affected in terms of morbidity, mortality, and loss of economic opportunity (2). These figures do not account for the health and economic burdens of the wide range and prevalence of mental health conditions, which are seen by many as leading NCDs.

The increasing importance of NCDs has several implications for development. First, unlike most acute infectious diseases, the often chronic and debilitating course of NCDs impedes social and economic development, deepening inequalities, and initiates a cycle of disability and health costs-related poverty (3,4). Second, as most NCDs share common major risk factors and present similar challenges for clinical management, an integrated response is required, avoiding the health care *"silos"* that have arisen as a consequence of the narrow focus on HIV, malaria, and tuberculosis (TB) by international donors: well-funded projects that operate in isolation from national health systems may fail to address wider health care needs (5,6).

Fifteen years ago, in the wake of rising concerns over the lack of progress in reducing global poverty, all 189 UN Member States committed themselves to eight goals aimed at reducing poverty (7). Yet despite the evidence of a strong association between NCDs and development, these diseases and their shared risk factors were not included in the Millennium Development Goals (MDGs) (8).

As the 2015 deadline for achieving the MDGs approaches, a new development agenda is being mapped out to advance the progress made towards the MDGs while addressing remaining gaps and meeting the complex political and economic governance challenges of the post-2015 landscape. Will the new *Sustainable Development Goals* (SDGs) be able to respond effectively to the rising tide of NCDs? In this paper we examine three major trends in global governance and their implications for post-2015 progress relating to NCDs.

1. Trend 1: Rise of the emerging economies. As we move into the second decade of the 21st century, global power is shifting yet again, two decades after the changes that followed the collapse of the USSR.

The power of a few rich countries (notably the USA, United Kingdom, Germany, and France) to shape the global agenda is being challenged by the growing economic power, of what have been termed the BRICS countries (Brazil, Russia, India, China, and South Africa) and the so-called CIVETs (Colombia, Indonesia, Vietnam, Egypt, and Turkey).

Table 27-1. *BRIC financial contribution to key global health institutions and amount received from Global Fund and GAVI (refs. 14-19). Displayed sums are cumulative to year 2012, expressed in US$ millions).*

	GLOBAL FUND CONTRI-BUTIONS	GLOBAL FUND AMOUNT RECEIVED	GAVI CONTRI-BUTIONS	GAVI AMOUNT RECEIVED	WHO CORE CONTRI-BUTIONS	WHO EXTRA-BUDGETARY CONTRI-BUTIONS
Brazil	0.0	39.1	0.0	0.0	7.5	0.03
Russia	297.0	372.0	24.0	0.0	7.4	6.1
India	10.0	1,019.9	0.0	94.0	2.5	0.015
China	25.0	763.3	0.0	38.7	14.8	0.4
S Africa	10.3	350.6	6.0	0.0	1.8	0.0

What does this mean for NCDs? On the one hand, NCDs are rising on the agendas of established international bodies. In 2011 the United Nations held a High Level Meeting on NCDs, only the second time that it had elevated health to this level (9). The first such meeting was on HIV/AIDS, following which the G8 took up the torch, creating new institutions such as the Global Fund to Fight AIDS, Tuberculosis and Malaria, and prioritizing certain issues such as universal access to anti-retrovirals. Yet it is not clear whether the High Level Meeting on NCDs, which was driven by a group of small countries, many in the Caribbean, will lead to similarly sustained action. Moreover, the G8 have not considered global health in either their 2011 or 2012 agendas (10) although the 2010 G8 meeting did result in the Muskoka Accord for maternal health. To the extent that health will feature on the G8's 2013 agenda, it is likely to be in the context of liberalization of trade in health services. Although the locus of global decision-making is considered to be shifting from the G8 to the G20, it is not clear that the latter body is willing to assume even the limited interest in global health governance seen with the G8 (11), despite hopes from the health community that it would do so (12). Moreover, it is not apparent from their previous engagement in global health debates that newer G20 states have a major interest in NCDs. Thus, having more emerging economies at the table does not necessarily mean clearer articulation of an effective NCD response.

Health has also been largely absent from the agendas of the BRICS countries, now forming a semi-official grouping. While they are increasingly influential in finance and trade, they have had only limited influence thus far in global health. The fact that the relatively economically stable BRICS have not stepped up their commitments to the Global Fund, the GAVI Alliance, or WHO has raised questions about their commitment to global health leadership in the long term (**Table 27-1**) (13–19). Domestically, Russia and to a lesser extent China, are the only two BRICS countries as of yet to address NCDs in a substantive manner.

There is some evidence of global health achieving a higher priority elsewhere, exemplified by the *Foreign Policy and Global Health Initiative*, which draws its leadership largely from the South and consists of five Southern (Brazil, Indonesia, Mexico, Senegal, and Thailand) and two Northern (France and Norway) countries. Yet, with the exception of the *Caribbean Community* (CARICOM) (20), it is uncertain whether the rise of newly emerging economies will mean global engagement with NCDs.

In summary, although emerging economies are clearly influential in global governance, there is little evidence of commitment to the NCD agenda, and it does not follow that they will advance the interests of poorer countries – or even health. To the extent that these countries do engage in health, it has been issue-specific, such as on access to essential medicines, technological cooperation, or on *Trade-Related Aspects of Intellectual Property Rights* (TRIPs) – all areas where health is incidental to trade concerns. Furthermore, global health engagement by emerging powers is often driven by regional concerns, which explains the re-invigoration and creation of regional bodies in health, particularly in Latin America. In this changing environment there is a danger of health slipping off the agenda of the traditional economic and political powers but not being taken up by the emerging ones.

2. Trend 2: Rise (and fall) of multi-bi financing. Over the past decade, most of the growth in multilateral funding has been through the channel of *"multi-bi aid"* (21). This refers to the practice of donors choosing to route non-core funding, earmarked for specific sectors, themes, countries, or regions, through multilateral agencies. At first glance the funding looks multilateral, but upon closer inspection, it is essentially bilateral. Examples of multi-bi aid include voluntary contributions within the WHO, trust funds within World Bank, the Global Fund, and the GAVI Alliance. Since 2002, global health donors have increasingly prioritized multi-bi aid at the expense of more traditional forms of multilateral aid as a proportion of all development assistance for health (22). Multi-bi aid increased as a proportion of all aid at a rate of approximately 1.5–2.0 percentage points per year over this time period (22).

The rise of multi-bi aid has three implications for the NCD agenda. First, an analysis of the WHO's expenditures shows a significant misalignment with the burden of disease, both globally and at regional levels, with the additional voluntary resources least well aligned (23). In 2008–2009 of the WHO's regular budget, 25% of funds were allocated to infectious disease, 8% for NCDs, and roughly 4.7% for injuries, which when compared with the global distribution of DALYs noted above indicates a disproportionate share of resources going to the first of these at the expense of the remaining two. However, the WHO's extra-budgetary funding for 2008–2009 is even further out of alignment, with 60% allocated primarily to infectious diseases, while only 3.9% was used for NCDs and 3.4% for injuries.

Second, the emergence of new multi-stakeholder global health funding institutions such as the Global Fund and the GAVI Alliance has signaled a major shift in global cooperation, one in which voting rights and board membership is granted to the private sector and philanthropic organizations and legitimacy is claimed through improving specific measurable health outcomes (21). Given the aggressive tactics the tobacco, alcohol, and food industries have used to oppose regulation addressing key NCD risk factors, it will be difficult to have industry at the table while addressing the root causes of the pandemic (24).

Third, an analysis by Grepin and Sridhar shows that the movement towards multi-bi aid reversed since the onset of the global financial crises with donors decreasing their contributions to the GAVI Alliance, the Global Fund, and UNAIDS since 2008 (22). This is particularly true of the ten largest global health donors, where this channel of funding decreased by nearly 6% of all development assistance for health during 2008–2009. Thus, it is unlikely that in the current financial climate new funds will be available to address NCDs. Given this situation, national governments will have to bear almost all the costs of responding to NCDs and will have little external incentive to prioritize these diseases (25).

3. Trend 3: Institutional proliferation. Since 2000, more and more global health institutions and initiatives have been created such as the GAVI Alliance, the Global Fund, and the Global Alliance for Improved Nutrition. However,

Table 27-2. *Political history of Universal Health Coverage (UHC).*

DATE	EVENT
1975	Health for All. (WHO)
1978	Declaration of Primary Health Care, Alma Ata. (WHO/UNICEF)
1987	Bamako Initiative on Health Financing. (UNICEF/WHO)
1993	World Development Report 1993: Investing in Health. (World Bank)
2000	World Health Report 2000. Health systems: Improving performance. (WHO)
2000	UN Millennium Declaration
2001	Adoption of Millennium Development Goals
2002	Commission on Macro-Economics and Health. (WHO)
2005	Paris Declaration on Aid Effectiveness. (OECD-DAC)
2005	GAVI Alliance Health Systems Funding Window. (GAVI)
2006	Global Fund to fight AIDS, TB and Malaria Health Systems Funding Window. (Global Fund)
2007	International Health Partnerships Plus (IHP+)
2007	Everybody's Business. Strengthening Health Systems to Improve Health Outcomes. WHO's Framework for Action. (WHO)
2007	Inaugural meeting of H8 (Health 8)
2008	World Health Report 2008. Primary Health Care: Now more than ever. (WHO)
2008	G8 Commitment to strengthening Health Systems, Toyako.
2009	High Level Taskforce on Innovative Financing for Health Systems
2009	Health Systems Funding Platform. (Global Fund/GAVI/World Bank/WHO)
2010	World Health Report 2010. Health systems financing: The path to universal coverage. (WHO)
2010	1st Global Symposium on Health Systems Research, Montreux.
2011	Universal Health Coverage, WHO General Assembly
2012	Bangkok Statement on Universal Health Coverage, Prince Mahidol Award Conference
2012	Mexico International Forum on Universal Health Coverage. (WHO)
2012	2nd Global Symposium on Health Systems Research, Beijing.
2012	UN General Assembly: Universal Health Coverage declared a UN global goal.
2013	World Health Report 2013. Research for universal health coverage. (WHO)

they remain largely uncoordinated, focused on vertical disease-specific programs, and lack rigorous assessment (26,27). Initiatives designed to support coherence among global players such as the International Health Partnership (IHP+) and Health 8 (H8) have remained largely focused on vertical global health program delivery rather than taking a role in leading governance for health as a global public good (28).

This institutional proliferation has two implications for the future NCD agenda. First, only a handful of these actors are interested in or focusing on the drivers of the NCD epidemic. According to the Institute for Health Metrics and Evaluation, only US$ 185 million of the US$ 28.2 billion spent globally on development assistance for health in 2010 was dedicated to NCDs (29). Donors spent US$ 300 for each year lost to disability from HIV/AIDS, US$ 200 for malaria, and US$ 100 for TB, but less than US$ 1 for NCDs. Nearly half of the development assistance for NCDs in 2010 derived from a single source: the Bloomberg Family Foundation (30).

Second, the drivers of NCDs are intricately connected with the policies of non-health sectors (30). Multi-sector participation has already begun on health issues at the state-level through inter-ministerial working groups focused on global health, the reduction of health inequities, and HIV/AIDS prevention in Australia, Canada, India, Norway, Sweden, Switzerland, Thailand, Uganda, United Kingdom, and United States (31–33). Institutional incentive structures to engage other sectors in negotiations about health are crucial to raising the profile of health-related priorities in other policy communities at the all levels of governance. However, the WHO and other global health agencies presently lack the resources and mechanisms to meaningfully participate in policy issues like trade, agriculture, security, and climate change (29).

4. Post-2015: Universal health coverage and healthy life expectancy. If NCDs are to be included in the new health goals, it seems most likely to be through the sector-specific target of universal health coverage (UHC) or access or the broad umbrella of healthy life expectancy. UHC has received particular prominence recently (**Table 27-2**). In January 2012, the Bangkok Statement on UHC committed to *"raise universal health coverage on the national, regional and global agendas, and to advocate the importance of integrating it into forthcoming United Nations and other high-level meetings related to health or social development"* (34). In April 2012 the Mexico City Political Declaration on UHC emphasized universal coverage as *"an essential component of sustainable development"* and its inclusion *"an important element in the international development agenda"* (35). In June 2012 the Rio+20 resolution explicitly recognized UHC, seeking *"to strengthen health systems towards the provision of equitable universal coverage"* (36). Later in 2012, a WHO Discussion Paper on the Post 2015 health agenda, identified UHC as a *"way of bringing all programmatic interests under an inclusive umbrella"* (37). On 12 December 2012 UHC received unequivocal endorsement from the UN General Assembly (including the United States) in approving a resolution on UHC, confirming the *"intrinsic role of health in achieving international sustainable development goals"* (38).

As the above developments indicate, the post-2015 health discussions have been centered on UHC and its link to WHO's revitalization of Primary Health Care. In our opinion, this enthusiasm has been tempered by confusion as to what UHC actually is, as well as the fear of failure from previous attempts such as *"Health for All"*. For example, in 2005 the World Health Assembly officially defined the achievement of UHC as *"access to key promotive, preventive, curative and rehabilitative health interventions for all at an affordable cost, thereby achieving equity in access"* (39). Yet, elsewhere, UHC has been construed as national service delivery, national service coverage, financial protection, and national health insurance and related reforms. We believe that it is unclear what health services UHC covers (e.g., whether it fully covers public health services such as sanitation, vector abatement, and tobacco control), and questions arise over whether UHC includes only services within a state's health sector or services and interventions outside the health sector (40,41).

If UHC is to become a new development goal, we argue that baselines for achievement of UHC must be agreed and developed in post-MDG negotiations and adapted to country circumstance, fiscal realities, and community priority. Currently it is not clear that policy-makers have considered how to integrate the response to NCDs with the scaling up of basic care through strengthening primary health care. For example, the USSR was successful in scaling up measures against infectious diseases, but failed to tackle the key drivers of NCDs (42). Most importantly, we feel that UHC will have limited impact on the rising tide of NCDs without targets and funding to reduce risk factors – requiring a prevention, public health, and *"all of society"* approach.

Recent discussions in Botswana highlight a move towards the broad umbrella of healthy life expectancy (HLE), or *"maximizing healthy lives"*, measured as *"reducing healthy years of life lost"* (43). But will HLE result in a better response to NCDs? Civil society organizations have started to champion HLE as the best vehicle to address the social determinants of health, thus creating space to address the root causes of the NCD crisis. On the other hand, HLE could also be used to push for individual responsibility for health and reframing unhealthy behaviors as personal choices, ignoring the circumstances within which those choices are made. HLE also makes it harder to tie health outcomes to state or institutional responsibility. Thus, could NCDs be addressed in such health goals? At face value, yes. But it is not clear in our view whether UHC or HLE as currently conceived will adequately incorporate the prevention and treatment of NCDs, which require alternative health system mechanisms and clear responsibility placed on the state for ensuring a healthy environment.

In the post-2015 debate, almost no attention has been given to the global governance structures necessary to support the attainment of the new goals. It is generally agreed that we need 21st-century innovative structures that go beyond the WHO *"command and control"* model, but little detail is given on institutional responsibility, monitoring, and evaluation and accountability (44). For NCDs in particular, the global response requires more than new funding or financing mechanisms. It requires global regulation of the key vectors of the epidemic, as well as linkages between health and the other areas discussed as part of the SDGs agenda such as agriculture and food security, environment, trade, urban development, energy policies, education, poverty alleviation, and gender equity. This necessity points to both the key role of the WHO as well as the inherent limitation in making the agency the focal point for the response. The WHO is the only global health body with the power to create international law, and given its success in legislating against tobacco (The Framework Convention on Tobacco Control), similar *"hard law"* mechanisms for other main drivers of the NCD epidemic such as alcohol and processed food are certainly feasible (45). At the same time, for multi-sectoral convergence to become a reality, various agencies of the UN must act in concert to catalyze, support, and monitor such collaboration (9).

While the epidemiological evidence is clear on the rising burden of NCDs across geographic boundaries, the current post-2015 discussions and larger global governance trends create challenges to addressing this burden effectively. These political and economic influences need to be considered carefully if NCDs are not to be left behind again.

Acknowledgement: *Originally published as: Devi Sridhar, Claire E. Brolan, Shireen Durrani, Jennifer Edge, Lawrence O. Gostin, Peter Hill and Martin McKee: Recent shifts in global governance: implications for the response to non-communicable diseases. Reprinted with permission from Public Library of Science (PLoS) under Creative Commons Attribution License (PLoS Medicine 2013; 10:e1001487). The authors thank Robert Marten for his comments and the Go4Health consortium members for their feedback on an earlier draft presented at the Dhaka virtual meeting.*

References

1. Horton R. GBD 2010: understanding disease, injury and risk. Lancet 2012; 380:2053–2054.
2. Commission on the Social Determinants of Health. Closing the gap in a generation: health equity through actions on the social determinants of health. Final Report of the Commission on the Social Determinants of Health. Geneva: World Health Organization, 2008.
3. World Health Organization. Commission on the Social Determinants of Health. Geneva: World Health Organization, 2008.
4. Suhrcke M, Rocco L, Mckee M, Mazzuoco S, Urban D, et al. Economic consequences of non-communicable diseases and injuries in the Russian Federation. London: European Observatory on Health Care Systems, 2007.
5. Spicer N, Walsh A. 10 best resources on ... the current effects of global health initiatives on country health systems. Health Policy Plann 2012; 27:265–269.
6. World Health Organization Maximizing Positive Synergies Collaborative Group. An assessment of interactions between global health initiatives and country health systems. Lancet 2009; 373:2137-2169.

7. United Nations. Road map towards the implementation of the United Nations Millennium Declaration: Report of the Secretary-General. New York: United Nations, 2001. Document A/56/ 326.

8. Rechel B, Shapo L, McKee M, Health, Nutrition, Population Group, ECA, the World Bank. Are the health Millennium Development Goals appropriate for Eastern Europe and Central Asia? Health Policy 2005; 73:339–351.

9. Sridhar D, Morrison JS, Piot P. Expectations for the United Nations high-level meeting on noncommunicable diseases. Bull World Health Organ 2011; 89:471.

10. Glassman A. What happened to health at the G-8? Washington: Center for Global Development, 2012. (Available from: http://blogs.cgdev.org/ globalhealth/2012/03/ what-happened-to-health-at-the-g8.php; Accessed: 22 January 2013).

11. Woods N, Betts A, Prantl J, Sridhar D. Transforming global governance for the 21st century: a UNDP Occasional Paper. 2013. (Available from: hdr.undp.org/en/reports/global/hdr2013/ occasional.../03_Woods.pdf; Accessed: 25 May 2013).

12. Chatham House. What is next for the G20? Investing in health and development. London: The Royal Institute of International Affairs, 2010.

13. Bliss K. Key players in global health: how Brazil, Russia, India, China and South Africa are influencing the game. Washington: Center for Strategic and International Studies, 2010.

14. Global Fund Pledges and Contributions. (Available from: http://www.theglobalfund. org/en/; Accessed: 25 May 2013).

15. Global Fund Grant Portfolio: Portfolio Overview. (Available from: http://portfolio. theglobalfund. org/en/Home/Index; Accessed: 25 May 2013).

16. Annual donor contributions to GAVI 2000-31 as of 31 December 2012. (Available from: http:// www.gavialliance.org/funding/donor-contributions-pledges/; Accessed: 25 May 2013).

17. GAVI disbursements to countries by type of support and year (2000–December 31, 2012). (Available from: http://www.gavialliance.org/results/disbursements/; Accessed: 25 May 2013).

18. Assessed contributions payable by member states and associate members. (Available from: http:// www.who.int/about/resources_planning/2012_ 2013_AC_summary.pdf; Accessed: 25 May 2013).

19. Schedule 4: Summary of voluntary contributions receivable – non-current and current (by age and contributor) as at 31st December 2012. (Available from: http://www.who. int/about/resources_ planning/A66_29add1-en.pdf; Accessed: 25 May 2013).

20. CARICOM Secretariat. CARICOM Summit on Chronic Non-Communicable Diseases (CNCDs). Port-of-Spain: CARICOM, 2007. (Available from: http://www.caricom.org/ jsp/community/chronic_ non_communicable_diseases/summit_chronic_ non-communicable_diseases_index.jsp; Accessed: 24 March 2013).

21. Sridhar D. Who sets the global health research agenda? The challenge of multi-bi financing. PLoS Med 2012; 9:e1001312.

22. Grepin K, Sridhar D. Multi-bi aid and effects of the 2008–10 economic crisis on voluntary development assistance for health contributions: a time series analysis. Lancet 2012; Abstracts: 3.

23. Stuckler D, King L, Robinson H, McKee M. WHO's budgetary allocations and burden of disease: a comparative analysis. Lancet 2008; 372:1563–1569.

24. Stuckler D, Nestle M. Big food, food systems, and global health. PLoS Med 2012; 9: e1001242.

25. Sridhar D, Gomez E. Health financing in Brazil, Russia and India: What role does the international community play? Health Policy Plann 2011; 26:12–24.
26. Garrett L. The challenge of global health. Foreign Affairs 2007; Jan/Feb Essay.
27. Unwin T. Partnerships in development practice: evidence from multi-stakeholder ICT4D partnership practice in Africa. Paris: UNESCO, 2005.
28. Kickbusch I. The 10 challenges of global health governance. Global Health Europe, 2010. (Available from: http://www.globalhealtheurope.org/index.php?option =com_content&view=article&id=306:the-10-challenges-of-global-health-governance&catid=60: your-opinion&Itemid=108; Accessed: 24 Jan 2013).
29. Institute for Health Metrics and Evaluation. Financing global health 2012: the end of the golden age? Seattle: IHME, 2012.
30. Bollyky T. Developing symptoms: non-communicable diseases go global. Foreign Affairs 2012; May/ Jun Essay.
31. Primarolo D, Malloch-Brown M, Lewis I. Health is global: a UK government strategy for 2008–2013. Lancet 2008; 373:443–444.
32. Torgersen T, Giaever O, Stigen O. Developing an intersectoral national strategy to reduce social inequities in health: the Norwegian case. Oslo, 2007.
33. Canada's Federal Initiative to Address HIV/ AIDS. Federal initiative to address HIV/ AIDS in Canada: Implementation Evaluation Report. Ottawa: Public Health Agency of Canada, 2009.
34. Bangkok Statement on Universal Health Coverage. Prince Mahidol Award Conference, 28 Jan 2012. (Available from: http://www.pmaconference. mahidol.ac.th/ index.php?option=com_content&view =article&id=525:2012-bkk-statement-final&catid=981:cat-2012-conference; Accessed: 16 Jun 2013).
35. Mexico City Political Declaration on Universal Health Coverage. Forum on universal health coverage: sustaining universal health coverage, sharing experiences and promoting progress. Mexico City, 2012. (Available from: http://www.who.int/health-systems/topics/financing/MexicoCityPoliticalDeclaration UniversalHealthCoverage. pdf).
36. United Nations. The Future We Want: outcome document adopted at Rio+20, 2012. UN Doc. A/CONF/216/l.1. (Available from: https://rio20.un. org/sites/rio20.un.org/ files/a-conf.216l-1_ english.pdf.pdf; Accessed: 30 Jun 2012).
37. World Health Organization. Discussion paper positioning health in the post-2015 development agenda. Geneva: WHO, 2012. (Available from: http://www. worldwe-want2015.org/health).
38. Oxfam. UN Resolution on Universal Health Coverage, 2012. (Available from: http:// www.oxfam. org/en/pressroom/reactions/un-resolution-universal-health-coverage; Accessed: 12 Dec 2012).
39. World Health Assembly. Sustainable health financing, universal coverage and social health insurance. 2005. (Available from: http://www.who.int/health_ financing/docu-ments/cov-wharesolution5833/en/; Accessed: 16 Jun 2013).
40. Editorial. Universal health coverage: access to what? Lancet 2009; 374:1946.
41. Fan VF, Glassman A, Savedoff WD, et al. A post-2015 development goal for health: should it be universal health coverage? BMJ Group Blogs, 2012.
42. McKee M. The health crisis in the USSR: looking behind the facade. Int J Epidemiol 2006; 35:1398–1399.

43. World We Want. Health in the post-2015 agenda: report of the Global Thematic Consultation on Health, 2013. (Available from: http://www. worldwewant2015.org/health; Accessed: 1 Jun 2013).

44. Ottersen OP, Frenk J, Horton R. The Lancet-Oslo Commission on Global Governance for Health. Lancet 2011; 378:1612–1613.

45. Gostin LO. A Framework Convention on Global Health: health for all, justice for all. JAMA 2012; 307:2087–2092.

CHAPTER 28.

Universal health coverage and the right to health: From legal principle to post-2015 indicators

1. Universal Health Coverage. Universal Health Coverage (UHC) rooted in the right to health is widely considered one of the front-runners to represent the health element of the post-2015 development agenda (1). On 12 December 2012 UHC received unequivocal endorsement from the UN General Assembly (including the United States) with the approval of a resolution on UHC that confirmed the *"intrinsic role of health in achieving international sustainable development goals"* (2). Yet despite UHC's growing prominence in the post-2015 agenda, there is not yet any single agreed definition of what it is and there is ongoing discussion about what indicators might measure progress towards it (3). While the 2005 World Health Assembly's definition of its achievement as *"access to key promotive, preventive, curative and rehabilitative health interventions for all at an affordable cost, thereby achieving equity in access"* (4) captures key elements and the World Health Report 2010 identified the three dimensions of who, what, and which proportion of the costs are covered (5), neither are easily operationalised for routine use. A notable exception is the 2014 World Health Organization/World Bank report which attempts to fill this gap by discussing possible targets and indicators from the three dimensions related to service delivery and financial protection (6).

In this paper we complement the WHO/World Bank approach by grounding UHC in the right to health. The right to health framework is a valuable starting point to develop measurable and achievable indicators of both process and outcome that can inform the ongoing post-2015 global negotiations and implementation as well as national debates on how to integrate UHC into domestic policies.

2. Six principles derived from the right to health. Our indicators of UHC are based on six principles pertaining to the right to health, as specified in General Comment 14 of the Committee on Economic, Social and Cultural Rights, which is tasked with monitoring compliance with the International Covenant on Economic, Social and Cultural Rights (7). This approach means that we can draw on a body of jurisprudence and authoritative interpretation of international human rights law that identifies the rights of individuals and the obligations of those who should secure their rights.

The first principle is that all states, no matter how poor, should offer a minimum core level of provision that should include *"at least the following obligations: (a) To ensure the right of access to health facilities, goods and services on a non-discriminatory basis, especially for vulnerable or marginalized groups; … (d) To provide essential drugs, as from time to time defined under the (World Health Organization) Action Programme on Essential Drugs; (e) To ensure equitable distribution of all health facilities, goods and services; (f) To adopt and implement a national public health strategy and plan of action, on the basis of epidemiological evidence, addressing the health concerns of the whole population; …"* (7).

The second principle is progressive realization of the right to health. This requires countries to move forward towards the right to health and, by implication, not to adopt measures that are regressive. In addition, each state should make progress *"to the maximum of its available resources"* (7). This implies an explicit comparison of what is being provided and what resources are available. If states claim they cannot provide health care to a level seen elsewhere, they are obliged to demonstrate why. And if states are able to move beyond their core obligations, they have a legal obligation to do so: core obligations constitute a universal floor, not a ceiling.

The third principle is that interventions should be cost-effective to maximise the benefit from available resources, derived from non-discrimination. *"Expensive curative health services which are often accessible only to a small, privileged fraction of the population, rather than primary and preventive health care benefiting a far larger part of the population"*, have been qualified as *"(i)nappropriate health resource allocation (that) can lead to discrimination that may not be overt"*, by the Committee on Economic, Social and Cultural Rights (Committee) in its General Comment on the right to health (7).

The fourth principle is that of shared responsibility among states. Article 2(1) of the International Covenant on Economic, Social and Cultural Rights prescribes that states *"take steps, individually and through international assistance and co-operation, especially economic and technical, to the maximum of its available resources, …"* (emphasis added), and when the Committee elaborated states' core obligations arising from the right to health, it explicitly referred to international assistance: *"For the avoidance of any doubt, the Committee wishes to emphasize that it is particularly incumbent on States parties and other actors in a position to assist, to provide "international assistance and cooperation, especially economic and technical" which enable developing countries to fulfil their core and other obligations…"* (7). Thus, there is an obligation on rich states to prioritize health care in their international assistance programmes.

The fifth principle is the imperative for participatory decision-making, the second derived from non-discrimination. National public health strategies and plans of action that states are required to adopt and implement *"shall be devised, and periodically reviewed, on the basis of a participatory and transparent process,"* according to the Committee on Economic, Social and Cultural Rights (7). Thus, *"the health concerns of the whole population"* should not simply be assessed from epidemiological data but should incorporate people's expressed priorities.

The sixth is that the needs of vulnerable or marginalized groups should be addressed explicitly, the last derived from non-discrimination. This derives from the statement by the Committee on Economic, Social and Cultural Rights that *"the process by which the strategy and plan of action are devised, as well as their content, shall give particular attention to all vulnerable or marginalized groups"* (7). Participation in the process of developing and monitoring national plans must specifically include marginalized populations in a meaningful way. Where particular health concerns disproportionately affect vulnerable or marginalized populations, it may be incumbent on the state to include interventions within its benefit package, even where the interventions needed are not considered cost-effective overall.

3. UHC indicators rooted in the right to health. The European Commission has set out criteria for any proposed post-2015 goals. They should be measurable, achievable and sustainable, and should consider the constraints of developing countries for improving health outcomes themselves (8). Bill Gates has also argued that the goals should be measurable, demonstrating tangible change in health status, but also operational, focused on extreme poverty and based in global consensus (9). There is a consensus on the right to health, as shown by the accession of all countries except South Sudan joining at least one treaty recognizing it (10). We now propose ten indicators that capture the achievement of the principles that flow from the right to health but which can also be operationalised to generate measureable, achievable, sustainable indicators.

The first is the existence of a legal mandate for universal health coverage in each country. This may take different forms, depending on the country's legal system, but its presence is easily determined. Thus, it may be incorporated in the constitution (as in South Africa), it may be established in national legislation, or it may exist because the country is one where the ratification of an international convention has direct effect in domestic law. These different instruments could be recorded in a proposed global health law repository (11). The existence of a legal basis is an important requirement for universal health coverage with empirical evidence illustrating that countries with such a mandate spend more on public health services (12).

The next three are the extent of coverage measured on three dimensions of depth (which services are covered), breadth (who is covered), and height (what proportion of the costs are covered) (5). The challenge then becomes how to operationalise these three dimensions. Currently available data on coverage of specific services refer largely to maternal and child health, such as antenatal care, delivery care and immunisation. This provides a starting point, but needs to be extended to other key areas of health care, such as non-communicable diseases, so as to include the main contributors to the burden of disease in a particular country. Breadth is arguably the simplest to measure, for example by asking in household surveys whether respondents consider that they are included in some insurance scheme or equivalent (although with the caveat that those least likely to be covered are least likely to be included in surveys, such as illegal migrants). This should also take account of equity, for example by capturing differences in coverage by wealth, gender or income quintile. This should also consider other markers of marginalization such as having a disability or being a member of an indigenous population. Height is also relatively straightforward and can be measured as a reduction in the share of out of pocket payments for health care below a fixed percentage, using data from the World Bank's Living Standards Measurement Surveys and similar household surveys.

The fifth indicator is the commitment of adequate resources to deliver universal health coverage. There is emerging evidence that the ability to deliver universal health care is associated with its ability to raise direct taxation (paper submitted). Accordingly, we propose the achievement of a fixed percentage of Gross National Product on health care, and not as in the Abuja Declaration (13), a percentage of government spending. We have considered, but rejected, the idea that the percentage should vary, from a low figure in the poorest countries to a higher one in the richest, as this would accentuate inequalities.

The sixth indicator relates to cost-effectiveness. Policy makers at national and sub-national levels have limited resources and must choose among many interventions that target different diseases and vulnerable populations (14). A possible indicator could be the use of expensive branded drugs when cheaper alternatives are available or the ratio of complex to basic items of equipment. However, cost-effectiveness of mortality reduction for the entire population does not necessarily mean that it will also be *"equitable"*, as these are two

Table 28-1. *Ten indicators for UHC based on the right to health.*

INDICATOR	UNDERLYING LEGAL PRINCIPLE	DATA SOURCE
1 The existence of a legal mandate for universal health coverage in the country	Minimum Core Obligation/ Progressive Realization	Global health law repository
2 The extent of coverage in terms of depth (which services are covered)	Minimum Core Obligation/ Progressive Realization	Household Survey Data
3 The extent of coverage in terms of breadth (who is insured) with attention to equity	Minimum Core Obligation/ Progressive Realization	Household Survey Data
4 The extent of coverage in terms of height (what proportion of costs are covered) with focus on reduction in share of out of pocket payments for healthcare	Minimum Core Obligation/ Progressive Realization	World Bank's Living Standards Measurement Surveys/Household Survey Data
5 The commitment of adequate resources to deliver UHC with focus on percentage of Gross National Product on healthcare	Minimum Core Obligation/ Progressive Realization	World Bank Statistics
6 Cost-effectiveness with attention to equity	Cost-effectiveness/ Non-discrimination	Data on use of branded/ generic drugs or high tech/ basic equipment
7 International assistance as a percentage of GDP	Shared Responsibility	OECD-DAC Database
8 Existence of an international development policy explicitly including specific provisions to promote and protect the right to health.	Shared Responsibility	
9 SARA assessment on participatory decision-making	Participatory Decision-Making/ Nondiscrimination	Extended SARA
10 SARA assessment on prioritisation of marginalised groups	Attention to Vulnerable and Marginalized Groups/Nondiscrimination	Extended SARA

separate dimensions. Deaths can be reduced in a highly cost-effective way when investments are targeting the wealthiest quintiles, just as when they are targeting the poorest. An appropriate indicator might be the number of deaths or disability-adjusted life years (DALYs) averted per cost of intervention scale-up in the poorest quintile of the population.

The next two indicators relate to financial and non-financial dimensions of shared responsibility. The first is international assistance as a percentage of GDP, using the widely accepted target of 0.7% of GDP. The second is the existence of an international development policy explicitly including specific provisions to promote and protect the right to health.

We finally consider the challenging issue of developing indicators for participatory decision-making, non-discrimination and prioritisation of marginalized groups. Rifkin, for example, notes that trying to capture these dimensions by indicators approved at the UN level may be meaningless or even counterproductive (15). Her main argument is that as soon as indicators are accepted, we are likely to see some tokenistic application of principles, which is likely to distract from the real issue, which is political willingness. The most feasible proposal is by O'Neill et al. to conduct *"Service Availability and Readiness"* assessments (SARA) as a baseline for UHC (16), and to be updated regularly as a way of monitoring progress. These underpin the ninth indicator, on participatory decision-making, and the tenth, on non-discrimination, and prioritisation of marginalised groups, adapted to the reality of each country.

4. Challenges in indicator development. Three major challenges face any exercise to set indicators post-2015: data availability as an essential criterion, the universality of targets, and the adaptation of global goals to local populations. Few developing countries have adequate data and there is growing recognition of the need for serious investment in data and sustainable information systems. These challenges should not be under-estimated and question the extent to which measuring progress made towards transformative goals can be achieved. Measurability will inevitably influence which targets and goals can be considered, thus potentially limiting the ambitious and transformative nature of the goals.

Second, universal goals may not capture the priorities of all countries. Spending time and money to collect data for indicators that are not relevant in specific contexts could lead to a neglect of problems associated with specific marginalised groups. In addition, developed countries have resisted universal goals given the political implications it has for their own domestic policies, in contrast to the MDGs which were applied to low and middle income countries (17).

Third, while some indicators might be universally relevant, such as maternal or child mortality, or life expectancy, others such as mortality from malaria are highly contingent. The choice of indicators may, therefore, directly affect people's health, meaning that peoples have the right to participate in deciding what the indicators are. While this should include decisions at the UN-level, as a practical and normative matter, to enable the most meaningful participation, it should also occur nationally (or even locally). And if the participation is to be meaningful nationally (or locally), then the results of the participation must have the possibility of having an impact, in this case, of affecting the nature of the indicator.

In this paper we have explicitly avoided setting specific targets to be achieved in terms of the individual indicators. Instead we note the principles that underpin any target setting exercise. Targets should be specific, measurable, accurate, realistic, and time bound (18). The process of determining targets will inevitably involve political considerations but it is also important that it is informed by technical ones. In some cases, the process is straightforward. Thus, we note that the target for the percentage of GDP spent on health proposed by the *Sustainable Development Solutions Network* is 5% (19). However, we also recognise that in the poorest countries this sum will be inadequate to provide universal coverage and will need to be supplemented by additional funds from development assistance. Crucially, we emphasise that whatever figure is chosen should be a minimum, not a maximum. A mid-term target might reasonably be to half the gap between the existing level of expenditure and the target. In other areas there is a need for modeling to determine feasible but challenging targets based on the starting conditions, effectiveness of policies to achieve the targets, and the time lags that apply.

Despite these challenges, for UHC to continue to gain momentum in the mainstream post-2015 agenda, attention must be given to the development of indicators that are universally accepted, implementable, and based on an agreed legal framework. It is only through law, and the right to health, that individuals and populations can claim entitlements to health services and that corresponding governmental obligations can be established and enforced (20). A crucial next step is to build on the WHO/World Bank report to measuring UHC by complementing with the right to health and the values that such a basis brings with it.

Acknowledgement: Originally published as: Devi Sridhar, Martin McKee, Gorik Ooms, Claudia Beiersmann, Eric Friedman, Hebe Gouda, Peter Hill and Albrecht Jahn: Universal health coverage and the right to health: From legal principle to post-2015 indicators. Reprinted with permission from SAGE journals (International Journal of Health Services, 2015; 45: 495-506). The authors thank Genevie Fernandes for her research assistance and Go4Health consortium members for their feedback on an earlier draft presented at the Antwerp workshop.

References:

1. Vega J. Universal health coverage: the post-2015 development agenda. Lancet 2013; 381:179-180.
2. UN General Assembly. Adopting consensus text, General Assembly encourages member states to plan, pursue transition of national health care systems towards universal coverage. 2012; Document GA/11326. (Available from: http://www.un.org/News/Press/docs//2012/ga11326.doc.htm; Accessed: 1 Apr 2014).
3. O'Connell T, Rasanathan K, Chopra M. What does universal health coverage mean? Lancet 2013; 383:277-279.
4. World Health Organization. Sustainable health financing, universal coverage and social health insurance. World Health Assembly A/5820. 2005. (Available from: http://apps.who.int/iris/bitstream/10665/20302/1/A58_20-en.pdf?ua=1; Accessed: 1 Apr 2014).
5. World Health Organization. Health systems financing: The path to universal coverage. Geneva: World Health Organization, 2010.
6. World Health Organization/World Bank. Monitoring Progress towards universal health coverage at country and global levels. Geneva: World Health Organization, 2014.
7. UN Committee on Economic, Social and Cultural Rights. General Comment No. 14: The Right to the Highest Attainable Standard of Health. E/C.12/2000/4, 2000. (Available from: http://www1.umn.edu/humanrts/gencomm/escgencom14.htm; Accessed: 1 Apr 2014).
8. GO 4 Health. Realizing the right to health for everyone: the health goal for humanity. Goals and Governance for health, Copenhagen, 2013. (Available from: http://www.go4health.eu/wp-content/uploads/Go4Health-interim-report-September-2013.pdf; Accessed: 1 Apr 2014).
9. Bill and Melinda Gates Foundation. Annual Letter 2013. (Available from: http://www.gatesfoundation.org/Who-We-Are/Resources-and-Media/Annual-Letters-List/Annual-Letter-2013; Accessed: 1 Apr 2014).
10. Gostin LO, Sridhar D. Global health and the law. N Engl J Med 2014; 370:1732-1740.
11. Attaran A et al. Healthy by law: The missed opportunity to use laws for public health. Lancet 2012; 379:283–285.
12. Stuckler D et al. The political economy of universal health coverage. Background paper for the global symposium on health systems research. Geneva: World Health Organization, 2010.
13. Organisation of African Unity. Abuja Declaration on HIV/AIDS, Tuberculosis and Other Related Infectious Diseases. 2001. (Available from: http://www.un.org/ga/aids/pdf/abuja_declaration.pdf; Accessed: 2 Apr 2014).
14. Chopra M, Campbell H, Rudan I. Understanding the determinants of the complex interplay between cost-effectiveness and equitable impact in maternal and child mortality reduction. J Glob Health 2012; 2:010406.
15. Draper A, Hewitt G, Rifkin S. Chasing the dragon: Developing indicators for the assessment of community participation in health programmes. Soc Sci Med 2010; 71:1102-1109.
16. O'Neill K et al. Monitoring service delivery for universal health coverage: the Service Availability and Readiness Assessment. Bull World Health Organ 2013; 91:923–931.
17. Fehling M, Nelson B, Venkatapurum S. Limitations of the Millennium Development Goals: a literature review. Glob Public Health 2013; 8:1109–1122.

18. Wismar M et al. Targets for health: uses and abuses. Brussels: European Observatory on Health Systems and Policies, 2008.
19. Sustainable Development Solutions Network. Health in the Framework of Sustainable Development: Technical Report for the Post-2015 Development Agenda. 2014. (Available from: http://unsdsn.org/resources/publications/health-in-the-framework-of-sustainable-development; Accessed: 2 Apr 2014).
20. Gostin LO. Global health law. Cambridge: Harvard University Press, 2014.

CHAPTER 29.

Global health and the law

The past two decades have brought revolutionary changes in global health, driven by popular concern over the acquired immunodeficiency syndrome (AIDS), new strain of influenza and maternal mortality (1). International development assistance for health — a crucial aspect of health cooperation — increased by a factor of five, from US$ 5.6 billion in 1990 to US$ 28.1 billion in 2012, with the private and voluntary sectors taking on an ever-increasing share of the total (2). Given the rapid globalization that is a defining feature of today's world, the need for a robust system of global health law has never been greater.

Global health law is not an organized legal system, with a unified treaty-monitoring body, such as the World Trade Organization. However, there is a network of treaties and so-called "*soft*" law instruments that powerfully affect global health, many of which have arisen under the auspices of the World Health Organization (WHO). Global health law has been defined as the legal norms, processes, and institutions that are designed primarily to attain the highest possible standard of physical and mental health for the world's population (3).

Global health law can affect multiple spheres, ranging from national security, economic prosperity, and sustainable development to human rights and social justice. Each global health problem is shaped by the language of rights, duties, and rules for engagement used in the law (see **Table 29-1**).

1. Understanding the law and Global Health. Safeguarding the population's health traditionally occurs at the national level, with a web of laws and regulations governing health services, injury and disease prevention, and health promotion (4). However, in a globalized world in which pathogens and lifestyle risks span borders, the need for collective action has intensified interest in international legal solutions (5). The law relating to global health rests primarily within the domain of public international law, which can be broadly characterized as the rules that govern the conduct and relations of countries, including their rights and obligations. Countries remain the major subjects of international law, but international organizations and (through human rights law) individuals are also considered to be subjects of international law.

There is a complex array of international norms, including those that are binding, or "*hard*" (e.g., treaties), and those that are nonbinding, or "*soft*" (e.g., codes of practice). Hard and soft legal instruments have many similarities and often take similar forms, since both forms of instruments are negotiated and adopted by countries, are administered by international organizations, and have similar compliance mechanisms, such as setting targets, monitoring progress, and reporting to governmental agencies. Soft instruments can influence domestic law and policy and are often viewed as part of the corpus of international law (**Figure 29-1**) (6).

In recent years, the international community has moved toward a new language of global governance (7). Neither global health law nor governance is well defined, but the central feature of global health law is the negotiation, adoption, and monitoring of normative rules among countries. Both law and broader governance require institutions to do much of the work, including creating norms, mobilizing resources, guiding multiple stakeholders to work collaboratively, and ensuring accountability for results. The WHO is the most important institution for negotiating international health agreements (8).

2. WHO as a normative agency. The WHO has constitutional authority to negotiate and monitor normative instruments – both treaties and soft instruments, such as recommendations. The constitution of the WHO enunciates the universal value of the right to health – a widely adopted international legal entitlement (9,10). The WHO uses a variety of policy tools to set soft norms, with varying levels of institutional support. A World Health Assembly resolution expresses the will of 194 member countries. The agency has constitutional authority to adopt formal recommendations; the two most prominent are the *International Code of Marketing of Breast-Milk Substitutes* (adopted in 1981) (11) and the *Global Code of Practice on the International Recruitment of Health Personnel* (adopted in 2010) (12). The Assembly has also adopted influential global strategies and action plans.

The treaty-making powers of the WHO are extraordinary, with separate processes for negotiating agreements, or conventions, and regulations. Member countries must accept or reject a convention within 18 months after its adoption by the Assembly (10). This is a powerful mechanism requiring countries to consider the treaty in accordance with national constitutional processes. The WHO, however, lacks the authority to enforce compliance and thus relies on governmental implementation through domestic law and policy. The WHO can negotiate regulations on a range of health topics, including sanitation and quarantine, nomenclatures of diseases, and standards for the safety, purity, and potency of pharmaceuticals. Regulations enter into force after adoption by the Assembly, except for members that notify the director-general within a specified time (10). Consequently, countries must proactively opt out or they are automatically bound. The first WHO regulations – on nomenclature for

Table 29-1. *Glossary of international health law.*

INTERNATIONAL LAW

Treaties are binding agreements between states intended to create legal rights and duties. Treaties can often have significant impacts on private parties such as corporations (e.g., trade law) and individuals (e.g., human rights).

Customary International Law refers to legal norms established by consistent state practice.

WHO TREATY-MAKING POWERS

The WHO has two constitutional powers to negotiate treaties:

Conventions: Article 19 empowers the Health Assembly to *"adopt conventions or agreements"* by a two-thirds vote. Article 20 directs members to *"take action"* by accepting or rejecting the convention within eighteen months after adoption. Member states must report annually on *"action taken"* (arts. 20, 62). The Framework Convention on Tobacco Control is the Assembly's only Convention.

Regulations: Article 21 empowers the Health Assembly to adopt regulations on a range of health topics. Regulations enter into force after due notice of adoption, except for member states that notify the Director-General of rejection within a specified time (art. 22). The two Assembly regulations are: (1) Nomenclature of Diseases and Causes of Death, and (2) International Health Regulations.

WHO "SOFT" LAW

"Soft" law instruments create health norms without the binding nature of international law. Article 23 empowers WHO to issue formal *"recommendations"*, but the Organization has developed norms through a range of *"soft"* instruments, such as global strategies, action plans, and guidelines.

WHO Recommendations: Article 23 empowers the Health Assembly *"to make recommendations to Members"*, while Article 62 requires states to report annually on the action taken. Two recommendations are: the International Code on the Marketing of Breast Milk Substitutes (1981) and the Global Code of Practice on the International Recruitment of Health Personnel (2010).

Global Strategies: offer a strategic vision of how to tackle health challenges, listing specific objectives and guidance to stakeholders – e.g., WHO's Global Health Strategy on HIV/AIDS, 2011–2015. Global strategies often stress WHO's comparative advantages, such as leveraging its strengths through partnerships and coordination.

Global Action Plans: outline specific steps or activities for a strategy to succeed – e.g., Global Non-Communicable Disease Action Plan 2013-2020. Global plans often specify detailed tasks, time horizons, and resources.

Guidelines: are approved by WHO's Guidelines Review Committee designed to promote evidence-based health policies or clinical interventions – e.g., WHO guidelines on patient safety.

INTERNATIONAL HUMAN RIGHTS LAW

The International Covenant on Civil and Political Rights: requires states to safeguard civil and political rights, including the freedom of expression and religion; freedom from slavery and torture; and rights to privacy.

The International Covenant on Economic, Social and Cultural Rights: guarantees *"the right to everyone to the enjoyment of the highest attainable standard of physical and mental health"*, as well as capturing social determinants: *"an adequate standard of living ... including adequate food, clothing and housing, and to the continuous improvement of living conditions"*.

General Comment 14: guides member states in implementing the right to health, including health goods, services and facilities that are available, accessible, acceptable, and of good quality.

diseases – date back to the late 19th century as the International List of Causes of Death; these regulations are now implemented through the International Classification of Diseases (13). The second WHO regulations date back to 1892, when European countries adopted the International Sanitary Convention, a predecessor to the International Sanitary Regulations (now called the International Health Regulations) (3). The constitution of the WHO creates ongoing governmental obligations to report annually on actions taken on recommendations, conventions, and regulations (10). Despite the normative powers of the WHO, modern international health law is remarkably thin, with only two major treaties adopted since the creation of the agency.

3. Framework Convention on Tobacco Control. The WHO did not negotiate a convention until the Framework Convention on Tobacco Control (FCTC), which was adopted in 2003 (14). The FCTC, which remains the only convention adopted by the World Health Assembly, was ratified by 177 countries that are home to 88% of the world's population, although the convention was not ratified by 2 countries, the United States and Indonesia, which have the third and fourth largest populations, respectively, worldwide (15). In 2012, the Secretariat of the FCTC estimated that nearly 80% of the 159 countries that submitted reports had strengthened national tobacco-control laws after ratification (16). However, overall progress masks unequal performance – for example, China showed *"an alarming lack of progress"*, whereas India's implementation was *"slow"* (16).

The FCTC created binding norms to reduce the demand for, and supply of, tobacco products and to share information and resources. Efforts to reduce demand include taxing and pricing guided by health objectives, the provision of 100% smoke-free environments, disclosures of contents and emissions of tobacco products, large warning labels on packaging of tobacco products, comprehensive marketing bans, and tobacco cessation and treatment programs. Reducing the supply of tobacco focuses on illicit trade (e.g., smuggling and counterfeiting), which was estimated to account for 11.6% of global cigarette consumption in 2009, resulting in lost tax revenues of US$ 30 to US$ 50 billion per year (17).

Despite the success of the FCTC in mobilizing governmental action and civil-society engagement, the treaty has major weaknesses. First, it contains ambiguous language, affording countries broad discretion in implementation. Second, it does not provide resources to give low-and middle-income countries sufficient capacity to implement and enforce policies outlined in the convention. In addition, the tobacco industry has fought back against the FCTC, bringing cases under the World Trade Organization and investment

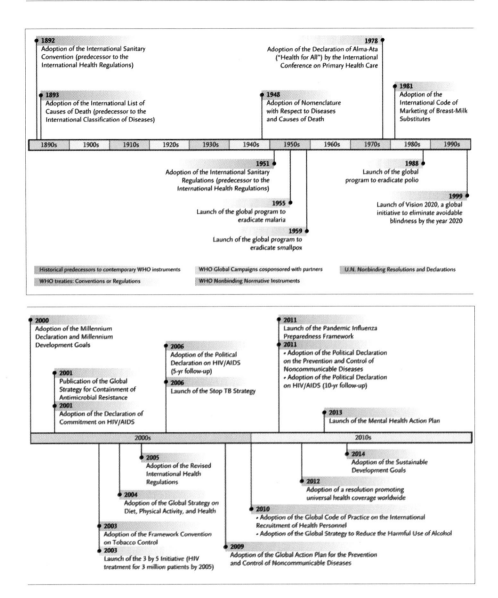

Figure 29-1a,b. *Timeline with the main events relevant to international health legislation.*

treaties against Australia and Uruguay for their use of plain packaging of tobacco products and adoption of tobacco-control legislation – a classic conflict between health and commerce regimes (18,19).

   4. International health regulations. The World Health Assembly adopted a substantially revised version of the International Health Regulations in 2005 in the aftermath of the severe acute respiratory syndrome (SARS) outbreak, establishing a framework for global health security (20). The aim of the regulations is to enhance the monitoring and reporting of international health threats and to improve the coordination of the response while avoiding unnecessary interference with traffic and trade (21). The regulations govern surveillance and containment of disease within countries, at borders, and in international travel (22).

The regulations encompass a broad spectrum of health hazards of international concern, regardless of their origin or source – biologic, chemical, or radionuclear. Using a decision instrument as a guide, governments must monitor health hazards and notify the WHO within 24 hours after events that may constitute a public health emergency of international concern. The director-general has the exclusive power to declare an emergency and has done so only once – during the 2009 influenza A (H1N1) pandemic. The regulations permit the WHO to take into account unofficial sources, such as nongovernmental organizations, scientists, and social networks in print and electronic media. Countries also agreed to develop core capacities – including legislation, national focal points, and pandemic planning – to implement the regulations.

5. Pandemic Influenza Preparedness (PIP) framework. Although not a treaty, the WHO PIP Framework is an innovative hybrid – a soft law instrument that nonetheless can create binding obligations. Adopted in May 2011, the PIP Framework resolved the nearly 5-year controversy that erupted when Indonesia refused to share samples of influenza A (H5N1) virus with WHO collaborating centers. Claiming sovereignty over a virus that was identified in their territory, Indonesian officials expressed concern that their country would not receive a fair share of the benefits of scientific discoveries (23,24).

The PIP Framework facilitates sharing of influenza viruses that have human pandemic potential and increases access to vaccines and anti-viral medications in developing countries. The agreement incorporates *"standard material transfer agreements"* between the WHO and biotechnology companies or universities. When such agreements are signed, they create contractual duties to provide certain benefits in exchange for access to biologic materials. Recipients of such materials make monetary and in-kind commitments, including commitments to donate vaccines to WHO stockpiles, offer products at affordable prices, and make intellectual-property rights available. Sharing the benefits of scientific progress is a vital aspect of global security and justice. However, the intellectual-property controversy associated with the novel coronavirus that causes the Middle East respiratory syndrome (MERS) reminds the international community that the PIP Framework applies only to pandemic influenza, with no WHO-negotiated agreement covering other emerging diseases (25).

6. International human rights law. The constitution of the WHO proclaims, "*The enjoyment of the highest attainable standard of health is one of the fundamental rights of every human being*" (10). Reflecting the same sentiment, the International Covenant on Economic, Social, and Cultural Rights, which complements the International Covenant on Civil and Political Rights and which 161 countries have accepted as binding international law, guarantees "*the right of everyone to the enjoyment of the highest attainable standard of physical and mental health.*" It also spells out governmental obligations to reduce infant mortality, promote the development of healthy children, improve environmental and industrial hygiene, prevent and treat diseases, and ensure the provision of medical services (26). In a demonstration of the universal value of such provisions, all countries except South Sudan have joined at least one treaty recognizing the right to health (27).

The right to health requires that governments meet "*minimum core obligations*", including the provision of health facilities, goods, and services, without discrimination and distributed equitably; nutritious and safe food; shelter, housing, sanitation, and safe and potable water; and essential medicines. Health goods, services, and facilities must be available in sufficient quantity, with public accessibility, ethnic and cultural acceptability, and good quality, as outlined in General Comment 14 of the U.N. Committee on Economic, Social, and Cultural Rights (28).

Whether human rights law influences governmental practices is disputed (29). However, health rights are incorporated into statutes and constitutions in many countries and have formed the basis for landmark judicial rulings (3). The real-world effect of human rights law depends on an active civil society, which can highlight governmental violations, lobby parliaments, and litigate health rights (30). The most successful national litigation has involved access to essential medicines. For example, in 2002, the Constitutional Court in South Africa struck down government limits on access to nevirapine for pregnant women with human immunodeficiency virus (HIV) infection. As a result of this ruling, the government had to begin to realize the rights of mothers and infants to HIV prevention (31).

Judicial decisions are increasing access to underlying determinants of health, such as food, water, and housing. In 2001, the Indian Supreme Court held that nutrition programs were legal entitlements and required that cooked meals be provided for primary school children. In later orders, the court set timetables for action on subsidized grain, maternal and child health, and food for the homeless and rural poor (3). **Table 29-2** shows country-level court cases that illustrate the effect of human rights law on health policy.

Table 29-2. *Human rights court cases showing the influence of international law on domestic health policy.*

CASE	YEAR	COUNTRY	BASIS FOR DECISION	COURT DECISION
Cruz del Valle Bermudez & Ors. v. Ministerio de Sanidad y Asistencia Social	1999	Venezuela	Freedom from discrimination; rights to health, security, life, and to the benefits of scientific progress	Requires government to cover treatment expenses for persons living with HIV and to develop information campaigns
People's Union for Civil Liberties v. Union of India	2001	India	Rights to health, food, and to life	Requires free and universal nutrition programs (mid-day meal), setting standards and timetables for action
Minister of Health v. Treatment Action Campaign	2002	South Africa	Right to health	Strikes down government limits on access to nevirapine for pregnant women
A.V. et al. v. Estado Nacional	2004	Argentina	Rights to bodily integrity, health, and to life	Mandates universal, free treatment for those living with HIV
Roa Lopez v. Colombia	2006	Colombia	Rights to life and to health	Finds unconstitutional a prohibition on abortions to protect life or health of the mother, or in cases of rape, even when fetus is not viable
Judgement T-760/08	2008	Colombia	Right to health	Requires government to unify two insurance schemes with fewer benefits for indigent persons into a single scheme with equal benefits for all
Lindiwe Mazibuko v. City of Johannesburg	2009	South Africa	Rights to water and sanitation	Finds no immediate duty to provide a specific amount of water, but only reasonable measures within the state's resources
Caceres Corrales v. Colombia	2010	Colombia	Rights to life and to heath	Upholds a complete ban on tobacco advertising and sponsorship

Table 29-2. *Continued.*

CASE	YEAR	COUNTRY	BASIS FOR DECISION	COURT DECISION
Canada (Attorney General) v. PHS Community Services	2011	Canada	Right to liberty and security of person, right to life	Finds unconstitutional failure to exempt drug users and staff at a supervised safe injection site from bans on possession and trafficking of illicit drugs
Matsipane Mosetlhanyane & Ors. v. The Attorney General	2011	Botswana	Freedom from torture and cruel, inhuman or degrading treatment, right to water and sanitation	Protects water rights of an indigenous community living in in the Kalahari Desert
5000 Citizens v. Article 3 of Law No.28705	2011	Peru	Right to health	Upholds a ban on smoking in all public places
British American Tobacco South Africa v. Minister of Health	2012	South Africa	Freedom of expression; rights to information, a clean environment, and to health	Upholds the constitutionality of tobacco advertising and marketing restrictions
Novartis AG v. Union of India	2013	India	Rights to health and to life	Invalidates patent for Gleevec because it was not materially better than existing drug

7. Challenges in Global Health law. Despite the potential of soft and hard instruments to set norms and mobilize multiple actors, global health laws have major limitations (**Table 29-3**). First, governments are loath to constrain themselves and, therefore, often reject international law or agree only to weak norms. Second, high-income countries are reluctant to finance capacity building in lower-income countries or to provide funding to the WHO without specific earmarks. And third, compliance mechanisms for such laws are often weak or nonexistent.

Because international law primarily addresses the rights and duties of countries, it cannot easily govern nonstate actors, which range from individuals and civil-society groups to foundations and private enterprises. Although newer global health institutions (e.g., UNAIDS, Global Fund, and GAVI Alliance) include civil-society representatives on their governing boards, the WHO has resisted nonstate participation in its governing structures (32).

The harmonization of governmental interests, moreover, can be difficult because of the disparate perspectives (33). Although high-income countries often favor trade liberalization, low and middle-income countries seek greater access to drugs and the fruits of technological progress. In 2001, World Trade

Organization members adopted the Doha Declaration on TRIPS (the Agreement on Trade-Related Aspects of Intellectual Property Rights) and Public Health, which allowed countries to issue a compulsory license during a public health emergency, granting to itself or a third party the right to produce or import a patented drug without authorization from the patent holder (34). So-called "TRIPS flexibilities" were designed to ensure that intellectual property should not prevent countries from providing affordable access to essential medications in a public health emergency.

Table 29-3. *Limitations of global health law.*

CHALLENGE	DESCRIPTION	EXAMPLE
National Sovereignty	States are reluctant to forego self-governance or cede authority to international actors.	Code of Practice on the International Recruitment of Health Personnel is voluntary despite active recruitment from high-income countries.
Rise of non-state actors	Businesses, foundations, and civil society have major health impacts, but are hard to govern at the international level.	Global Strategy on Diet, Physical Activity and Health does not govern marketing of food.
Divergent interests of emerging economies and high-income states	The Global "North" defends trade liberalization (e.g., intellectual property), while the "South" focuses on health justice (e.g., access to medicines and fair allocation of scientific benefits).	Pandemic Influenza Preparedness Framework struggled to reconcile Indonesia's claim for fair sharing benefits with high-income states' desire to receive viral samples.
'Multi-bi' Financing	States route assistance through WHO and other multilaterals, but hold tight control over its use—limiting WHO's control of its resources and ability to set priorities. Multi-bi financing diminishes WHO's perceived independence.	~80% of WHO's funding is voluntary, which is incongruent with Assembly priorities and the major causes of disability and death.
Funding for Capacity-building	Global health law rarely requires high-income states to build capacities in lower-income states to fulfill international obligations.	Committee on IHR Functioning (2011) found many states lacked capacity and could not fulfill their obligations.
Compliance and Incentives	WHO norms (whether soft or hard) rarely contain effective methods of holding states and stakeholders accountable.	Global Strategy to Reduce Harmful Use of Alcohol does not require state action or prevent industry lobbying against alcohol control.
Adjudication and Enforcement of Norms	WHO lacks power to adjudicate most disputes and enforce norms.	Tobacco industry uses WTO and investment treaties to challenge plain packaging and tobacco control.

Increasingly, the reconciliation of these interests occurs at the national level. For example, in 2013, the Supreme Court of India held that Novartis did not have a valid patent in India on the lucrative cancer drug *Gleevec* (35). The court ruled that Indian law grants patents only to new compounds and that modified drugs must improve treatment for patients. The decision could embolden other emerging economies to reject similar intellectual-property claims. At the same time, developed countries are seeking stricter intellectual-property protection in trade agreements, such as the Trans-Pacific Partnership, which seeks to promote trade and investment among the partner countries (36).

Trust in international organizations to act impartially and demonstrate leadership is crucial to the future of global health law. As new health security challenges arise, the integrity and efficient functioning of the WHO becomes ever more important. The WHO, however, is struggling with a small group of donors that contribute approximately 80% of its total budget (37). The term for this type of financing is "multi-bi" aid – donors' earmarking of noncore funding for specific sectors, diseases, or regions through multilateral agencies (38). Since the leadership of the WHO is unable to control most of its budget, these aid arrangements endanger the perceived independence and normative influence of the WHO.

Financing is intricately related to the challenge of building capacity to fulfill duties created by global health law. The 2011 review committee on the functioning of the International Health Regulations stressed that many countries lacked capacity and were not on a path to fulfill their obligations (39). The same failure to mobilize resources has plagued WHO normative development in such areas as achieving ambitious goals set forth in action plans on non-communicable diseases and mental health (40-42).

8. Strategy for Global Health laws. Given the undoubted need for global cooperation, international norms are accepted as important global health tools. The more difficult question is whether to pursue hard or soft routes to address health challenges. This debate plays out in international forums ranging from alcohol control and biomedical research to broader reforms such as the Framework Convention on Global Health (30,43-45). However, there are strengths and weaknesses to both approaches. Soft agreements are easier to negotiate, with countries more likely to accede to far-reaching norms if there is no formal obligation to comply.

Countries can assent to a soft norm without the national constitutional processes entailed in ratifying a treaty. In addition, soft norms can be negotiated more quickly with the use of fewer resources. Resolutions of the WHO Health Assembly represent a major expression of political will and can lead to progressive deepening of norms — enacted into domestic law, referenced by treaty bodies, or incorporated into international law. The WHO, moreover, is building accountability mechanisms into soft agreements, with targets, monitoring, and timelines for compliance.

However, national governments can largely ignore soft instruments, and as a result, civil society often urges treaty development (30). No hard norms have been enacted, for example, relating to food, alcohol, physical activity, injuries, pain medication, or mental health. If the WHO acts principally through voluntary agreements, while other sectors develop hard law, this weakens and sidelines the agency. Civil society often points to the obligatory nature of international trade law and its binding dispute-settlement mechanism, which often trumps WHO norms (46).

Even with all the funding and celebrity power that has entered the global health space, key health indicators lag, whereas the health gap between rich and poor has barely abated (47,48). A renewed attention to lawmaking efforts by the WHO and the human right to health are crucial elements of progress. It is only through law that individuals and populations can claim entitlements to health services and that corresponding governmental obligations can be established and enforced. It is through law that norms can be set, fragmented activities coordinated, and good governance ensured, including stewardship, transparency, participation, and accountability. Global health law, despite its limitations, remains vital to achieving global health with justice.

Acknowledgement: Originally published as: Lawrence O. Gostin and Devi Sridhar: Global health and the law. From New England Journal of Medicine, 370:1732-1740, Copyright © 2014 Massachusetts Medical Society. Reprinted with permission from Massachusetts Medical Society.

References

1. Brandt AM. How AIDS invented global health. N Engl J Med 2013; 368:2149-2152.
2. Institute for Health Metrics and Evaluation. Financing global health: the end of the golden age. Seattle: Institute for Health Metrics and Evaluation, 2012.
3. Gostin LO. Global health law. Cambridge: Harvard University Press, 2014.
4. Idem. Public health law: power, duty, restraint. 2nd ed. Berkeley: University of California Press, 2008.
5. Cohen IG. The globalization of health care: legal and ethical issues. New York: Oxford University Press, 2013.
6. Abbot K, Snidal D. Hard and soft law in international governance. Int Organ 2000; 54:421-456.
7. Frenk J, Moon S. Governance challenges in global health. N Engl J Med 2013; 368:936-942.

8. Burci GL, Vignes C-H. World Health Organization. The Hague, the Netherlands: Kluwer Law International, 2004.

9. Friedman EA, Gostin LO. Pillars for progress on the right to health: harnessing the potential of human rights through a Framework Convention on Global Health. Health Hum Rights 2012; 14:E4-E19.

10. WHO Constitution. Geneva: World Health Organization. (Available from: http://www.who.int/ governance/eb/constitution/en).

11. International code of marketing of breast-milk substitutes. Geneva: World Health Organization, 1981. (Available from: http://www.who.int/nutrition/publications/ infantfeeding/9241541601/en).

12. WHO global code of practice on the international recruitment of health personnel. Geneva: World Health Organization, 2010. (Available from: http://www.who.int/hrh/ migration/code/full_text/en).

13. International statistical classification of diseases. Vol. 2. 10th rev. Geneva: World Health Organization, 2010. (Available from: http://www .who.int/classifications/icd/ ICD10Volume2 _en_2010.pdf).

14. Roemer R, Taylor A, Lariviere J. Origins of the WHO framework convention on tobacco control. Am J Public Health 2005; 95:936-938.

15. Parties to the WHO Framework Convention on Tobacco Control. Geneva: World Health Organization (Available from: http://www.who.int/fctc/signatories_parties/en).

16. Global progress report on implementation of the WHO Framework Convention on Tobacco Control. Geneva: World Health Organization, 2012. (Available from: http:// www.who.int/fctc/reporting/2012_global_ progress_report_en.pdf).

17. Joossens L, Merriman D, Ross H, Raw M. The impact of eliminating the global illicit cigarette trade on health and revenue. Addiction 2010; 105:1640-1649.

18. McGrady B. Implications of ongoing trade and investment disputes concerning tobacco: Philip Morris v. Uruguay 2012. In: Voon T, Mitchell A, Liberman J, Ayres G, eds. Public health and plain packaging of cigarettes: legal issues. Northampton, MA: Edward Elgar, 2012. (Available from: http://papers.ssrn.com/sol3/papers.cfm?abstract_ id= 2046261).

19. Voon T, Mitchell A. Time to quit? Assessing international investment claims against plain tobacco packaging in Australia. J Int Econ Law 2012; 14:515-552.

20. Fidler DP. SARS, governance and the globalization of disease. Houndmills, United Kingdom: Palgrave Macmillan, 2004.

21. International Health Regulations: Article 2. Geneva: World Health Organization (Available from: http://www.who.int/ihr/publications/9789241596664/en/index.html).

22. Fidler DP. From international sanitary conventions to global health security: the new international health regulations. Chin J Int Law 2005; 4:325-392.

23. Fidler DP, Gostin LO. The WHO pandemic influenza preparedness framework: a milestone in global governance for health. JAMA 2011; 306:200-201.

24. Kamradt-Scott A, Lee K. The 2011 pandemic influenza preparedness framework: global health secured or a missed opportunity? Polit Stud 2011; 59:831-847.

25. Fidler DP. Who owns MERS? The intellectual property controversy surrounding the latest pandemic. Foreign Affairs, 2013. (Available from: http://www.foreignaffairs. com/articles/139443/david-p-fidler/who-owns-mers).

26. International covenant on economic, social and cultural rights. Geneva: World Health Organization. (Available from: http://www.who.int/ hhr/Economic_social_cultural.pdf).

27. Zuniga J, Marks SP, Gostin LO. Advancing the human right to health. Oxford, UK: Oxford University Press, 2013.

28. United Nations, Office of the High Commissioner for Human Rights. General comment 14L: the right to the highest attainable standard of health. Adopted at the 22nd Session of the Committee on Economic, Social, and Cultural Rights, Geneva, August 11, 2000.

29. Singh JA, Govender M, Mills EJ. Do human rights matter to health? Lancet 2007; 370:521-527. (Erratum, Lancet 2007; 370:1686).

30. Gostin LO, Friedman EA, Buse K, et al. Towards a framework convention on global health. Bull World Health Organ 2013; 91:790-793.

31. Minister of Health v. Treatment Action Campaign, 2002 (5) SA 721 (CC) (S. Afr.).

32. Silberschmidt G, Matheson D, Kickbusch I. Creating a committee C of the World Health Assembly. Lancet 2008; 371:1483-1486.

33. Feldbaum H, Michaud J. Health diplomacy and the enduring relevance of foreign policy interests. PLoS Med 2010; 7:e1000226.

34. World Trade Organization. Doha WTO Ministerial 2001: TRIPS, WT/MIN(01)/DEC/2, 20 November 2001: Declaration on the TRIPS agreement and public health, adopted 14 November 2001 (Available from: http://www.wto.org/english/thewto_e/minist_e/min01_e/mindecl_trips_e.htm).

35. Kapczynski A. Engineered in India — patent law 2.0. N Engl J Med 2013; 369:497-499.

36. Bollyky T. Regulatory coherence in the TPP talks. In: Lim CL, Elms D, Low P (eds). Trans-Pacific Partnership: a quest for a twenty-first century agreement. New York: Cambridge University Press, 2012.

37. Sridhar D, Gostin LO. Reforming the World Health Organization. JAMA 2011; 305:1585-1586.

38. Sridhar D. Who sets the global health research agenda? The challenge of multi-bi financing. PLoS Med 2012; 9:e1001312.

39. Implementation of the International Health Regulations (2005): report of the Review Committee on the Functioning of the International Health Regulations (2005) in relation to pandemic (H1N1) 2009. Geneva: World Health Organization, 2011. (Available from: http://apps.who.int/gb/ebwha/pdf_files/ WHA64/A64_10-en.pdf).

40. Magnusson RS. Non-communicable diseases and global health governance: enhancing global processes to improve health development. Global Health 2007; 3:2.

41. Morain S, Mello MM. Survey finds public support for legal interventions directed at health behavior to fight non-communicable disease. Health Affairs (Millwood) 2013; 32:486-496.

42. Becker AE, Kleinman A. Mental health and the global agenda. N Engl J Med 2013; 369:66-73.

43. Taylor AL, Dhillon IS. An international legal strategy for alcohol control: not a framework convention — at least not yet. Addiction 2013; 108:450-455.

44. Sridhar D. Health policy: regulate alcohol for global health. Nature 2012; 482:302.

45. Røttingen JA, Chamas C. A new deal for global health R&D? The recommendations of the Consultative Expert Working Group on Research and Development (CEWG). PLoS Med 2012; 9:e1001219.

46. Friedman EF, Gostin LO, Buse K. Advancing the right to health through global organizations: the potential role of a Framework Convention on Global Health. Health Hum Rights 2013; 15:71-86.

47. Garay J. Global health (GH)=GH equity=GH justice=global social justice: the opportunities of joining EU and US forces together. Berkeley: University of California, European Union of Excellence, 2012 (Available from: http://eucenter.berkeley.edu).

48. Garrett L. Money or die: a watershed moment for global public health. Foreign Affairs. March 6, 2012 (Available from: http://www.foreignaffairs.com/articles/137312/laurie-garrett/money-or-die).

CHAPTER 30.

Improving access to essential medicines: How health concerns can be prioritised in the global governance system

1. Access to essential medicines: The debate. Patents are often viewed as a technical issue, one to be discussed and contested by intellectual property lawyers who are familiar with the complex language used in drafting agreements and briefs. However, as the past 10 years have shown, patents are actually a critical health issue and, as Pogge (2007) has argued, an important moral issue of our time (1). The agreements made at the global level within the World Trade Organisation (WTO) and in bilateral trade negotiations have enormous local implications, especially among the global poor.

In this paper, I discuss the politics of access to essential medicines and identify "*space*" in the current system where change can be made. I would like to start by stating the obvious problem: the current state of access to essential medicines among the global poor is unacceptable. Every year there are over 18 million preventable deaths and tens of millions more cases of increased morbidity due to poverty-related causes and arguably the unavailability of essential medicines. Why in a world of plenty do we still have so much suffering? This leads us to a moral question: what are our moral duties to those who are suffering from preventable and treatable illnesses due to the unavailability of pharmaceuticals, or, when they do exist, a lack of access to them? The current situation constitutes a violation of the human rights of millions of the world's poorest people.

At a global level, there is a systematic weakness of health concerns relative to trade and tensions between the governance of trade and health (2). For example, human rights and health activists have argued that patent protection prevents access to essential medicines, resulting in unnecessary, excessive and unjust mortality and morbidity. However, this argument has been dismissed by pharmaceutical industry representatives and their host countries, who have argued that patent protection, such as that afforded by the WTO Agreement on Trade-Related Aspects of Intellectual Property Rights (TRIPS), is necessary to incentivize research and thus save lives in the long term. In terms of patent protection barring access to drugs, they point to research such as Attaran's (2004) article, which argues that patent protection for AIDS medications has little effect on the distribution of drugs, to argue that it is other factors in developing countries that result in limited access to essential medicines (3).

The patent regime notwithstanding, there are structural and wider societal factors in developing countries that impede access to medicines. Morbidity and mortality are often the result of underlying social inequality, poverty, gender inequality, caste/class discrimination and lack of access to clean water and adequate sanitary facilities. Thus there is an argument to be made for paying attention to the forces that produce and aggravate the social conditions that impede access to essential medicines. Indeed, this line of argument has been used by pharmaceutical companies, lobbyists and the US government to stall action on generic drug production and uphold patent protection, such as that afforded by TRIPS.

There is no question that structural factors are important. Most developing countries do need better health systems and infrastructure, more health workers, clean water and proper sanitation and better institutions. They do need equitable economic growth, job creation and poverty reduction. Few would question this. But the importance of these factors does not reduce the significance of the barriers to access to essential medicines at reasonable prices that are created through patent laws. The focus on structural factors in developing countries is often an excuse for the lack of progress in trade negotiations. In addition, when access to essential medicines is blocked by two barriers (patent protection and structural factors in developing countries), we cannot absolve one of responsibility on the basis that the other exists. This would provide perverse incentives for those who would block attempts to address structural factors to ensure that there is a second barrier to patent protection also in place. And it would provide no moral incentives to remove either barrier (as each is innocent of the harm they together produce).

Barriers to improving access to essential medicines exist at different levels, including research on one hand and production and pricing on the other. In terms of research, Pogge has proposed a complementary patent arrangement called the Health Impact Fund (HIF), which focuses on incentivizing pharmaceutical companies to develop drugs for diseases that predominantly afflict the poor (1). As Ravvin (2008) notes, *"Under this plan, instead of receiving profits from selling patented drugs at high monopoly prices, innovators could opt to register any newly patented medicine with the HIF, which would provide a guaranteed payment stream in proportion to the incremental impact of the innovative drug on the global burden of disease (GBD) during its first 10–12 years on the market"* (4). I return to this proposal later in this paper. In terms of pricing and production, I will focus on the room in the current system for health concerns to be prioritised.

This issue is addressed from a global governance perspective focusing on the main actors who can make a difference. These include developing country coalitions and citizens in developed countries.

2. The role of developing countries. I turn now to examine the important role that developing countries can play in the prioritisation of health relative to trade concerns. It is first important to understand the inner workings of the WTO. As Patel (2007) describes, despite the existence of a voting structure, WTO decisions are reached through *"consensus"* within restricted inner-group meetings, known as *"Green Room"* meetings (5). Historically, the four members included in these meetings were USA, Japan, the EU and Canada. Because of this informal and exclusive governance arrangement, the WTO has been criticised for its lack of transparency and marginalisation of developing country concerns. An example of this marginalisation is TRIPS, where organised and coordinated intellectual property stakeholders, most significantly large pharmaceutical companies, came together to press for certain conditions such as stringent intellectual property rights in all countries regardless of their state of development. (It should be noted that private interests are of course informally represented at WTO negotiations; officially, negotiations are conducted among states.)

Why did developing countries, which had the most to lose, agree to TRIPS? Some have explained the agreement of developing countries to TRIPS by pointing to the elites that govern them, who do not always represent the needs of the poorest citizens. While I recognize the validity of this argument in some cases, I argue that government should nonetheless be the key actor in development if its legitimacy is derived from democracy and an electoral process. Thus I take the perspective that developing country governments with democratic legitimacy should have the authority and capacity to represent their countries' interests in trade negotiations, and should be able to do so on fair terms with wealthy countries. In brief, ownership and control of trade negotiations by developing country governments are important for three distinct reasons: effectiveness and sustainability, democracy and self-determination and the alignment of accountability with effectiveness (such that those who make the key decisions also bear the risk if policies have detrimental effects).

Pogge offers an alternative explanation (1). He argues that most poor countries lacked the bargaining power to resist the conditions of TRIPS that were imposed by rich countries. This situation raises the question of how relatively weak developing countries can negotiate on a fair basis with the powerful, developed states within the WTO. Using a political-economic perspective, we can choose a country that has achieved a certain level of success in pharmaceutical trade negotiations, such as India, and try to understand what factors facilitated the process. Drawing on interviews with Indian government officials involved in the negotiations, I identify four main factors: financial independence from wealthier states, a clear plan, strong leadership and technical expertise in intellectual property law. (India is, of course, unique as it has a large population and economic independence from donor countries).

Countries that enter trade negotiations without these four elements face a significant disadvantage. This can be overcome through developing countries organising and forming a coalition and pushing forward their collective agenda. Developing country coalitions have built and used coalitions to improve their bargaining power. This analysis draws on the important work of Patel, as well as Sell and Odell (5-7). As Patel describes, this pooling of bargaining resources has improved the technical and lobbying capacity by which developing countries engage in the WTO (5). These coalitions are highly visible, formalized and co-ordinated and focus on working within the WTO and existing trading structures to proactively engage in the negotiation process with the purpose of improving outcomes for developing countries.

Patel outlines three benefits of developing country coalitions (5). First, countries can share the costs of negotiating in the WTO. Developed countries have many negotiators based in Geneva, while developing countries have much fewer. For example, Carolyn Deere has noted that the USA, Canada, Japan, and the EU have roughly two Geneva negotiators per 10 million citizens while developing countries have just one. These numbers do not capture the fact that many of the delegates from developing countries are also responsible for covering other international organisations that are based in Geneva (e.g. World Intellectual Property Organisation, International Labour Organisation). Second, coalitions enable collaboration among countries so that they are able to compensate for their individual capacity limitations by sharing the tasks of technical and legal analysis. Third, coalitions can increase representation of developing countries. In 2004, 33 developing countries that were WTO members had no permanent representatives to the WTO based in Geneva, and so were unable to be present at a number of trade negotiations. More negotiations can be monitored when formal delegates are elected to represent groups of developing countries (e.g. African Group; African, Caribbean and Pacific Group of States (ACP); Least Developed Countries Group (LDC)).

I would add a fourth benefit of developing country coalitions. By aligning with emerging countries such as China, India and Brazil, less powerful countries can better handle the bullying tactics of certain developed states. I would like to elaborate on the final point, as it is critical to understanding the implementation of TRIPS. While most parties involved have seen TRIPS as a maximum standard of compliance, the USA has viewed it as a minimum. The USA has used its power to enforce TRIPS and bully countries into complying. Beyond this, the USA has used bilateral free trade agreements to extend the reach of TRIPS and increase patent protection beyond the provisions of TRIPS; these agreements are referred to as TRIPS-plus. Caroline Thomas (2002) quotes an NGO staff member in Washington, DC (8):

"The problem for developing countries is not whether the compulsory licensing of pharmaceuticals is legal, because it clearly is legal. It is the political problem of whether they will face sanctions from the U.S. government, for doing things that they have a legal right to do, but which the U.S. government does not like".

Similarly, Ralph Nader and James Love have spoken about the *"weight of the US power, short of military warfare, on South Africa to prevent that country from implementing policies to obtain cheaper sources of essential medicines"* (8). For example, in 1997 and 1998, Thailand, in the face of the HIV/AIDS crisis, attempted to use TRIPS articles 30 and 31 to pursue compulsory licensing of generic medicines. However, Thailand dropped these plans when threatened with sanctions by US trade officials (supported by the lobbying organisation PhRMA, the Pharmaceutical Research and Manufacturers of America).

3. The role of citizenship. The other main group of actors, citizens in developed countries, are especially important in light of the attitudes that developed countries take towards trade negotiations and enforcing trade agreements. The main multilateral trade institution, the WTO, consists of member-states. The government of each state, at least the democratic ones (which also happen to include the developed countries), are accountable to their citizens. Thus, those of us living in the wealthier countries have considerable influence over our governments' decisions and are therefore to a certain extent responsible for its actions, regardless of whether they take place in a multilateral forum or through bilateral agreements.

How can an individual influence his or her government's trade policy? Citizens can organise and form consumer groups, such as Knowledge Ecology International run by James Love, or join and financially support civil society organisations (CSOs) advocating for access to essential medicines. Citizens can write to their senators, representatives, or members of Parliament arguing why a change in foreign policy is necessary. Perhaps most effectively, citizens can make health and human rights a key electoral issue and apply pressure during presidential and senatorial campaigns. The upcoming 2008 US presidential election provides an opportunity for citizens to lobby for access to essential medicines as candidates attempt to avoid bad press.

4. Doha declaration on TRIPS and public health. Developing countries and citizens in developed countries represented by CSOs working together can increase the voice and interests of those most in need of affordable medicines. This was demonstrated in November 2001 when the WTO adopted the Doha Declaration on TRIPS and Public Health. In this agreement, a coalition of developing countries sought explicit assurance that they would not be subject to WTO penalties under TRIPS for addressing certain health crises by issuing compulsory licenses and extending for 10 years the deadline by which least developed members must provide patent protection for pharmaceuticals (7). How were the developing countries able to achieve this despite the powerful opposition from pharmaceutical companies and their host countries?

Four key factors can be identified (7). First, intellectual property was framed as a public health issue about saving lives by civil society organisations, which captured the attention of mass media in industrialised countries. CSOs, such as MSF (Medecins Sans Frontieres), TAC (Treatment Action Campaign), ACT UP Paris, Oxfam GB and Health Action International, pushed the issue to the forefront, indicating the role that these organisations and networks can play in supporting the agenda of developing countries and lobbying on their behalf. In addition, citizens lobbied their governments and gained the attention of prominent officials. During the 2000 US elections, when Al Gore announced he was running for president, health activists interrupted his speech chanting *"Gore's Greed Kills"*. The media picked up this story, and then the White House reached out to activists and started discussions.

Second, the developing country coalition did not fragment and pursued a common objective in WTO negotiations. Even in the face of US concessions to the African Group in the hope that it would withdraw, the coalition stayed together. Third, the coalition was large, including the African Group, Brazil, India, Pakistan, Bangladesh, Indonesia, Thailand, Sri Lanka, Philippines and 11 other Latin American and Caribbean states, and thus could not be easily dismissed. The inclusion of Brazil was important as the country was already a leader in the generic production of antiretrovirals and could play a key role in the negotiations. Fourth, the coalition eventually made a compromise and went after what was achievable given the existing trading structures, not what was ideal. While perhaps imperfect from an ideal moral perspective, compromise was arguably necessary to achieve agreement on the Declaration, which was highly preferable to no Declaration at all. One can see these four factors as forcing the pharmaceutical manufacturers and their home governments to compromise and agree to the Declaration.

5. Mixed news since 2001. Despite the general disappoint with the patchy implementation of the 2001 Declaration (9), there has been some positive news from individual developing countries on the prioritisation of health. For example, Thailand and India have become strong examples for what can be achieved for other developing countries. In November 2006 the government of Thailand announced that it would issue a compulsory license to the Government Pharmaceutical Organisation of Thailand so that the company could produce the AIDS drug *efavirenz* (*Storcrin*), which was still under patent by Merck. Then, in January 2007, the government of Thailand issued a compulsory license on patents for clopidogrel bisulfate, a heart disease drug, as well as compulsory licenses on patents on the AIDS drug sold by Abbott under the name of *Kaletra*.

In addition, in 2006, India rejected Novartis' patent application for the cancer drug *Gleevec*. Under Indian law, patents are only given for medicines invented after 1995, or for new and more efficacious versions of older drugs. The law in effect upholds scope for the production of generic medicines. India rejected the patent application because the drug that Novartis wanted to patent was not more efficacious than older versions. Novartis challenged the decision in a court in Chennai as the company argued that the decision, and the criteria used to make the decision, violated WTO law and could set a precedent that would make it very difficult to patent new drugs. In 2007, the court ruled against Novartis and in favour of Indian law, and more importantly for those concerned with public health, in favour of public health interests over intellectual property law. The Novartis case has set an important precedent. GlaxoSmithKline recently withdrew patent applications for its antiretroviral drugs *Abacavir* and *Trizivir* in India due to concerns about Novartis' patent rejection and about challenges to its patent applications by CSOs MSF and I-MAK. GlaxoSmithKline thought it better to withdraw the applications rather than receive a rejection because a rejection could weaken the country's chances of receiving patents in other developing countries.

Pharmaceutical companies have argued that facilitating compulsory licensing and patent rejection by certain developing countries undermine incentives for research in neglected diseases. GlaxoSmithKline states, "*Use of compulsory licensing... would significantly undermine the benefits to be gained from patents (which are real) without having a significant beneficial impact on access*" (10). These fears, however valid, provide more reason to favour a systematic solution to this problem, such as that provided by the Health Impact Fund (4,11). The implementation of this proposal would go some way toward abating fears that compulsory licensing and patent rejection will decrease the amount of research into neglected diseases.

6. The way forward. Despite the agreement reached on the 2001 Doha Declaration on Public Health, as of the end of 2007, nothing agreed upon has yet been launched, and USA is increasingly turning to bilateral agreements outside the WTO in order to thwart the power of negotiating coalitions. These bilateral agreements erode the gains made in the 2001 declaration. In addition, the use of bilateral agreements such as Economic Partnership Agreements (EPAs) has resulted in negotiations taking place outside the WTO. These agreements have been notoriously difficult for the WTO and CSOs to monitor. The politics of trade negotiations have therefore changed to preserve the negotiating advantages of developed countries through the use of bilateral agreements that circumvent the WTO.

What is the way forward? To improve access to essential medicines, six C's are needed: *coalitions, civil society, citizenship, compromise, communication and collaboration*. All six elements came together when the 2001 Doha Declaration was agreed upon. First, developing countries must form a coalition that comes together to achieve a very specific objective and does not fragment. Second, CSOs committed to health issues must continue to push the issue onto the political agenda. Third, citizens in developed countries need to pressure their governments to prioritise health concerns through lobbying, protesting and supporting CSOs. Fourth, the various stakeholders must compromise to a certain extent so that progress can be made. Fifth, health activists must communicate to the media, so that the media can frame the issue of access to essential medicines in an appealing manner. Finally, developing countries, CSOs and citizens in developed countries must collaborate to ensure that the barriers to access to essential medicines are overcome.

I conclude this paper by focusing on the issue of power: who gets what, when and how. As citizens we must think about what part each of us will play as we move forward into the twenty-first century. We need to think about who has power, how they use it and how we, as concerned actors in our respective roles as academics, practitioners, policy-makers, activists and citizens, can ensure that our governments and international institutions function with attention to the moral duty to reduce the obstacles to access to essential medicines.

Acknowledgement: Originally published as: Devi Sridhar: Improving access to essential medicines: How health concerns can be prioritised in the global governance system. Public Health Ethics 2008; 1:83-88. Reprinted by permission of Oxford University Press. The author would like to acknowledge the assistance of Thomas Pogge, Marcel Verweij, Mike Ravvin, Matt Peterson, Ngaire Woods, Sonali Srivastava, Carolyn Deere, Mayur Patel and Arunabha Ghosh.

References

1. Pogge T. Montreal Statement on the Human Right to Essential Medicines. Cambridge Quarterly Healthcare Ethics 2007; 16:97–108.
2. Lee K, Sridhar D, Patel M. Bridging the divide: the global governance of trade and health. Lancet 2009; 373: 416–422.
3. Attaran A. How do patents and economic policies affect access to essential medicines in developing countries? Health Affairs 2004; 23:155–166.
4. Ravvin M. Incentivizing access and innovation for essential medicines: A survey of the problem and proposed solutions. Public Health Ethics 2008; 1:110–123.
5. Patel M. New faces in the Green Room: Developing country coalitions and decision-making in the WTO. Global Economic Governance Programme Working Paper, 2007/33, 2007. (Available from: http://www. globaleconomicgovernance.org/docs/ Patel Main%20 tex new.pdf)
6. Sell S. TRIPS and the access to medicines campaign. Wisconsin International Law Journal 2002; 20:510.
7. Odell J, Sell S. Reframing the issue: The WTO coalition on intellectual property and public health, 2001. In: Odell J (ed.): Negotiating trade: Developing countries in the WTO and NAFTA. Cambridge, UK: Cambridge University Press, 2006.
8. Thomas C. Trade policy and the politics of access to drugs. Third World Quarterly 2002; 23:251–264.
9. Love J. Doha + Five: The Doha Declaration on the TRIPS agreement and public health, after five years. CP Tech, 2006. (Available from: http://www.cptech. org/blogs/ipdis-putesinmedicine/2006/11/ cptech-statement-on-doha-plus-five.html).
10. http://www.iprcommission.org/ graphic/Views articles/GlaxoSmithKline.htm
11. http://www.patent2.org/index.html

CHAPTER 31.

Global health: Who can lead?

It seems that the main responsibility for global health should lie with the United Nations specialist agency, the World Health Organization (WHO), established in 1948 to aid all peoples in the attainment of the highest possible level of health. It was created to be the chief director and coordinator of global health. However, since its inception, and especially over the past two decades, the WHO has become increasingly marginalised because of three significant changes in the global health system.

1. Too many players, too many initiatives. The past fifteen years have witnessed an explosion in the number as well as type of actors involved with health. Since its 1993 World Development Report *"Investing in Health"*, and arguable even since 1980, the World Bank has become the most influential global health actor in the UN. This reflects its financial power as a lender, its access to senior decision-makers in ministries of planning and finance and reputation for intellectual prowess.

Other than the WHO and World Bank, there has been an exponential growth of civil society organisations and of the private sector in global health, as well as increasing involvement by charitable foundations, research institutes, regional development banks, regional organisations, such as the European Union, and various partnerships and networks. In addition to the increase in the number of players, there has been a constant deluge of initiatives, focusing on specific diseases or issues, such as the United States President's Emergency Plan for AIDS Relief (PEPFAR), STOP TB, Roll Back Malaria, UNAIDS, the H-8, and most recently the International Health Partnership. While some of these have been housed in the WHO, the vast majority exist entirely outside, such as the Joint UN Programme for HIV/AIDS.

2. Go-it-alone bilateral aid. The second trend has been a move away from multilateral aid towards bilateral health programmes. This has been driven largely by the administration of former President George Bush. In 2002, the Global Fund to Fight HIV/AIDS, Tuberculosis and Malaria was established to serve as a financial instrument, managing and providing resources through an independent, technical process. A year later, Bush launched PEPFAR, the $15 billion five-year plan for AIDS relief which is the largest ever bilateral health programme to target a particular disease. Funds were allocated to fifteen countries chosen by the Bush administration, the large majority in sub-Saharan Africa.

Last July, PEPFAR was re-authorised with $48 billion to be spent by 2013. While PEPFAR has done an enormous amount of good, it operates entirely outside the UN system and only allocates a small proportion of funding to the Global Fund. The move away from multilateral cooperation seems also to be occurring in emerging powers, such as China, India and Brazil. These countries show a tendency to use regional, plural or bilateral mechanisms to engage in global health, rather than relying solely on the WHO.

3. Gates empire. The third change in the global health system has been the incredible increase in the amount of money pledged for global health, rising from a few hundred millions in the early 1990s to an estimated $20 billion last year. Other than the US government, the most significant new player is the Bill & Melinda Gates Foundation which, with the donation from Warren Buffet, is the global health donor with the largest endowment, roughly US$ 67 billion, and with annual disbursements of roughly US$ 3 billion. This compares with the WHO's biennial funding of US$ 3.3 billion for 2006-2007.

The Gates Foundation has been donating an enormous amount of money to global health, resulting in almost every university department, think-tank, civil society group and partnership working in this area, receiving funding from it directly or indirectly. This generosity has extended even to the UN system: while 30% of the WHO's budget is funded by assessed member contributions – roughly half a billion – the remaining 75% is from extra-budgetary funds from member states and philanthropic bodies. Alongside the US and British governments, the Gates Foundation is the third largest contributor to the WHO.

One of the consequences of a limited pool of donors with an increase in the number of actors and initiatives, is competition among the various parties, for the same pots of money. As a former health minister in sub-Saharan Africa noted, *"Everyone is chasing the money-reputable universities, the UN agencies, partnerships, civil society groups, so who is actually doing what developing countries really need, rather than what donors want?"* Much of the increase in funding has been directed at HIV/AIDS, malaria and tuberculosis. A recent study of the four biggest donors noted that in 2005, funding per death varied widely by disease, from US$ 1029.10 for HIV/AIDS to US$ 3.21 for non-communicable disease. The result is that while indicators for certain targeted diseases shows striking improvement, in some situations, primary care has deteriorated and other less *"fashionable"* diseases, such as child diarrhoea, have gone unnoticed. Most of the new money pouring into poorer countries is radically skewing public health and medical programmes towards the issues of greatest concern to the donors, but not necessarily of top priority for people in recipient states.

4. Strengthening WHO? The question then of who leads on world health is not an easy one to answer. Many experts argue that there is no single leader, nor strategic vision for where the global health community should be going. While the WHO was created to be the lead agency, a number of factors have eroded its ability to be the focal institution. Some hope that with the change in US administration, there will be renewed use of multilateral mechanisms and political commitment to reform and strengthen existing UN bodies. While it is far from perfect, there seems little doubt that the WHO should be the leader, and given certain reforms, it could manage the chaotic and crowded landscape and play a key role as coordinator.

Acknowledgement: Originally published as: Devi Sridhar: Global health: Who can lead? Reprinted from Chatnam House World Today, 2009.

PART 5.

Improving international organizations

CHAPTER 32.

Healthy governance:
How the WHO can regain its relevance

After 15 years of heralded progress on pandemic preparedness, tuberculosis control, tobacco regulation, and health metrics, the World Health Organization faces confusion over its future. In 2011, after a yearlong consultation with member states, WHO Director-General Margaret Chan described the agency as overextended and unable to respond with speed and agility to today's global health challenges. The most serious examples: the WHO's inability to address noncommunicable disease (NCD) prevention globally, to improve access to health systems, and to set global priorities in health.

In the years after the WHO was founded in 1948, the organization plucked a lot of low-hanging fruit. It helped governments improve hygiene and environmental health. It also supported the development and application of new technologies to control major infectious diseases such as malaria, syphilis, tuberculosis, and yaws. These missions largely went hand in hand with postwar reconstruction efforts. The WHO's most cited success from its early years was its initiative to eradicate smallpox, which began in 1958 and was certified complete in 1979.

Yet even in this golden era, the WHO struggled with an internal debate over its fundamental mission. There was an ongoing tension between a *"vertical"* approach, which tackled specific diseases without addressing general health services and prevention needs, and a *"horizontal"* one, which looked to strengthen whole health systems and support basic-care services that would deliver broad-based, integrative, and long-term improvements in public health. Bilateral donors in particular favored vertical interventions because measurable results were easier to demonstrate over a short time frame, by quantifying, say, the number of bed nets delivered or vaccines administered. These programs are also easier to control, given that they typically have separate funding proposal and allocation processes, delivery systems, and budgets. However, champions of primary care believed the WHO should dedicate resources and efforts to a horizontal approach because short-term advances in certain diseases or vaccination coverage run the risk of fragmenting general health services and weakening the role of governments as the main stewards of national health systems.

Like a pendulum, the vertical-versus-horizontal debate has regularly swung over the past 50 years. The result: The WHO has embraced elements of both approaches. There are vertical programs for AIDS, tuberculosis, and malaria. At the same time, the WHO pushes for universal health coverage and improved health systems in many countries, focusing especially on broad issues such as maternal and child health.

Yet, over the last two decades, as globalization expanded, urbanization accelerated, and lifestyles grew more sedentary, a baseline shift transformed the public's health demands. NCDs such as diabetes, cardiovascular disease, cancer, and depression started to displace the classic diseases of poverty and child mortality: Rising wages reduced the former, and successful health campaigns lowered the latter. Of course, emerging and developing countries must still cope with both. Brazil, for example, has had to create policies and health services to tackle maternal mortality and depression; India struggles with widespread undernutrition and type II diabetes; South Africa and Eastern Europe, meanwhile, must fight multidrug-resistant tuberculosis while combating alcohol abuse. According to data from 2005, the most comprehensive and recent available, NCDs account for three out of five deaths worldwide, with 80% of these deaths occurring in low and middle-income countries.

Underscoring the point, in 2011 the prevention and control of NCDs were the focus of a dedicated high-level meeting of the UN General Assembly. The talks resulted in the adoption of a major political declaration that called on governments, nongovernmental organizations (NGOs), and the private sector to commit to reducing risk factors and creating health-promoting environments, strengthening national policies and health systems, bolstering international cooperation and partnerships, and promoting research and development.

But the WHO has been unable to adapt its practices. WHO-promoted health services still focus on acute episodic care and not on long-term needs. And NCD prevention is not adequately addressed. The General Assembly may have adopted a declaration, but member states have not funded the WHO's work on the issue in earnest, and most countries have not implemented concrete prevention and treatment strategies to combat the four main risk factors: diet, smoking, alcohol, and physical inactivity. Unlike the first UN General Assembly special session on HIV/AIDS in 2001 – in which mobilized NGOs, the private sector, and UN agencies were coordinated by UNAIDS to press for specific financial, policy, and leadership commitments – the NCD summit was characterized by fragmentation among key actors. The WHO was sidelined.

The main problem is that the agency has not captured the political support of key governments in high-income and emerging economies. Unlike infectious diseases, which are well within the expertise of ministries of health, the new health challenges require a whole-of-government approach, one in which ministries of agriculture, transportation, finance, and foreign affairs have a say. Addressing NCDs' specific risk factors requires buy-in from ministries that are not within the WHO's sphere of influence. For example, ministries of finance need to develop innovative fiscal policies that incentivize individuals and companies to adopt and maintain healthy behaviors, and ministries of agriculture must help eliminate national and regional subsidies that disfavor healthy foods. Ministries of trade should prioritize public health while negotiating trade and investment treaties. And ministries of urban planning must keep the focus on physical activity when designing walkways, bike paths, roads, and transportation grids.

To be effective, the WHO needs to assert the importance of health in decision-making at the national level. Its mandate requires that it does so, and moreover, the organization's biggest advantage is that it has the data to back up its arguments. The WHO needs to be at the table when global trade and financial decisions are negotiated. Stronger diplomatic abilities adapted from the trade and finance regimes, in addition to a well-articulated case for linkage to major global debates on sustainable development, human rights, and security, will earn the WHO its right in settings where health can truly flourish. And this also needs to occur at the country level, where the WHO works directly with local health ministries.

Improving health is not just about better medical services or cutting-edge technology but also about better government. For example, one of the most effective ways to curb NCDs is to reduce smoking. The best way to do that is by taxation – a responsibility of finance ministries. Similarly, improving under- and over-nutrition in the long term requires significant changes to agricultural policies that drive which foods are grown and how they are processed and marketed.

There are already good models to follow. Julio Frenk, during his tenure as Mexico's minister of health, demonstrated that clear economic and epidemiological evidence can be used to convince other parts of government to invest in health. Under his stewardship, the ministry employed academic analysis to argue that lacking health insurance was driving families into poverty. Drawing on evidence-based policy to build consensus across party lines, Frenk was able to promote a major legislative reform establishing comprehensive national health insurance. The scheme, *"Seguro Popular"*, has covered 40 million people as of 2010, and Mexico is on track to achieving universal health coverage before the end of this year.

The WHO also needs to embrace the private sector. By giving responsible partners in industry a seat at the table, the agency will benefit from their expertise in science, operations, financing, and marketing. Unlike the tobacco and alcohol industries, which market and sell dangerous products, the food and beverage, pharmaceutical and medical, and sporting goods industries have clear interests in being part of the conversation. Firms recognize that markets are stronger when they are populated with healthier consumers. To embrace industry, the WHO will have to overhaul its budget process and rally support within the World Health Assembly. But given resistance from member states to open governance processes to nonstate actors, this has been a tough sell. In recent years, the World Economic Forum has played a leadership role in bringing the private sector together with the WHO to develop common approaches to NCDs.

But no agency can fulfill its mandate if it is not given the resources. And in the WHO's case, nearly 80% of its funding comes from short-term extrabudgetary sources that are earmarked for specific diseases or purposes, rather than core UN-assessed contributions. In this climate, the WHO secretariat is forced to compete to raise funds with NGOs, academics, and other multilateral organizations such as the Global Fund and the GAVI Alliance. Instead, the WHO should create a central fundraising unit so that the best scientific minds can focus on technical and normative work, while the people with the right skills can raise money. With an appropriate mandate and the resources to carry it out, the WHO can be the leader in global heath that it needs to be.

Acknowledgement: *Originally published as: Devi Sridhar, Lawrence Gostin and Derek Yach: Healthy governance: How the WHO can regain its relevance. Copyright © 2012 Council for Foreign Relations. Reprinted with permission from Foreign Affairs, 2012.*

CHAPTER 33.

Reforming the World Health Organization

In December 2010, Jack Chow, the former World Health Organization (WHO) Assistant Director-General (1), asked, *"Is the WHO becoming irrelevant?"* A month later, the WHO's executive board considered the agency's future within global health governance. After a year-long consultation with member states on its financing, Director-General Margaret Chan called the WHO overextended and unable to respond with speed and agility to today's global health challenges (2). The crisis in leadership is not surprising to those familiar with the WHO. As its first specialized agency, the United Nations (UN) endowed the WHO with extensive normative powers to act as the directing and coordinating authority on international health. Yet modern global health initiatives (e.g., the Global Fund to Fight AIDS, Tuberculosis and Malaria and the GAVI Alliance – formerly the Global Alliance for Vaccines and Immunisation), bilateral programs (e.g., US President's Emergency Plan for AIDS Relief (PEPFAR)), and well-funded philanthropies (e.g., the Bill and Melinda Gates Foundation) often overshadow the agency. The WHO can be subject to political pressure, and its relationship with industry and civil society is uncertain (3).

Given the importance of global health cooperation, few would dispute that a stronger, more effective WHO would benefit all. The WHO's internal reform agenda must be bold to ensure its future. In this Commentary, we offer five proposals for reestablishing the agency's leadership.

1. Give real voice to multiple stakeholders. As a UN agency, the WHO consists solely of member states, which govern through the World Health Assembly (WHA) and the executive board. Yet nonstate actors have become major stakeholders in global health, often shifting their resources to new initiatives with governance structures reflecting their power. Known in international relations as *"forum shopping"*, stakeholders choose specific institutions to pursue their interests. In contrast to the WHO, representatives from civil society, the private sector, and foundations sit on the boards of the Global Fund and the GAVI Alliance. Even UN agencies such as the Joint United Nations Programme on HIV/AIDS engage civil society through advisory committees.

The WHO would be more effective by giving voice and representation to key stakeholders, including philanthropies, businesses, public/private partnerships, and civil society. While actively engaging with the private sector, the WHO should also set standards for and ensure compliance of key private partners such as the food, pharmaceutical, and biotechnology industries. At the same time, conflict-of-interest rules for expert committees and contractors require clarity and enforcement.

The director-general is taking a major step in proposing a global health forum, which would include regular multistakeholder meetings under the guidance of the WHA (2). The global health forum must afford stakeholders real voice and representation, effectively shaping the WHO's decisions. The WHA should also pass a resolution lowering the bar to official nongovernmental organization status. Meaningful stakeholder engagement would instill confidence and spark investment in the agency.

2. Improve transparency, performance, and accountability. Good governance also requires clear objectives, transparent decision-making, information dissemination, monitoring progress, and accountability. Stakeholders demand clarity on how their resources will achieve improved health outcomes as they shift toward results-based financing and performance-based measures. Yet a recent evaluation of multilateral organizations graded the WHO as weak on key parameters such as cost-consciousness, financial management, public disclosure, and fulfilling development objectives (4). To improve its standing, the WHO must make it easier for stakeholders to monitor achievements and demonstrate that activities effectively translate into better health outcomes.

3. Closer oversight of regions. The WHO's decentralized, regional structure poses a significant challenge in demonstrating results and delivering on priorities. The 6 WHO regional offices are uniquely independent within the UN system, with full power over regional personnel, including appointment of country representatives. Regional committees meet annually to formulate policies, review the regional program budget, and monitor the WHO's collaborative activities for health. The WHA and the executive board formally approve decisions, but in practice do not provide tight policy and budgetary control.

The headquarters of the WHO should exercise more oversight and control over regional personnel and decision-making. Minimally, the agency should fully disclose the funds held within each regional office and how regions meet health objectives, with monitoring and benchmarks of success. Even if decentralized decision making remains the norm, the WHO should apply the same yardstick across regions to assess efficiency and effectiveness.

4. Exert legal authority as a rule-making body. The WHO's constitution grants the agency extraordinary rule-making powers, but the agency has promulgated only 2 major treaties in more than 60 years: the International Health Regulations and the Framework Convention on Tobacco Control. The

WHO could take a more active role in regulating for the world's health on key issues, including counterfeit medicines, alcoholic beverages, food safety, and nutrition. It could be far more engaged and influential in international regimes with powerful health impacts such as trade, intellectual property, arms control, and climate change.

The agency could exert normative power through innovative treaties (e.g., a Framework Convention on Global Health) or through soft power (e.g., codes of practice) with strong incentives for compliance (5). The WHO must offer leadership for urgent challenges facing the global health system such as the need to set clear priorities, facilitate coherence among currently fragmented actors, and ensure fair burden sharing among states.

5. Ensure predictable, sustainable financing. The WHO is financed through 2 main streams. First, member states pledge a specified proportion of total assessed contributions calculated according to each country's wealth and population. The WHA then unanimously approves a core budget. The second stream is through voluntary contributions often earmarked for specific diseases, sectors, or countries. The development assistance committee of the Organisation for Economic Co-operation and Development calls extrabudgetary funding "*multi-bi*" aid (i.e., donors routing non-core funding allocated for specific purposes through multilateral agencies) (6).

The WHO's biennial budget more than doubled from US$ 1.6 billion in 1998-1999 to US$ 4.2 billion in 2008–2009, but the agency has a dire budget deficit of US$ 300 million this year. More importantly, its extrabudgetary budget increased from 48.8% to 77.3% during that period (7). It is not sustainable to have voluntary funding represent nearly 80% of the agency's budget. Moreover, extrabudgetary funding skews global health priorities. Assessed contributions are more aligned with the actual global burden of disease than extrabudgetary funding. For example, in 2008–2009, the WHO's extrabudgetary funding was primarily for infectious diseases (60%) and had negligible allocations for noncommunicable diseases (3.9%) and injuries (3.4%) (7). Yet noncommunicable diseases account for 62% of all deaths worldwide (8), and injuries account for 17% of the global burden of disease (9).

The director-general's report proposes broadening the base for flexible, unearmarked funding by attracting new donors such as foundations, emerging economies, and the private sector (2). Although worthwhile, these stakeholders are unlikely to behave differently than traditional donors, and probably will prefer to control their funds through earmarks. The ideal solution would be for the WHA to set higher member state contributions. Member states must become genuine shareholders in WHO's future, act collectively, and refrain from exerting narrow political interests. Failing decisive WHA action, the WHO could consider charging overheads of 20% to 30% for voluntary contributions to supplement its core budget. Although overheads are a familiar model in academia, the WHO would have to guard against the risk that charges might drive donors toward other multilateral organizations.

6. Global health leadership. If the WHO is to hold its rightful place as the leader in global health governance, the organization must undergo fundamental reform. There is no substitute for the WHO, with its progressive constitution and global legitimacy. It is not likely that the same powers would be granted to an international organization if it were created today. Consequently, while remaining true to its normative and bold vision of health for all, the WHO must adapt to a new political climate, demonstrate global leadership, and deliver results.

Acknowledgement: Originally published as: Devi Sridhar and Lawrence O. Gostin: Reforming the World Health Organization. Reprinted with permission from the American Medical Association (JAMA 2011; 305:1585–1586). Copyright © 2011 American Medical Association. All rights reserved.

References

1. Chow JC. Is the WHO becoming irrelevant? (Available from: http://www.foreignpolicy.com /articles/2010/12/08/is_the_who_becoming_irrelevant; Accessed: 18 Mar 2011).
2. World Health Organization. Future of financing for WHO. (Available from: http://apps.who .int/gb/ebwha/pdf_files/EB128/B128_21-en.pdf; Accessed: 18 Mar 2011).
3. Godlee F. WHO in crisis. BMJ 1994; 309:1424–1428.
4. Department for International Development. Multilateral aid review. (Available from: https: //s3-eu-west-1.amazonaws.com/media.dfid.gov.uk/multilateral_aid_review_full_linked.pdf; Accessed: 18 Mar 2011).
5. Gostin LO, Heywood M, Ooms G, et al. National and global responsibilities for health. Bull World Health Organ. 2010; 88:719–719A.
6. Organisation for Economic Co-operation and Development; Development Assistance Committee. 2010 DAC (development assistance committee) report on multilateral aid. (Available from: http://www.oecd.org/dataoecd/23/17/45828572.pdf; Accessed: 18 Mar 2011).
7. Sridhar D, Woods N. Trojan multilateralism: the changing face of global cooperation. Paper presented at: International Studies Association 52nd Annual Convention; March 16, 2011; Montreal, Canada.
8. World Health Organization. World Health Statistics 2010. Geneva: World Health Organization, 2010.
9. World Health Organization. Global Burden of Disease. Geneva: World Health Organization, 2010.

CHAPTER 34.

Global rules for global health: Why we need an independent, impartial World Health Organization

Over the past few years the World Health Organization (WHO) has been undergoing substantial reform. The immediate trigger was a budget crisis in 2010 that spurred massive staff cuts. But at a more fundamental level, deeper systematic changes in global health governance have made reform imperative (1). Though WHO reform draws relatively little attention outside diplomatic circles in Geneva, at stake are critical concerns that will affect public health everywhere.

The essential role of WHO is most often appreciated when outbreaks of infectious disease cross borders, such as the newly identified Middle East respiratory syndrome (MERS) coronavirus, which has infected 636 people since 2012 and has a death rate of about one in three (2). With an increasing number of cases being reported, fears exist that it could infect thousands of people, similar to the SARS (severe acute respiratory syndrome) coronavirus in 2002–2003 (3).

The international response to MERS has been more rapid than to SARS at least partly because of global structures that have facilitated epidemiological assessment, international information sharing, and the development of potential treatments. In an increasingly interconnected and interdependent world, global rules negotiated among governments are crucial for facilitating international cooperation and for protecting the health of the world's population. Sometimes adhering to these rules requires governments to forgo some of their sovereignty and to trust an international organisation to act impartially and independently for the common good. One of the fundamental reasons for the creation of WHO in 1948 was to ensure that governments would *compromise their short-term differences in order to attain the long-run advantages of regularized collaboration on health matters*" (4). Although many global health problems can be dealt with outside of WHO, the negotiation, agreement, and monitoring of compliance with global health rules can realistically take place only in WHO's main decision making body, the World Health Assembly. WHO possesses unique political legitimacy because its membership encompasses all countries in the United Nations. This legitimacy allows WHO to convene governments and others (such as civil society, experts, and business) to negotiate rules, resolve differences, and reach consensus – all key elements of stewardship, a core function of the global health system (5). MERS exemplifies at least three areas of global rule making that are crucial for protecting global health: rapid information sharing on new infectious threats, fair arrangements for access to drugs and vaccines, and research and development of technologies and other interventions.

1. Rules for information sharing on infectious disease. MERS is just the most recent illustration of the fact that states acting in isolation cannot control the spread of infectious disease across their borders. Global collective action is vital not only to protect health but also to secure trade and human rights. Global rules can help ensure prompt identification and control of disease through an interconnected global network of information and surveillance.

The stature and impartiality of WHO is crucial to its success in monitoring and disseminating information. Countries need to trust an international agency to report and use health information impartially in the interests of public health. The revised International Health Regulations (2005) require states to report certain public health events of international concern to WHO and establish procedures that WHO and its members must follow to uphold global public health security (6). WHO member states adopted the regulations to balance their sovereign rights with a shared commitment to prevent the international spread of disease.

The regulations require countries to strengthen their existing capacities for public health surveillance and response, while calling on higher income states to provide help with capacity building. Here again, WHO draws on its expertise to work closely with governments and partners to provide technical guidance and to mobilise the resources needed to implement the new rules effectively. The regulations do not include mechanisms to enforce compliance, and countries do not always fully or immediately report relevant data. But there are strong diplomatic and political pressures to conform to global rules, and each act of state compliance increases the normative force on other states to do the same.

2. Rules for access to health technologies in pandemics. More recently, WHO negotiated a highly contentious framework concerning the sharing of influenza viral samples and fair access to vaccines and treatments in the event of a pandemic. This was prompted by the Indonesian health minister's refusal to supply H5N1 virus samples to WHO Collaborating Centres for analysis and vaccine preparation in 2007, amid concerns about an outbreak of avian flu. She claimed that any vaccines or drugs derived from its viral samples were unlikely to be available to developing countries (7) and invoked the principle of viral sovereignty to defend her decision to withhold samples until a more equitable system for access to vaccines in a pandemic could be established.

If developing countries were to withhold viruses from WHO Collaborating Centres, it would pose a threat to global health security and the ongoing risk assessment for influenza. After multiple tense negotiations, member states agreed the Pandemic Influenza Preparedness (PIP) Framework for the sharing of influenza viruses and access to vaccines and other benefits in 2011. Though imperfect, the agreement balanced the goals of improving and strengthening the sharing of influenza viruses with efforts to increase access to vaccines and other pandemic related supplies by developing countries (8). The framework was adopted at the 64th World Health Assembly.

In negotiating the PIP Framework and the International Health Regulations, WHO served as a respected international intermediary to set vital global rules. These achievements could happen only because of WHO's international legitimacy, impartiality, and technical independence. WHO also used its position to negotiate more equitable access to other drugs.

3. Rules for generating innovation and access to medicines. New research findings were recently published that identified a compound that could potentially protect humans from MERS and other coronaviruses by inhibiting their replication (9). While it is too early to draw conclusions on the effect of this discovery, it is a timely reminder of the central importance of research for global health. The 15 coauthors of the publication were based at academic institutions in the Netherlands, Switzerland, Sweden, and Germany, and the work was funded by research institutes based in Europe and Japan. Once their results were announced, they became a valuable global public good of potential use to governments, drug developers, and health workers not only in the Middle East but in all countries at risk of infection.

However, research and development for emerging infections and globally equitable access to drugs, vaccines, and diagnostics remains one of the most contentious issues in global health. Although such technologies have the potential to prevent or treat deadly diseases, they also require costly investments in research and development. In the past, the governments of wealthy countries and the multinational drug industry largely financed such investments, with patients ultimately reimbursing the costs by paying high prices for new medicines. With the globalisation of patent rules in the 1990s through the World Trade Organization (WTO) agreement on Trade Related Aspects of Intellectual Property Rights (TRIPS), it became easier for companies to charge high prices for medicines in developing countries. As a result, drugs were often priced at unaffordable levels and access to medicines became a sensitive political issue. Companies now sell some cancer drugs, for example, for prices as high as US$ 70,000 in India, where two thirds of the population live on less than US$ 2 a day.

Concern about access to drugs, which first drew global attention with the HIV/AIDS crisis, prompted governments to amend global norms on intellectual property. An addition to TRIPS in 2001 stated it *"can and should be interpreted and implemented in a manner supportive of WTO Members' right to protect public health and, in particular, to promote access to medicines for all"* (10). This came after health ministers at WHO's World Health Assembly in 1996 insisted that health concerns be better incorporated into intellectual property rules (11). WHO was also instrumental in government negotiations to tackle shortcomings of the existing research and development system, which too often required difficult trade-offs between incentives for research (by keeping prices high) and ensuring widespread access (by keeping prices low) (12). The 2008 Global Strategy and Plan of Action on Public Health, Innovation and Intellectual Property paved the way to explore new global rules for encouraging, financing, coordinating, and ultimately sharing the benefits of research and development. A WHO expert group in 2012 recommended that governments start negotiating such rules within a proposed global treaty (13). After yet another round of difficult negotiations at WHO, in May 2013 governments agreed to test new approaches to innovation that would pay for research and development with public funds, so that costs do not need to be recuperated through high prices. And at the 2014 World Health Assembly, governments agreed to establish a pilot international fund to finance research and development, mobilising public funds from countries across the income spectrum.

Once research and development has been paid for, drug prices can be set at the lowest possible levels (a concept known as de-linkage, as it breaks the link between high drug prices and research financing). WHO member states are now exploring international coordination mechanisms to improve the efficiency of global research by reducing duplication and providing incentives for rapid and open sharing of research findings, and they are testing out some of these principles in demonstration projects (14).

4. WHO financing and stature. As new challenges arise that threaten health security across the world, the independence and neutrality of WHO become even more important. But WHO is struggling. Its core budget, which was intended to provide guaranteed, long term, predictable financing through assessed contributions by all WHO member states, has atrophied. Powerful stakeholders are increasingly funding WHO through voluntary contributions, which now make up 80% of WHO's total budget (15). In 2013, the Gates Foundation and the US and UK governments were the top three financial contributors to WHO. Roughly five sixths of UK funds and two thirds of US funds were channelled as voluntary contributions, which means the country has control over how it is spent (1). Top donors that channel a higher percentage of funds through core contributions are Japan, Germany, and France. Less wealthy countries rightfully question whether WHO has become an agent for powerful countries that have clear political incentives such as retaining tight control over the agency's priorities and operations for providing funding in this way (16).

Because discretionary funding is given to disease specific causes rather than to cover core normative functions such as rule making, the agency must plead with donor countries and organisations for needed resources. Voluntary funding, moreover, often is unconnected to the global burden of diseases (17). In addition, countries may choose to go entirely around the WHO through regional or small group bodies (18). For example, Brazil, Russia, India, China, and South Africa now convene an annual meeting of health ministers to strengthen cooperation on issues of shared interest among the five countries, such as technology transfer for medicine production and universal health coverage (19). Although WHO could benefit from additional resources, the greater challenge is that it needs a larger proportion of its budget guaranteed. The US made the prospect of financial stability within WHO virtually impossible by adopting a policy of zero nominal growth – a decline in real terms – for the core budget of UN agencies such as WHO in the 1999 Helms-Biden Act.

Amending this law and similar provisions in other countries to allow an increase in the core budget is critical to strengthen the independence and neutrality of WHO and requires strategic advocacy to frame it as an important national security concern given the agency's importance in managing new disease outbreaks (20). Core funding has not yet received the attention it deserves in the US Congress and other national legislatures. In addition, countries in arrears should be further pressured to meet their financial obligations to WHO. WHO is the only international agency that can broker global rules that protect the health of all, but is badly underfunded to perform this core function. The ongoing MERS outbreaks offer a critical opportunity to reform WHO financing so that it can perform its vital normative functions.

Acknowledgement: Reproduced from BMJ (Global rules for global health: Why we need an independent, impartial World Health Organization. By Devi Sridhar, Julio Frenk, Lawrence Gostin and Suerie Moon. Volume 348, pages 38–41, Copyright © 2014, BMJ

Publishing Group Ltd, reprinted with permission). We thank Genevie Fernandes of the University of Edinburgh for research help and acknowledge insights gained from participation in the Chatham House high level working groups on WHO reform and sustainable financing convened by David Heymann, of which all four authors were members.

References

1. Clift C. What's the World Health Organization for? Chatham House, 2014.
2. World Health Organization. Middle East respiratory syndrome coronavirus (MERS-CoV)—update. Disease Outbreak News 2014. (Available from: www.who.int/csr/don/2014_05_28_mers/en).
3. Garrett L. Why MERS virus is so scary. CNN, 2 Jun 2013. (Available from: http://edition.cnn.com/2013/05/31/opinion/garrett-mers-virus).
4. Allen C. World health and world politics. Int Organ 1950; 4:27–43.
5. Frenk J, Moon S. Governance challenges in global health. N Engl J Med 2013; 368:936-942.
6. Gostin L. Global health law. Cambridge, MA: Harvard University Press, 2014.
7. Sedyaningsih ER, Isfandari S, Soendoro T, Supari SF. Towards mutual trust, transparency and equity in virus sharing mechanisms: the avian influenza case of Indonesia. Ann Acad Med Singapore 2008; 73:482–488.
8. Kamradt-Scott A, Lee K. The 2011 pandemic influenza preparedness framework: global health secured or a missed opportunity? Polit Stud 2011; 59: 831–847.
9. Lundin A, Dijkman R, Bergström T, Kann N, Adamiak B, Hannoun C, et al. Targeting membrane-bound viral RNA synthesis reveals potent inhibition of diverse coronaviruses including the Middle East respiratory syndrome virus. PLoS Pathog 2014; 10:e1004166.
10. World Trade Organization. Declaration on the TRIPS agreement and public health, 2001. Document WT/MIN(01)/DEC/2. (Available from: www.wto.org/english/thewto_e/minist_e/min01_e/mindecl_trips_e.htm).
11. 't Hoen E. The global politics of pharmaceutical monopoly power. AMB Publishers, 2009:17.
12. Moon S, Bermudez J, 't Hoen E. Innovation and access to medicines for neglected populations: could a treaty address a broken pharmaceutical R&D system? PLoS Med 2012; 9:e1001218.
13. WHO Consultative Expert Working Group on Research and Development: Financing and Coordination. Research and development to meet health needs in developing countries: strengthening global financing and coordination. Geneva: WHO, 2012.
14. Rottingen J, Moon S, Tangcharoensathien V. Multistakeholder technical meeting on implementation options recommended by the WHO consultative expert working group on research & development: financing and coordination. Cambridge, MA: Harvard Global Health Institute, 2012.
15. Sridhar D. Who sets the global health research agenda? The challenge of multi-bi financing. PLoS Med 2012; 9:e1001312.
16. Sridhar D, Woods N. Trojan multilateralism: global cooperation in health. Global Policy 2013; 4:325–335.
17. Nozaki I. WHO's budgetary allocation and disease burden. Lancet 2013; 382:937–938.

18. Woods N, Betts A, Prantl J, Sridhar D. Transforming global governance for the 21st century. UNDP Human Development Report Office, 2013. (Available from: http://hdr. undp.org/sites/default/ files/hdro_1309_woods.pdf.)

19. Barbosa da Silva J, Desiraju K, Matsoso P, Minghui R, Salagay O. BRICS cooperation in strategic health projects. Bull World Health Organ 2014; 92:388.

20. Mackey TK, Novotny TA. Improving United Nations funding to strengthen global health governance: amending the Helms-Biden agreement. Glob Health Gov 2012; VI.

CHAPTER 35.

Economic ideology and politics in the World Bank: Defining hunger

"A Virginia planter advised in the 1837 "Farmers' Register" that the most important subject in slave management was sufficiency of food: The master who gives his field hands half a pound of meat per day and two quarts of meal... is better compensated by slave labour, than those who give the ordinary quantity".

– Alan Berg, First Nutrition Advisor to the World Bank in 1974 (1)

"Health is too important to leave it to the health people" – Jean Louis-Sarbib
"Like war and the generals" – Philip Musgrove

– Conversation between the Bank's Senior Vice-President and a former health economist at the World Bank (2)

In the last 35 years, the World Bank has become the largest financial contributor towards health related and nutrition projects, committing more than one billion dollars annually towards the Health, Nutrition and Population sector (HNP). Other than as a lending agency, the Bank has innumerable unofficial functions such as an advisory body, an intellectual research institute, and a training centre for developing country civil servants. Symbolically, the World Bank is the arbiter of development norms and meaning combining intellectual prestige and financial power. Its annual World Development Report (WDR) and staff working papers have established it as an intellectual powerhouse whose research represents the cutting edge of development.

Given the significant role the World Bank plays in the global nutrition community, an analysis of the policy process for nutrition-related lending is critical. This paper examines the interlacing of economic ideology and politics in World Bank nutrition policy. It is an attempt to uncover the workings of power through a close look at the structures, discourses and agencies through which nutrition policy operates, and in particular to discuss the process by which nutrition has remained an area of concern at the Bank.

The Bank began to fund stand-alone nutrition projects under the Presidency of Robert McNamara who brought to the Bank an agenda outlining the moral imperative of foreign aid both for humanitarian and national security purposes. The first section of this paper examines the ways in which the Bank justified involvement in nutrition in the 1970s and the role of economic principles, such as the reliance on market forces, in shaping the Bank's involvement in this issue. The history of why the Bank chose to make loans for nutrition is extremely relevant as it partially explains the significance of economic models in the HNP sector. This section explains how in the late 1970s, nutrition was transformed from a medical issue to a concern for economists and how an *"econometrics of suffering"* was developed.

To publicize its new role as a development agency, the Bank focused its 1980 World Development Report on the importance of investing in the social sector since improved health and nutrition would accelerate economic growth. The Bank then adopted an economic theory on the individual which is commonly referred to as human capital theory. This framework justifies nutrition loans on the basis that they are an investment in the future productivity of a nation. The second section of this paper examines the underlying tenets of human capital theory, as well as the implications for health resource allocation.

This shift towards addressing health and nutritional issues was firmly established by the 1993 WDR *"Investing in Health"* which was the first annual report to be devoted entirely to health. The 1993 WDR launched a new Bank framework for applying economic principles to health through the use of cost-effectiveness and introduced other cost-benefit analyses. Turning to the evaluation of potential nutrition projects, the third section of this paper examines how the Bank has used the tool of cost-effectiveness in health either to justify spending or to identify failures. While the importance of lending for nutrition is constantly in flux at the Bank, the Bank's approach to addressing this issue has remained essentially the same over the past 35 years. The final section of the paper addresses the question, *"Why does nutrition have to be looked at in this way in the World Bank?"*. In particular, it examines the ideological and political factors that have influenced lending for nutrition.

There is increasing interest in the use of anthropological methodologies to study the World Bank, such as by Robert Wade on environmentalism, Gerhard Anders on good governance technologies, and Diane Stone and Chris Wright on internal reform (3–7). This paper aims to add to the growing literature by revealing how economic analysis and politics intertwine in the World Bank's nutrition operations. Research for this paper consisted of semi-structured interviews with current and former Bank staff, consultants and associates between June 2005 and January 2006 as well as critical discourse analysis of key Bank documents.

1. Mainstreaming nutrition into an economics-dominated organization: 1971-1980. In 1971, experts from various fields and government officials from several countries gathered at the Massachusetts Institute for Technology (MIT) for the first International Conference on Nutrition, National Development and Planning. That same year Alan Berg, then working for Food for Peace, published a paper in *Foreign Affairs* arguing that nutrition planning was crucial for development. This led to the Council for Foreign Relations sponsoring Berg for a year at the Brookings Institution to write a book on nutrition and national development. Published in 1973, Berg's *"The Nutrition Factor"* is viewed as catalysing the emergence of food and nutrition policy and nutritional planning on the international stage. Berg gave a presentation on his book to the Board of Brookings, which included Bank President McNamara.

McNamara was intrigued by the economic arguments Berg presented regarding the urgency of addressing undernutrition in developing countries. He contracted Berg to write a policy note on nutrition and economic development. This brief was crucial as it convinced the Bank's Board of Executive Directors and several senior managers that the Bank should start lending for nutrition. Berg made two arguments to the Bank. The first was that nutrition was a development concern that had an impact on productivity. It was not just a medical or social welfare issue. Second, he argued that nutrition needed the involvement of managers. It needed to move away from its association with *"medical, biochemist, welfare"* types. The latter issue, the move from the medically oriented approach to the development planners approach positioned nutrition in the domain of economics. Berg argued that there needed to be a switch to *"macronutrition"*. By this term he meant the transition of nutrition from the clinic and laboratory to development planning in institutions such as the World Bank. The mainstreaming of nutrition in development brought it into the domain of economists who dominate the development apparatus in the Bank.

The Bank management were hesitant to engage with nutrition because of its complexity, its inter-sectoral nature and *"the nature of the Bank's system for assessing and rewarding staff"* (8). Health-related projects were viewed as a *"bottomless pit"*. However with McNamara's urging, the Bank's Board decided to finance the implementation and evaluation of certain largely experimental actions in countries with high priority. Berg and others involved in nutrition during the 1970s and 1980s recount how difficult it was to convince the senior economists to lend for nutrition, calling it an *"uphill battle"*. As one staffer noted, *"Nutrition has always occupied a strange position, I mean, economists think it's too complicated and there are no clear demonstrations of success. They think the evalua-*

tions are ineffective and that food subsidies are a bad idea. During the retreat on this, sceptics want to trash the nutrition programmes so we have to fight quite hard for it. Nutrition goes through cycles at the Bank. The biggest problem is the complexity, and task managers and leaders not knowing how to do it, how to get the project approved, how to push through such a complicated thing".

Similarly, another staffer explained, *"The bureaucratic politics of main-streaming nutrition, what a story. There were very very high objections and resistance on the part of senior economists who were more concerned with transferring money than what you did with it. They wanted a return. So the nutritionists turned arguments against them and created productivity numbers, they wanted numbers so we played that game".*

Returning to the emphasis on numbers, several nutrition staff would argue that the Bank's main contribution to nutrition was quantifying the economic and social benefits of involvement in this sector. Econometrics is defined as the application of statistical and mathematical methods in the field of economics to describe the numerical relationships between key economic forces such as capital, interest rates and labour. In the push to convince Bank managers to fund nutrition in the late 1970s, a new metrics of nutrition was created in which theoretical models were used to draw relationships between nutritional gains, labour, discount rates and productivity. Using these models, the previously unquantifiable such as the value of adequate nutritional status could be numerically expressed and thus enter into calculations. Economists were uncomfortable with the complexity of nutrition and the difficulty in evaluating the economic gains from nutrition projects. To make nutrition comprehensible to senior economists, production functions were employed such as:

Equation 1: $Q = A * L^l * K^k$

In **Equation 1**, Q stands for output, A stands for conversion coefficient, L is labour, K is capital, l is the percent increase in output per 1% increase in labour, and k is the percent increase in output per 1% increase in capital (9). Once this was established, a second equation was derived that included food consumption as a proxy for nutritional status:

Equation 2: $N\,(df) = N\,(dy) * (dc/dy) * (dq/dc)$

In **Equation 2**, N *(df)* stands for the expected number of low income individuals who move from *"poor"* diet to *"fair"* diet, N *(dy)* is the number of low income individuals at risk multiplied by the change in real income of each participant, dc is the change in participant food consumption associated with a change in real income, dy is the family income, dq is the estimated proportion of households with *"poor diets"*, and *dc* is the current level of food consumption (9). Once *N (df)* is estimated, then the change in labour can be estimated and entered into **Equation 1**. Using these two equations, a direct mathematical link can be drawn between an increase in food consumption and an increase in output per person, or productivity.

In addition, by using the proxy of food for nutrition in this time period, Berg could gain the attention of economists: *"(E)conomic distinction commonly is made between food and nutrition-ranking food "high", nutrition "low"; or food "essential", nutrition "welfare". Food has obvious tangibility features that nutrition lacks. Food costs and supplies can be measured, subjected to economic analysis, and entered into the national accounts. Nutrition in contrast often is invisible and dimly understood, and it seldom commands a price, especially among those who need it most"* (1).

Berg had difficulty convincing the senior economists that the Bank should make loans for nutrition. For example, his initial policy paper for President McNamara was neglected for many months since there was an oil crisis in 1971 that diverted attention away from nutrition. (Although a major shock to economists, it was also of grave concern to nutritionists as the price of food increased dramatically). Since this time, the numerical equations used to describe productivity gains from investment in nutrition have increased in complexity. Economic functions have been continually used to justify Bank involvement in nutrition as well as to increase the likelihood of management approval of nutrition lending.

Concerning nutrition metrics, since this time period, the Bank has emphasised the use of production functions to justify involvement in nutrition. This dialogue is the only one that is permitted and used. This can be viewed as an *"econometrics of suffering"*, the situation where mathematical analysis of production relationships is used to determine the magnitude of nutritional deprivation and provides justification for spending to alleviate this destitution. Quantification makes hunger real to economists and to planners.

The previous section has discussed how the language of nutrition metrics is one defining influence economists have had on nutrition-related projects. This section examines another influence: how the economic principle of information asymmetry led to a particularly favoured intervention by the Bank to improve nutritional status in developing countries. One of the key concerns in economics is the nature and extent of public sector involvement (10). The Bank tends to favour the private sector as *"public sector institutions have often been found to operate less efficiently than those in the private sector"* (11). The World Bank argues that government involvement can only be justified in specifically defined cases. These include where there are identifiable failures in the market (i.e. the private sector), which arise in the case of public goods, externalities, and imperfect information, or where income redistribution is considered desirable (10).

Bank nutritionists have perceived market failure as one of the key reasons why malnutrition rates are extremely high in South Asia (12). In this framework, government expenditure on nutrition has been justified on the basis that markets have failed (13). Information, in the form of nutrition education, mass communication or counselling, has been viewed as an adequate government response to this market failure. Behaviour modification is expected to occur through nutrition education. This approach is still evident today. As a 2006 Bank report states, *"People do not always know what food or what feeding practices are best for their children or themselves…the need to correct these "information asymmetries" is another argument for government intervention"* (12). Since the pilot projects of the late 1970s, nutrition education, using the tools of growth monitoring and supplementary feeding, has been the base of the Bank project design. The underlying assumption has been that once individuals and households have the necessary information, behavioural change will occur and malnutrition rates will drop (1). Proponents of this perspective have used *"positive deviance"* (children who grow much better than the median of their community) to argue that even in conditions of deprivation, households can adopt strategies to improve the nutritional status of their children. As a 1996 Bank document notes, *"Improvements in child nutrition so often depend on changing feeding and care-giving behaviours in the home"* (14). Thus, the economic influence on Bank nutrition project design is apparent through the emphasis on nutrition education to correct the information asymmetry as well as the significance of rate of return on investment.

2. Health as a commodity and health as an investment: 1980–1993. As a result of McNamara's Presidency, which ended in 1981, the Bank moved closer towards the role of a development agency. The 1980 WDR solidified the rhetoric that the involvement of the Bank in health and nutrition was justified on the grounds that investing in the social sector would accelerate economic growth. The Bank adopted an economic theory on the individual which is commonly referred to as *"human capital theory"*. Human capital theory employs an instrumental, rather than intrinsic, approach to project beneficiaries. This will now be explained.

In general, health economists have used two alternative models for describing the attainment of *"good health"* (11). The first is health as one of several commodities over which individuals have well-defined preferences, the intrinsic approach. The second approach to health is the human capital approach which constructs health as stock, or a future investment in an individual, the instrumental approach (11). The economic definition of human capital theory is that individuals allocate resources at one point of time in order to bring about certain outcomes at another point of time (15). In this model, health and good nutritional status are valuable because the body is used as a productive resource. The more health one is able to acquire, the more valuable this will be in the future.

As noted earlier, health as investment was first emphasized by the Bank in the 1980 WDR on poverty (2). Since this time, the Bank has predominantly relied on the human capital framework to lobby governments to take loans for nutrition-related projects. Applying the concept of human capital to health, Alan Berg argued in 1981 that nutrition and national economy were linked through investment in human beings: "*Recently...the concept of capital has been extended to human beings. Development of the new theory was prompted by the discovery that "increases in national output have been large compared with the increases of land, man-hours and physical reproducible capital." Investment in human capital is probably the major explanation for this difference*" (16).

Berg then described the many economic benefits of investment in child nutrition (1). The first is that of savings on medical costs through reduced demand for curative medical services (e.g. hospitalisation). The second benefit is that of reduced productivity losses caused by the debility of the labour force: "*The failure to meet basic needs for nutrition means higher death rates and a less productive population*" (16). Although conceding that the assumptions were "*heroic*", Berg noted that productivity losses could be measured through a comparison of a country's average caloric need to average national caloric consumption. A country's average caloric need could be calculated through the occupational distribution of the labour force. The shortfall in national working capacity could be used to estimate the productivity losses from nutritional deficit.

However, Berg acknowledged the methodological difficulties with estimating productivity losses. First, using an indicator such as physical growth is made complicated because of infection, possible genetic factors as well as the reference used for comparison. Second, using an input-based indicator has problems due to recall, intrahousehold allocation of resources, the special needs of individuals, micronutrient deficiencies as well as food waste. Third, nutritional status is seasonally dependent indicating that it is hard to relate it to human performance at any given time. Finally, the relationship between income and nutritional status has been shown to be weak.

The third benefit of investment in child nutrition is the extension of working years, malnutrition reducing the number of productive working years. Other economic benefits of nutrition investment include a decrease in the incidence of infectious disease, better care for children, and returns on other investments in human capital such as education. Thus an economic case was made to *"upgrade the potential productivity of those masses of unskilled, landless, adult workers who have dim prospects of gainful employment"* (1). Nutritional investment and subsequent economic development will *"get the person out of the isolated village and change their fears, beliefs and attitudes"* (9).

Thus, in the human capital framework, initially propagated by the Bank in the early 1980s, child nutritional well-being and health are directly tied to future labour and productivity. This approach is still employed today. For example, in 2005, the World Bank estimated that malnourished children have at least a 10% reduction in lifetime earnings. Thus, investing in child nutrition will have fruitful payoffs in the future when the child becomes an adult member of the workforce.

A 2005 Bank document titled, *"To Nourish a Nation: Investing in Nutrition with World Bank Assistance"* which is used for lobbying governments states, *"The challenges of development require a strong human resource base – a workforce that is physically strong, mentally alert, and healthy. But malnutrition robs a country of these resources"* (17). It continues with the following section titled, *"Children's Growth = Economic Growth"* which discusses how *"Children with retarded growth become stunted adults who are less productive… these problems have implications for human achievement and economic development"* (17). It then presents data on how iron deficiency, anaemia, causes, *"a 10–15% reduction in work output in many different occupations. Thus, the productivity of entire populations is needlessly reduced"* (17). Using this framework, the Bank estimates that returns to nutrition investment are as high as 84-to-1 (17).

In the case of countries like India, the World Bank estimates that Gross Domestic Product (GDP) lost to malnutrition is as high as 2–3%. Worldwide, the Bank estimates that malnutrition costs at least US$ 80 billion per year, and for India, at least US$ 10 billion (18). Thus, health and nutrition have been directly linked to economic growth. The initial productivity arguments that Alan Berg used to convince the Bank's Board to initially invest in nutrition-related projects are still being employed today.

Using productivity gain estimates and the human capital framework in the 1980s, the Bank created *"target groups"* of individuals who should be the beneficiaries of nutrition projects (19). Since their creation for the pilot projects, the composition of target groups has essentially remained the same. These target groups should be viewed as economic constructs. They were defined by the age and gender that would most impact on economic growth in the future. In the creation of target groups, individuals were identified as a beneficiary or an individual "*at risk*" based on a single characteristic, such as age or pregnancy status. The beneficiaries were chosen based on their instrumental importance for the economy, rather than for their intrinsic worth as individuals.

World Bank nutrition projects have generally specified three main target groups as beneficiaries: preschool children and pregnant and lactating women (10). Preschool children have been targeted because it is during the first few years of life that a child's most rapid physical and intellectual growth occurs (17). Thus the "*benefits of nutrition and other inputs are…maximised when they are timed accordingly*" (17). A World Bank paper titled "*Nutrition and Economic Sector work*" (2005) states: "*Undernutrition's most damaging impact occurs during pregnancy and in the first two years of life, and the effects of this early damage on health, brain development, intelligence, educability, and productivity are largely irreversible. Actions targeted at older ages have little, if any impact… Governments with limited resources are therefore best advised to focus actions on this small 'window of opportunity', between conception and 24 months of age*" (20).

The World Bank has targeted its projects at preschool children because improving their nutrition and investing in their human capital will have the strongest impact on productivity. Similarly, during the nine months of pregnancy and six months of lactation, a woman becomes the target of nutrition interventions. The predominant reason for this inclusion is that it is during these stages that a woman is constructed as a mother or future mother. She must ensure the health of a future member of the work force. Her nutritional status is valued instrumentally, not instrincally. If her health was valued solely then a woman would receive health services and food supplements regardless of pregnancy status. However, this is not the case as non-pregnant, non-lactating women have not been included as beneficiaries in nutrition project design.

Pregnant women have been viewed as instrumentally important to decrease the incidence of low-birth weight infants (21). The most critical determinant of low-birth weight is maternal malnutrition, specifically protein-energy and iron deficiencies. (Other determinants include smoking and alcohol use by mother, genetics, congenital abnormalities or infections, and age of mother). Well-nourished women gain, on average, 10 kilograms during pregnancy. Low nutrient intake and high caloric expenditure can compromise the health of the developing baby. Lactating women have been viewed as instrumentally important to ensure that an infant is healthy during its first six months of life. Physiologically, breast milk is the best food for the child during this period, preventing infection while also developing the immune and digestive system. The main interventions that the Bank offers are nutrition counselling (breast-feeding promotion) and supplementary feeding (21). Although a moderately undernourished woman can produce an adequate amount of breast milk, a severely malnourished woman may produce 20–30% less breast milk than her well-nourished counterpart. To address this problem, the Bank nutrition projects offer food supplements which replenish a woman's nutrient stores and ensure the child is being breastfed sufficiently (22).

The second benefit of targeting lactating women is that breastfeeding acts as a contraceptive. Physiologically, infant suckling inhibits ovulation (23–24). In addition, cultural factors can result in post-partum avoidance of intercourse. For example, Ayurvedic humeral ideology states that food is progressively transformed from a series of body substances from blood, flesh and bone to breast milk and semen (*"dhatu"* – *"semen"* refers to the substance that both women and men release during intercourse). As *dhatu* reserves in the form of semen become depleted through sexual experience, the body attempts to replenish these reserves. This leads to a reduction in the amount of breast milk produced (25). Other cultural beliefs in India include that a mother's breast milk spoils if she has intercourse while lactating (25). Thus family planning could also have been a factor in the creation of the target group of nursing women in the 1980s.

3. The tool of cost-effectiveness: 1993–2006. Since the 1993 WDR, cost-effectiveness in health has become the flagship tool of the Bank to evaluate various nutrition schemes. The report attempted to reconcile the specificity of health with the traditional methods of economics (2). The Bank argued that the tool of cost-effectiveness was essential in making the *"right choices among sectors and among designs for any given policy and institutional context"*. It was necessary to evaluate the different policy options to *"eradicate"* hunger and determine which was the most efficient (17). While attractive in rhetoric, the identification and measurement of costs and benefits for projects has been difficult for the Bank to operationalise. Prior to the 1993 WDR, a 1992 World Bank report on cost-effectiveness and nutrition presented limited information on the cost per death averted of select nutrition interventions then concludes that the existing data on cost-effectiveness is inadequate to properly assess projects. It notes: *"existing studies tend to cite over and over again data from the same few projects"* (26).

Within the Bank, since the turn towards cost-effectiveness, there has been confusion surrounding an exact formula for measurement of costs and benefits. Discussing cost-benefit analysis, a 1994 Bank document states: *"Al-*

though it would be desirable to have a standard cost-benefit methodology with precise rules for calculation for every situation, this is not the present case… (A)lthough the conceptual methods for identifying and measuring benefits are well-established, the application of these methods depends crucially on a variety of judgements on both the measurement of benefits and their values" (27).

The basic method for estimating benefits is first to identify the positive effects of an intervention on areas such as mortality, morbidity, work output and productivity (27). The benefits of reduced mortality are generally considered to be the value of lost productivity, for morbidity the value of lost productivity plus the savings in health care, and for work output and productivity the additional days of productive work and the additional productivity per day. The key step is the application of monetary values to each of these areas. **Table 35-1** adapted from the *"World Bank Nutrition Toolkit"* illustrates the process.

Table 35-1. *Benefit-cost ratio of providing food to malnourished children (adapted from ref. 10).*

INFORMATION	VALUE
Transfer of 50,000 calories to malnourished children leads to a height increase of:	1 cm
Cost per 1,000 calories	$0.20
Cost per centimeter of height gain in adults	$10
Average adult height	160 cm
Increase in 1cm as percentage of average height	0.625%
Elasticity of labor productivity with respect to height	1.38
1 cm increase in height is associated with an increase in wages of	0.86%
Annual current income	$750
Increase in annual wages from an increase in height of 1cm	$6.45
Discount rate	0.03
Real wage increase	0.02
Productive years	18–55yrs
The present value of additional lifetime earnings from an increase in height of 1 cm	$174
Benefit-Cost Ratio	17.4

Since 1993, the World Bank has emphasised the indicator *"cost per death averted"* and since 1993 the *"cost per Disability-Adjusted Life Year (DALY) averted"* as useful measures of the cost-benefit of a project (28). (For nutrition, other indicators used include *"cost per case of child stunting averted"*, *"cost per 0.1 kg increase in birth weight"*, *"cost per child removed from third degree malnutrition"*, etc.) (28). World Bank staffers claim that *"Computing the cost per disability-adjusted life year (DALY) of interventions provides an objective measure"* (29). **Table 35-2** provides an example of a typical Bank cost-effectiveness analysis. The source given for the information in the table is *"based on author's assumptions"*.

When presenting a tentative loan for approval to senior managers, the focus has been on whether the design of the project is the most efficient, the most cost-effective, to achieve the desired impact. For nutrition, projects have been assessed on the cost per death or the cost per DALY averted. The assumptions by which these numbers were computed are seldom investigated. These analyses are based on theoretical models and quantification which are presentable and understandable to the economist managers. An example of this from **Table 35-1** is the use of the indicator *"the present value of additional lifetime earnings from an increase in height of 1 cm"* in which height has become a form of capital such as land. The body has been commoditised to have a certain economic value. Bank staff acknowledge the lack of rigorousness of these indicators and the implicit value judgments that they are based on. However, those in the HNP sector have been forced to present projects in this manner in order to conform to the Bank mandate as well as the related ideology of the Bank.

Table 35-2. *Cost per Death/DALY Averted in Iron Interventions (from ref. 27).*

PARAMETER	IRON SUPPLEMENTATION OF PREGNANT WOMEN	IRON FORTIFICATION
Target group	Pregnant women	All people
Number	4,000	100,000
Average rate (percent)*	63	50
Program effectiveness (percent)	75	75
Deaths averted	10	10
Immediate productivity gains (percent)	20	20
Program duration (days)	200	Year round
Program costs (US$)	8,000	20,000
Discounted wage gains (US$)	221,280**	1,682,720***
DALY gained	624****	4,520*****
Wage gains divided by program cost	27.7	84.1
Cost per DALY (US$)	12.8	4.40
Cost per death averted (US$)	800	2,000

*Rate of anemia for iron supplementation of pregnant women; rate of iron deficiency for iron fortification; **Calculated as the product of the number of anemic participants times disability times wages times effectiveness times employment, plus the product of number of deaths times wage times employment times productive life expectancy; ***Calculated as the product of the number of adult participants times disability times effectiveness times employment times wages, plus the product of number of deaths times wage times employment times productive life expectancy; ****Calculated as the product of the number of deaths times life expectancy, plus the product of disability times number of malnourished participants times effectiveness; *****Calculated as the product of number of adult participants times the rate of anemia times disability times effectiveness, plus the product of the number of deaths times life expectancy

Both cost-benefit and cost-effectiveness analyses in nutrition suffer from methodological difficulties in practice. First, the impact of nutrition interventions normally occurs over a long period of time compared to immunisation or other short-term health interventions (26). In addition, most nutrition interventions do not occur in isolation. Nutrition education, growth monitoring and supplementary feeding often occur in conjunction with health services, food subsidies, and school feeding programmes. This makes it difficult to conduct a proper assessment of the nutritional impact of a project. Third, the use of the indicator *"cost per death averted"* is an extreme measure of outcome neglecting the toll of malnutrition on well-being and general health. It does not include a measurement of the quality of life for survivors or the *"dark side of child survival"* which refers to excessive morbidity (30). Other problems with analysis are difficulties with data collection in the field and the use of different standards for measuring malnutrition which are both part of the general problem of large-scale quantitative analysis in nutrition.

Given these methodological problems some academics have argued that the use of cost-effectiveness in decision-making processes can be essentially useless. Development economist Alice Sindzingre notes that models and econometrics work at such a high level of aggregation and use such broad categories that although they may always be proven true (non-falsifiable), they are still meaningless (31). Although cost-effectiveness can serve a useful allocative function, the conclusions reached are dependent on the values entered into the equation. For example, suppose that two projects are being evaluated to determine which is more efficient in achieving a death averted. If there is a clear preference for one, it is possible to first determine what the outcome should be then work the equation backwards to determine the value of the variables to achieve the preferred options. Reflecting on this, William Ascher notes *"The staff member can, consciously or unconsciously, convert personal disagreement with policy into technical caveats about the applicability of the policy in specific cases"* (32).

Despite its limitations, cost-effectiveness is still a key determinant of a project's approval by the World Bank. The 1993 WDR used the term over 200 times to reiterate the Bank's contribution to health, namely in quantification of costs and benefits. Due to its subjective nature and value-added calculation, the label *"cost-effective"* has served as the Bank's ambiguous symbol. It has been purposefully ambiguous such that it could reflect a diversity of interests and approaches. In each particular situation, depending on certain circumstances, cost-effectiveness could assume the form needed to justify involvement and garner support or to indicate a flawed design. In addition, *"Power relations may use this very indeterminacy to select particular descriptions and present them as "the truth" (scientific) because the claim of scientificity (of being the exclusive truth) is a helpful tool for the exercise of power"* (31). Cost-effectiveness has not been employed as a conceptual tool; it has been used as a tactical one.

The Bank presents its operations as being technical and objective, and based on sound, economic analysis. However, the assumptions entering calculations include several value judgments taken by Bank staff, both during McNamara's Presidency and today. These have been disguised in models and productivity functions which can be used to justify a particular involvement by the Bank in a nutrition project. As Paul Nelson notes, *"Economic doctrine helps the Bank shape discourse about development around technique and science rather than values and politics. The presentation of economic theories as scientific formulations shields them from criticism, permitting the Bank to exert financial leverage to promote not 'its' way but a certifiably 'correct way'"* (33).

4. Ideology and politics in the Bank: 1971–2006. During the negotiations with economists over nutrition-related lending in the 1970s, nutrition staff had to make tactical concessions which pushed them towards econometric models. And, to ensure the survival of lending for nutrition, HNP staff have continued to translate their case into economic terms: *"the weapon of choice was numbers"*.

As the evidence presented in this paper demonstrates, nutrition has been framed within the Bank as an issue of human capital. In nutrition projects, the worth of project beneficiaries has been based on their contribution to the economy and thus to social welfare. This can be demonstrated by the economist function that puts a monetary value on years lost to mortality through using the individual's expected wages and by the creation of target groups. The target group of preschool children has attracted considerable health investment. This has been justified by the World Bank on the grounds that proper nutrition is crucial for both *"physical and mental functioning"* in their adult years (12). A healthy child has been defined as a *"public good"* in that *"it"* (the child) has welfare effects for society as a whole (12). Likewise, the target group of pregnant and lactating women has been given importance because of the functional role of mothers in raising children to be productive adults.

The human capital framework for nutrition within the Bank is a general reflection of the dominance of economics in public health development projects, which can be viewed as the *"economic gaze"*. The economic gaze refers to the process by which those individuals working within the Bank on public health as well as the beneficiaries of public health projects have been disciplined and regulated through the constraints of economic theory. This has resulted in a situation where staffers design projects in a manner consistent with human capital and other economic principles if they would like to gain loan approval from senior managers as well as be promoted.

Within the Bank, the discipline of economics can be viewed as hegemonic, the only way of examining problems, of defining their essential features and suggesting solutions. The strength of economic knowledge is seen to lie in its ability to manage the details of a local issue, reduce the complexity, and extract indicators and specific policy goals (34). Local knowledge is considered messy, complicated, political, and incomprehensible to the institution. Thus, an economic approach reduces problems, such as nutrition, to their core elements so that the professional expertise can digest them objectively and prescribe solutions.

For the above reasons, the Bank has been described as an *"economic fortress"* by its staff (19) where internal operations and activities are dominated by economic paradigms and frameworks. This is true within the Bank's HNP sector which has often been run by an economist who ensures that potential project loans are designed to be consistent with the Bank's economic framework and legal mandate. This principle is a constraining factor on HNP staff who would like to justify loans or Bank involvement on other, i.e. human rights, grounds. It has been argued that economists are diverse, so classifying them into a single group is misleading. While this critique is acknowledged, within the Bank, there is an overwhelmingly Anglo-Saxon approach to economics (35). Unlike other United Nations agencies, English is the working language of the Bank. (Early in the history of the international financial institutions, the United States ensured there would be no national quotas for hiring and that English would be the working language) (36). Thus, this requirement favours graduates of institutions that teach in English. As fluency in English is *"tended to be correlated with preferred economic and social status"*, the Bank's composition primarily is composed of elites (35). A 1991 study of the high-level staff in the Policy, Research and External Affairs Departments of the Bank shows that roughly 80% had trained in economics and finance at institutions in the United States and United Kingdom (37). Ascher notes that the economists in the Bank behave very much alike, whether they are Indian, Brazilian, English, or Canadian (32). Thus ideological divisions within the Bank do not reflect a conflict between North and South as much as between the Chicago School and the Sussex School.

The Bank has also been described by its staff as a *"church protecting an orthodox bureaucracy"*. One of these principles, a legacy of McNamara's Presidency, is quantification and measurability. As one staffer put it, *"If you can't measure it, then it doesn't exist"*. The emphasis on quantitative language has resulted in staff becoming bureaucratic entrepreneurs and attempting to develop packages that can be sold to the economists on the operational teams. Alan Berg was a master of this. In the 1970s, he convinced economists that nutrition was an issue of lost productivity and brought a health issue into the realm of capital and economic growth. Bank nutrition staff gained the attention of senior economists through presenting *"hard numbers"* and models. Nutrition is an issue within the Bank that has not had a stable or powerful position. Some economists have argued that the Bank should be a bank and not a health development agency and that it suffers from *"mission creep"*. They have argued that the Bank is a financial institution. It was created to address solvable problems with measurable returns using lending instruments. One staffer noted that there has been continual resistance on the part of senior economists who have been more concerned with transferring money and delivering lending on time rather the quality of lending.

Despite the push to lend fast, economists have wanted a measurable return. This leads to a further problem that economists have had with nutrition: the effects of nutrition interventions are generally hard to discern, difficult to measure, and long-term. In the Bank, Task Managers need to sell a package internally and ensure that it is judged successful by the Operations Evaluation Department. Thus staff are urged to think *"backwards"*, to pay attention to assessment. However, nutritional status is a complex outcome of multiple forces thus making short-term returns unrealistic to obtain. Reflecting on this tension, one staffer noted, *"It is much harder for the Task Leader to target and follow the money... In countries with weak capacity or failing governments, it is impossible to show results"*.

Over the past 35 years, the approval of a project, as well as the career and survival of a staffer, has depended on his/her marketing success in making social problems economic ones. This has been done by creating equations and models out of complex issues. However, economic ideology alone does not explain the Bank's approach to nutrition. The internal politics of the Bank has been just as critical. The importance given to nutrition lending has constantly been in flux at the Bank. It has never been as prominent in the Bank as it was with Berg. During the 1970s, Alan Berg was highly successful at marketing nutrition using McNamara's support advantageously. This big name gave his projects credibility. One anthropologist within the Bank stated that this was the *"pragmatist"* way to get things done, to go through unofficial channels using celebrity names to garner support. However, nutrition continued to be important during the 1980s under the leadership of Anthony Measham, a savvy translator between nutritionists and economists. In the 1990s the Bank's HNP department turned its attention towards health systems evidenced by a decline in Bank lending for nutrition (38). Part of the reason for the loss of interest in nutrition has been the difficulty in showing impact as discussed earlier.

Nutrition has also had to compete with other social issues for attention. For example, one staffer noted that due to the leadership of the United Kingdom in the G-8 in 2006, the primary focus has been on debt relief and HIV/AIDS in Africa. However, as a result of the centrality of health to the Millennium Development Goals and their international importance, nutrition has been able to keep its place at the table. The Acting Director for HNP explained this trend: *"Right now, to illustrate the centrality of this discussion and how meaningful it is to us and why we're attaching the kind of important that we are, we will be having… what we call the Annual Strategic Forum. It's a small gathering of Mr. Wolfensohn, our Managing Directors, our Vice Presidents from all over the institution, and a few other Bank staff to try to set out the strategic tone… And the exclusive topic… is around how the Bank can do its part to contribute to faster progress on the Millennium Development Goals… And within the Millennium Goals and the way in which the corporate priorities of the Bank have been defined, there are several themes where nutrition figures very, very prominently… (These things) are really preoccupying Mr. Wolfensohn as he entered the middle of his second term and looks at what kind of legacy he'll leave to the Bank and in development. It's very clear to us who work closely with him or hear from those who work closely with him that trying to make the focus of what he does over the next couple of years and what his institution does very much around not just measuring the Millennium Goals but trying to do something to change what happens by 2015"* (39).

As the Acting Director's comments reflect, for nutrition to be important within the Bank, it must be framed in a way that attracts the interest of the President and senior management. The position of nutrition within the Bank seems to depend highly on the nutrition spokesperson within the Bank, his/her charisma and his/her ability to form personal connections and manoeuvre the system. As a Bank consultant noted, nutrition requires a Task Manager who is *"capable of making the economic arguments for investing in nutrition, and who has networking skills and an entrepreneurial approach"* (38).

5. Conclusion. This paper has examined the interlacing of economic ideology and politics in World Bank nutrition policy. These two factors affect HNP staff who must design projects and work within the Bank in a manner that will ensure project approval and their sector's survival. They must produce designs that fit the operational guidelines of the Bank, while also pleasing senior management. They must make align themselves with the prevailing ideology, the social must be made economic, while also navigating their project through the internal politics.

Within these structures, staff have shown considerable agency. The translation of nutrition into economic terms along with garnering the support of former President McNamara in 1971, and former President Wolfensohn in 2004, can be viewed as a triumph of ingenuity and good will. Money that would have instead been allocated to loans for infrastructure projects has been acquired to help the undernourished. Powerful incentives and limitations, as well as clever negotiating of the system by certain individuals, define how staff work and approach development issues.

Given the significant role the World Bank plays in the global nutrition community, both as a financier and as a norm setter, it is critical to understand how policy is formulated within the institution. My key point is that nutrition policy is a reflection of the political pressures and institutional constraints operating within the Bank. Technical economic expertise is moulded by the political, institutional, and bureaucratic incentives. The prevailing policy is ultimately shaped by *"economic analysis, institutional constraints, and bureaucratic organisation"*. (34)

Acknowledgement: Originally published as: Devi Sridhar: Economic ideology and politics in the World Bank: Defining hunger. Copyright © 2007 Routledge Taylor & Francis (New Political Economy 2007; 12:4). Reprinted with permission. The author would like to acknowledge helpful comments by David Gellner, Ngaire Woods, Stanley Ulijaszek, Gerhard Anders, the editors of this journal, and two anonymous referees. I am also grateful to my informants on the World Bank for their candidness and generosity with their time.

References

1. Berg A. The nutrition factor: Its role in national development. Brookings Institute, 1973.
2. Musgrove P. Ideas versus money: A conversation with Jean-Louis Sarbib. Health Affairs 2005; W5:341–352.
3. Wade R. Greening the bank: The struggle over the environment, 1970-1995. In: Kapur D, Lewis J, Webb R (eds): World Bank: Its first half century. Brookings Institute, 1997.
4. Anders G. Good governance as technology: Towards an ethnography of the Bretton Woods institutions. In: Mosse D, Lewis D (eds): The aid effect: Giving and governing in international development. Pluto Press, 2005.
5. Stone D, Wright C (eds.): The World Bank and governance: A decade of reform and reaction. Routledge, 2007.

6. Miller-Adams M. The World Bank: New agendas for a changing world. Routledge, 1999.
7. Boas M, McNeill D (eds.), Global institutions and development: Framing the World. Routledge, 2004.
8. Berg A. Malnutrition: what can be done? Lessons from World Bank experience. World Bank, 1987.
9. Wilson D. Economic analysis of malnutrition. In: Berg A, Scrimshaw N, Call D (eds): Nutrition, national development and planning. MIT Press, 1973.
10. Phillips M, Sanghvi T. The economic analysis of nutrition projects: Guiding principles and examples. Nutrition Toolkit 3. World Bank, 1996, p. 15.
11. Jack W. Principles of health economics for developing countries. World Bank Institute, 1999, p. 271.
12. World Bank. Repositioning nutrition as central to development. World Bank, 2006.
13. Behrman J. Household behavior, preschool child nutrition, and the role of information. In: Pinstrup-Andersen P, Pelletier D, Alderman H (eds). Child growth and nutrition in developing countries. Cornell University Press, 1995.
14. Griffiths M, Dicken K, et al. Promoting the growth of children: What works? Rationale and guidance for programs: Nutrition toolkit 4. World Bank, 1996.
15. Davis J. The theory of the individual in economics: Identity and value. Routledge, 2003.
16. Berg A. Malnourished people: A policy view. World Bank, 1981.
17. World Bank. To nourish a nation: Investing in nutrition with World Bank assistance. World Bank, 2005.
18. Measham A, Chatterjee M. Wasting away: The crisis of malnutrition in India. World Bank, 1999.
19. Cernea M. "Culture? At the World Bank?" Letter to a Friend. Paris, 2004.
20. World Bank. Nutrition and economic sector work. World Bank, 2005.
21. Elder L, Kiess L, Beyer J. Incorporating nutrition into project design. Nutrition Toolkit 1. World Bank, 1996.
22. King F, Burgess A. Nutrition for developing countries. 2nd Ed. Oxford University Press, 1993.
23. Delgado H, Lechtig A, et al. Nutrition, lactation and postpartum amenorrhea. Am J Clin Nutr 1978; 31:322–27.
24. Huffman S, Chowdhury AK, et al. Postpartum amenorrhea: how is it affected by maternal nutritional status? Science 1978; 200:1155–7.
25. Nichter M, Nichter M. Anthropology and international health: Asian case studies. Gordon and Breach, 1996.
26. Horton S. Unit costs, cost-effectiveness and financing of nutrition interventions. World Bank, 1992.
27. World Bank. Enriching lives: Overcoming vitamin and mineral malnutrition in developing countries. World Bank, 1994.
28. Levinson FJ, Rogers B, et al. Monitoring and evaluation: A guidebook for nutrition project managers in developing countries. Nutrition Toolkit 8. World Bank, 1999.
29. de Beyer J, Preker A, et al. The role of the World Bank in international health: Renewed commitment and partnership. Soc Sci Med 2000; 50:169–76.
30. Huffman S, Steel A. Do child survival interventions reduce malnutrition: the dark side of child survival. Centre to Prevent Childhood Malnutrition, 1990.

31. Sindzingre A. "Truth", "Efficiency" and Multilateral Institutions: A political economy of development economics. New Polit Econ 2004; 9:233–49.
32. Ascher W. New development approaches and the adaptability of international agencies: The case of the World Bank. Internat Organ 1983; 37:415–39.
33. Nelson P. The World Bank and non-governmental organizations: Limits of a political development. MacMillan, 1995.
34. Woods N. The Globalizers: The World Bank, the IMF and their borrowers. Cornell University Press, 2006.
35. Woods N. The challenge of good governance for the IMF and the World Bank Themselves. World Development 2000; 28:823–41.
36. Woods N. The United States and the international financial institutions: Power and influence within the World Bank and the IMF. In: Foot R, MacFarlane N, Mastanduno M (eds): US hegemony and international organizations. Oxford University Press, 2003.
37. Stern N, Ferreira F. The World Bank as "intellectual actor". London: LSE, 1993.
38. Heaver R. Good work but not enough of it: A review of the World Bank's experience in nutrition. World Bank, 2006.
39. The World Bank: transcript from the meeting.

CHAPTER 36.

Coordinating the UN System: lessons from UNAIDS

1. Introduction. Few would contest that the United Nations (UN) as a whole is in serious need of reform particularly on the issue of global health. The authors propose the establishment of a UN Global Health Panel to coordinate existing initiatives within the UN as well as leverage key stakeholders outside of it. While the new Panel aims to link and coordinate existing bodies, rather than create a new one, it is questionable whether this is realistic.

Do *"coordinating"* initiatives that attempt to leverage the resources and comparative advantage of the various parts of the system work? To probe these issues, I use the case study of the Joint UN Programme on HIV/AIDS (UNAIDS). UNAIDS is an important example since it was explicitly established to test whether UN reform in coordination would be feasible, and to assess whether such a model could be rolled out to other issue areas within the UN. The material and data that are used in this paper are based on both primary and secondary sources. 52 interviews were carried out in total, 19 by me, and the remaining by collaborators on a larger project. In addition, supporting sources included a full media review undertaken using LexusNexus, internal and external UNAIDS evaluations, the UNAIDS Chronicle, and academic literature related to UNAIDS in key governance, health and development journals.

2. UNAIDS. UNAIDS emerged from the World Health Organization's (WHO) special Global Programme on HIV/AIDS (GPA). The WHO first become formally involved with HIV/AIDS in 1986 when it established the Control Programme on AIDS under the leadership of Dr. Jonathan Mann, a widely respected HIV/AIDS activist and health and human rights expert. In 1987, the programme was re-named the Special Programme on AIDS, and more than a year later, in January 1988, it was again re-named GPA. An external review of GPA led, eventually, to the official decision to replace the programme with a new body that would coordinate the work of the UN on AIDS as well as provide an experiment in whether UN reform could work. The external review concluded that *"no single agency is capable of responding to the totality of the problems posed by AIDS; and as never before, a cooperative effort, which is broadly based but guided by a shared sense of purpose, is essential"* (1).

In 1994 it was agreed that a joint and cosponsored initiative would be established. The initiative would not be an agency in itself but leverage the resources of its co-sponsoring UN agencies. The original six co-sponsors were UNICEF, UNDP, UNFPA, UNESCO and the World Bank, because they were at the time members of the GPA Management Committee. However this was later expanded to ten co-sponsors including the ILO, UNODC, WFP, UNHCR and most recently UN Women. The first UNAIDS Executive Director, Dr. Peter Piot, was appointed in 1995.

3. Advantages of a UNAIDS model. The case of UNAIDS provides important lessons for UN reform. What advantages does such a coordinating mechanism provide? First, a stand-alone coordinating entity can raise awareness and financing for that one issue if the leadership is given seniority within the UN system. A body such as UNAIDS enables the leader to focus on one specific issue and devote all resources towards that aim. UNAIDS has made an enormous contribution to placing AIDS on the global agenda as a high-priority disease and a disease of *"exceptional"* importance thus deserving unparallelled financial resources, political attention and institutional response. Through its policy and practice recommendations, UNAIDS has made a strong case regarding the exceptionality of HIV/AIDS as a disease, drawing attention to its rapid spread into pandemic levels, the associated stigma and discrimination, the underlying gender imbalance, its impact on social structures, and its clinical complexity. In part through its own design as a programme linking together a diverse group of co-sponsors, UNAIDS has successfully promoted the notion that HIV/AIDS is not just a health issue but also a social and political issue requiring a multi-sectoral response. This distinction does not exist for almost all other disease areas.

The exceptionality of HIV/AIDS has resulted in an exceptional response, which is demonstrated in several different ways. Unparallelled levels of new resources have been pledged for HIV/AIDS research, surveillance and programming for prevention and treatment. It is estimated that spending on HIV/AIDS rose from about US$ 300 million in 1996 to US$ 10 billion in 2007 (2). Although UNAIDS does not play a role in financing HIV/AIDS activities directly, the sizable new resources for HIV/AIDS, and global health more generally, may not have been made available without UNAIDS constant lobbying of donors and key decision-makers. UNAIDS has also paved the way for new financing initiatives within the UN family that may not have come to pass without the momentum of the programme and buy-in from others, for example, the development of the innovative financing mechanism UNITAID which uses the levys raised on air tickets to reduce the price of essential medicines. Within countries, UNAIDS has promoted an exceptional institutional response through the creation of autonomous National AIDS Councils that often sit above Ministries of Health.

The second major achievement of UNAIDS is becoming the key source of information on HIV/AIDS for donors, developing country governments and academics. With WHO's assistance, UNAIDS compiles epidemiological data on the HIV epidemic at the global, regional and national levels. The UNAIDS report on HIV/AIDS draws on the best available data from countries to provide an overview and commentary on the epidemic and the international response.

Third, UNAIDS has been credited with a more inclusive governing body, the Programme Coordinating Board (PCB) relative to WHO, as well as providing real engagement with civil society groups. The PCB comprises 22 member states elected from among the member states of the co-sponsoring UN agencies: Western Europe and Others have 7 seats, Africa 5 seats, Asia and Pacific 5 seats, Latin America and Caribbean 3 seats, and Eastern European/Commonwealth of Independent States 2 seats. The terms of membership of the 22 members is three years, with approximately one third of the membership replaced annually. While member states are the only voting members, each of the co-sponsors has a seat on the PCB, as well as 5 NGOs, three from developing countries and two from developed countries. In contrast to the WHO, five NGOs are able to sit on the PCB and thus provide real input into the decision-making process. In addition, UNAIDS has built good relationships with civil society and the private sector.

4. Limitations of the UNAIDS model. However, establishing a new coordinating initiative also has several drawbacks. First, although a body might be established as a small, focused coordinating initiative, institutions tend to grow and become bureaucracies. Eventually they become an agency in themselves and then tend to compete with the other UN agencies rather than coordinate. There is little incentive for partner UN bodies to relinquish control and participate meaningfully. Adding to difficulties of coordinating is that as initiatives grow, they tend to spread into areas beyond their initial focus resulting in replication and inefficiency within the entire system. One of the consequences of a limited pool of donors with an increase in the number of actors and initiatives is competition among the various parties, for the same pots of money. Given that the leaders of new initiatives need to fundraise for voluntary contributions, initiatives are highly dependent on donors, which affects their perceived or real independence. And is it enough to be just a co-ordinating body? As a respondent noted, "*We need a very hard headed normative mode, which is interdisciplinary, and working with system engineers and business* *strategists, and business experts to look at what kind of system can be built with this money. UNAIDS is not technical, it is not normative like WHO, it is not a funding agency – what are they doing? Coordinating? I don't know if the world is going to be happy to spend $250 million to sing cumbaya."*

The second major criticism relates to whether UNAIDS has been able to coordinate effectively given internal competition within the UN system. UNAIDS was described by respondents as a *"victim of the UN system"* with politics among its co-sponsoring agencies holding back progress. A DFID report noted, *"UNAIDS works well with the UN although they can sometimes appear constrained by their co-sponsors"* (3). This friction with co-sponsors has been evident since UNAIDS was first created in 1995. Given the reservations that the co-sponsors expressed about the establishment of a new initiative, the compromise reached was that UNAIDS would not have real authority over the co-sponsors. A Swedish assessment of UNAIDS notes: *"One weakness of UNAIDS is that the Board does not have any real power to get the ten co-sponsors to execute Board decisions, which do actually apply to the whole "UNAIDS family". While the Board is active and constructive, has the ability to take decisions that have real influence and is pressing forward with important issues, it currently has too little impact on the rest of the system"* (4). This raises an issue of authority over both what the UNAIDS Secretariat can hold others accountable for, and conflict over who they themselves are accountable to.

The challenges at the global level are replicated at the country level; limited resources (both human and financial) available to UNAIDS at country level leads to inadequate capacity to encourage the various co-sponsors to work effectively through Joint Teams and Programmes on AIDS or to coordinate their support to the National AIDS Councils or government ministries. At the country level, it is unclear what mechanism exists to hold bilateral donors to account for coordination. For example, despite a call by the PCB in 2006 for donors to fund Joint Programmes of Support on AIDS (pooled monies), some donors continue to fund the individual co-sponsors of UNAIDS through Trust Funds or for specific program implementation (3). The vast monies available to fund vertical HIV/AIDS programs also create incentives for the co-sponsors to implement separate and uncoordinated HIV activities.

5. Conclusion. To conclude, as the UNAIDS example has shown, at a particular time in history for a particular disease, its unusual structure was highly effective in making progress against HIV/AIDS. As the UN creates new coordinating mechanisms such as the UN High-Level Taskforce on the Global Food Security Crisis, serious thought must be given to the drawbacks of establishing new initiatives for coordination. While a UN Panel on Global Health is an innovative approach to addressing the absence of global leadership in global health, history has shown that the politics of global health governance need to be taken into consideration. As the case of UNAIDS demonstrates, small, focused coordinating initiatives can become over time just another UN body in need of reform.

Acknowledgement: Originally published as: Devi Sridhar: Coordinating the UN System: lessons from UNAIDS. Reprinted with permission from Elsevier (Social Science in Medicine 2013; 76:21-7). Background research for this paper was supported by a grant from the Center for Global Development. The author would like to acknowledge the assistance of Ngaire Woods, Ruth Levine, Danielle Kuczynski as well as the research assistance of Edward Joy and Danny George. The author is grateful to those who gave their time in interviews.

References

1. GPA Management Committee. Report of the ad hoc Working Group of the GPA Management Committee. GPA/GMC (8)92.5. Geneva: WHO, 1992.
2. UNAIDS. Unified Budget and Workplan 2008; e09. Geneva: UNAIDS, 2008.
3. UK DFID. UNAIDS development effectiveness summary. London: DFID, 2007.
4. Ministry of Foreign Affairs, Sweden. Swedish assessment of multilateral organisations – the UN Joint Programme on HIV/AIDS. 2009. (Available from: http://www. sweden. gov.se/sb/d/3365/a/121949; Accessed: 10 Sep 2012).

CHAPTER 37.

Expectations for the United Nations high-level meeting on noncommunicable diseases

The United Nations General Assembly's decision to convene a high-level meeting on the prevention and control of noncommunicable diseases (NCDs) worldwide in September 2011 is a major, timely opportunity to elevate chronic diseases onto the global stage and to encourage action by individual governments (1). Just as the 2001 United Nations General Assembly Special Session on HIV/AIDS was a pivotal moment in the global response to AIDS, there is hope that the September session on NCDs will become an historic rallying point. How shall we judge the success of the meeting? If Member States can address the following five critical elements, then new measurable goals and means of building accountability may be within reach.

First, the meeting should put a spotlight on the true scale of morbidity and mortality caused by NCDs and the economic consequences for households, health systems and national economies. It should result in an endorsement of the World Health Organization (WHO) Action plan for the global strategy for the prevention and control of noncommunicable diseases (2) and a commitment to a study of their projected economic impact as well as the cost of preventive action.

Second, governments should commit to developing national NCD plans by convening, for example, a multisectoral national task force or commission to elaborate country-specific strategies and targets. WHO could support countries in this process. These plans should be required by 2013, with updates on specific targets by 2015 and continuous monitoring by the United Nations.

The third key element of success is financing. It is unlikely that there will be new funds pledged at the meeting. In fact, it could be detrimental to focus on raising a specific amount of funding as this might distract governments from other key tasks. Rather than establishing a new institution such as a Global Fund for NCDs or expanding the mandate of the Global Fund to Fight AIDS, Tuberculosis and Malaria, we suggest three feasible financial avenues. These are: (i) seeking joint financing mechanisms such as public–private partnerships (3); (ii) investing in health system reform to deal better with NCDs, e.g. supply of essential drugs and devices, health worker retention, provision of diabetes care through primary providers; and (iii) including NCDs as a line item in government health budgets and donor reporting systems to help monitor budgetary allocations.

A fourth requirement is the commitment of governments to strengthening national regulation of NCD risk factors, including pushing for change in the food and beverage industry. This should put into force regulatory frameworks to reduce consumption of trans-fatty acids, salt, alcohol and sugar.

Finally, incentives and mechanisms to encourage cross-sectoral action and coordination are central to sustained progress. Finance ministries need to budget sufficient funds; agriculture ministries to reduce subsidies for harmful crops; trade ministries to enlarge access to essential medicines; urban planning and transport ministries to create opportunities for greater physical activity; and education ministries to ensure that school environments provide healthy diets through banning the sale and distribution of harmful foods in schools and promoting health education.

Tobacco control efforts could lead discussions in each of these areas given that there have been considerable policy gains. These include the WHO Framework Convention on Tobacco Control and the practical assistance provided to governments through WHO's MPOWER resources; commitments of more than US$ 500 million from the Bloomberg Family Foundation and the Bill & Melinda Gates Foundation; and increasing attention to the role of tobacco in bilateral trade agreements, in taxation policy and in agriculture.

Despite such progress, there is still much work required to curb tobacco use as it is the single most important risk factor for NCDs and kills an estimated 5 million people annually. If the United Nations Secretary-General makes a strong declaration to support the WHO Framework Convention on Tobacco Control in New York this year, this will add significant weight to previous commitments to the Convention made in Geneva. While tobacco use is declining in most wealthy countries, it is increasing in many poor countries of the world, with profound consequences for the future of public health and development. As stock prices for tobacco continue to rise – underscoring the confidence of the markets in tobacco – clear decisions must be made on overcoming barriers to implementation of the WHO Framework Convention on Tobacco Control. These include: investment treaties and associated pressures to open markets; agriculture and loss of employment, and subsidies for harmful crops; difficulties in regulating the private sector; illicit trade in cigarettes and tobacco smuggling; and constraints to implementing tobacco taxation.

We hold high expectations for what can be achieved at this high-level meeting, especially if Member States are willing to develop and support a strong outcomes document with agreed set targets and reporting mechanisms to ensure accountability to commitments. This is a crucial first step in stemming the global epidemic in NCDs.

Acknowledgement: Originally published as: Devi Sridhar, J Stephen Morrison and Peter Piot. Expectations for the United Nations high-level meeting on noncommunicable diseases. Reprinted with permission from the World Health Organization (Bulletin of the World Health Organization 2011; 89:471).

References

1. United Nations General Assembly Resolution on the prevention and control of non-communicable diseases (Agenda item 114 (A/64/L.52)). New York: United Nations, 2010.
2. 2008–2013 Action plan for the global strategy for the prevention and control of non-communicable diseases. Geneva: World Health Organization, 2009.
3. Yach D. The challenge of noncommunicable disease in emerging powers. New York: Council on Foreign Relations, 2010.

CHAPTER 38.

Vertical funds in the health sector: Lessons for education from the Global Fund and GAVI

1. Introduction. There are over 230 international organizations, funds, and programmes providing development aid throughout the world (1). Philanthropic development aid is heavily concentrated in the health sector and has been growing over the past decade: about half of all international aid from private sources is invested in global health (2). The majority of international health aid is delivered for specific uses or programmes, commonly called "*vertical*" funding. Vertical funding specifies and targets resources for particular diseases, services, or interventions in the health sector of a given country and usually focuses on interventions that are considered cost-effective with measurable results. Vertical interventions typically have separate funding proposal and allocation processes, delivery systems and budgets with varied structural, funding and operational integration in the broader country health system (3). Vertical approaches initially emerged as natural channels for developing government action in severely resource-constrained and donor-dependant countries and were considered interim strategies to achieve improved health outcomes (4). More recently, philanthropic vertical funding in the health sector adheres to businesslike values with problem-oriented strategies that focus on performance goals. Examples of vertical health programmes include the U.S. President's Emergency Plan for AIDS Relief (PEPFAR) and the GAVI Alliance's Hib initiative. Health aid financing can also be delivered to countries through "*horizontal*" approaches. Horizontal funding in the health sector is a traditional mode of healthcare delivery that focuses on primary healthcare. Horizontal funding approaches are broad-based, integrative, and offer long-term public improvements in overall health outcomes delivered through primary care services. For example, the World Health Organisation (WHO) strengthening health systems initiative and sector-wide programmes (SWAPs) are examples of horizontal health programmes.

Discussion about the comparative effectiveness of vertical versus horizontal approaches can be traced over the past 50 years. In 1978, the International Conference on Primary Health Care was convened by the WHO and United Nations Children's Fund (UNICEF) in Alma Ata, Kazakhstan. Representatives from all nations attended this conference, and for the first time, healthcare challenges in disadvantaged countries were seriously examined and linked with development opportunities. The conference generated the Alma-Ata Declaration which strongly emphasized: health as a basic human right; the role of the state in the universal provision of health care; and community participation as a fundamental prerequisite for effective health care (5). The declaration acknowledged the importance of community-oriented comprehensive primary healthcare for all nations, as well as the required changes needed in economic, social, and political structures to enable equitable healthcare access.

Soon after Alma-Ata, the financial crisis in the early 1980s initiated a move toward selective primary care. The horizontal health funding approaches that originated from Alma-Ata concepts were criticized as being unattainable, especially in resource-deprived countries, due to vague implementation strategies, immense costs, and the need for a large trained workforce. Vertical strategies that focused on medical interventions, such as vaccinations were proposed to achieve more immediate results. Although WHO's *"Health for All by 2000"* initiative in the late 1980s aimed to achieve comprehensive global primary healthcare based on horizontal delivery of basic services, failing to achieve its goals further fueled a paradigm shift from horizontal to vertical funding strategies for health services. In conjunction, greater support for vertical health funding grew given the success of smallpox eradication (3) and the looming AIDS epidemic. Interest in horizontal versus vertical health funding again peaked with the release of the World Bank's 1993 World Development Report *"Investing in Health"*, which focused on Disability Adjusted Life Years (DALYs) gained by particular vertical disease interventions. In response, Vincent Navarro and others (6) criticized an increasingly narrow focus on diseases rather than general health systems. The United Nations Millennium Development Goals (MDGs) in 2000 specified indicators that have further encouraged the development and growth of multiple vertical programmes to target specific health interventions, thus reinforcing funding approaches that target specific diseases.

Discontentment among developing country governments grew in the early 21st century, and donors became increasingly aware of the influx of aid missions and projects deployed in developing countries. Thus, in early 2004, the Paris Declaration on Aid Effectiveness was adopted by the Organisation for Economic Co-operation and Development (OECD) countries, which inspired a broader call for greater aid effectiveness and focused on the principles of harmonization, alignment and coherence. In 2008, the Paris Declaration was re-affirmed in Accra by key donors, and in homage to the 30th anniversary of Alma Ata, WHO focused its annual World Health Report on primary care.

Like a pendulum, the vertical versus horizontal financing debate has swung back and forth many times over the past 50 years. This condensed and incomplete historical account of vertical and horizontal funding approaches in the health sector highlights just a few major events that have influenced health aid funding today. While there is near universal consensus that optimal health systems are the key to improving health and that donors must move from vertical towards horizontal financing, current practice continues to focus on vertical financing strategies (7). In fact, there has been an incredible rise, especially in the past decade, in the number and type of funds allocated through vertical funding mechanisms. As of 2008, there were over 90 global health partnerships (8) that overwhelmingly target health interventions for disease-specific projects. These new vertical health aid donors often have successful business aptitude, apply private sector investment techniques to aid monies (e.g. the GAVI Alliance's International Finance Facility for Immunisation) and utilize effective public relations strategies. Much of the increase in monies for global health has been directed to address HIV/AIDS, malaria and TB. A recent study of the four major donors in global health noted that in 2005, funding per death varied widely by disease area, from US$ 1029 for HIV/AIDS to US$ 3 for non-communicable disease (see discussion on HIV/AIDS and UNAIDS later in this article) (7). This finding suggests that donors do not base their decision-making processes on morbidity or mortality data. The study also noted the difficulty in discerning the amount of aid money that flows vertically versus horizontally in the health sector given the complicated manner in which donors categorize their aid.

Despite the rhetoric of various mechanisms for health aid funding, why does most health aid flow to vertical programmes? We put forth several plausible explanations. First, the recent shift to vertical health funding might be attributable to the values and businesslike strategies of major philanthropic donors. These private donors (e.g. Bill & Melinda Gates Foundation) strive for timely and quantitative results and revise their grants based on performance indicators. For these donors, vertical funding mechanisms are ideal to achieve their goals and to leverage concurrent investments from the public and private sector. Vertical funding may remain relatively nonexistent in other sectors due to the lack of private philanthropist donors as seen in the health sector.

Second, the imperative for donors to fund programmes that demonstrate measurable results in a short time-frame demonstrates a preference for vertical health funding. Since it is difficult to accurately monitor and evaluate the impact of horizontal interventions (e.g. primary healthcare), donors have very little incentive to fund broader health systems (9). For example, the global health community does not have accurate non-disease-specific mortality estimates, which creates a lack of data to quantitatively assess the success or failure of horizontal funding approaches. Specifically, information is unavailable about the mortality rate due directly or indirectly to a lack of access to health systems. This insufficiency of current health metrics to determine results of, and improvements to, horizontal health funding, also fails to determine and evaluate community (as well as regional and national) health needs. In other words, the lack of measurement tools impacts both broader health system and preventive public health financing and strategies. This leads to considerable uncertainty among researchers and donors in deciding how best to invest monies. With the current health system driven by data collection of disease-specific causes of death, investing in broader health systems is seen as a bottomless pit, where there is no universally accepted proxy for the impact of health systems investment on mortality. However, when incentives (e.g., through data-driven feedback or widespread public advocacy) are aligned towards funding health systems, *"vertical"* donors have demonstrated a willingness to incorporate horizontal funding programmes into their initiatives. Ultimately, the tension still remains between the recognized importance to improve health systems and fund horizontal activities with the current reality of immense financing for vertical interventions led by the business acumen of private donors.

In order to shed light on the successes and limitations of vertical approaches in the health sector, this paper describes and assesses the design of two of the largest global health initiatives, the Global Fund to Fight AIDS, Tuberculosis, and Malaria (Global Fund) and the GAVI Alliance (GAVI). Both organisations function as international public-private partnerships that funnel capital into low-income countries for specific vertical health programmes and are based on the concept of performance-based funding. While these global partnerships share many similarities, both have achieved varying degrees of success and have divergent priorities and governance strategies.

2. The Global Fund. The Global Fund was created in 2001 to serve as a financing mechanism for HIV/AIDS, TB and malaria. Although it is officially a Swiss foundation, it receives administrative support from the WHO and fiduciary support from the World Bank as a trustee (10). The World Bank's role is limited to disbursing funds to Principal Recipients upon receiving instruction to disburse from the Global Fund secretariat. Since its inception in 2002, the Global Fund has committed over US$ 14.9 billion to more than 140 countries. Disbursements have tended to lag behind grant approvals; the target length of time between commitment and disbursement is 8 months, but in practice, this process tends to take a few more months (i.e. between 9–11 months).

The idea of the Global Fund was first discussed at the 2000 G-8 meeting in Okinawa and again at the 2001 Abuja African leaders summit. In Abuja, Kofi Annan, then Secretary-General of the UN, called for the creation of a global fund to provide a new channel for additional resources to target HIV/AIDS, tuberculosis and malaria. He called for a *"war chest"* of US$ 10 billion per year to fight HIV/AIDS and other infectious diseases (11). In June 2001, a UN General Assembly Special Session concluded with a commitment to create such a fund, which the G-8 supported and helped finance at their 2001 meeting in Genoa. In January 2002, a permanent secretariat was established, and just three months later, the Global Fund approved its first round of grants.

The new initiative was created to not only significantly increase the resources available to countries to address these three diseases, but also to ensure that allocation was demand-driven, aligned to country ownership and performance oriented. (While country ownership is a cornerstone of the Global Fund, the in-built priorities of the Fund – HIV/AIDS, TB and Malaria – result in countries being limited in what they can apply and use funds for). Since its inception, the concept of country ownership has been a key pillar of the Fund's work. Through the country coordinating mechanism (CCM) each country is responsible for determining its own needs and priorities (within the three diseases), based on consultation with a group of diverse stakeholders including national and local governments, NGOs, the private sector and people living with, or affected by, the diseases.

The majority of funding has come from the governments of industrialized countries, mostly the G8 (see **Table 38-1**). The US alone has given close to 30% of funding and in 2009, President Obama pledged an additional US$ 900 million. It is important to note that US law requires that US contributions to the Fund do not exceed 33% of total Fund receives. While the Fund is keen to draw private sector contributions, it does not accept in-kind donations (e.g. drugs) or earmarked funds. It only accepts unconditional funds.

Table 38-1. *List of contributors to the Global Fund – cash pledged (12).*

DONOR	PLEDGE TIMETABLE	TOTAL AMOUNT (IN US$ MILLION)
Australia	2004–2010	168
Belgium	2001–2010	115
Brazil	2003–4, 2006–7	0.2
Brunei Darussalam	2007	0.05
Cameroon	2003, 2007	0.1
Canada	2002–2010	834
China	2003–2010	16
Denmark	2002–2010	212
European Commission	2001–2010	1427
Finland	2006–2009	16
France	2002–2010	2493
Germany	2002–2010	1273
Greece	2005, 2007, 2009	2
Hungary	2004–6, 2008	0.06
Iceland	2004–2010	1.1
India	2006–2010	11
Indonesia	2008–2012	37
Ireland	2002–2010	228
Italy	2002–2010	1365
Japan	2002–2009	1406
Korea (Republic of)	2004–2009	11
Kuwait	2003, 2008	2
Latvia	2008	0.01
Liechtenstein	2002, 2004–2009	0.6
Luxembourg	2002–2010	24
Mexico	2003, 2005	0.2
Netherlands	2002–2010	648
New Zealand	2003–2005	2
Nigeria	2002–3, 2006	20
Norway	2002–2010	347
Pakistan	2009–2012	28
Poland	2003–06, 2008	0.2
Portugal	2003–2010	16
Romania	2007–2008	0.5

Table 38-1. *Continued.*

DONOR	PLEDGE TIMETABLE	TOTAL AMOUNT (IN US$ MILLION)
Russia	2002–2010	289
Saudi Arabia	2003–06, 2008–10	28
Singapore	2004–2008	1
Slovenia	2004–2008	0.13
South Africa	2003–2008	10.3
Spain	2003–2010	837
Sweden	2002–2010	547
Switzerland	2002–2010	47
Thailand	2003–2012	10
Uganda	2004–2007	2
United Kingdom	2001–2015	2286
United States	2001–2008	5428
Other Countries	2001–2004	3
Total		20191
Other		
Bill & Melinda Gates Foundation	2002–2004, 2006–2010	650
Communitas Foundation	2007–2009	3
Debt2Health – Germany	N/A	32
UNITAID	2007	39
Chevron Corporation	2008–2010	30
Idol Gives Back	2007–2009	17
(PRODUCT) RED™ and Partners: American Express, Apple, Converse, Dell + Windows, GAP, Giorgio Armani, Hallmark, Motorola Foundation, Motorola Inc. & Partners, Starbucks Coffee, Media Partners and (RED) Supporters[11]		
Hottokenai Campaign (G-CAP Coalition Japan)	2006	0.3
Other UNF Donors	various	4
Other Donors	various	
Total		775
Grand Total		20966

The Global Fund does not directly work in-country or implement pro-grammes. Rather, it serves as a financial instrument, managing and disbursing resources through an independent and technical process. It operates transparently, must demonstrate accountability, and employs a rapid grant-making process. Proposals are reviewed by a Technical Review Panel and assessed based on fulfilling certain eligibility criteria. Grants are awarded based on *"rounds of funding"*, with a total of eight completed rounds since its inception. High-quality proposals are recommended to the Board for funding, and recommendations have been made for approximately 40% of proposals submitted.

Countries submit proposals to the Global Fund through a Country Coordinating Mechanism (CCM). CCMs are country-level partnerships that develop and submit grant proposals, which do not have to be previously endorsed, to the Global Fund based on priority needs at the national level. After grant approval, they oversee progress during implementation. CCMs usually consist of representatives from governments, NGOs, donors, people living with the diseases, faith-based organisations, the private sector and the academic community. For each grant, CCM nominates one or two organisations to serve as Principal Recipient. Since the CCM is a committee and not an implementing agency, it allocates the oversight and responsibility for the grant to the Principal Recipient. The Principal Recipient is responsible for local implementation of the grant, including oversight of sub-recipients of grant funds, and communication with the CCM on grant progress. In South Africa, for example, the Ministry of Finance is the Principal Recipient given that all sources of external funding must first go through its doors. The Ministry of Health is a sub-recipient that then further allocates the funding to civil society groups for implementation. Principal Recipients also work with the Global Fund Secretariat to develop a two-year grant agreement that sets programme goals to be achieved over time. Local Auditors are also contracted to assess the capacity of the Principal Recipient to administer grant funds and be responsible for implementation. The main auditors are *PriceWaterhouseCoopers*, *KPMG*, *Emerging Markets Group*, and the *Swiss Tropical Institute*.

There are a number of guidelines for the CCMs: CCM members from the nongovernmental sector must be selected in a documented, transparent manner; CCMs must provide evidence that they include representatives of communities living with the disease; CCMs must put in place a transparent and documented process soliciting submissions and ensuring the input of a broad range of stakeholders in the proposal development and grant oversight process; CCMs must have a transparent, documented process for the nomination of the Principal Recipient; and CCMs must have a written plan in place to mitigate against conflict of interest in situations where the Chair or Vice-Chair of the CCM and the Principal Recipient are from the same entity. About two-thirds of all Principal Recipients are government institutions, but most recently, the Global Fund has worked towards *"dual track financing"*, where the grant is split across different Principal Recipients (13).

CCMs have faced a number of problems (14). These include: (i) The CCM's role and operating methods are not clearly defined, and are not clearly understood by CCM members and outsiders; (ii) The CCM is dominated by government members. Civil society and people living with the diseases are underrepresented and have little influence; (iii) CCM members who are supposed to represent NGOs are not chosen by the NGO sector and do not properly represent them; (iv) CCM members are not involved in choosing the CCM Chair or in selecting the Principal Recipient; (v) The CCM Chair also serves as Principal Recipient and thus has a conflict of interest; (vi) There is no genuine involvement by CCM members in the CCM decision-making process. Decisions are made in advance by the CCM Chair and a few others; (vii) CCM members are asked to sign a proposal to the Global Fund even though they had no input into its preparation and little prior knowledge of its content; (viii) The CCM does not have access to sufficient money, practical resources or expertise to operate effectively; (ix) CCM officers do not share information within and outside the CCM; (x) CCM members do not know whether the project funded through the Global Fund grant is being effectively implemented

The problems that CCMs face vary by country; in general, they are not seen as being *"donor-driven"*. However, there is anecdotal evidence that given inadequate technical expertise to put together a grant proposal, there has been heavy reliance on consultants and staff from the WHO and UNAIDS. This is because at the country level, the Global Fund does not itself provide technical assistance and capacity-building support. Instead, partner organizations provide this, such as UNAIDS, WHO, World Bank, as well as other UN and bilateral agencies. To address mixed capacity at the country level, in 2005, the Global Fund created the Global Implementation Support Team (GIST), which is a group that meets once every few months to coordinate a response to implementation bottlenecks in HIV/AIDS grants. GIST was initially composed of seven partners (WHO, UNFPA, UNICEF, UNDP, the World Bank, the UNAIDS Secretariat and the Global Fund) but was expanded in 2006 to include PEPFAR, GTZ (now GIZ), the International Council of AIDS Service Organisations, the International HIV/AIDS Alliance, the International Coalition on AIDS and Development and the Brazilian International Centre for Technical Cooperation. The GIST Secretariat is based in UNAIDS and consists of a Chair (currently

UNFPA), Co-Chair (currently Global Fund), a Coordinator (UNAIDS) and host (UNAIDS). GIST has developed a set of Principles for Technical Support and is developing a global-level database known as CoATS (Coordinating AIDS Technical Support). GIST also applies research and analysis on overcoming systematic obstacles to improved technical support.

As noted above, the Global Fund has adopted a performance-based funding scheme. New programmes are evaluated at two years (referred to as Phase 2) to assess progress in meeting coverage targets, and continued funding is contingent on positive evaluation, which has been associated with a number of predictive factors (15). Most grants that are approved initially are also approved for Phase 2, save for a few exceptions. Of the first 124 grants reviewed by the Global Fund Secretariat, 119 received Phase 2 funding (16). The Fund uses a four-tier measurement framework to assess operational and grant performance, systems effects and impact on the three diseases. If programmes are positively evaluated, they are approved for a further three years. There have been concerns about what happens with grants at the end of their five-year term. As part of its 2007–2010 strategy, the Global Fund announced the introduction of the Rolling Continuation Channel (RCC), which provides continued funding of high-performing grants for up to an additional six years. This helps facilitate the expansion of successful programmes, reduce the risk of gaps in funding, and remove the costs of putting together a new proposal.

The Board, which oversees the Global Fund, is responsible for its overall governance, development of new policies and the approval of grants. The Chair and Vice-Chair of the Board each serve two-year terms with the positions alternating between representatives from the donor constituency and from the recipient delegation. The Board itself is made up of a total of 24 members; the 20 voting members include 7 representatives from developing countries (one from each of the six WHO regions and an additional representative from Africa), 8 from donor countries, 3 from civil society, 1 from private sector, and 1 from the Gates Foundation. In addition, there are four non-voting members whom are key partners, such as the WHO, UNAIDS, World Bank and a Swiss citizen (as the Fund is legally a Swiss Foundation). Civil society seats are for one developed country NGO representative, one developing country representative and one person who represents the communities affected by the diseases. The Board has been viewed as a good model of governance (17).

The secretariat of the Global Fund is based in Geneva and consists of around 250 staff members. There are no staff members in developing countries. The emphasis on a relatively lean secretariat results in overhead costs consuming less than 3% of donor contributions Richard Feachem was the first

Executive Director from July 2002 until April 2007. After much wrangling between developed and developing countries representatives on the Board, Michel Kazatchkine was appointed as his successor.

The Global Fund has been praised for its transparency (17). It provides detailed financial information about commitments and disbursements, as well as donor pledges and contributions. An electronic library provides internal and external evaluations of the Fund. The Global Fund Observer, which is a newsletter produced by the NGO Aidspan, reports on the financing of the Global Fund, monitors its progress; comments on the approval, disbursement and implementation of grants; provides guidance for stakeholders within application countries; and reports and comments on board meetings. The Global Fund also works closely with the regional branches of the NGO, Friends of the Global Fund, which lobbies donor governments to increase their contributions.

In terms of how grants are used, almost two-thirds of funds are spent by governments; almost a third by NGOs and multilateral organisations; and the remainder by faith-based organisations, the private sector and communities affected by the disease. Almost half of award funding is used for the purchase of medicines and commodities (48%); a third is used to strengthen infrastructure (11%) and expand training (22%); and the remainder is allocated towards monitoring and evaluation (2%), administration (11%) and other expenses (6%). In response to criticism that the Fund is not building in-country capacity, Richard Feachem noted that roughly 35% of funds contribute to health systems strengthening. Michel Kazatchkine claimed that vertical funds for AIDS, malaria and TB have strengthened systems; provided, refurbished and renovated infrastructures; and financed training and salaries of workers. He estimated that the Global Fund has committed roughly US$ 4 billion to support the health workforce in both the public sector and civil society.

From 2002 to 2007, 57%, 15% and 27% of grant funding were allocated to HIV/AIDS, TB and malaria, respectively. The Global Fund provides 20% of overall resources for HIV/AIDS, 45% for TB and roughly 67% for malaria. More funding is allocated towards treatment rather than to prevention of these diseases. The Fund works in over 140 countries worldwide. However, given that HIV/AIDS, TB and malaria are concentrated in Sub-Saharan Africa, between 2002 and 2007, over half of grant funds (55%) were given to Sub-Saharan Africa. When stratified by income, 64%, 28%, and 8% of disbursements went to lower, lower-middle and upper middle income countries, respectively (18).

In terms of its aid to fragile states, the Global Fund estimates that it has disbursed US$ 2.9 billion in fragile and conflict-affected states since its creation in 2001 (19). The Global Fund is the second largest donor in Equatorial Guinea, providing 11% of official development assistance. According to the Global Fund's 2008 Progress Report, 70% of programmes in fragile states are performing well, and the overall effective performance of all countries supported by the Global Fund is only slightly higher at 75%. The Global Fund admits, however, that performance improvements for fragile states and countries with weaker health systems require a focused effort from partners. In 2005, the Global Fund published a report of its grants to states that *"cannot or will not deliver core functions to the majority of its people, including the poor"*. Core functions include territorial control, safety and security, capacity to manage public resources, delivery of basic services and the ability to protect and support the ways in which the poorest people can sustain themselves. The report notes that in its first four rounds of funding, the Global Fund has invested one-third of committed funds in 45 fragile states, financing a total of 123 programmes. Given their lack of capacity, the performance by grants in fragile states was surprisingly comparable to that of the 55 grants implemented in stable states. Most of the grants in fragile states (14 out of 19) were managed by Principal Recipients from the government sector, and these grants performed equally well as those managed by non-government Principal Recipients. The report concludes that if further assessment validates these early results, the Global Fund may offer a unique, performance-based model within which other donors can engage with fragile states in health and other sectors.

   3. The GAVI Alliance. The GAVI Alliance (GAVI), formerly the Global Alliance for Vaccines and Immunisation, was launched at the World Economic Forum in January 2000 and received a start-up grant from the Gates Foundation. GAVI aims to reduce the mortality rate in children under five targeted by the UN MDGs through immunisation strategies. GAVI is a public-private partnership of major stakeholders in immunisation to finance and speed delivery of new and improved vaccines for children in low-income countries. Partners in the GAVI Alliance include: developing and industrialised country governments, research and technical health institutes, industrialised and developing country vaccine industries, civil society organisations, the Gates Foundation and other philanthropy organisations, the WHO, UNICEF and the World Bank Group.

   As of January 2008, 67% of donor governments made multi-year (covering three years or more) donations to GAVI, which was twice the amount of contributions from donor governments in 2005. Donor contributions to GAVI can be made through direct donations, long-term pledges, and pledges to specifically support the development and manufacture of vaccines. GAVI has been directly financed by 14 governments to date: Australia, Canada, Denmark,

European Commission, France, Germany, Ireland, Luxembourg, Netherlands, Norway, Sweden, United Kingdom, U.S., and Spain (see **Table 38-2**). Through the end of December 2008, total donor contributions to GAVI were over US$ 3.8 billion. Private industry donated almost a third of that amount, with the remaining balance originating from both direct contributions and long-term commitments from various governments.

GAVI provides funding to national governments based on country income (i.e. countries with gross national income per capita below US$ 1000), which describes half the world's population. There are currently 72 countries eligible to apply for GAVI support – half of which are located in Sub-Saharan Africa (21). GAVI's immunisation funding varies by country in its extent of vertical funding: while there are separate funding channels that rely extensively on donor funding, immunisation services are delivered through the same network of service providers as most other health services in GAVI-eligible countries.

Grants are made based on a rigorous application process; an Independent Review Committee (IRC) comprised of experts drawn from a broad geographic base reviews country proposals. IRC members are not connected with GAVI and are selected (primarily from low and middle income countries) for their expertise in public health and specific knowledge of vaccines and immunisation. Grant applications may undergo multiple rounds of revisions between GAVI and recipient countries before GAVI approves the grant; on average, 50% of proposals are approved at their first submission, 37.1% of proposals are approved after the second submission, 11.3% of proposals are approved after the third submission, and 1.6% of proposals are approved after the fourth submission. There are varying application and submission guidelines for GAVI programmes. For example, GAVI's support to Health System Strengthening (HSS) will have two application rounds in 2009: May 1 and September 11. It currently takes around 6 months from the time of HSS application submission to funds arriving in recipient countries. The length of this fund disbursement process could be reduced if country submissions do not have to be revised. On average, GAVI takes 3.65 months from the first proposal submission to the grant approval. After the grant is approved, it takes approximately 1.5 –2.5 months for funding (not disbursement).

About 22 GAVI-eligible countries are considered to be "*fragile states*" based on the World Bank's classification system for Low Income Countries Under Stress that may be in active or post-conflict situations. In general, GAVI offers greater support for these fragile states due to their lower country vaccine co-financing, greater opportunity for immunisation coverage awards, and increased need for health system and immunisation services support.

Table 38-2. *List of contributors to GAVI – cash received (20).*

Donor	Pledge Timetable	Total amount (in US$ million)
Australia	2006–2008	15
Canada	2002–2006	149
Denmark	2001, 2004–2007	17
European Commission	2003, 2007–2008	29
France	2004, 2006	19
Germany	2006–2007	11
Ireland	2002–2008	23
Luxembourg	2005–2008	4
Netherlands	2001–2005, 2007–2008	160
Norway	2001–2008	376
Spain	2008	41
Sweden	2001–2008	72
United Kingdom	1999/2000, 2002–2007	122
United States	2001–2008	494
Total Direct Contributions	1999/2000–2008	1530
IFFIm	2006–2008	1226
Bill & Melinda Gates Foundation	1999/2000–2001, 2003–2005, 2007–2008	1063
Other Private	1999/2000, 2002–2008	16
Private and Institutions	1999–2000–2008	1079
Grand Total		3835

Over the past few years, GAVI has acknowledged the special needs of fragile states by strengthening their health system capacity to create sustainably the infrastructure to administer immunisation programmes. However, while GAVI tries to support primary health through its HSS initiative started in 2007, its efficacy in fragile states is difficult to evaluate. For example, the fragile state of Liberia has demonstrated great increases in vaccine coverage and was able to increase DTP3 immunisation to 87% by 2005, but information is unavailable about the specific outcomes of HSS support in Liberia awarded in July 2007. Unarguably, the incorporation of a health systems approach for fragile states is critical for the proper functioning of vertical health interventions and for broader in-country health systems improvement. In many parts of Africa, vaccine infrastructure has been suboptimal, and adoption of new vaccines into national epidemiology programmes has been obstinate due to lack of support for routine vaccine delivery throughout the continent (21). Vertical health interventions need to be implemented in conjunction with broader health system approaches, given that logistical and operational factors in fragile states are barriers that require substantial continuous investments in human capital, equipment, and financing.

GAVI's history can be separated into two phases. The principal objective of GAVI's first five-year work phase (2000–2005) was to disburse rapidly funds to countries extending the reach and quality of immunization programmes. Funding was focused on the supply of three underused vaccines (Hib, hepatitis B, and yellow fever) and on strengthening vaccine delivery systems. Support was provided in five-year grants with the expectation that countries would increase their own contribution, eventually financing their own immunization programmes. GAVI created incentives for countries to increase immunisation through performance-based cash rewards: GAVI's Immunisation Services Support (ISS) allocated additional money to countries for every additional child immunised.

In its second phase of operation (2005–2010), two primary factors caused GAVI to review its strategy and priorities: a critical need to improve country health systems and the inability of recipient countries to sustain long-term funding. Since December 2005, GAVI has moved toward a broader health perspective that strives to improve the general health sector of recipient countries in addition to increasing immunisation services. One of GAVI's recently revised strategic goals is to strengthen the capacity of countries' health systems in order to deliver immunisation and other health services in a sustainable manner. GAVI now offers a new form of support funding – Health System Strengthening (HSS) and acknowledges that improved immunisation service delivery in many countries has been impeded by broader health system constraints. GAVI is investing US$ 800 million in developing countries' health systems between 2006 and 2015. This investment is flexible and long-term, since barriers to immunization vary from country to country. Health ministries also need flexibility in planning improvements to best suit their needs. Frequently, barriers to greater immunisation coverage include: limited local management and supervisory skills, infrastructure failures (transport or equipment), workforce numbers and training.

Another change in GAVI's policies during its second operational phase concerns the sustainability of immunisation programmes. GAVI formally implemented co-financing of vaccines in 2007 and requested recipient countries to co-finance the introduction of new vaccines and to co-finance existing vaccines beyond the first five years (or equivalent) of GAVI support. This new co-financing policy aims to gradually increase countries' share of vaccine costs to facilitate the sustainability of country immunisation programmes. In addition, GAVI-eligible countries are requested to contribute a set amount for the first new vaccine, according to their funding capability classification. For each subsequent new vaccine, the co-financed amount increases by a minimum of US$ 15 cents per dose. Countries are expected, if possible, to scale up co-financing by 15% annually. Other recipient countries can maintain current co-financing levels until 2010 after which they will increase gradually. In its new sustainability plan, GAVI sets a sunset clause for grant support and sponsors the preparation of a financial sustainability plan alongside its grants to assess whether or not a recipient country will be able to cover financing after a grant expires.

GAVI utilizes two mechanisms for disbursing funds that draw heavily on private-sector mechanisms: the Advance Market Commitment (AMC) and the International Finance Facility for Immunisation (IFFIm). AMC provides a method of accelerating the development and manufacture of vaccines. Through the AMC, donors commit money to guarantee vaccine prices once they are developed (per demand from GAVI-eligible countries), provided that they meet stringent, pre-agreed criteria on effectiveness, cost and availability. The AMC also helps sustained vaccine usage by recipient countries, since it also guarantees a long-term price. IFFIm was proposed to the Group of Seven countries by the UK government in 2005. Wealthier donor countries provide immediate and long-term aid usually in 10–20 year, legally binding aid commitments. IFFIm borrows against these pledges on capital markets, raising funds that can be disbursed in an optimal way. The aim of IFFIm is to raise US$ 4 billion on capital markets over the next 10 years – enough to support the immunization of half a billion children through immunisation campaigns.

GAVI provides reward-based support through Immunisation Services Support (ISS) that aim to increase coverage of vaccines through performance-based incentives. ISS support, representing 11% of GAVI's business, responds to country proposals and represents flexible cash that countries can use to improve immunisation performance (22). ISS payments are disbursed in proportion to the numbers of additional children immunized (beyond original immunisation targets) and are calculated according to country achievements in surpassing previous year targets. GAVI does not prescribe conditions for the use of cash rewards but imposes strict performance requirements and relies on governments and inter-agency coordinating committees to set goals and monitor progress. Currently, due to over-reporting of immunisation coverage by many recipient countries, GAVI has suspended further ISS payments until they complete a review of countries with significant data variance in immunisation coverage.

The GAVI Alliance Board establishes all policies, oversees operations and monitors programme implementation of GAVI. Board membership is drawn from a range of public and private partner organisations, as well as experts from the private sector. The Board's representative members ensure that institutions and constituencies provide formal input in the development of GAVI's policies and the management of its operations. The GAVI Alliance Board is comprised of four permanent seats for representatives from the Bill & Melinda Gates Foundation, UNICEF, WHO, and the World Bank. In addition, there are 18 rotating Board members who are representatives from various constituency groups: developing country governments (5 seats), donor governments (5 seats), research and technical health institutes (1 seat), industrialized country vaccine industry (1 seat), developing country vaccine industry (1 seat), and civil society organizations (1 seat). The Board also includes unaffiliated Board members with no professional connection to GAVI's work in order to bring independent and balanced scrutiny to the Board's deliberations – currently, there are 10 unaffiliated Board members. The GAVI Alliance Board meets twice a year and holds periodic teleconferences to review progress and policies.

The GAVI Alliance Board is supported by a secretariat with offices in Geneva and Washington. The GAVI Secretariat is responsible for GAVI's day-to-day operations including: mobilizing resources to fund programmes, coordinating programme approvals and disbursements, and managing legal and financial issues. The Secretariat is led by Executive Secretary Dr Julian Lob-Levyt and is supported by a number of teams. GAVI's 2009 administrative budget is about US$ 42.4 million and has a current total of about 123 personnel in its Geneva and DC offices. 83% of funds GAVI receives goes toward its grant programmes, 7% funds its work plan, 5% funds administrative costs of the Secretariat, and the remaining 5% funds IFFim interest expenses (i.e. financial cost of front-loading).

GAVI has experienced success in bringing together committed partners, mobilizing investments, and increasing the numbers of immunised children. It has revitalized international concern for, and knowledge about, immunisation in resource-deprived countries, as well as developing effective instruments for dispensing money it raises (23). Since its creation in 2000, GAVI has helped to significantly increase vaccine coverage for children around the world. From 2000–2007, GAVI has made available more than US$ 3.7 billion for immunisation in GAVI-eligible countries. As a result, immunisation levels have increased dramatically, and the WHO estimates that 2.8 million premature deaths have been averted in 2000–2007 through use of GAVI-supported vaccines. During the same period, WHO estimates that GAVI protected 172 million children with new and underused vaccines. GAVI is also credited with achieving large-scale introduction of hepatitis B vaccination throughout the developing world.

4. Challenges faced by Global Fund and GAVI: Distortion of health sector priorities. Both the Global Fund and GAVI have been criticized for distorting developing country health sector priorities. Critics allege that vertically targeting three diseases (HIV/AIDS, TB and Malaria) and immunisation cause distortions in weak and under-funded health systems (24). Short-term advances in certain diseases or vaccination coverage run the risk of fragmenting health services.

The Global Fund has been criticized for focusing attention on three high-profile diseases at the expense of primary care and the social determinants of health. **Table 38-3** provides a snapshot of the five countries where fund grants made up the biggest proportion of total health expenditure between 2003 and 2005.

Table 38-3. *Contributions of the Global Fund (GF) to national expenditure on health (17).*

COUNTRY	GF DISBURSE-MENTS (US$ MILLION)	GF DISBURSEMENTS AS % OF TOTAL HEALTH EXPENDITURE (PUBLIC + PRIVATE)	GF DISBURSEMENTS AS % OF PUBLIC HEALTH EXPENDITURE
Burundi	21.8	31.8	118.2
Liberia	14.2	17.6	28.0
Dem. Rep. Congo	48.3	15.3	31.1
Rwanda	53.1	12.6	22.4
Gambia	10.4	12.4	46.0

This critique ties into a more serious concern that the Global Fund might be further fragmenting and weakening country health systems. To address this, the Board created a separate category for health systems strengthening in the fifth round (25). However, the separate category was discontinued due to the view that this was not the reason for the Global Fund's creation, nor its comparative advantage. Thus, while the Global Fund encourages applications to budget for health systems within disease-specific grant proposals, it states that these activities must be *"essential to reducing the impact and spread of disease"* (17,26–28).

As the Executive Director of the Global Fund has argued, perhaps a natural by-product of disease-specific grants is the strengthening of health systems. The WHO Report, The Global Fund Strategic Approach to Health Systems Strengthening, identifies seven countries where this has clearly occurred. In addition, Gorik Ooms (29) has argued that *"...critiques implicitly blame the Global Fund for having too narrow a mandate... These critiques are blaming the Global Fund for the successes of its exceptional approach in part because their authors want this exceptional approach to exist for primary health care in general. I would argue that instead of critiquing the Global Fund's success they should be pushing for its approach to be expanded"*. Ooms argues that the Global Fund should expand its mandate to become a *"Global Health Fund"*, with broader health aims and not merely focused on HIV/AIDS, TB and Malaria.

GAVI has also been criticized for distorting health sector priorities through prioritizing immunisation programmes over improvements in primary health care systems. While increasing vaccine coverage reduces the incidence of, and mortality from, various diseases, immunisation service delivery needs to be strengthened and better integrated into routine general health services to ensure that more children receive needed vaccines (30). In recent years, GAVI has tried to engage in a greater systems approach to public health development, while continuing to prioritize immunisation. GAVI now includes new funding for health systems support, but the implementation of this approach has been criticized by both health systems support advocates and critics. Advocates for this approach point out that in order to obtain health systems support funding, countries are required to complete extensive, burdensome analyses and plans. Specifically, they need to provide an analysis of health system constraints, demonstrate the process for identifying those constraints, address how those constraints will be addressed, and provide budget plans that demonstrate the link between those actions and increased immunisation coverage. Critics of the move towards a greater health systems approach argue that GAVI should focus on vaccines to avoid distractions from its original mission.

Vaccines chosen by GAVI may not necessarily be the most appropriate for all recipient countries given varying financial and health system constraints. Health budgets in many recipient countries are still far from what is required to provide decent minimal health services. Many GAVI-eligible countries and in-country workers would not necessarily place new children vaccines at the top of their national health priorities, because these resource-deprived countries typically have a host of other pressing health challenges. In GAVI's second phase of operations (2005–2010), it added two new vaccines (pneumoccoal and rotavirus) to its portfolio. GAVI is also developing a new investment strategy to determine which vaccines to offer to countries in the future. The shortlist of vaccines under evaluation targets four deadly diseases: cervical cancer, Japanese encephalitis, rubella, and typhoid. While these new vaccines may prove to be important and beneficial in GAVI-eligible countries, it is unclear if the shift to these new vaccines is appropriate and effective for all countries. It is also unclear to what extent GAVI-eligible countries are able to influence decisions about the development of new vaccines.

In addition, GAVI may provide inadequate support for technological shifts, for implementation, and for explanation and communication of new information to recipient countries. Tying funding to policy shifts due to new and improved vaccines has created uncertainty and a sense of coercion of recipient countries. William Muraskin (23,31) argues that when a policy has shifted toward a newer vaccine, stakeholders in recipient countries have received insufficient information about the decision. Often, they do not receive evidence (e.g. cost-benefit analyses), information about whether the policy is flexible, or the logistics and trade-offs of using new vaccines. GAVI also prioritizes certain vaccines over others, and this prioritization can change and shift over time without adequate accommodating support for recipient countries.

5. Challenges faced by Global Fund and GAVI: Raising funding/sustainability. Both the Global Fund and GAVI face challenges of raising funding and ensuring sustainability. The Global Fund holds *"replenishment"* meetings every two years to discuss future funding. In March 2009, Michel Kazatchkine noted that the Global Fund needs an additional US$ 4 billion to address its budget needs through 2010. While it is doubtful in the current financial climate that aid budgets will increase, he argued that the governments of developing countries need external financial assistance now more than ever, and thus *"the crisis is one more reason to increase aid to development"*.

While the U.S. has been one of the largest contributors to the Global Fund, it has been criticized for channeling funding through its own bilateral initiative, PEPFAR rather than through the Global Fund (32,33). PEPFAR was a hallmark initiative of the former President Bush, which disbursed US$ 15 billion for HIV/AIDS prevention, treatment and care to 15 target countries from 2003–2008. PEPFAR was renewed for US$ 48 billion in 2008 for another five years. Richard Feachem, former Executive Director of the Global Fund, has referred to the Fund as the *"multilateral arm"* of US efforts.

GAVI also experiences problems with raising funds. Although its AMC initiative gained seed funding of US$ 1.5 billion in 2007, GAVI estimates that it would need US$ 35 billion to carry out its existing programmes through

2015 (34). In addition, IFFIm bonded debt will continue far into the future negatively affecting donor ability and willingness for continuing country immunisation programmes (31).

There are also issues of long-term financial sustainability of immunisation in GAVI-eligible countries. GAVI historically strived to leverage the drug industry to produce cheaper and greater quantities of vaccines to ultimately lower the cost of vaccines (35). Given its assumption of decreased vaccine costs, GAVI believed that recipient countries would be able to eventually afford immunisation coverage without GAVI support. Given these two assumptions, GAVI expected a complete transition of immunisation coverage to national government partners. The first assumption has since 2000 proved to be false. While GAVI expected a drop in vaccine prices due to greater demand, the guaranteed vaccine market, reliable financing, and strong delivery systems have been slow to occur. GAVI initially failed to understand the situation it faced in the vaccine marketplace: procurement decisions were made on well-intentioned assumptions about supply, demand and market realities but without the benefit of analyses and comparisons of optional approaches and likely results. The second assumption is also flawed; upon closer look at government budgets, even if immunisation is a national priority, many recipient countries have no financial means to sustain vaccine coverage and costs. If positive market changes for immunization do not materialise and recipient countries continue to be unable to take over responsibility for immunisation by 2015, then the problem of sustainability will be exaggerated further than alleviated (31).

6. Challenges faced by Global Fund and GAVI: Performance-based incentives. The Global Fund and GAVI utilize performance-based incentives with the aim to ensure health financing is effective, accountable and transparent. Incentives focus on outcomes, reward solutions, and manage results of health programmes (36). There have been concerns that performance-based funding might penalize poorer countries, reduce the predictability of aid, and increase incentives to distort reported indicators. The Global Fund has not faced these problems on a large scale. On average, Global Fund grants are 90% disbursed at the scheduled end of grant compared with about 80% for World Bank. However, there are notable exceptions. In 2005, the Global Fund suspended grants to Uganda following reports of mismanagement and irregularities in procurement and subcontracting (37). In 2006, the Fund suspended two grants in Chad and phased out its grants to Myanmar. This, tensions still remain between ensuring stable/reliable financing and implementing performance-based incentives.

Under its Immunisation Services Support, GAVI offers support in a reward phase, which begins from the third year after grant approval. Payments are calculated according to country achievements in surpassing previous year immunisation targets. To calculate financial rewards, GAVI uses a performance indicator and a baseline appropriate to the respective year. The performance indicator is the number of additional children aged less than one year who have received a given vaccine compared to the baseline. The baseline for the first reward is the number of additional children who were targeted to receive a given vaccine in the first year after approval of GAVI support. The baseline for subsequent rewards is the number of additional children who were reported to have received a given vaccine in the previous year. GAVI then calculates the reward each year by multiplying the performance indicator by US$ 20.

In contrast, GAVI has experienced setbacks and negative repercussions from its performance-based policies. The majority of GAVI's recipient countries have been inflating the number of children who have received vaccines, which has increased the amount of cash reward governments receive (38). Over-reporting the number of additional children immunized occurs in two ways: vaccine coverage at the baseline year can be lowered; and vaccine coverage after the baseline year can be inflated, particularly from the third year when reward payments begin (39). The number of children receiving vaccines is based on official reports from countries to WHO and UNICEF – these reports are largely based on artificially inflated administrative data from health service provider registries. The quality of administrative data on immunization coverage remains problematic due to measurement problems and performance-based payment systems such as GAVI's ISS that encourages health-service providers to over-report coverage.

A recent study which examined the number of children receiving Diphteria-Pertussis-Tetanus vaccines in 193 countries from 1986 to 2006 found that vaccination estimates from countries' official data were much higher than immunization estimates based on surveys (39). Overall, recipient countries reported 13.9 million newly vaccinated children while surveys indicate that the actual number is closer to 7.4 million. At US$ 39 per child, GAVI allocated US$ 290 million, which is nearly double the US$ 150 million that would have been justified at the established cost of US$ 20 per additional child immunized (38). In light of this recent study, GAVI officials created a task force to make recommendations to improve GAVI's data collection and performance. As a result of this study, GAVI suspended further ISS payments until they have completed a review of the countries where there is a significant data variance in reporting of immunization coverage.

Some argue that the inherent cause of over-reporting is not due to GAVI's use of incentives to improve vaccine coverage, but rather due to GAVI's failure to implement a better monitoring system that tracks recipient countries to prevent them from over-reporting immunisation coverage (38). GAVI implements data quality audits (DQAs) that try to assess the accuracy of immunisation reports from health centres to districts to the national level by comparing this number against a re-count of paper records in health centres (39). Although GAVI requires countries to pass a DQA of their administrative data system to be eligible for reward payments, over-reporting remains a concern. Lim et al. (39) note that there is an urgent need for independent monitoring and tracking of vaccination coverage to reduce over-reporting abuses. They continue that the incentive to over-report progress whether intentional or unintentional will always exist with performance based payments, so counteracting this problem requires independent monitoring and a system based on rigorous, empirical measurements using the best scientific methods available. They suggest that GAVI could implement a monitoring system that benchmarks vaccine coverage with periodic surveys either as a condition or component of GAVI support to provide timely information and to inform size of required payments. Countries that receive funding from GAVI and the Global Fund often need to have two separate health information systems to appropriately report progress on certain health indicators (40). This leads to inaccuracies in data collection and increased economic and human capital costs. It has been suggested that the Global Fund and GAVI consider standardizing and coordinating their reporting structures and health information systems in developing countries, which will help with international comparability of data and indicators.

7. Conclusion. Global public-private partnerships like the Global Fund and GAVI finance initiatives to address many public health challenges throughout the world. There is, however, room for improvement so that vertical interventions can optimally operate in highly resource-constrained environments with limited infrastructure, weak basic health systems and severe healthcare service shortages (41). The Global Fund and GAVI may consider having more flexibility throughout their operations to address the specialised needs for strong performing countries, as well as fragile states. The vertical fund model for health has important lessons for other issue areas such as education. Two areas that vertical funds can make significant progress in, as demonstrated by the Global Fund and GAVI, are increased monies for global health challenges and a focus on results and progressive achievements. However, introducing vertical funding into low-income countries has its drawbacks and a number of negative externalities for recipient countries (42). First, recipient countries are burdened with multiple processes, funding requirements, and reporting structures, which make it difficult for them to holistically strategize health sector priorities. Second, vertical health funding has led to situations where programmes compete for scarce resources and human capital. The discrepancy in salaries between regular public sector jobs and comparable jobs with better-funded vertical health programmes and projects has exacerbated the human resource crisis in fragile health systems (3). Third, while performance-based funding was developed in the 1970s in the education sector (36), distortion of results (e.g. over-reporting or under-reporting) is an important consideration in implementing vertical programmes in the education sector. Finally, there is limited integration of vertical programmes with general health services in recipient countries, which lead to duplicated efforts where inefficiencies in health care delivery and fragmentation of health system occur. The positive as well as detrimental impact of vertical funds in the health sector must be taken into account before looking at whether mechanisms such as the Global Fund and GAVI could be expanded to other sectors.

Acknowledgement: Originally published as: Devi Sridhar and Tami Tamashiro: Vertical funds in the health sector: Lessons for education from the Global Fund and GAVI. Reprinted from 2010 UNESCO Global Monitoring Report Background Paper.

References

1. O'Keefe J. Aid – from consensus to competition. Presented at: Brookings Blum Round-table 2007. Washington, DC: Brookings Institute, 2007.
2. Marten R, Witte JM. Transforming development? The role of philanthropic founda-tions in international development cooperation. Global Public Policy Institute, 2008.
3. Atun RA, Bennett S, Duran A. When do vertical programmes have a place in health systems? In: Permanand G (ed). World Health Organization Regional Office for Eu-rope and European Observatory on Health Systems and Policies, 2008.
4. World Health Organization. World Health Report Primary Health Care: Now More Than Ever. Geneva: WHO, 2008.
5. Maciocco G, Stefanini A. From Alma-Ata to the Global Fund: the history of interna-tional health policy. Revista Brasileira de Saúde Materno Infantil 2007; 7: 479–486.
6. Navaro V; personal communication.
7. Sridhar D, Batniji R. Misfinancing global health. Lancet 2008; 372:1185–1191.
8. McColl K. Europe told to deliver more aid for Health. Lancet 2008; 371: 2072–2073.
9. Sridhar D. Battle against hunger. Oxford: OUP, 2008.
10. Available from: http://www.theglobalfund.org/documents/6_pp_fiduciary_ arrange-ments_4_en.pdf
11. Annan K. Secretary-General proposes global fund for fight against HIV/AIDS and other infectious diseases at African Leaders Summit. 2001. (Available from: www.un.org/News/Press/docs/2001/SGSM7779R1.doc.htm).

12. Available from: http://www.theglobalfund.org/en/pledges/?lang=en; Accessed: 31 Aug 2009.
13. Mataka E. In: The Global Fund: How CCMs can be made more effective. 2004. (Available from: www.gtz.de/de/dokumente/en-ccm-satellite-july04.pdf)
14. Lawson P. In: The Global Fund: How CCMs can be made more effective. 2004. (Available from: www.gtz.de/de/dokumente/en-ccm-satellite-july04.pdf)
15. Radelet S, Siddiqi B. Global Fund grant programmes: an analysis of evaluation scores. Lancet 2006; 369: 1807–1813.
16. Schocken C. Overview of the Global Fund to Fight AIDS, Tuberculosis and Malaria. 2009. (Available from: http://www.cgdev.org/doc/HIVAIDSMonitor/OverviewGlobal-Fund.pdf)
17. Global Health Watch 2. The Global Fund to Fight AIDS, TB and Malaria. 2008.
18. Grubb I. Global Fund to Fight AIDS, Tuberculosis and Malaria. 2007.
19. Organisation for Economic Co-operation and Development (OECD). Ensuring fragile states are not left behind: Summary Report, 2009.
20. Available from: http://www.gavialliance.org/support/donors/index.php; Accessed: 3 Jun 2009.
21. Jamison DT, Feachem RG, Makgoba MW, Bos ER, Baingana FK, Hofman KJ, Rogo KO (eds.) Disease and mortality in sub-Saharan Africa. The World Bank: Washington, DC, 2006.
22. Lob-Levyt J. Vaccine coverage and the GAVI Alliance immunization services support initiative. Lancet 2009; 373: 209.
23. Muraskin W. Crusade to immunize the World's children. USC Marshall Global Bio-Business Initiative, 2005.
24. Garrett L. Challenge of global health. Foreign Affairs 2007; 86:14–38.
25. Sidibe M, Ramiah I, Buse K. The Global Fund at five: what next for universal access for HIV/AIDS, TB and malaria? J Royal Soc Med 2007; 99: 497–500.
26. Global Fund Website: What we do, Principles. 2005. (Available from: http://www.theglobalfund.org/en/publications/whoweare)
27. Global Fund. Global Fund investments in fragile states. 2005. (Available from: http://www.theglobalfund.org/documents/replenishment/london/fragile_states_3rdreplenishment.pdf).
28. Global Fund. Guidelines for proposals, Round 7, 2007.
29. Ooms G. From the global AIDS response to global health? Discussion paper prepared for the Helene de Beir foundation and the International Civil Society Support group. 2009.
30. Ryman TK, Dietz V, Cairns KL. Too little but not too late: Results of a literature review to improve routine immunization programs in developing countries. BMC Health Serv Res 2008; 8:134.
31. Muraskin W. The Global Alliance for Vaccines and Immunization: Is it a new model for effective public-private cooperation in international public health? Am J Publ Hlth 2004; 94: 1922–1925.
32. Public Broadcasting Service. Frontline: The Age of AIDS. Interview with Richard Feachem. May 30, 2006. (Available from: http://www.pbs.org/wgbh/pages/frontline/aids/interviews/feachem.html).
33. Sridhar D. Global Health: Who can lead? Chatham House World Today, 2009. 65:25–26.

34. Chokshi DA, Kesselheim AS. Rethinking global access to vaccines. BMJ 2008; 336:750–753.
35. Brown H. Great expectations. BMJ 2007; 334:874–876.
36. Low-Beer D, Afkhami H, Komatsu R, et al. Making performance-based funding work for health. PLoS Med 2007; 4:1308–1311.
37. Bass E. Uganda is learning from its Global Fund grant suspension. Lancet 2005; 366:1839–1840.
38. Sternberg S. Study: Nations inflate vaccine numbers to get more aid. USA Today, 2008.
39. Lim SS, Stein DB, Charrow A, Murray CJL. Tracking progress towards universal childhood immunisation and the impact of global initiatives: a systematic analysis of three-dose diphtheria, tetanus, and pertussis immunisation coverage. Lancet 2008; 372:2031–2046.
40. Aiga H, Kuroiwa C, Takizawa I, Yamagata R. The reality of health information systems: challenges for standarization. BioScience Trends 2008; 2:5–9.
41. Bill & Melinda Gates Foundation. Global health partnerships: Assessing country consequences. McKinsey & Company, 2005.
42. Horton R. Venice statement: Global health initiatives and health systems. Lancet 2009; 374:10–12.

PART 6.

Improving research prioritization

CHAPTER 39.

Setting priorities in global health research investments: Assessment of principles and practice

Among the many challenges in global child health today, the main is that 10.6 million children younger than 5 years still die each year (1,2). In The World Health Report in 2002, the World Health Organization (WHO) identified the leading health risks in developing countries as underweight, unsafe sex, unsafe water, sanitation and hygiene, iron deficiency, and indoor smoke from solid fuels (3). Each of those risks heavily affects children in a more or less direct way. However, many health interventions that could reduce this burden are available. Globally, the coverage for most of those interventions is below 50%, and the children who do not receive them are usually also the poorest and those exposed to multiple risk factors listed above (4).

1. The UN's Millennium Development Goal 4. At a turn of the Millennium, United Nations defined its 8 priorities for further development – *"Millennium Development Goals"* (5). One of these goals is to reduce child mortality by two-thirds between 1990 and 2015. Achieving this goal required a reliable assessment of the main causes of child deaths. In 2001, the WHO established the external Child Health Epidemiology Reference Group (CHERG) to develop estimates of the proportion of deaths attributable to each of the main causes in children under 5 years of age. This was needed as a starting point in further planning and setting priorities, because previous estimates varied widely with certain organizations or research groups overemphasizing the importance of some diseases (1). After reviewing all the available information, CHERG estimated that, over the period 2000–2003, six causes accounted for 73% of deaths in children younger than 5 years: pneumonia (19%), diarrhea (18%), malaria (8%), neonatal pneumonia or sepsis (10%), preterm delivery (10%), and asphyxia at birth (8%) (2,6). Undernutrition, as a major risk factor in children, was estimated to represent the underlying cause of 53% of all child deaths globally (5).

Jones et al (4) estimated that, if the existing interventions for which there is sufficient or limited evidence of the effect, and which are feasible for delivery at high coverage in low-income settings, were made available universally, a disproportionately high figure of 63% of child deaths would be prevented each year. Subsequently, Bryce et al (7) demonstrated that there were no financial obstacles to fund such an effort given the amount of funding available, but there is lack of knowledge on how to do it. Strategies are needed to reach the poor and deprived children and to sustain their coverage, and they need to be developed through further research.

2. **Research agenda in global child health.** Although the interventions and the financial resources needed to achieve Millennium Development Goal 4 seem available, more than half of the period (1990–2015) set by the UN has passed and mortality of children globally has not decreased enough. It is becoming apparent that the achievement of this goal may soon be out of reach. Why is this the case? One of the answers may lie in current practices in which funding priorities are being set in global child health research. Pneumonia and diarrhea, as an example, are jointly responsible for nearly 40% of all child deaths globally, which is about the same as the number of deaths from smoking, double the number of deaths from HIV/AIDS, and is 25 times the number of deaths from war globally (3). Interventions (antibiotics and oral rehydration therapy) have been developed and have been shown to be highly cost-effective in preventing deaths from both diseases in the mid 1980s (7), but this appears to be where research interest ended (**Figure 39-1**).

There is considerably less interest in research on how to implement these interventions in the context of health services in countries with limited resources. Implementation research is not ranked highly by the scientific community or by most funding agencies. As it is rarely considered a research priority, research on new interventions far exceeds that on delivery. A vaccine against measles has been available for decades and it is highly cost-effective and deliverable, but even in this case only about 50% of world's children have been vaccinated (4). Research funding for global child health currently favors opening new frontiers with their attractive promises over realizing the full public health impact of the interventions which led from past advances in knowledge (8–11). Even if work on new research avenues proves successful, the beneficiaries are only those who can afford the results of the research success. This further increases already unacceptable levels of inequity. The methodology for setting investment priorities is needed which could carefully balance between long-term investments and supporting research on better use of the existing knowledge (12–15).

3. **Instruments (domains) of health research.** Current areas of progress in health research can be classified into four large (and to some extent overlapping) categories from the perspective of their potential to reduce persisting mortality and morbidity burden (16). Assessment of existing and averted

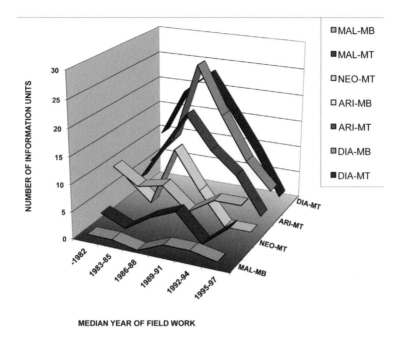

Figure 39-1. *Number of papers with policy-relevant information on epidemiology of specific childhood illnesses in developing countries identified by Child Health Epidemiology Reference Group shows depleting interest in diseases that continue to kill most children. MAL – malaria; NEO – neonatal causes; ARI – acute respiratory infections; DIA – diarrhea; MB – morbidity; MT – mortality (7).*

disease burden can be achieved through epidemiological research. Further reduction of disease burden can then be achieved through health policy and systems research, research to improve existing interventions, and research for development of new health interventions. The key challenge in setting investment priorities for health research is to find the right balance of investments into those 4 different *"instruments"* of health research. The aim should be to achieve maximum gains in disease burden reduction with improved health information, efficiency of health systems, and deliverability of available interventions, while still supporting long-term strategic investments into new interventions with large potential to remove the existing disease burden.

4. A history of priority setting in global health research investments. In 1990, *"Commission on Health Research for Development"* was set up. The Commission is usually referred to as the first truly significant international initiative aimed toward systematic approach to setting priorities in global health research. It reviewed global health needs and priorities for health research and identified great inequity in the allocation of research funds globally – the

"10/90" gap, where less than 10% of global health research funds is devoted to 90% of the world's health problems. This led to subsequent promotion of the concept of Essential National Health Research (ENHR), in which countries take responsibilities to delineate a research agenda by themselves (17).

In 1994, *"Ad Hoc Committee (AHC) on Health Research Relating to Future Intervention Options"* was assembled. This is the second major initiative in similar direction, which came from the World Health Organization (WHO), when the Ad Hoc Committee on Health Research Relating to Future Intervention Options (AHC) was formed. The Committee's mandate was to address: (i) priorities for health research and development, (ii) prospects for funding, and (iii) institutional changes that might enhance the output of ongoing research and development investments at the time. In 1996, Ad Hoc Committee presented a report *"Investing in Health Research and Development"*, that recommended policies for investments into research and development of particular relevance to poor nations (16). Ad Hoc Committee is also credited with conceptual framework showing the relationship between different *"instruments"* of health research and their potential to reduce different components of disease burden, as presented in the previous section (16).

In 1998, the *"Global Forum for Health Research"* (GFHR) began its operations with the main focus on helping to correct this "10/90" gap. It had been holding annual conferences at which ideas and strategies for correcting the *"10/90 gap"* were exchanged. Working as a consultant for Global Forum for Health Research, Hyder wrote a report on priority investments in research and development (*"best buys"*) identified by Ad Hoc Committee (16). Through structured interviews and comprehensive review of the literature, and a number of other methods that took into account issues such as dynamic nature of *"best buys"*, time factor, baseline status, and research intensity, 17 research and development priorities were identified and classified as either *"Strategic research"*, *"Package development and evaluation"*, and *"New tool or intervention development"*.

Examples of *"Strategic research options"* were *"Sequencing genomes of major pathogens responsible for disease burden"* or *"Investigating factors influencing the development of anti-microbial resistance"* (16). Examples of *"Package development and evaluation"* were *"Evaluating and refining the package for the Integrated Management of Childhood Illness"* and *"Developing, evaluating and refining the Mother-Baby package for pregnancy, delivery and neonatal care"* (16). Finally, the examples of proposed *"New tool or intervention development"* research options were *"Evaluating the efficacy and dosage of candidate rotavirus vaccine in low-income countries"*, *"Evaluating the efficacy of candidate conjugate pneumococcal vaccine and conducting trials in low-income countries"*, *"Developing malaria vaccine"* and *"Developing HIV vaccine"* (16).

In 2000, *"Council on Health Research and Development"* (COHRED) was formed. In October 2000, an International conference on health research and development was held in Bangkok, Thailand. The conference was chaired by an international organizing committee formed by the representatives of the WHO, The World Bank, Global Forum for Health Research, and the Council on Health Research and Development. COHRED reviewed experiences and lessons from developing countries (10). The issues addressed were systematically categorized into the processes and methods for priority setting, assessing the results of Essential National Health Research strategy, defining who sets priorities and how to get participants involved, the potential functions, roles, and responsibilities of various stakeholders, information and criteria for setting priorities, strategies for implementation, and indicators for evaluation (10).

The next major global initiative emerged at the World Economic Forum, held in Davos, Switzerland, in January 2003. Bill and Melinda Gates Foundation (BMGF) announced the release of US$ 200 million to support the initiative of *"The Grand Challenges in global health research"*. This was based on a model formulated by the mathematician David Hilbert, who defined ultimate problems in mathematics and prizes were then offered to anyone who would succeed in solving them. This initiative resulted in more focused research by scientists in mathematics and resulted in major progress in the field at the time (11).

The identification of *"Grand Challenges"* was achieved with financial support from BMGF and the National Institutes of Health. It gathered a scientific board of 20 scientists and public health experts from 13 countries (including some developing countries), while the scientific community supplied ideas for challenges. *"Grand Challenge"* was described as *"...a call for a specific scientific or technological innovation that would remove a critical barrier to solving an important health problem in the developing world with a high likelihood of global impact and feasibility"* (11). More than 1,000 submissions were received from scientists and institutions in 75 countries, and scientific board reached the decision on declaring 14 submissions as *"Grand Challenges"* (11). Grants of up to a total of US$ 20 million were then made available by Bill and Melinda Gates Foundation to remove these major obstacles to progress against diseases that disproportionately affect the developing world (11). All of the identified *"Grand Challenges"* fell into 7 broad categories, as follows: *"Improving childhood vaccines"*, *"Creating new vaccines"*, *"Controlling insects that transmit agents of disease"*, *"Improving nutrition to promote health"*, *"Improving drug treatment of infectious diseases"*, *"Curing latent and chronic infections"* and *"Measuring disease and health status accurately and economically in poor countries"* (11).

The *"17 Best Buys"* and the *"14 Grand Challenges"* addressed very similar problems and some of them entirely overlapped. The key difference was that the *"17 Best Buys"* were generally very specific technologies or interventions already under a certain degree of development and targeted at specific diseases, while the *"Grand Challenges"* were more broadly and generally defined and could impact several diseases and conditions.

In 2004, to improve the process in which the respected scientists discuss and decide on funding priorities based on their own views and knowledge, Global Forum for Health Research developed a useful tool, the *"Combined Approach Matrix"* (CAM). The tool has proven to be highly useful for systematic classification, organization, and presentation of the large body of information that is needed at different stages of priority setting process, so that the decisions made by the members of decision-making committees could be based on all relevant and available information, rather than their own personal knowledge and judgment.

CAM incorporates *"economic"* dimension of priority setting process along one axis, and *"institutional"* dimension along the other, thus covering the information on the determinants of health at the population level. Components of *"economic dimension"* are *"disease burden"*, its *"determinants"*, *"present level of knowledge"*, *"cost and effectiveness"* and *"resource flows"*. Components of *"institutional dimension"* are *"the individual, household and community"*, *"health ministry and other health institutions"*, *"sectors other than health"* and *"macroeconomic policies"*. CAM can be applied at the level of disease, risk factor, group or condition, and also at local, national, or international level (18).

"Research challenges to improve maternal and child survival" (2007): Over the past several years, *The Lancet* journal bravely engaged into advocacy of international health issues through publication of several series of papers focusing on main priority areas in international health. Recently, *The Lancet* expanded this effort through conducting a Delphi process similar to the one that had led to the *"Grand Challenges"* among a wide range of academics and professionals who had experience in developing countries (19). The coordinators of the process ranked by their perceived importance a limited number of very general and broad research themes in child health, maternal health, health systems, and community development (19).

5. Assessment of the outcomes of previous attempts to define priorities in health research investments. All the initiatives from the past aiming to set priorities in health research investments resulted in apparent benefits and successes. The benefits were that discussions over these issues were taking place and highlighted many important factors relevant to setting health research priorities. The successes were that a more specific research focus was agreed, which then attracted attention of many researchers groups. The investments began to follow the specified goals. Such situation was more favorable than having no priorities, when each research group followed its own path.

However, the past approaches were also not free from certain shortcomings. Identified interventions and research questions that were outlined as the priorities were not compiled in a truly systematic way, using scientifically convincing conceptual framework and objective and repeatable methods, but rather through consensus reached by panels of experts. This often made it difficult to present the identified priorities to wider audiences as legitimate and fair, as the decisions could be seen as driven by research interest bias of individual experts.

Also, the claim of *"best buys"* was not supported by scientific and repeatable arguments. The *"best buys"* were not consistent or informative with respect to their potential for targeted disease burden reduction. The category of *"package development"* represented a mix of health policy and systems research options and options to improve the existing interventions. Similarly, some items among the *"best buys"* listed as *"new tools or interventions"* were clearly research options addressing the improvement of efficacy, affordability, deliverability, or sustainability of existing interventions. More fundamentally, the claim that the proposed items are indeed *"best buys"* was not convincingly demonstrated in a scientifically based, repeatable manner.

The decision-making process leading to the concept of *"Grand Challenges"*, although better designed, informed, explained, and documented, had a somewhat biased focus from the start. The whole process was designed so that it largely promoted very difficult upstream technology developments. Among the *"challenges"*, there is hardly any that addressed the improvement of efficacy, effectiveness, deliverability, affordability, and sustainability of the existing interventions, so that these important instruments of health research were nearly ignored. This is particularly unfortunate, because one of motivations behind the *"Grand Challenges"* initiative was to promote equity. Equity, however, is best promoted through delivery of the already existing and effective interventions to all children.

One of the conclusions of the recent *Lancet*'s Child Survival series was a concern that global child health is perhaps losing its focus (4,8). Amid the large number of new interventions advertised and validated, levels of attention and effort directed at new, complex, and expensive interventions seem to be receiving higher profile and funding priority than the efforts to save millions of children by applying insecticide-treated materials, oral rehydration therapy, or promoting breastfeeding, all at a tiny fraction of costs of the former (4).

"*Combined Approach Matrix*" was launched, aiming to ensure that decision-makers are better informed about these facts and realities when making their decisions (18). However, the CAM also has its shortcomings. Although it is an extremely helpful tool for gathering and organizing information needed for priority setting process, it does not in itself represent an algorithm for making the decisions on the priorities by ranking or separating the competing investment options. Therefore, in the absence of reliable information, which is usually very scarce for developing countries, most of the decisions will still be based on discussions and agreements within the panels of experts. The recent effort by *The Lancet* made a step further in specifying broad research avenues that should be considered priorities, but did very little to point to more specific research programs or research questions which should be initiated or addressed urgently (19).

6. A need for systematic methodology for priority setting in global child health research investments. Today, investments into health research on new interventions far exceed those on delivery in spite of the evidence that emphasizes large potential contribution of the latter to mortality burden reduction (4,8). The dominant model of research priority setting is driven by criteria such as interests of different advocacy groups, media exposure, interests of donors, individual biases of the members of policy-making panels, attractiveness of research results, novelty of proposed research and potential for publication in high-impact journals. We are concerned that continuing application of these criteria in decisions over investments into health research is resulting in gross under-achievement of potential disease burden reduction and is actually generating further health inequity. Even when new research avenues succeed in the development of new interventions, the initial beneficiaries usually are those who can afford the results. More complete coverage of the population in need often lags decades behind (20).

The current model of research priority setting is a closed circle set to increasingly favor basic research and generate ever-increasing inequity. A major underlying problem is lack of clear criteria and principles that would guide health research investments based on a vision of what the endpoints of such investments should be. If we can agree that the ultimate endpoint of any health research should be reduction of disease burden and improvement of health, then some of the criteria needed for prioritization of investments should include: (i) usefulness of the proposed research in terms of its potential to lead to development of new or improved health interventions; (ii) true effectiveness of those interventions; (iii) their deliverability, affordability, and sustainability in the context of interest; and (iv) their maximum potential to reduce persisting disease burden in an equitable way.

In addition, there is growing need to make decisions on research priorities not only globally, but also at lower levels – regional, national, and local community levels, and at single health facilities. Because of this, a methodology proposed to assist in health research priority setting should ideally have a form of an algorithm, that would be able to rank the priorities in very specific research programs or questions in a given setting (global, regional, national, and local) and for a given disease, risk factor, or a set of diseases and risk factors. Such methodology should also be simple enough for application, so that it could gain popularity among the users. It should provide simple, intuitive, and easily understandable answers, so that they could be presented to policy-makers from different regions of the world and be understood in the similar way. The methodology should be able to incorporate the available information relevant to priority setting (such as that compiled by "*Combined Approach Matrix*").

The future application of this new methodology in the area of child health would greatly benefit from a particularly favorable knowledge base, represented in recently defined global burden of disease and death in children based on collective review of over 17,000 sources and references published over the past two decades, that was performed by WHO Child Health Epidemiology Reference Group (CHERG) (2,7,21–25). It would also have a solid base for comparatively evaluating the competing interventions, through the recently completed "*Disease Control Priorities Project II*" (26).

7. Designing a new methodology respecting the principles of fair and legitimate priority setting. There are several fundamental principles that need to be respected in order to develop, promote, and implement priority setting methodology that would have a chance to become widely accepted and used. To begin with, Daniels and Sabin (27) defined two main principles that must underlie any process of setting priorities – legitimacy and fairness. Legitimacy can only be insured by involving a large and diverse range of stakeholders from different regions and with different backgrounds into development of such methodology.

Respecting the principle of fairness is an equally difficult, but in many ways even more complex problem. There are different perspectives from which prioritizing between two or more competing options for health research investments can be made (e.g., medical, economical, legal, ethical, social, political, rational, philosophical, stakeholder driven, and others). Even if each process from each single perspective was driven through *"perfect"* decisions, the outcomes will necessarily conflict each other. Therefore, developing methods for setting priorities fairly will be a highly complex and multidimensional process that will require wide agreement of numerous experts from different disciplines working collaboratively to produce such methods.

A standard multidisciplinary approach, where researchers work in parallel from their respective disciplinary bases to address a common problem (as has been usually done in the past), would not have a capacity to address this particular problem. A transdisciplinary approach, where researchers of different backgrounds work jointly, using shared conceptual frameworks to draw together disciplinary specific knowledge and address common problems, will be significantly more likely to meet the target (28). Encouraging steps in providing theoretical guidelines for achieving success in transdisciplinary priority setting were made by Gibson et al (29), who managed to merge ethics principles on how priority-setting should be made (*"Accountability for reasonableness, A4R"*) with empirical observations on how priority setting is made in absence of any guidelines (*"The diamond model"*) into a single model. Their further collaboration with leading representatives of economy-based model of priority setting (*"Program budgeting and marginal analysis"*) resulted in the development of a joint model that incorporates principles and knowledge from all three disciplines – theory of ethics, theory of economy, and qualitative assessment of how model-free priority setting is made in practice – into a satisfactory general model (30). The task for Child Health and Nutrition Research Initiative (CHNRI) experts will be to collaborate with those experts and continue to expand their work by incorporating the principles from medical dimension (e.g., public health reasoning), social dimension (e.g., concern about equity), and public opinion dimension (e.g., respecting stakeholders' views) into an even more general transdisciplinary framework that could be useful in setting health research priorities at all levels. It would also remain open to emerging ideas, such as recently presented decision theory and *"value of information"* (VoI) concept (31).

8. Conclusion. The dominant model of priority setting in health research investments today continues to result in gross under-achievement of potential disease burden reduction among world's children and is actually generating further health inequity. There is growing need for a sound and informed process to make decisions on health research priorities, both globally and at lower levels – regional, national, and local community levels, and at single health facilities. A methodology in a form of algorithm that would enable this and that would be simple and practical enough to gain wider acceptance is much needed. In the series of papers that will follow this assessment of the past approaches, Child Health and Nutrition Research Initiative will propose a methodology for prioritization in global and national child health and nutrition research that attempts to satisfy most of those requirements. The proposed methodology will not seek to replace the existing methodologies, but will attempt to build upon their experiences, supplement them with input of knowledge and concepts from new and different perspectives, and seek to bring them all together and enhance transdisciplinary approach.

Acknowledgement: Originally published as: Igor Rudan, Jennifer L. Gibson, Lydia Kapiriri, Mary Ann Lansang, Adnan A Hyder, Joy E Lawn, Gary L Darmstadt, Simon Cousens, Zulfiqar A Bhutta, Ken H Brown, Sonja Y Hess, Maureen Black, Julie Meeks Gardner, Julie Webster, Ilona Carneiro, Daniel Chandramohan, Margaret Kosek, Claudio F Lanata, Mark Tomlinson, Mickey Chopra, Shanti Ameratunga, Harry Campbell, Shams El Arifeen, Robert E Black on behalf of Child Health and Nutrition Research Initiative (CHNRI): Setting priorities in global health research investments: Assessment of principles and practice. (Croat Med J 2007; 48:595–604). Child Health and Nutrition Research Initiative (CHNRI) of the Global Forum for Health Research was supported by The World Bank in conducting this work.

References

1. Black RE, Morris SS, Bryce J. Where and why are 10 million children dying every year? Lancet 2003; 361:2226–2234.
2. Bryce J, Boschi-Pinto C, Shibuya K, Black RE; WHO Child Health Epidemiology Reference Group. WHO estimates of the causes of death in children. Lancet 2005; 365:1147–1152.
3. World Health Organization. The World Health Report 2002. Geneva: WHO, 2002.
4. Jones G, Steketee RW, Black RE, Bhutta ZA, Morris SS; Bellagio Child Survival Study Group. How many child deaths can we prevent this year? Lancet 2003; 362:65–71.
5. Millennium Project. (Available from: http://www.unmillenni umproject.org/goals/index.htm. Accessed: 20 Oct 2006).
6. Bryce J, Victora CG; Conference Organizing Group. Child survival: countdown to 2015. Lancet 2005; 365:2153–2154.
7. Rudan I, Lawn J, Cousens S, Rowe AK, Boschi-Pinto C, Tomaskovic L, et al. Gaps in policy-relevant information on burden of disease in children: a systematic review. Lancet 2005; 365:2031–2040.
8. Bryce J, Black RE, Walker N, Bhutta ZA, Lawn JE, Steketee RW. Can the world afford to save the lives of 6 million children each year? Lancet 2005; 365:2193–2200.
9. Global Forum for Health Research. The 10/90 report on health research, 1999. Geneva: GFHR, 1999.
10. The Working Group on Priority Setting. Priority setting for health research: lessons from developing countries. Health Policy Plann 2000; 15:130-136.

11. Varmus H, Klausner R, Zerhouni E, Acharya T, Daar AS, Singer PA. Grand challenges in global health. Science 2003; 302:398–399.

12. Rudan I, El Arifeen S, Black RE. A systematic methodology for setting priorities in child health research investments. In: Child Health and Nutrition Research Initiative (CHNRI). A new approach for systematic priority setting in child health research investments. Dhaka: CHNRI, 2006.

13. Rudan I, El Arifeen S, Black RE, Campbell H. Childhood pneumonia and diarrhoea: setting our priorities right. Lancet Infect Dis 2007; 7:56–61.

14. Tomlinson M, Chopra M, Sanders D, Bradshaw D, Hendricks M, Greenfield D, et al. Setting Priorities in child health research investments for South Africa. PLoS Med 2007; 4:e259.

15. Nuyens Y. Setting priorities for health research: lessons from low and middle-income countries. Bull World Health Organ 2007; 85:319–321.

16. Hyder A. Research and development in priority investments ("best buys") identified by the Ad Hoc Committee on Health Research Relating to Future Intervention Options 1996–1998. Progress Report. Geneva: Global Forum for Health Research, 1998.

17. Commission on Health Research for Development. Health research: essential link to equity in development. Geneva: CHRD, 1990.

18. Ghaffar A, de Francisco A, Matlin S (eds). The combined approach matrix: a priority-setting tool for health research. Geneva: Global Forum for Health Research, 2004.

19. Costello A, Filippi V, Kubba T, Horton R. Research challenges to improve maternal and child survival. Lancet 2007; 369:1240–1243.

20. Victora CG, Hanson K, Bryce J, Vaughan JP. Achieving universal coverage with health interventions. Lancet 2004; 364:1541–1548.

21. Williams BG, Gouws E, Boschi-Pinto C, Bryce J, Dye C. Estimates of world-wide distribution of child deaths from acute respiratory infections. Lancet Infect Dis 2002; 2:25–32.

22. Rudan I, Tomaskovic L, Boschi-Pinto C, Campbell H; WHO Child Health Epidemiology Reference Group. Global estimate of the incidence of clinical pneumonia among children under five years of age. Bull World Health Organ 2004; 82:895–903.

23. Boschi-Pinto C, Tomaskovic L. Methods and assumptions for diarrhoea mortality estimates. (Available from: http:// www.who.int/child-adolescent-health/New_Publications/ CHILD_HEALTH/EPI/CHERG_Diarrhoea_Mortality.pdf; Accessed: 20 Oct 2006).

24. Rowe AK, Rowe SY, Snow RW, Korenromp EL, Schellenberg JR, Stein C, et al. The burden of malaria mortality among African children in the year 2000. Int J Epidemiol 2006; 35:691–704.

25. Lawn JE, Cousens S, Zupan J; Lancet Neonatal Survival Steering Team. 4 million neonatal deaths: when? Where? Why? Lancet 2005; 365:891–900.

26. Jamison DT, Breman JG, Measham AR, Alleyne G, Claeson M, Evans DB, et al. Disease control priorities in developing countries. 2nd ed. Washington (DC): Oxford University Press and The World Bank, 2006.

27. Daniels J, Sabin JE. Setting limits fairly: can we learn to share medical resources? Oxford: Oxford University Press, 2002.

28. Gibson JL, Martin DK, Singer PA. Priority setting for new technologies in medicine: a transdisciplinary study. BMC Health Serv Res 2002; 2:14.

29. Gibson JL, Martin DK, Singer PA. Setting priorities in health care organizations: criteria, processes, and parameters of success. BMC Health Serv Res 2004; 4:25.

30. Gibson J, Mitton C, Martin D, Donaldson C, Singer P. Ethics and economics: does programme budgeting and marginal analysis contribute to fair priority setting? J Health Serv Res Policy 2006; 11:32–37.
31. Claxton K, Ginnelly L, Sculpher M, Philips Z, Palmer S. A pilot study on the use of decision theory and value of information analysis as part of the NHS Health Technology Assessment programme. Health Technol Assess 2004; 8:1–103.

CHAPTER 40.

Structure, function and five basic needs of the global health research system

In the past four years, two major initiatives that were set up with the aim to support global health research efforts have been largely discontinued. The first is the Global Forum for Health Research, which was established in Geneva in 1998 to support WHO's focus on health research (1). The second is WHO's Department for Research Policy and Cooperation (WHO RPC), which ceased its operations in 2012 during the WHO's internal reform. Almost ironically, the annual WHO World Health Report for 2012 announced its theme as: "*No health without research*" and was to be coordinated by the WHO RPC (2). The journal *PLoS Medicine* agreed to publish a special series on health research in parallel to the release of the World Health Report, as discussed in the journal's editorial to the series, entitled: "*The World Health Report 2012 that Wasn't*" (3). Eventually, the report was retitled "*Research for Universal Health Coverage*" and published in 2013 (4).

These developments provide an interesting case study into the factors that contribute to the sustainability of initiatives to support global health research in the 21st century. A timeline of key events that set the current context is shown **Figure 40-1**. In this viewpoint, we will map the structure of the global health research system as it has evolved under the funding increases of the past decade. Bearing in mind its structure, core functions and dynamic nature, we will propose a framework on how to effectively support the system to increase its efficiency.

1. The evolving structure of the Global Health Research System (GHRS). Over the past two decades, the funding available for health research has increased rather dramatically from US$ 50 billion in 1993 to $ 240 billion in 2009 (5), but this did not happen in any planned or coordinated way. Those who tried tracking this funding – such as the Global Forum for Health Research in its annual reports, G-FINDER, the Institute for Health Metrics and Evaluation and other academics, provided rather different figures (5-9). This discrepancy is largely due to the difficulty in distinguishing research funding from broader development assistance for health. There is also lack of consensus on whether the funding invested in high-income countries to study health challenges that may be relevant to low and middle-income countries should also be included. Still, under any assumption, the interest in funding global health research is growing, and the structure of this system is rapidly evolving.

In **Figure 40-2**, we show the simplified representation of the key stakeholders and processes, based on how the funds flow through the system. At the beginning of the system is the source of the funding – with donors being either public, private, or the emerging *"class"* of donors – the large philanthropies, such as the Bill and Melinda Gates Foundation (BMGF), the Carlos Slim Foundation, and the Rockefeller Foundation. They all provide financial support for the projects of researchers employed in universities, research institutes, international organizations, biotech companies and small and medium enterprises (SME are a growing *"class"* of recipients). They also fund stakeholders with research capacity in low and middle-income countries that can help carry out the research projects as equal partners. Eventually, the responsibility for spending the funds is passed down to research teams and their international consortia, which conduct research to generate new knowledge in several generic areas: measuring a problem; understanding its cause(s); elaborating solutions; translating the solutions or evidence into policy, practice and products; and/or evaluating the effectiveness of solutions (10).

The decision over the channel of dissemination of this knowledge is made by a new set of stakeholders (**Figure 40-2**), which may involve research committees of public institutions, journal editors, reviewers, donor representatives, company managers or owners. The bulk of work will end up published by research journals, where editors and reviewers, and sometimes even private publishers, influence decisions on the shape and form of publication. The funders increasingly require researchers to publish in open-access journals. Some of the findings do not get published because placing the knowledge in the public domain would invalidate patent applications and subsequent financial profits. This new knowledge can also be presented at conferences, published

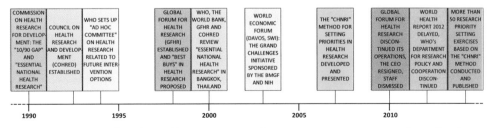

Figure 40-1. *A timeline of several important events relevant to governance, support and co-ordination of global health research that determined the current context.*

as a report to the funder, as *"grey literature"*, or simply posted on the internet. Finally, in many cases, new knowledge does not get published in any way – perhaps due to insufficient relevance or novelty, concerns over its quality, or simply a lack of a positive result. In the end, the published knowledge can be professionally evaluated and replicated, with a growing industry of companies offering those services. Moreover, universities have set up structures to help researchers to commercialize their work and set up spin-out companies.

2. The core functions of the Global Health Research System (GHRS). There should not be much controversy over the main function of the global health research system: it is there to use donors' funding to support experiments that address pertinent health research questions. In this way, through answering those questions, new knowledge is continuously being generated. This knowledge is then translated into both clinical and public health practice in order to reduce the burden of disease in the population and improve health-related outcomes.

The effectiveness of the global health research system to perform its main function will depend on the efficiency of several of its sub-components (**Figure 40-2**). First, donors need to be *motivated* to continue investing; *informed* to understand the targets; and *coordinated* to avoid over- and under-funding certain areas. This, in turn, ensures efficiency of their investments. Second, researchers need to prioritize research ideas well, to balance those that could benefit the public relatively soon with more speculative and downstream ones. They need to design and conduct the experiments carefully to ensure that their efforts are useful even when the result is negative. Third, managers, journal editors and media need to recognize important progress accurately to ensure efficiency in selection of work that receives attention. Fourth, publishers need to ensure broad open access to all new knowledge that results from health research and rapid accessibility of information without exception. Fifth, the effectiveness of translation of the new knowledge into practice needs to be evaluated. This is important because it could help recognizing the most promising research projects and ideas earlier in the process. It would also allow comparisons of returns on investments in health research with other competing investments that could also improve health, such as development assistance, infrastructure projects, or simply increased purchase and coverage of existing interventions.

After the relatively stagnant nature of the global health research system throughout most of the second half of the 20th century, the system evolved rapidly over the past decade and took a life of its own in all of its segments. Attempts to support and co-ordinate such a dynamic and unpredictably evolving system using a *"top-down"* approach may have seemed a feasible and sustainable mission from the perspective of the post-World War II world, when the

UN was established. However, the 21st-century global health research system has developed in a *"bottom-up"*, *"laissez-faire"* manner, in which the stakeholders themselves are continuously inventing improved practices and introducing changes in the models that worked well in previous decades. This is happening at all levels – with emerging big donors, innovative finance mechanisms, creative organization of large international consortia of research teams and their collaborations on *"big science"*. There are now many web-based routes to publication, new tools and measures of assessment of research output (like *Google Scholar, Scopus, Research Gate* and *H-index* metric), and increased support mechanisms for rapid translation, commercialization and implementation of research results. In such a dynamic system, any attempt to influence the relevant stakeholders and processes from the *"outside"* by a group of experts who drive their legitimacy exclusively from a fact that they are employees or affiliates of the UN is largely unrealistic and outdated.

3. **Five basic needs of the Global Health Research System (GHRS) and proposed solutions to improve its efficiency.** We now propose an alternative route to improved efficiency of the global health research system that would

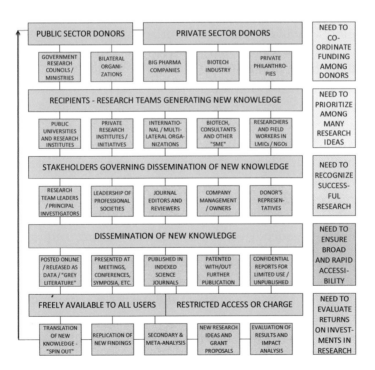

Figure 40-2. *The structure of the global health research system and the five basic needs to ensure its efficient performance.*

be primarily needs-based, and therefore likely welcomed by the stakeholders in the system. At the top of **Figure 40-2**, it is clear that the emergence of new donors is certainly a positive development, but it requires their sustained motivation and also carries a large risk of becoming un-coordinated and unbalanced, with high preference towards certain topics and neglect of others. This is a real risk that has already been exposed in even the most basic analysis of funding flows (7). To help the system develop and grow in an equitable way at this level, there is a need to continuously track funding using an internationally agreed methodology, preferably by more than one agency/institute. Beyond simply tracking funding, a tool is needed to ensure that no areas are neglected in comparison to areas of strong donor preference, thus assisting policy-makers and donor representatives. As a possible solution, we are working to propose a *"Stock Market for Global Health Research Investment Options"* – a tool that would use analogy to real-time stock markets to compare the burden of different health problems with the investments being committed to those problems, using the most recent available information.

The main need at the level of the recipients in the system – the communities of researchers (**Figure 40-2**) – is to find ways to communicate and agree on their own field's research priorities, so that a more balanced and unified case on funding priorities could be presented to donors from the *"cutting edge"* of research. As a possible solution, *"the CHNRI method"* developed by Child Health and Nutrition Research Initiative (CHNRI) of the Global Forum for Health Research seems to be an example of this need being met rather effectively (11). This *"crowd-sourcing"* approach to generating and managing research ideas, while balancing short-term and long-term vision and different instruments of health research, has been validated through many applications (12-15). The results from 50 conducted research prioritization exercises have been published by mid-2015, and many further exercises are being conducted presently (15). A recent independent review showed that 18% of prioritization exercises in global health research in recent years used the CHNRI methodology, which made it the most frequently used specific priority-setting method (16).

Then, at the level of stakeholders who govern dissemination of research results (**Figure 40-2**), there is a need for a tool, process or a system that would recognize important research, promote and reward it appropriately (17). Interestingly, journal editors operate such systems already while reaching their decisions on which papers to publish. Given that many of them select less than 10% of submissions for publication, the journals that manage to maintain high quality and substantial impact over time have clearly developed well-performing systems. We propose to learn more of their decision-making systems and processes and review the results of their work – both at the level of journal's impact, and of individual papers – over long periods of time. This should allow development of a system that would be highly sensitive to important research and ensure its publication, but also quite specific, reducing the amount of published work that is not relevant.

Clearly, it is difficult to predict the impact that research articles may have in the future at the point at which they are being evaluated. However, in the new world of *"big data"*, it is possible to conduct massive exercises in available databases of research papers and their received citations to search for common patterns that are shared among those papers that have most impact. Recently, the journal *Nature* devoted a special news feature to analysis of the 100 most cited papers of all time (18). In a related feature, titled *"Is your most cited work your best?"*, Ioannidis et al. tried to capture the key dimensions that need to be addressed to make any biomedical research *"exceptional"*. They asked about 400 most cited biomedical scientists in the world (123 of whom responded) to score their 10 most cited papers from 0-100 for each of the six criteria that they hypothesized may be inherent to truly exceptional work. They termed these six criteria *Continuous Progress, Broader Interest, Greater Synthesis, Disruptive Innovativeness, Surprise* and *Publication Difficulty* (19). Their exercise made some of the first steps towards a more systematic and transparent framework that could allow capturing the exceptional nature of biomedical research articles at the time they are evaluated, rather than having to wait for many years to determine their importance through impact they generated and citations they received (19).

At the next level – dissemination of new knowledge (**Figure 40-2**) – the need for broad and rapid access to new knowledge is presently being addressed through the *"open access"* movement, world wide web development, IT-based solutions for publication, dissemination and search engines, social networks and internet-based media (20). The success of *PLoS One* journal can be used as an excellent example. We believe that the journal succeeded in a very short time, and well beyond expectations, precisely because it provided an effective solution to this particular need of the global health research system. It is enough to state that in the year of its inception, in 2006, it published 137 papers; in 2007 it already published 1,230 papers, and in 2013 a staggering 31,498 papers, with the number per year still growing strongly. At the same time, given an unprecedentedly large denominator, it still manages to keep a very decent impact factor of around 4.0 in the past several years. Clearly, many participants in the global health research system have recognized PLoS One as a solution that addresses one of the system's major needs.

Finally, at the level of research outputs, a tool is needed that could evaluate returns on investments in global health research, and what is seen as the value for money gained through those investments (21). The tool should also monitor success rates in translation and implementation of the outcomes into products and programmes, all the way to measurable benefits for global public health. Such a tool would allow a proper understanding of the actual value of investing in health research, in comparison to alternative forms of investments that can also benefit health – e.g. community infrastructure projects, improved education, safety, social welfare, and transportation. It is perhaps time to get some understanding on whether the many trillions invested in health research have been a reasonable investment – especially in the wake of Big Pharma largely closing down their R&D departments, which may provide an indication that they are concerned about the feasibility of those investments in comparison to alternatives. This need will be the most difficult to address, but we aim to propose a draft solution and keep improving it over time.

4. Conclusion. The global health research system has evolved rapidly and spontaneously. It has not been optimally efficient, but it is possible to identify solutions that could improve this. There are already examples of effective responses for the need of prioritization of research questions (e.g. *the CHNRI method*), rapid recognition of important research (e.g., systems used by editors of the leading journals) and quick and broadly accessible publication of the new knowledge (e.g. *PLoS One* journal as an example). It is still necessary to develop tools that could assist donors to co-ordinate funding and ensure more equity between areas in the provided support, and to evaluate the value for money invested in health research.

Acknowledgement: Originally published as: Igor Rudan and Devi Sridhar: Structure, function and five basic needs of the global health research system. Reprinted with permission from Edinburgh University Global Health Society under Creative Commons Attribution License (Journal of Global Health 2016; 1:010505).

References:

1. B. Peterson-Stearns. Why has the global forum for health research collapsed? SciDev. Net, 15 November 2010. (Available from: http://www.scidev.net/global/health/opinion/why-has-the-global-forum-for-health-research-collapsed-.html).
2. Pang T, Terry RF, The PLoS Medicine Editors. WHO/PLoS Collection "No health without research": A call for papers. PLoS Med 2011; 8:e1001008.
3. The PLOS Medicine Editors. The World Health Report 2012 that wasn't. PLoS Med 2012; 9:e1001317.

4. World Health Organization. Research for universal health coverage: World Health Report 2013. Geneva: WHO, 2013.

5. Rottingen JA, JA Regmi S, Eide M, Young AJ, Viergever RF, Ardal C. Mapping of available health research and development data: what's there, what's missing, and what role is there for a global observatory? Lancet 2013; 382:1286–1307.

6. Burke MA, Matlin SA. Monitoring financial flows for health research 2008: Prioritizing research for health equity. Global Forum for Health Research, Geneva, 2008. (Available from: http://announcementsfiles.cohred.org/gfhr_pub/assoc/s14888e/s14888e.pdf).

7. Moran M, Guzman J, Ropars AL, McDonald A, Jameson N, Omune B, et al. Neglected disease research and development: How much are we really spending? PLoS Med 2009; 6:e1000030.

8. Institute of Health Metrics and Evaluation. Financing global health 2012: The end of the golden age? Seattle: Institute of Health Metrics and Evaluation, 2012. (Available from: http://www.healthmetricsandevaluation.org/publications/policy-report/financing-global-health-2012-end-golden-age).

9. Sridhar D, Batniji R. Misfinancing global health: a case for transparency in disbursements and decision-making. Lancet 2008; 372:1185-1191.

10. World Health Organization. WHO's role and responsibilities in health research: Draft WHO strategy on research for health. World Health Assembly A63/22. Geneva: World Health Organization, 2010. (Available from: http://www.wpro.who.int/health_research/policy_documents/draft_who_strategy_on_research_for_health.pdf).

11. Rudan I, Gibson JL, Ameratunga S, El Arifeen S, Bhutta ZA, Black M, et al. on behalf of Child Health and Nutrition Research Initiative (CHNRI). Setting priorities in global child health research investments: guidelines for implementation of the CHNRI Method. Croat Med J 2008; 49:720–733.

12. Fontaine O, Kosek M, Bhatnagar S, Boschi-Pinto C, Chan KY, Duggan C, et al. Setting research priorities to reduce global mortality from childhood diarrhoea by 2015. PLoS Med 2009; 6:e41.

13. Rudan I, El Arifeen S, Bhutta ZA, Black RE, Brooks A, Chan KY, et al, the WHO/CHNRI Expert Group on Childhood Pneumonia. Setting research priorities to reduce global mortality from childhood pneumonia by 2015. PLoS Med 2011; 8:e1001099.

14. Tomlinson M, Swartz L, Officer A, Chan KY, Rudan I, Saxena S. Research priorities for health of people with disabilities: an expert opinion exercise. Lancet 2009; 374:1857–1862.

15. Rudan I. Global health research priorities: mobilizing the developing world. Public Health 2012; 126:237–240.

16. McGregor S, Henderson KJ, Kaldor JM. How are health research priorities set in low and middle income countries? A systematic review of published reports. PLoS One 2014; 9:e108787.

17. Editorial. The maze of impact metrics. Nature 2013; 502:271.

18. Van Noorden R, Maher B, Nuzzo R. The top 100 papers. Nature 2014; 514:550–553.

19. Ioannidis JP, Boyack KW, Small H, Sorensen AA, Klavans R. Bibliometrics: Is your most cited work your best? Nature. 2014; 514:561–562.

20. Wolpert AJ. For the sake of inquiry and knowledge — the inevitability of open access. N Engl J Med 2013; 368:785–787.

21. Lane J, Bertuzzi S. Measuring the results of science investments. Science 2011; 331:678–680.

CHAPTER 41.

Childhood pneumonia and diarrhoea: Setting our priorities right

WHO highlighted the continuing scandal of unacceptably high levels of maternal and child deaths in developing countries in their World Health Report for 2005 (1). The report shows that 30,000 children under 5 years of age still die every day. In recent years, malaria, tuberculosis, and HIV/AIDS have received global attention in high profile scientific publications and major international disease control initiatives (e.g., the Roll Back Malaria Partnership, the Stop TB Partnership, directly observed treatment, short course (DOTS) strategy, and the 3-by-5 Initiative) (2-4). This international response has been reinforced by substantial new funding mechanisms and sources such as the Global Fund to Fight AIDS, Tuberculosis and Malaria, and the major financial contributions from the Bill and Melinda Gates Foundation to the development of new vaccines against these scourges. However, malaria, tuberculosis, and HIV/AIDS account for only about 11% of all child deaths globally, whereas pneumonia and diarrhoea are jointly responsible for nearly half of all child deaths (**Figure 41-1**) (5). This value is about the same as the global number of deaths from smoking, double the global number of deaths from HIV/AIDS, and 25 times the number of deaths from war. Despite this huge mortality, we recently found a steep decreasing trend in research publications on the global extent of these problems, reflecting reduced research interest and investment over the past two decades (**Figure 41-2**) (6). This trend was in line with the report of the Global Forum for Health Research for 2004 (7), where it was shown that diarrhoea and pneumonia research receive markedly lower investments than those allocated to other diseases that contribute substantially to global child mortality.

Why should there be depleted scientific interest in field studies trying to better understand these two conditions – childhood pneumonia and diarrhoea – at a time when WHO has again shown that they remain two of the most important causes of global burden of disease in children? Why do these two diseases continue to be responsible for almost half of all child deaths globally, when interventions exist to prevent most of these deaths, interventions that were developed and proven highly cost effective more than two decades ago (8,9)? It is clear that these interventions are not being delivered to the children who need them most (10). Programmes aiming to deliver these

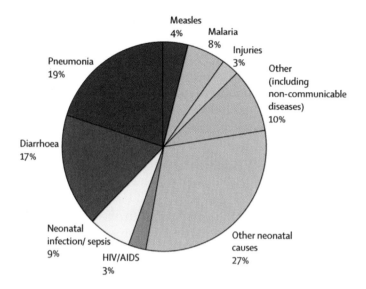

Figure 41-1. *Causes of an estimated 10.6 million deaths that occur every year in children under 5 years of age globally. (Adapted from reference 5. Pneumonia and diarrhoea combined are directly responsible for 36% of deaths in children under 5 years of age. With neonatal infection/sepsis added to that figure, because it is most frequently caused by pneumonia, a total share of the two causes approaches 45% of all child deaths – the left vs. the right side of the chart).*

interventions have been inadequately funded, of poor quality, not sustained, and not expanded from initial pilots that often took place in the least deprived regions (11). Our failure in delivering the interventions is caused by our lack of understanding of how to do it efficiently and creatively in low-resource settings, and it is a challenge for research to generate this required knowledge.

We propose that a major reason for these failures has been the lack of recognition that low coverage is a challenge for health research, to identify effective and efficient context – specific delivery mechanisms in health services of countries with limited resources. The development and proof of effective interventions has been seen in the past as the legitimate endpoint of research. Implementation research that needs to follow (including health policy and systems research, and delivery research) is methodologically challenging and might require long-term studies. It has not been ranked as highly by the scientific community or by most funding agencies as new work in basic science or intervention development. This has tragic consequences. It has been shown that globally, up to two-thirds of deaths in children under 5 years of age could be prevented today if available and cost-effective interventions were delivered to those in need (10). Such a reduction in child deaths would achieve UN's Millennium Development Goal 4, and is affordable within current global financial resources (10,12).

We believe that this experience with these two forgotten killers, where highly cost-effective interventions to fight childhood pneumonia and diarrhoea were developed decades ago but then failed to be implemented, is a good predictor of what can be expected to occur in the future if the current research investment model is to persist (**Figure 41-3**). Effective new interventions such as vaccines against AIDS, tuberculosis, or malaria might be developed in the coming decade, but the same challenge will then be faced: how to make those vaccines cheaper and more cost-effective, and how to deliver them to those people most in need? The potential public-health effect of these new interventions will not be realised without research on implementation.

The dominant model of research priority setting is resulting in gross under-achievement of potential disease burden reduction and is actually generating further health inequity. Current major global funding initiatives favour the areas of research interest of the scientists involved in basic research, thus investing into options that have received the greatest level of advocacy and

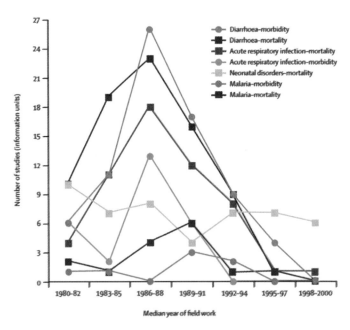

Figure 41-2. *Number of papers with policy-relevant information on epidemiology of specific childhood illnesses in developing countries. (Papers identified by WHO Child Health Epidemiology Reference Group. Figure shows decreasing interest in diseases that continue to kill most children. Reproduced from reference 6).*

media coverage and whose future potential outputs appear most attractive to these communities and the agencies that support them. Investing in basic research but also in future funding is further encouraged by the greater potential for publication in high-impact journals, which is a major indicator of research quality, and also funding in the current research policy model (**Figure 41-3**). When these new research avenues lead to the successful development of new interventions, the initial beneficiaries are usually those who can afford the results of the research. More complete coverage of the population in need often lags decades behind (12–14). It is apparent that global research priorities and media pressure fuelled by an interest in highly unusual individual cases or emerging but uncertain threats are bound to generate ever-increasing inequity. We believe that a major underlying problem is lack of clear principles for health research investment on the basis of a vision of what the endpoints of such investments should be. We need a framework that values investment not only in generating new knowledge, but also in research that seeks to define how to implement and make better use of the existing knowledge leading to a public-health effect on burden of disease.

The Commission on Health Research for Development was the most striking initial development in setting research priorities globally (15). It reviewed global health needs and priorities for health research in 1990 and concluded that "*...less than 10% of global health research funds is devoted to 90% of the world's health problems*" (13). A number of subsequent initiatives addressed this problem by attempting to set priorities in global health research, including the recommendations from the "*Ad Hoc Committee on Health Research Relating to Future Intervention Options*" in 1996 (16), the "*Council on Health Research and Development*" in 2000 (17), the "*Grand Challenges in Global Health*" supported by the Gates Foundation that emerged from World Economic Forum in 2003 (18) and the "*Combined Approach Matrix*" tool by the Global Forum for Health Research in 2004 (19). All these approaches are useful methods for gathering information relevant to setting research priorities, but the process itself eventually depends on a limited number of technical experts who collect this information and then recommend priorities, which makes it highly susceptible to their own individual opinions, and personal interests and biases.

The Child Health and Nutrition Research Initiative (CHNRI), an initiative of the Global Forum for Health Research, is now leading a project that seeks to overcome these concerns. The major conceptual advance in this initiative is the recognition that there should be a broader definition of "health research option" as an activity that is not only limited to producing new knowledge, but also has a vision of implementation of this knowledge, which ultimately should help to reduce disease burden. From this recognition it follows that it

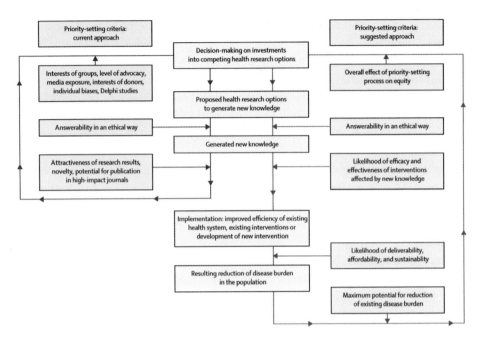

Figure 41-3. *Priority setting in health research investments to achieve UN's Millennium Development Goal 4—reducing child mortality by two-thirds by 2015; (Criteria used in setting priorties in global health research investments: the current approaches (left), and the approach proposed by the Child Health and Nutrition Research Initiative (right)).*

is important not to consider the endpoint of research as "generating new and interesting knowledge or insight", because this might favour more fundamental research. Rather, the process of research priority setting should have a clear theoretical framework based on multiple endpoints coupled to a systematic process of scoring and ranking competing research options. In figure 3, we show the alternative model proposed by CHNRI, which addresses several components of a research option that can be used as criteria for setting research priorities: (1) likelihood that the research option would be answerable in an ethical way; (2) likelihood that the resulting intervention would be effective in reducing disease burden; (3) deliverability, affordability, and sustainability of the resulting intervention; (4) maximum potential of the intervention to reduce disease burden; and (5) effect of disease burden reduction on equity in population. We believe it is also important to acknowledge that there are three different instruments of health research (**Figure 41-4**).

For example, health policy and systems research will reduce disease burden by improving efficiency of health systems in delivering the interventions; implementation research will aim to improve existing non-affordable interventions to make them feasible and affordable in low-income settings; whereas other types of research will seek new and non-existing interventions. The former two types of research are not as innovative and attractive as the latter one, and their results are unlikely to be publishable in journals of high impact, but they nevertheless carry a great potential to reduce disease burden.

We are concerned that the current research priority decision making is not driven by an explicit framework and value system, and thus is too open

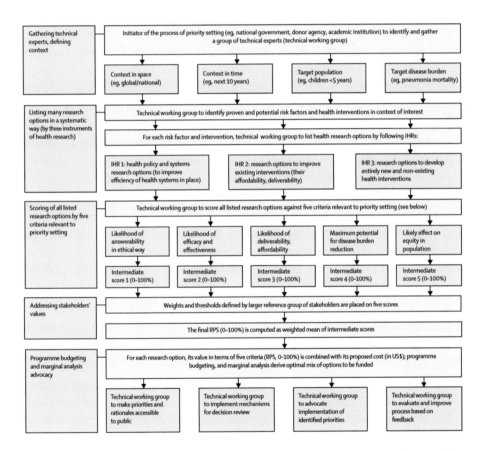

Figure 41-4. *Steps of the proposed CHNRI methodology at a glance. (The steps are: gather a working group of technical experts who are expected to define the context (space, time, population and disease burden addressed); list research options systematically based on potential risk factors, interventions and 3 instruments of health research (IHR); score the competing research options independently and in a highly structured way, according to 5 criteria relevant to priority setting; address the input from stakeholders; and perform program budgeting and marginal analysis, to define the optimal mix of assessed overall value of research for invested funding; RPS = research priority score).*

to research interest bias of individuals who influence funding priorities in large donor agencies without an unbiased vision focused on reducing disease burden and improving global health inequities. The six main advantages of the CHNRI methodology presented in **Figure 41-4** over the alternative approaches are: (i) it is systematic, and technical experts involved in setting research priorities are asked to list and score competing research options in a highly structured way – this limits the influence of their own personal biases on the outcome, which is frequently a problem in Delphi studies; (ii) the methodology is entirely transparent – all rationales for decision making and input from each person involved from the initial to the final stages are recorded, displayed, and can be viewed and challenged at any later point in time; (iii) the experts submit their input into the process independently from each other, and the results are based on their collective opinion in a true sense, thus avoiding the possibility of some individuals among them directing the process; (iv) the final result is a simple quantitative outcome (research priority score), which measures the value of each research option when all the criteria and stakeholders' views are taken into account. This value can then be combined with the proposed cost of research for programme budgeting and marginal analysis, to derive a best possible mix of research options to be funded from a fixed budget; (v) the methodology is well suited to simultaneously evaluate and score different types of research (e.g., health policy and systems research, implementation research, and research on new interventions) using the same set of criteria; and (vi) unlike all previous approaches, this methodology incorporates an efficient means of considering the voice of stakeholders and the wider public, who are given the power to place thresholds and weights upon intermediate scores (which are based on the collective opinion of technical experts) and in this way considerably shape the final outcome (see **Figure 41-4**).

This methodology has recently been implemented with success at both international and national levels. At the global level, CHNRI and the WHO Child and Adolescent Health Department are now working together using this methodology and global childhood mortality burden estimates (provided by the WHO Child Health Epidemiology Reference Group) to define research priorities for each of the eight main causes of child deaths (5). This methodology has also been applied at the national level. Sixty-three health research options addressing seven main causes of child deaths in South Africa were listed (nine options per cause of death) and scored by local technical experts, with their results adjusted by local stakeholders (Tomlinson M, personal communication). In the table, we present final scores and rankings of those research options that addressed pneumonia and diarrhoea. Eight research options addressing these two diseases were placed among the top 13 research priorities, thus correctly recognising the magnitude of their effect on mortality burden in South Africa. Furthermore, the priorities identified were dominated by health policy and systems research options to increase the coverage of the simplest and most cost-effective interventions, such as handwashing, breastfeeding, and increased use of antibiotic treatment for pneumonia (**Table 41-1**).

Table 41-1. *Selected results from research priority setting exercise conducted in April 2006 to address South African child health research priorities. (Results cover 7 major causes of child deaths in the country: HIV/AIDS, malnutrition, neonatal problems, diarrhoea, pneumonia, congenital and genetic disorders, accidents and injuries; For each cause of death, 9 research options were proposed for scoring by local experts – 3 for each of the three instrument of health research, IHR; The final research priority scores (RPS) were based on scoring by technical experts and adjusting the scores according to the system of values of 30 members of larger reference group representing the stakeholders in the country. The rankings of 18 research options that addressed childhood pneumonia and diarrhoea are presented).*

RPS (x100)	RANK	DISEASE	IHR	RESEARCH OPTION
87.8	2/63	Diarrhoea	1	Health policy and systems research to increase handwashing with soap
87.7	3/63	Pneumonia	1	HPSR to achieve increased usage of antibiotic treatment for pneumonia
84.2	5/63	Diarrhoea	1	HPSR and education/behaviour modification research to increase exclusive breastfeeding in first 6 months
83.5	6/63	Pneumonia	1	HPSR to improve existing ways of training health workers to deliver pneumonia standard case management
83.3	7/63	Diarrhoea	1	HPSR to increase awareness of indications for treatment and access to ORS sachets at all times and sites
80.3	10/63	Diarrhoea	2	Research to reduce costs /improve deliverability and sustainability of piped safe water systems
77.6	12/63	Diarrhoea	2	Research to develop ways of sewage treatment systems affordable to developing countries
75.6	13/63	Pneumonia	1	HPSR to increase zinc supplementation coverage
68.4	24/63	Diarrhoea	3	Low cost no electrical/no fuel consuming refrigerators to storage food at home level
68.3	25/63	Diarrhoea	2	Increasing availability of appropriate complimentary foods
67.5	26/63	Pneumonia	2	Reducing the cost of Hib vaccine
63.0	37/63	Diarrhoea	3	Develop interventions that will reduce bacterial contamination of crops irrigated with contaminated water
61.8	40/63	Pneumonia	2	Developing existing vaccines with needle-free delivery
59.2	41/63	Diarrhoea	3	Developing shigella vaccines
58.0	44/63	Pneumonia	3	Developing RSV vaccine
56.9	47/63	Pneumonia	3	Developing "common protein" pneumococcal vaccine
54.4	52/63	Pneumonia	3	Developing new antibiotics that would overcome bacterial resistance
49.7	59/63	Pneumonia	2	Research to reduce the costs of oxygen therapy and make it more available to the general public

Although all initiatives aiming to set priorities and invest in child-health research in developing countries are welcome, it is important to understand that without an explicit consideration of the issues listed above, the health gains that can be achieved will be limited. There are signs that these issues are beginning to gain attention. Some examples include the Research Assessment Exercise in the UK, a major driver of research priorities in the public sector, debating how to respond to criticisms that the system undervalues health systems research; the European Commission, announcing that there will be a new funding stream for health policy and systems research in the forthcoming 7-year research programme; and, in the field of pneumonia, the grants by the Global Alliance for Vaccines and Immunization for public-private partnerships and related research to achieve high levels of population coverage of immunisation with the new Haemophilus influenzae type b and pneumococcal protein conjugate vaccines. These initiatives are welcome but there is a need for a new framework for global health research priority setting, especially in child-health research. We believe that only in this way will proper attention be given to delivery of proven interventions to reduce the high childhood mortality caused by pneumonia and diarrhoea.

Acknowledgement: *Originally published as: Igor Rudan, Shams El Arifeen, Robert Black and Harry Campbell: Childhood pneumonia and diarrhoea: Setting our priorities right. Reprinted with permission from Elsevier (Lancet Infectious Diseases 2007; 7:56–61). We thank Mark Tomlinson and Mickey Chopra, Medical Research Council, Cape Town, South Africa, for providing selected results of national level application of CHNRI methodology presented in the table.*

References

1. WHO. World Health Report 2005. Geneva: World Health Organization, 2005. (Available from: http://www.who.int/whr/2005/en/index.html; Accessed 13 Nov 2006).
2. Snow RW, Guerra CA, Noor AM, Myint HY, Hay SI. The global distribution of clinical episodes of Plasmodium falciparum malaria. Nature 2005; 434:214–217.
3. Piot P, Feachem RG, Lee JW, Wolfensohn JD. Public health. A global response to AIDS: lessons learned, next steps. Science 2004; 304:1909–1910.
4. Schwartzman K, Oxlade O, Barr RG, et al. Domestic returns from investment in the control of tuberculosis in other countries. N Engl J Med 2005; 353:1008–1020.
5. Bryce J, Boschi-Pinto C, Shibuya K, Black RE, the WHO Child Health Epidemiology Reference Group. WHO estimates of the causes of death in children. Lancet 2005; 365:1147–1152.
6. Rudan I, Lawn J, Cousens S, et al. Gaps in policy-relevant information on burden of disease in children: a systematic review. Lancet 2005; 365:2031–2040.

7. Sazawal S, Black RE. Effect of pneumonia case management on mortality in neonates, infants, and preschool children: a meta-analysis of community-based trials. Lancet Infect Dis 2003; 3:547–556.

8. WHO. The treatment of diarrhoea. A manual for physicians and other senior health workers. Geneva: World Health Organization, 1995. (WHO/CDR/95.3.)

9. Global Forum for Health Research. The 10/90 Report on Health Research 2004. Geneva: Global Forum for Health Research, 2004.

10. Jones G, Steketee RW, Black RE, Bhutta ZA, Morris SS, the Bellagio Child Survival Study Group. How many child deaths can we prevent this year? Lancet 2003; 362:65–71.

11. Victora CG, Fenn B, Bryce J, Kirkwood BR. Co-coverage of preventive interventions and implications for child-survival strategies: evidence from national surveys. Lancet 2005; 366:1460–1466.

12. Bryce J, Black RE, Walker N, Bhutta ZA, Lawn JE, Steketee RW. Can the world afford to save the lives of 6 million children each year? Lancet 2005; 365:2193–2200.

13. Victora CG, Hanson K, Bryce J, Vaughan JP. Achieving universal coverage with health interventions. Lancet 2004; 364:1541–1548.

14. Global Forum for Health Research. The 10/90 Report on Health Research 1999. Geneva: Global Forum for Health Research, 1999.

15. Commission on Health Research for Development. Health research: essential link to equity in development. New York: Oxford University Press, 1990.

16. Hyder A. Research and development in priority investments ("*best buys*") identified by the Ad Hoc Committee on Health Research Relating to Future Intervention Options 1996–1998. Geneva: Global Forum for Health Research, 1998.

17. The Working Group on Priority Setting (COHRED). Priority setting for health research: lessons from developing countries. Health Policy Plann 2000; 15:130–136.

18. Varmus H, Klausner R, Zerhouni E, Acharya T, Daar AS, Singer PA. Grand challenges in global health. Science 2003; 302:398–399.

19. Ghaffar A, de Francisco A, Matlin S, eds. The Combined Approach Matrix: a priority-setting tool for health research. Geneva: Global Forum for Health Research, 2004.

CHAPTER 42.

Who sets the global health research agenda? The challenge of multi-bi financing

A major challenge in the governance of research funding is priority-setting. As a former health minister in sub-Saharan Africa noted: *"Everyone is chasing the money – reputable universities, the UN agencies, partnerships, civil society groups, so who is actually doing what developing countries really need, rather than what donors want?"* (1) The past 15 years have been called revolutionary in global health in terms of the funding raised and the number of initiatives launched. One of the side effects of having more money, institutions, and initiatives in global health is increased competition among the various parties. And, the priorities of funding bodies largely dictate what health issues and diseases are studied.

In this Essay, I argue that the challenge of agenda-setting that occurs in research funding is a consequence of a larger phenomenon in global health, *"multi-bi financing"*. Multilateral funding refers to monies given to an organization that involves two or more governments or other institutions, the prime example being the United Nations; bilateral funding refers to monies given from one government or institution to another such as the US Agency for International Development (USAID) grants to Haiti. Multi-bi financing refers to the practice of donors choosing to route non-core funding – earmarked for specific sectors, themes, countries, or regions – through multilateral agencies and to the emergence of new multistakeholder initiatives. Drawing on insights from political science and international relations, I put forward an explanation for why these developments are occurring and discuss the consequences for global health research governance.

1. Multi-bi financing. At first glance, the story of international cooperation in health seems straightforward. Driven by widespread concerns about HIV/AIDS, maternal mortality, and flu pandemics, the past two decades have witnessed an exponential growth in health funding both for service provision, estimated at US$ 27.73 billion in 2011, and for research, estimated at US$ 3 billion in 2010 (2,3). The growth in funding by governments and international agencies has been accompanied by new forms of multistakeholder cooperation such as the Global Alliance for Improved Nutrition (GAIN) and new institutions including private philanthropists with large endowments such as the Bill & Melinda Gates Foundation.

On the face of it, the rise in funding and plurality of institutions in global health looks like increased support for multilateral cooperation. Existing analyses of global health spending and development assistance that focus on multilateral versus bilateral spending and programs, done by the Institute for Health Metrics and Evaluation and the World Bank, for example, show that over the past 15 years there has been an increase in the budget and commitments of the WHO and World Bank (2). The WHO program budget has doubled. The World Bank's lending for health has trebled.

Alongside increases in funding for global health, a major change in international cooperation has been the emergence of new multistakeholder institutions such as the Global Fund to Fight AIDS, Tuberculosis and Malaria and the GAVI Alliance. The new initiatives are marked by a structure of governance that differs in five important ways from traditional multilateral institutions (such as the WHO and the World Bank). First, while traditional multilateral institutions are governed by boards solely comprising member states, the Global Fund and GAVI are governed by boards on which sit the representatives of civil society, the private sector, and the Bill & Melinda Gates Foundation. Second, unlike the broad mandates of the WHO (*"the attainment by all people of the highest possible level of health"*) and the World Bank (*"to alleviate poverty and improve quality of life"*), both the Global Fund (*"to attract and disburse additional resources to prevent and treat HIV/AIDS, TB and malaria"*) and GAVI (*"to save children's lives and protect people's health by increasing access to immunisation in poor countries"*) have narrowly defined mandates that are problem-focused. A third attribute of the new multistakeholder initiatives is that they are entirely funded by voluntary contributions. Fourth, unlike the WHO and World Bank, which work through government agencies and have offices and personnel in recipient countries, neither the Global Fund nor GAVI work directly in-country. Finally, both the Global Fund and GAVI derive their legitimacy from their effectiveness in improving specifically defined health outputs and outcomes in contrast to traditional multilateral agencies, which rely on claims to representation and state-centric deliberation.

But, the story of increasing multilateral funding for global health does not end here. As a recent OECD/DAC report noted, about 40% of the multilateral funding is given through, what it calls, *"multi-bi"* aid (4). Changing fastest is the discretionary funding of programs within the WHO and World Bank. Within WHO, the biennial (2 year) budget has more than doubled in the past decade from US$ 1.647 billion in 1998– 1999 to US$ 4.227 billion in 2008–2009. Most of the growth, however, has been in extra-budgetary funding, which has risen from 48.8% in 1998–1999 to 77.3% in 2008–2009. In 2007, the top six donors of extra-budgetary funding were US (25%), UK (24%), World Bank-GAVI affiliate (16%), Canada (12%), Bill & Melinda Gates Foundation (11.8%), and Commission of European Communities (10.2%) (5).

Within the World Bank's activities in health, total commitments have increased from US$ 1.7 billion in 1998-1999 to US$ 5.2 billion in 2006–2007 (6). However, a large part of this growth is due to the trust fund portfolio. Trust funds are similar to the voluntary contributions of the WHO in that they are a financing arrangement set up with contributions from one or more donors. A trust fund can be country-specific, regional, or global in its geographic scope, and it can be free-standing or integrated into existing programs. While growth has occurred in both core and trust fund budgets, it is the trust fund portfolio for health that has experienced the most dramatic growth from US$ 95 million in 2003–2004 to US$ 2.4 billion in 2006–2007, which is almost equal to the core funding provided through the World Bank's International Bank for Reconstruction and Development and the International Development Association (US$ 2.8 billion). For both the WHO and World Bank, voluntary contributions are increasing while core budgets are flat or fluctuating (see **Figure 42-1**).

2. What is driving the new patterns of global health funding and governance? The above analysis highlights that an increasing proportion of the new funding for global health has been by contributions that are discretionary (in terms of amount and timing of payment) to fund a specific priority (as opposed to the general purposes of the organization), and to fund implementation through a third party. What explains the shift towards multi-bi financing? It likely reflects a desire by participating governments and other stakeholders such as philanthropic foundations and non governmental organizations, to control and monitor multilateral organizations more tightly.

First, multi-bi financing permits governments and other stakeholders to realign the objectives of multilateral initiatives with their own. Rather than working through the governance of existing organizations, individual governments can use new funding mechanisms as a way to define a separate mandate and to push specific goals. Second, multi-bi financing permits governments and other stakeholders to tie contributions to performance. For example, the Global Fund and GAVI explicitly link performance to replenishment and must show results to attract donor interest. Similarly, within the WHO and World Bank, negotiations for the amount and time period of voluntary contributions take place outside the official decision-making structures. Thus, through providing tied funding to specific departments, donors can ensure that their funding is used to influence the activities and direction of the organization.

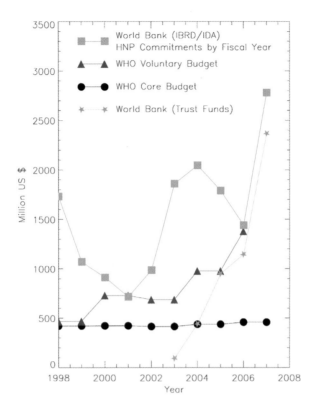

Figure 42-1. *Funding patterns of the WHO and World Bank (5,6,11).*

Third, multi-bi financing permits donors to finance and deliver assistance in ways that allow for closer monitoring when they delegate actions to a global fund or agency. One of the main challenges in monitoring the WHO relates to its regional structure, which in practice makes tight policy and budgetary control impossible. In contrast, the Global Fund and GAVI provide detailed financial information about commitments and disbursements, as well as donor pledges and contributions.

3. Why does this matter for global health research? There are three possible consequences of multi-bi financing for global health research governance. First is the risk that difficult choices about priority-setting in health will be made in the marketplace of global initiatives, rather than in the community that will have to live with those choices. Developing country health ministers have alleged that this funding mechanism imposes the priorities of powerful states and institutions on poorer countries, whose populations have little recourse to demand accountability or to influence these priorities (1).

As previous work has noted (7–10), core funding of WHO is used for the purposes decided by member states at the World Health Assembly (WHA) while the use of extra-budgetary funding is decided by specific donors. In 2008–2009, of WHO's regular budget, 25% of funds were allocated to infectious disease, 8% to non-communicable diseases, and roughly 4.7% to injuries. These purposes align roughly with the global burden of disease. By contrast, most of the extra-budgetary funding of WHO for 2008–2009 was used for infectious disease (60%), while only 3.9% was for non-communicable diseases and 3.4% for injuries (5).

A similar picture emerges at the World Bank. In 2005, the core budget in the health, nutrition, and population sector was focused on infrastructure in health, with the major priorities being health systems (34%), water and sanitation (22%), injury (18%), and disease-specific strategies followed by infectious disease (15%) and non-communicable disease (2%) (5). In contrast, the trust fund portfolio is largely focused on disease-specific strategies with funds including the Global Partnership to Eradicate Poliomyelitis, Programs for Onchocerciasis Control, the Avian and Human Influenza Facility, and the Global Partnership for TB Control. The Global Fund is the largest trust fund and received 35% of 2008 contributions to trust funds (**Figure 42-2**) (11).

Second is the risk that multi-bi financing may create mechanisms that permit donors to favor short-term gains over longer-term public health goals. The advantage of traditional multilateral organizations is that their relative autonomy permits them to bring transparency and discipline to difficult choices: the rationale for creating WHO was to ensure that nations would compromise their short-term differences in order to attain long-term advantages of regularized collaboration and decision-making on health matters. A successful example of this is the International Health Regulations, which require countries to report certain disease outbreaks and public health events. A recent failed attempt was the proposed binding treaty on research and development (R&D) discussed at the World Health Assembly in May 2012. The instrument would have outlined the necessary funding and coordination to promote the R&D that is needed to address the diseases that disproportionately affect developing countries and that constitute a common global responsibility (3,12).

The third risk is that multi-bi financing will erode global capacities to create, collate, and disseminate information, the cornerstone of research. To some extent, working off the back of several decades of core multilateral funding, donors are still benefitting from a wider, previously built, technical expertise in agencies such as the World Bank or the WHO. However, this knowledge capacity is likely to erode as funding is narrowed to discretionary activities and contributions to core budget are reduced.

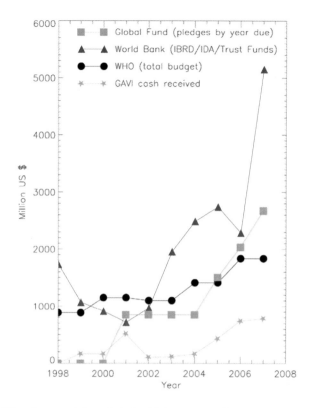

Figure 42-2. *Old and new multilaterals in health (5,6,11,15,16).*

But to conclude on a positive note, one major impact of multi-bi financing has been to shine a clear light on how and where multilateral institutions, such as the World Bank and WHO, might do better. Both organizations have been criticized for being slow to act, difficult to monitor, and overly bureaucratic (13,14). Multi-bi financing is forcing these institutions to reflect on how to reform to remain more appealing to the wider set of stakeholders and interests at play.

Acknowledgement: Originally published as: Devi Sridhar: Who sets the global health research agenda? The challenge of multi-bi financing. Reprinted with permission from Edinburgh University Global Health Society under Creative Commons Attribution License (PLoS Medicine 2012; 9:e1001312). The author would like to acknowledge insights gained from a long-term project on global governance with Ngaire Woods and the research assistance of Gabrielle Krapels and Layla Yuezen.

References

1. Global Economic Governance Programme. High-level working group of developing country health ministers, meeting report, 2008. (Available from: http:// www.globaleconomicgovernance.org/wp-content/ uploads/Working%20Group%20Report%20 May% 202008.pdf. Accessed: 31 Jan 2011).
2. Institute for Health Metrics and Evaluation. Financing global health. 2011. (Available from: http://www. healthmetricsandevaluation.org/publications/policy-report/financing-global-health-2011- continued-growth-mdg-deadline-approaches; Accessed: 15 Jul 2012).
3. Moon S, Bermudez J, Hoen E. Innovation and access to medicines for neglected populations: could a treaty address a broken pharmaceutical R&D system? PLoS Med 2012; 9:e1001218.
4. OECD/DAC. DAC report on multilateral aid, 2010. (Available from: www.oecd.org/ dataoecd/23/17/45828572.pdf; Accessed 31 Jan 2011).
5. WHO. Programme budgets. Geneva: WHO, 2012. (Available from: http://apps.who. int/gb/archive/; Accessed 31 Jan 2011).
6. World Bank. World Bank HNP lending, 2012. (Available from: http://web.worldbank.org/WBSITE/EX TERNAL/TOPICS/EXTHEALTHNUTRITION ANDPOPULATION/ EXTDATASTATISTICSH NP/EXTHNPSTATS/0,contentMDK:21198454; Accessed: 31 Jan 2011).
7. Vaughan JP, Mogedal S, Kruse SK, Lee K, Walt G, et al. Cooperation for health development: extrabudgetary funds in the World Health Organisation. Published by the Governments of Australia, Norway and the United Kingdom. Geneva: WHO, 1995.
8. Vaughan JP, Mogedal S, Walt G, Kruse SK, Lee K, et al. WHO and the effects of extrabudgetary funds: is the Organization donor driven? Health Policy Plann 1996; 16:253–264.
9. Vaughan JP, Mogedal S, Stein-Erik K, Lee K, Walt G, et al. Financing the World Health Organization: global importance of extra-budgetary funds. Health Policy 1996; 35:229–245.
10. Stuckler D, King L, Robinson H, McKee M. WHO's budgetary allocations and burden of disease: a comparative analysis. Lancet 2008; 372:1563–1569.
11. The World Bank Group. Partnership & trust fund annual report. Washington, 2008. (Available from: http://siteresources.worldbank.org/CFPEXT/ Resources/TFAR_2008. pdf; Accessed: 14 Aug 2012).
12. Røttingen J-A, Chamas C. A new deal for global health R&D? The recommendations of the Consultative Expert Working Group on Research and Development (CEWG). PLoS Med 2012; 9:e1001219.
13. Woods N. The globalizers. Ithaca, NY: Cornell University Press, 2006.
14. Godlee F. The World Health Organization: WHO in crisis. BMJ 2004; 309:1424.
15. Global Fund. Grant portfolio, 2012. (Available from: http://portfolio.theglobalfund. org/en/ DataDownloads/Index/; Accessed: 31 Jan 2011).
16. GAVI. Donor contributions and pledges, 2012. (Available from: http://www.gavialliance.org/funding/ donor-contributions-pledges/; Accessed: 31 Jan 2011).

CHAPTER 43.

Setting priorities in global health research investments: Universal challenges and conceptual framework – the CHNRI method

Increasingly, there is a need for national governments, public-private partnerships, private sector and other funding agencies to set priorities in health research investments in a fair and transparent way. A process of priority setting is always an activity driven by values of wide range of stakeholders, which are often conflicting. This process always occurs in a highly specific context (e.g., agreed policies and targets in terms of disease burden reduction and time limit, defined geographic space, population and specific health problems).

Child Health and Nutrition Research Initiative (CHNRI) held a series of expert meetings during which a list of 20 universal challenges inherent to research prioritization was identified. Based on these challenges, several key concepts were proposed and defined, including the boundaries of health research, its main domains, and possible criteria for prioritization between competing research investment options. If accepted, these concepts could form a basis for a transparent decision-making framework for setting priorities in health research investments.

CHNRI first proposed that *"health research"* funded by public funds should be regarded as an activity undertaken to generate presently non-existing knowledge that will eventually be used to reduce the existing disease burden (or other health-related problem) in the population that provided funding. Three universal and non-overlapping domains of health research were proposed as follows: (i) research to assess the burden of disease and its determinants; (ii) research to improve performance of the existing capacities to reduce disease burden; and (iii) research to develop new capacities to reduce the disease burden (or other problem). The focus on disease burden is aligned with internationally agreed goals, but it can also be changed to address differences in interests of the investors, such as patentable products for private sector. An approach to systematic listing of all competing research avenues, options, and questions is suggested along with a framework for identifying criteria that can discriminate between characteristics of research questions (e.g., answerability, ethics, effectiveness, deliverability, affordability, sustainability, maximum potential impact on disease burden, equity, and others).

CHNRI proposes a new approach to undertaking health research priority setting in a fair and transparent way, respecting principles of risk-neutral investing. The process brings together the investors, a group of technical experts, and a larger number of representatives for various other stakeholders. Investors are a part of the process from the outset; they are assisted in defining the context, expected *"returns"* on the investments, and their risk preferences. The role for technical experts is to systematically list the competing research investment options and to use a set of criteria to discriminate between research options according to their likelihood of reaching the targets. The stakeholders can then weigh different criteria according to their system of values to inform the investors on research priorities.

It is estimated that more than US$ 130 billion are invested globally in health research each year and the amount has been increasing steadily over the past decade (1). Still, proposals for health research funding are far exceeding the available resources. Increasingly, there is a need to set priorities in health research investments in a fair and legitimate way, using a sound and transparent methodology. In 2005, CHNRI launched a project to develop a systematic methodology for setting priorities in health research investments and to apply it to child health (2). This effort was motivated by a notion that current research investment prioritization approaches suffer from many shortcomings, which may partly be responsible for the persisting high levels of mortality in children globally (3–5). Commission on Health Research for Development stated that *"only 5% of global spending on health research in 1986 was devoted to health problems in developing countries, where 93% of the world's burden of 'preventable mortality' occurred"* (6). Leroy et al. (3) determined the proportion of research on childhood mortality directed toward better medical technology (i.e., toward improving old technology or creating new technology) compared with research on technology delivery and utilization. They found that 97% of grants were allocated to developing new technologies, which could reduce child mortality by 22% – a one-third reduction of what could be achieved if the existing technologies were fully utilized (3). Furthermore, in terms of financial support for health systems and policy research, the *"10/90 gap"* persists and health systems research receives very little funding (7). The World Report on *"Knowledge for Better Health: Strengthening Health Systems"* reported similar conclusions (8). All these sources implied that large disproportion existed between the investments in different types of health research, different diseases contributing to overall burden, and between the health needs of the wealthy and the poor.

One of the trends that have been observed is that certain type of research has persistently been awarded funds and, therefore, attracted scientists, while other crucial research, such as child health epidemiology, which many not be as attractive and likely to be funded remained neglected (5,9). Our concern is that the past several decades of rewarding new, attractive, and original ideas, whereby little concern was given to the usefulness of the generated new knowledge for reduction of persisting disease burden in the society, has led to a dramatic increase in the number of basic research studies and growth of impact factors of the journals that publish such research (5). This process inevitably led to an opening of many new and exciting research avenues, but there have been only few examples where the full potential of the new knowledge was realized at the level of public health, i.e., used to meet the needs of the community/society. This is particularly unwelcome because the contributions from taxpayers are frequently the main source of funding for health research investments, and it may (to an extent) explain the ongoing lack of progress toward achieving substantial disease burden reduction across the developing world (3). Only recently, these issues have gained more attention (10–12).

The examples above point to the dangers of the status quo, inconsistencies, and imbalances in investing, relative lack of transparency, accountability to high-level goals and strategic directions, difficulties in determining where particular research fits in the process of knowledge translation, and similar issues. Since May 2005, CHNRI organized a series of meetings and workshops that involved more than 100 experts in global child health from different backgrounds. During those meetings, a review of existing principles and practice of research priority setting was undertaken (4) and a strategy of involving all the stakeholders in the process was defined (13). Those two papers were the first in the series of five papers describing the CHNRI methodology that was prepared as a result of the meetings.

The meetings also highlighted a need for defining some universally observed challenges and agreeing on several key concepts that could be helpful in resolving the challenges. A consensus over those concepts would enable systematic, transparent, and rational solutions to the challenges that were identified with respect to research investment priority setting. In this paper, which is the third paper of the series on CHNRI methodology, we exclusively focus on those universal challenges and propose a solution in a form of conceptual framework that should serve to surmount the challenges through the CHNRI priority setting process. Information on the historic approaches, current principles, and practice of priority setting, strategies of involving the stakeholders, specific guidelines for implementing the CHNRI methodology, and its validation and comparison with other similar methodologies can be found in other papers of this series (4,13), and these issues are not a focus of this particular paper.

1. Universal challenges in setting priorities in health research invest-ments. Discussions between experts of different backgrounds were moderated by CHNRI at several meetings and workshops during 2005 and 2006. They highlighted some universal challenges that any priority setting exercise in health research investments will eventually have to face (**Table 43-1**). The first challenge is deciding who should be involved in the process of setting research priorities. It was agreed that one important requirement should be that the priority setting process involves those who invest in health research from the outset. The shortcoming of several previously proposed methodologies driven by technical experts was that, although they resulted in sound recommendations, they were rarely implemented by the investors subsequently (4). It is therefore important that investors are involved in the process from the start. Still, they should seek assistance from technical experts and numerous other stakeholders to better understand the context in which investments are performed. This context involves time frame (long-term vs short-term expectations), space (geographic boundaries likely to be affected by investments), magnitude and urgency of the problem (i.e., burden of disease, disability, or death), and existing and agreed investment policies and targets to which political commitment has been made.

Based on the understanding of the context, investors can make informed decisions in terms of expectations from their investments and their risk preferences. Discussions with technical experts and stakeholders should assist them in addressing three further universal challenges – defining what constitutes a health research investment option/opportunity; defining what constitutes an expected "*return*" on this investment; and defining what constitutes a potential "*risk*" in this investment. The CHNRI's solution to defining what constitutes a "*research investment option*" has been described in detail in our earlier work (2,5). We proposed previously (5) that an investment option in health research where public funds are used should be defined as a research activity that not only produces new knowledge but also incorporates a vision of implementation of this knowledge to reduce the burden of disease and disability and improve health. However, different investors will have different expectations on "*returns*" from such investment options. While those who are in charge of public funds may be interested in reduction of the persisting disease burden as an appropriate "*return*" of their health research investment, funders of academic institutions may be seeking "*high impact*", visible publications, while

Table 43-1. *Twenty "universal challenges" in setting priorities in health research investments, according to CHNRI expert group (3).*

1. Deciding who should be involved in the process of setting research priorities
2. Defining what constitutes a health research investment option opportunity
3. Defining what constitutes the expected *"return"* on the investment
4. Defining what constitutes a potential *"risk"* in the investment
5. Finding a way of dealing with uncertainty of health research outcomes
6. Defining health research, its boundaries, and its levels of *"depth"*
7. Systematic listing of many competing research investment options
8. Defining what is meant by *"priority setting"* in the context of health research
9. Defining criteria relevant to priority setting in health research investments
10. Comparing different domains of health research using the same criteria
11. Development of a simple quantitative way to rank competing research options
12. Limiting the potential of personal biases to substantially influence the outcome
13. Ensuring that priority-setting process is fully transparent
14. Ensuring that it can be repeated and validated
15. Ensuring that it is flexible and adjustable to all contexts and levels of application
16. Ensuring that it is iterative with a feedback loop, instead of a one-way process
17. Ensuring that it is perceived by the users as legitimate and fair
18. Ensuring that it is simple and intuitive enough to become popular among the users
19. Linking quantitative ranks of research options with specific investment decisions
20. Involving stakeholders from the wider community into the process

funders from the industry may be primarily interested in patentable products that could have commercial value.

A further universal challenge is finding a way of dealing with uncertainty of health research outcomes. This challenge reflects perceived difficulties in comparing long-term strategic basic research that offers great promise in reducing disease burden (although the final outcome is very uncertain) with short-term research in order to define more efficient means of delivering existing interventions that are known to be effective. At this point, it would again be reasonable for the investors to consult technical experts, whose knowledge and expertise can be used to assess likelihoods related to answerability of different research investment options (i.e., the likelihood that the endpoints of the research can be reached) within a precisely defined context.

Further challenges include systematic listing of a seemingly endless spectrum of competing research investment options and comparing different domains of health research using the same criteria. Again, the CHNRI's solution to this problem has been described in detail in implementation exercises

of CHNRI priority setting process in South Africa (at the national level) and
for zinc as a risk factor (at the global level) (14,15) (**Table 43-2**). Potential profits and risks from investing in research options from epidemiological research,
research on new interventions, or health systems and policy research can be
compared to each other according to several criteria, which should always include (but are not limited to) their answerability, their usefulness (in terms of
effectiveness, deliverability, affordability, and sustainability), potential impact
on persisting disease burden, and effect on equity. A further challenge is deciding whether those most fundamental criteria need refinement or addition of
some other criteria.

Table 43-2. *Child Health and Nutrition Research Initiative's proposed framework for systematic listing of investment options in health research, which takes into account the varying "depth" of proposed
research: the three most fundamental and mutually exclusive research domains; very broad research
avenues within those domains; more specific research options; and very specific research questions.*

RESEARCH DOMAIN	RESEARCH AVENUE	RESEARCH OPTION	RESEARCH QUESTION
Health research to assess burden of health problem (disease) and its determinants	Measuring the burden Understanding risk factors (in terms of their relative risks) Measuring prevalence of exposure to risk factors Evaluating the efficacy and effectiveness of interventions in place Measuring prevalence of coverage of interventions in place	Many research options within each of the avenues; research options should correspond to the level of 3-to-5-y research programs	Several very specific research questions within each of the research avenues should correspond to the title of individual research papers
Health research to improve performance of existing capacities to reduce the burden	Health policy analysis Health system structure analysis Financing/costs analysis Human resources Provision/infrastructure Operations research Responsiveness/recipients Improving existing interventions (their affordability and deliverability)		
Health research to develop new capacities to reduce the burden	Basic, clinical, and public health research to advance existing knowledge to develop new capacities Basic, clinical, and public health research to explore entirely novel ideas to develop new capacities		

For example, in different contexts addressing of the *"answerability"* crite-rion may also require a separate assessment related to ethics, existing research capacity, or public acceptance of research results. The *"usefulness"* (relevance) criterion will, in different contexts, be split into criteria that will separately assess effectiveness, deliverability, affordability, sustainability, and whether a critical gap in knowledge is being addressed. The *"potential impact"* will occasionally not only assess the quantity of potential burden reduction, but also its quality – i.e., whether this reduction is targeting those most heavily affected in the population. **Table 43-3** lists some of the possible criteria that can be used for setting priorities between different research investment op-tions and questions about each option that could address these criteria well.

Table 43-3. *Some of the possible criteria (and related questions) proposed by Child Health and Nutrition Research Initiative that can be used to discriminate between any two (or more) health research options that compete for investments in order to set research priorities. The outcomes of the different criteria will necessarily conflict each other.*

Acceptability: How likely is the proposed research to be approved, taking into account any possible resistance based on ethical or political grounds and public opinion?
Affordability: How likely is it that the results will improve affordability of existing policies and programs?
Answerability: How likely is it that the objectives will be met given the current state of science and the size of the gap in knowledge?
Applicability: How likely is it that the results will be immediately applicable for guiding poli-cies and programs?
Deliverability: How likely is it that the results will improve the delivery of existing policies and programs?
Equity: How likely is it that the proposed research will benefit those who are most vulnerable to poor child development?
Feasibility: How likely is it that the cost of the proposed research will be a feasible investment?
Potential effect on disease burden: How likely is the proposed research to lead to significant improvement in disease burden reduction?
Sustainability: How likely is it that the results will improve sustainability of existing policies and programs?
Usefulness: Given the quality of existing evidence, how likely is it that the proposed research will fill a critical gap in knowledge?
Existing research capacity: How likely is it that that the objectives will be met given existing research capacity?
Alignment with other policies: How well are the objectives aligned with other existing poli-cies in the society?
Generation of commercial products: How likely is it that the proposed research will lead to patents and generate commercial products?
Competitiveness and publication impact: How likely is it that the results of the research will be seen as competitive against other ongoing work and be accepted for publication in the journals with the highest impact factor?

The next challenge is development of a simple quantitative (and intuitive) way to score and rank all competing research options while addressing all relevant criteria. CHNRI recommends that appropriate questions to address the chosen criteria need to be developed and then posed by the investors to technical experts, who will then answer them independently from each other. In this way, their expertise will be used to discriminate between competing research options based on strictly defined criteria and their collective optimism toward compliance of each research option with each criterion will be measured. It will also limit the potential of personal biases to substantially influence the outcome, which was seen as another universal challenge.

Namely, personal opinions of members of research panels and the undue influence of certain members of the panel can have large effect on the decision-making process on research grant awards. The proposed conceptual framework for CHNRI methodology ensures that technical experts provide their input independently of each other, and that the final scores for each competing research option are computed in a highly structured, transparent, and systematic way. This ensures that priority setting process is fully transparent and that it could be repeated and validated. Through application of agreement statistics methods, the CHNRI methodology can also identify controversial issues (i.e., responses with a large variation in scores among experts).

The above characteristics of the CHNRI process should also deal with several other universal challenges. The flexibility in the choice of criteria should ensure that the methods are adjustable to all contexts and levels of application. They also enable a feedback loop, as the process can be repeated after some preset periods of time and priorities will then change with the changing context. Its transparency and clarity of the necessary steps should ensure that it is perceived by the users as legitimate and fair.

Finally, the following proposed solutions should eventually ensure that the process is seen as simple and intuitive enough to become popular among its users. Many experts from different backgrounds should undertake scoring independently from each other and intermediate scores for each investment options could then be expressed as the percentage of maximum possible points to get awarded for each criterion. The final score can then be computed as a mean value of the five intermediate scores, expressed as a number between 0 and 100%. This simple and intuitive quantitative score assigned to each research investment option to capture its overall value can easily be presented to policy-makers to guide their decisions and can also be combined with the proposed cost of research to assess cost-effectiveness of all possible research options and derive optimal mix of funded options through program budgeting and marginal analysis (16). This is a way of linking quantitative ranks of research options with specific investment decisions.

The final challenge, identified as *"universal"*, was how to address opinions and systems of values of stakeholders other than investors and technical experts (such as government representatives, health workers, journalists, legal experts, recipients from the wider community, and others). While stakeholders' representatives may lack technical expertise to list and score research options, they could still prioritize between the chosen criteria by setting specific weights on intermediate scores for each research option, based on their perception of the relative importance of each priority-setting criterion in comparison with others. The rank orders of competing research avenues may change with the modifying of weights. These can also be revised as a result of a feedback process or substantial changes in the dynamic environment in which the priority setting process is being performed. The problem of involving stakeholders is a very complex one and CHNRI have recently published a separate paper that presented different strategies to involve stakeholders into health research priority setting process (13).

2. Conceptual framework for setting health research priorities proposed by CHNRI. CHNRI experts agreed that all identified challenges could eventually be dealt with in a satisfactory way through introduction of a new and systematic methodology for setting priorities in health research investments. However, a prerequisite for such a methodology/process is that an agreement is reached on a very limited number of key concepts. We present these concepts in further text, as they form the basic framework of the CHNRI priority setting method.

3. Defining health research. In the framework proposed by CHNRI, health research is defined as *"any activity that is undertaken to generate presently non-existing knowledge that will eventually be used to reduce the existing disease burden (or other health-related problem) in human population"*. This definition is intended mainly to guide the investments of public funding and not-for-profit organizations. Instead of disease burden, the endpoint may also be another health problem, such as health promotion necessary to address improvements in child development. For private donors, however, the end-points may be patentable products that would have commercial value.

The definition of health research stated above, which applies to public funding, should be carefully considered, because it has two important implications as follows:

(i) It defines disease burden reduction as the perceived *"return"* of investments in health research. This is because the agreed targets and policies for spending public and not-for-profit funds are typically defined in terms of burden of disease reduction within a specified time frame. This methodology assists investment choices to reach those targets in an effective way.

(ii) It sets limits to what should be considered health research. Setting these limits may also attract criticism, but it is an essential first step that eventually enables a constructive and fair priority setting in health research investments in the real world. For example, a number of activities in construction, environment, and communication technology could eventually prove to have considerable positive collateral effects on population health. However, if it was not possible to envisage and predict these effects on disease burden reduction at the time when the activities were proposed for funding, then they should not be considered health research. Also, research on genetics of drosophila flies or yeast can bring fascinating new insights. However, if there is no vision at all (if even a blurred or distant one) on how the new knowledge generated by those activities can be used to achieve disease burden reduction in human populations, then those activities cannot be considered health research and should not be considered a funding priority by the organizations that invest in health research.

4. Defining main domains of health research. It has already been proposed by the Commission on Health Research for Development that, with respect to their potential to reduce existing disease burden, there are three broad and general domains of health research: (i) health policy and systems research; (ii) research on improvement of the existing health interventions, and (iii) research on development of new interventions (6). The recent work by CHNRI has shown that these domains of health research, although very useful, are neither mutually exclusive nor universally applicable, which would both be desirable properties for a research domain (2,4,5,14,15).

For example, if the health research proposed for funding is relevant at the global level, such as improvement of existing vaccines to increase coverage, then a domain *"health research to improve deliverability or affordability of an existing intervention"* will only be relevant to some countries, but not the others, depending on their contexts and level of investment in health care. Also, *"improving of the effectiveness of existing interventions"* cannot be entirely addressed through health policy and systems research, as suggested in the previous conceptual frameworks (6). Furthermore, epidemiological research features all three domains, and it is a necessary and important component of health research needed to inform any priority setting process, but it did not receive enough attention.

Much of the *"improvement of the existing interventions"* is reliant on the issues of deliverability or affordability. This qualifies it as the question for health systems and policy research, which is a different research domain from *"improvement of existing interventions"*. Finally, development of new interventions is not always achieved through identifying an entirely novel line of research, but also through scientific advancements on the existing lines of work, which overlaps with the domain of *"improvement of existing interventions"*.

Because of those limitations in the existing framework (6), we propose an extension of that framework in which there are 3 universal and non-overlapping domains of health research as follows:

(i) Health research to assess burden of health problem (disease) and its determinants; (ii) Health research to improve performance of existing capacities to reduce the burden;

(iii) Health research to develop new capacities to reduce the burden.

By capacities we consider any means of conducting health research – from health facilities and other infrastructure and equipment to available interventions and human resources. We believe that these three domains of health research are universally applicable in all contexts and also mutually exclusive. All possible health research questions should be easily categorized under one of the three domains, which is the advancement over previous approaches. For practical reasons, the second general domain could be further split into *"health policy and systems research"* and *"research to improve the existing interventions"*.

5. Defining priority setting (rationing, resource allocation). In most human communities, ranging from the nuclear family to global human population, the needs and demands of the individuals or groups are greater than the resources that are available to fulfill them. Therefore, setting investment priorities for meeting those needs and demands becomes one of the most important issues for the development of any policy. Because not everyone can immediately get their demands fulfilled, some will be fulfilled immediately with existing resources, while others will be delayed.

These choices are especially difficult to make in developing countries, where delaying investments often means that a price would continue to be paid in human suffering, illness, and death. Because of this, priority setting requires transparent, legitimate, and fair approaches and explicit debate about the principles and criteria that would be used to make such difficult decisions. Some authors define priority setting as *"who gets what at whose expense"*. The *"what"* can be either organs from donors, available drugs, or, most commonly, funding for different suggested activities. Although there is growing interest in priority setting, there is little consensus on the best way to carry it out in a fair and legitimate way at different levels (individual, community, national, or global) (4,17,18).

An important concept that we propose here is understanding that priority setting is not an exact science, process, or method. The reason for introducing this concept are the experiences with alternative priority-setting methods, such as *"Combined Approach Matrix"*, *"value of information"* approach, or the tools used by *"Council on Health Research for Development"* (4). These methods have all been carefully developed and validated with the aim to become very exact, consistent, and repeatable. However, the variety of contexts in which priority setting occurs and *"returns"* on investments expected by different donors are so large, that we believe it would not be possible to develop a *"one-fits-all"* method with a fixed set of criteria and processes. The successful method that will have a chance to become accepted and popular will need to show very large flexibility in design to be readily tailored to different contexts and purposes. Priority setting is a *"science"* intending to serve the needs of a community or a society at a specific point in time, within given policy, context, time limit, and financial constraints. It is value-driven and there are many interested stakeholders who will necessarily promote a diverse set of opinions and values. There are also many possible criteria according to which priorities could be set, some of them conflicting each other.

The community of health researchers is already used to the process of priority setting in which they submit their research proposals for funding and most of them get rejected or delayed until some later point in time. Only the minority of *"priority research projects"* get funded. Therefore, priority setting for investments into health research is already implemented for many decades by governmental and private donor agencies. The key question is whether it can be done in a more legitimate, fair, transparent, and replicable way (19).

6. Choice of relevant criteria for priority setting in health research investments. The decisions made regularly by investors in health research on supporting some of the proposed research grants are based on some criteria that separate priority projects, that get funded from those that get delayed or rejected. The key question is how much those criteria are compatible with what priority setting should be about within our conceptual framework, i.e., *"serving the needs of a community or a society at a specific point in time, within given policy, context, time limit and financial constraints"*.

We have witnessed a publication of several millions of research papers as a product of investments in health research over the past several decades.

Table 43-4. *Elements of the Child Health and Nutrition Research Initiative methodology for setting priorities in health research investments – it is a process driven by the investors and assisted by technical experts and numerous stakeholders, that results in the following seven outcomes.*

1. Understanding the context in which investments are performed (by funders)
2. Agreeing on expected profits and risk preferences (by funders)
3. Defining main criteria for priority setting (by funders)
4. Systematic listing of many competing research investment options (by experts)
5. Transparent valuation of each research option against each criterion (by experts)
6. Adjustment of this valuation according to values of the society (by stakeholders)
7. Combining this adjusted valuation with predicted cost, expected profits and risk preferences to decide on the optimal investment strategy (by funders)

Have those papers really been what society needed most in order to reduce its present disease burden? Did they really generate the new knowledge that was most needed and useful in reducing the persisting disease burden? Have they eventually led to reductions in disease burden over the past several decades that justified the immense investments made into health research over that time period? The criteria most often used by panels of experts evaluating the research grant proposals is answerability (mainly by judging track record and capacity of the group suggesting to undertake the research) and attractiveness of the new knowledge that is proposed to be generated (mainly in terms of potential for later publication in journals with high impact factors). Very rarely the panels judge the usefulness of the knowledge proposed to be generated in terms of its potential to contribute to reduction of the persisting disease burden in the society, although this should be one of the main criteria within CHNRI's conceptual framework for health research priority setting. The stakeholders can then weigh different criteria chosen by the investors and applied by technical experts. This weighing will reflect their system of values and guide the investors' decisions on research priorities. The technical aspects of the weighing have been addressed in detail in our previous work (13).

7. Conclusions. CHNRI proposes a new approach to undertaking health research priority setting in a fair and transparent way, respecting principles of maximizing the returns in terms of burden of disease reduction for invested funding. The approach is systematic and it attempts to overcome a larger list of universal challenges through introduction of several key concepts and proposal of a process that could become useful and popular among the users. It is transdisciplinary and it incorporates principles ranging from medical (e.g., public health reasoning), social (e.g., concern about equity), public opinion (eg, respecting stakeholders' views), ethical (*"accountability for reasonable-*

ness"), and economic (*"program budgeting and marginal analysis"*) disciplines. The agreed desirable elements of this new process are summarized in **Table 43-4**. Target audience for the proposed CHNRI methodology are national governments, public-private partnerships, international not-for-profit agencies, large research funding donors, and policy-makers, but it can also be adapted to the needs of private sector. We hope that these concepts will lead to improved accountability and increased attention to evaluation of returns on health research investments. In principle, it should be possible to evaluate the outcome of investment prioritization using a framework such as CHNRI's vs. an alternative framework (e.g., continuation of existing practices or using some alternative priority-setting tool). The countries increasingly measure and quantify their disease burden in metrics such as disability adjusted life years. If a reduction in disease burden is agreed as a target that could partly be achieved through health research investing, then the design of randomized controlled trial should be applicable in assessing the reduction in this burden achieved through different investment practices – those guided by priority setting tools vs. alternative approaches. After a time frame of 5-10 years, the differences should become apparent and detectable. At that point, if a substantial advantage of the use of framework such as CHNRI's could be demonstrated, investing in health research could become a discipline guided by sound, transparent, and fair methods and practices.

Acknowledgement: *Originally published as: Igor Rudan, Mickey Chopra, Lydia Kapiriri, Jennifer Gibson, Mary Ann Lansang, Ilona Carneiro, Shanthi Ameratunga, Alexander C. Tsai, Kit Yee Chan, Mark Tomlinson, Sonja Y. Hess, Harry Campbell, Shams El Arifeen, Robert E. Black on behalf of Child Health and Nutrition Research Initiative (CHNRI): Setting priorities in global child health research investments: Universal challenges and conceptual framework. Reprinted with permission from Croatian Medical Journal under Creative Commons Attribution License. (Croat Med J 2007; 126:237-240). The authors would like to thank Craig Mitton (University of British Columbia, Vancouver, Canada), Dean T. Jamison (Disease Control Priorities Project), Simon Lewin (London School of Hygiene and Tropical Medicine), Rajiv Bhal, Olivier Fontaine, and Jose Martines (Child and Adolescent Health Department of the World Health Organization, Geneva, Switzerland) for their comments that helped advancing this methodology at various stages of its development, and Nancy Hughart, Deborah Horner, and Carolina Cueva Schaumann for their outstanding secretarial support.*

References

1. De Francisco A, Matlin S (eds). Monitoring financial flows for health research 2006: The changing landscape of health research development. Geneva: Global Forum for Health Research, 2006.

2. Rudan I, El Arifeen S, Black RE. A systematic methodology for setting priorities in child health research investments. In: Child Health and Nutrition Research Initiative: a new approach for systematic priority setting. Dhaka: Child Health and Nutrition Research Initiative, 2006.

3. Leroy JL, Habicht JP, Pelto G, Bertozzi SM. Current priorities in health research funding and lack of impact on the number of child deaths per year. Am J Public Health. 2007; 97:219–223.

4. Rudan I, Gibson J, Kapiriri L, Lansang MA, Hyder AA, Lawn J, et al. Setting priorities in global child health research investments: assessment of principles and practice. Croat Med J 2007; 48:595–604.

5. Rudan I, El Arifeen S, Black RE, Campbell H. Childhood pneumonia and diarrhoea: setting our priorities right. Lancet Infect Dis 2007; 7:56–61.

6. Commission on Health Research for Development. Health research: essential link to equity in development. Geneva: CHRD, 1990.

7. Currat LJ, de Francisco A, Al-Tuwaijri S, Ghaffar A, Jupp S. The 10/90 report on health research 2003–2004. Geneva: Global Forum for Health Research, 2004.

8. World Health Organization. The world report on knowledge for better health: strengthening health systems. Geneva: World Health Organization, 2004.

9. Rudan I, Lawn J, Cousens S, Rowe AK, Boschi-Pinto C, Tomaskovic L, et al. Gaps in policy-relevant information on burden of disease in children: a systematic review. Lancet 2005; 365:2031–2040.

10. Global Forum for Health Research. The 10/90 report on health research 1999. Geneva: Global Forum for Health Research, 1999.

11. Nuyens Y. Setting priorities for health research: lessons from low and middle-income countries. Bull World Health Organ 2007; 85:319–321.

12. Costello A, Filippi V, Kubba T, Horton R. Research challenges to improve maternal and child survival. Lancet 2007; 369:1240-1243.

13. Kapiriri L, Tomlinson M, Chopra M, El Arifeen S, Black RE, Rudan I; Child Health and Nutrition Research Initiative (CHNRI). Setting priorities in global child health research investments: addressing values of stakeholders. Croat Med J 2007; 48:618–627.

14. Tomlinson M, Chopra M, Sanders D, Bradshaw D, Hendricks M, Greenfield D, et al. Setting priorities in child health research investments for South Africa. PLoS Med. 2007;4:e259.

15. Brown KH, Hess SY, Boy E, Gibson RS, Horton S, Osendarp SJ, et al. Setting priorities for zinc-related health research to reduce children's disease burden worldwide: an application of the Child Health and Nutrition Research Initiative's research priority-setting method. Public Health Nutr 2009; 12:389–396.

16. Mitton CR, Donaldson C. Setting priorities and allocating resources in health regions: lessons from a project evaluating program budgeting and marginal analysis (PBMA). Health Policy 2003; 64:335–348.

17. Kapiriri L, Norheim OF. Criteria for priority-setting in health care in Uganda: exploration of stakeholders' values. Bull World Health Organ 2004; 82:172–179.

18. Gibson JL, Martin DK, Singer PA. Setting priorities in health care organizations: criteria, processes, and parameters of success. BMC Health Serv Res. 2004; 4:25.

19. Daniels N, Sabin JE. Setting limits fairly: can we learn to share medical resources? Oxford: Oxford University Press, 2002.

CHAPTER 44.

Setting priorities in global health research investments: Guidelines for implementation of the CHNRI method

This article provides detailed guidelines for the implementation of systematic method for setting priorities in health research investments that was recently developed by Child Health and Nutrition Research Initiative (CHNRI). The target audience for the proposed method are international agencies, large research funding donors, and national governments and policy-makers. The process has the following steps: (i) selecting the managers of the process; (ii) specifying the context and risk management preferences; (iii) discussing criteria for setting health research priorities; (iv) choosing a limited set of the most useful and important criteria; (v) developing means to assess the likelihood that proposed health research options will satisfy the selected criteria; (vi) systematic listing of a large number of proposed health research options; (vii) pre-scoring check of all competing health research options; (viii) scoring of health research options using the chosen set of criteria; (ix) calculating intermediate scores for each health research option; (x) obtaining further input from the stakeholders; (xi) adjusting intermediate scores taking into account the values of stakeholders; (xii) calculating overall priority scores and assigning ranks; (xiii) performing an analysis of agreement between the scorers; (xiv) linking computed research priority scores with investment decisions; (xv) feedback and revision. The CHNRI method is a flexible process that enables prioritizing health research investments at any level: institutional, regional, national, international, or global.

Proposals for health research funding are far exceeding available resources. Increasingly, there is a need to set priorities in health research investments in a fair, transparent, and systematic way. In 2005, Child Health and Nutrition Research Initiative (CHNRI, www.chnri.org), an initiative of the Global Forum for Health Research, launched a project to develop a systematic method for setting priorities in health research investments and to apply it to global child health (1). This effort was motivated by a notion that current research investment prioritization approaches suffer from many shortcomings which may partly be responsible for persisting high levels of mortality in children globally (2–4). The target audience for the proposed method are international agencies, large research funding donors, and national governments and policy-makers. The CHNRI method is a flexible process that enables prioritizing health research investments at any level: institutional, regional, national, international, or global.

1. Selecting managers of the process. CHNRI method is a process managed by a relatively small team of persons. This team needs to appropriately represent investors in health research, their interests, and visions. Like any other investing, health research funding is associated with possible gains and profits, but also risks and losses. The key concept of CHNRI's methodology is that all health research should have a common ultimate goal, which is to reduce existing burden of disease and disability and improve health. Future reductions in the existing disease burden that will result from supported health research are considered *"profits"*. However, because of many uncertainties inherent to health research, many investments will never sufficiently contribute to reduction in disease burden to justify the investments.

The purpose of the CHNRI priority setting method is to inform the investors in health research about the risks associated with their investments. Each research investment option needs to be judged according to a set of criteria. Those criteria will assess likelihood that proposed research option could realistically contribute to disease burden reduction within the context in which investments are taking place (4).

2. Specifying context and risk management preferences. Priority setting in health research investments is not an abstract, theoretical exercise with a single possible correct outcome, such as a mathematical problem. It is a process that occurs within complex circumstances of the real world. The decisions will, therefore, strongly depend on the context in which the process takes place and on risk preferences of the investors. At this point, a small group of process managers (who represent the investors) needs to specify the context and their risk preferences. The context is specified by thoroughly discussing and carefully defining the following: (i) context in space; (ii) disease, disability, and death burden; (iii) context in time; (iv) stakeholders; and (v) risk management preferences. **Table 44-1** provides guidelines on how this should be done.

3. Discussing criteria for setting health research priorities. There is a large number of nearly independent criteria that can be used to discriminate between any two competing *"health research investment options"*, giving one of them preference over the other. The central challenge is that the decisions on investment priorities based on different criteria will necessarily conflict each other.

Table 44-1. *Guidelines on defining the context in which research priorities will be set.*

(i) *Context in space:* What is the population in which the investments in health research should contribute to disease burden reduction and improved health? (e.g., all developing countries/all children under 5 years of age/people exposed to a specific risk factor);
(ii) *Disease, disability, and death burden:* What is known about the burden of disease, disability, and death that will be addressed by supported health research? Can it be measured and quantified (e.g., in disability-adjusted life years – DALYs – or in some other way)?
(iii) *Context in time:* In how many years are the first results expected (in terms of reaching the endpoints of health research, translating and implementing them, which is then expected to achieve detectable disease burden reduction)?
(iv) *Stakeholders:* Who are the main groups in the society whose values and interests should be respected in setting health research investment priorities?
(v) *Risk management preferences:* What will be investment strategy in health research with respect to risk preferences? Will all the funding support a single (or a few) expensive high-risk high-profit research options (eg, vaccine development), or will the risk be balanced and diversified between many research options which will have different levels of "risks" and "profits" associated with them?

This means that, when choosing between any two proposed research options, some criteria will give preference to one of them, while other will prefer the other.

At this point, managers of the priority setting process should try to list possible criteria appropriate to their specific context. **Table 44-2** provides a list of criteria that can serve as an example and starting point. There is no real limit to a number of priority setting criteria that may seem appropriate to different contexts. However, with inclusion of more criteria to the list, they will begin to overlap with the already listed ones, so their potential usefulness as independent criteria will soon begin to decrease.

4. Choosing a limited set of the most useful and important criteria. In this step, managers of priority setting process need to select a set of priority setting criteria from the longer list that should be sufficiently informative to discriminate between the competing research options. **Figure 44-1** shows an example of how this can be done. Competing research options are expected to initially generate new knowledge, which then needs to be translated into health intervention. This translation may either lead to improvement of an existing intervention, or development of a new one. The implementation of that intervention will eventually reduce disease burden, which is the ultimate aim of any health research investment (**Figure 44-1**).

The criteria that assess the likelihood of the progress through this simple framework are: (i) answerability, (ii) effectiveness, (iii) deliverability, (iv) maximum potential for disease burden reduction, and (v) the effect on equity.

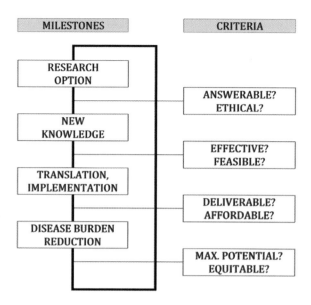

Figure 44-1. *A simple framework developed by CHNRI that identifies some of the apparent criteria that can be used for setting priorities between the proposed health research options.*

CHNRI recommends these five criteria to be used in almost all contexts. Some of them may even be merged – e.g., *"effectiveness"* and *"deliverability"* criteria could be merged in some contexts into a more general criterion called *"usefulness"*. Also, *"maximum potential for disease burden reduction"* and *"effect on equity"* criteria can be merged into a more general criterion called *"impact"*.

Additional criteria (those shown in **Table 44-2**, or any other useful criteria) may be added to these ones suggested here, if the management team decides that they are important within their context. It is entirely up to the team of process managers to decide on the final list of criteria that will be useful for their particular exercise in priority setting in health research investments. Examples on how this was achieved in practice can be found in some published examples of implementation (5,6).

5. Developing means to assess the likelihood that proposed health research options will satisfy selected criteria. After the managers selected the criteria, they should invite a group of technical experts. The experts should take the process through the next three steps (listing, checking, and scoring research options), working closely with the management team.

The first task for technical experts is to develop a set of three simple questions that will address each of the selected criteria. These questions should

Table 44-2. *Examples of the possible criteria which can be used for setting priorities in health research investments.*

Answerability? (some health research options will be more likely to be answerable than the others)

Attractiveness? (some health research options will be more likely to lead to publications in high-impact journals)

Novelty? (some health research options will be more likely to generate truly novel and non-existing knowledge)

Potential for translation? (some health research options will be more likely to generate knowledge that will be translated into health intervention)

Effectiveness? (some health research options will be more likely to generate/improve truly effective health interventions)

Affordability? (the translation or implementation of knowledge generated through some health research options will not be affordable within the context)

Deliverability? (some health research options will lead to / impact health interventions that will not be deliverable within the context)

Sustainability? (some health research options will lead to / impact health interventions that will not be sustainable within the context)

Public opinion? (some health research options will seem more justified and acceptable to general public than the others)

Ethical aspects? (some health research options will be more likely to raise ethical concerns than the others)

Maximum potential impact on burden? (some health research options will have a theoretical potential to reduce much larger portions of the existing disease burden than the others)

Equity? (some health research options will lead to health interventions that will only be accessible to the privileged in the society/context, thus increasing inequity)

Community involvement? (some health research options will have more additional positive side-effects through community involvement)

Cost and feasibility? (all other criteria being equal, some research options will still require more funding than the others and thus be less feasible investments)

Likelihood of generating patents/lucrative products? (some research options will have greater likelihood of generating patents or other potentially lucrative products, thus promising greater financial return on investments, regardless of their impact on disease burden)

---

jointly help to assess the likelihood that proposed research options will satisfy the selected criteria. It is recommended that the questions should be simple, sufficiently informative, easily understandable, and answerable simply as *"yes"* or *"no"*. **Table 44-3** shows an example of how the questions were developed in some of the conducted exercises to address the set of 5 criteria: *answerability, effectiveness, deliverability, maximum potential for disease burden reduction,* and the *effect on equity* (5,6).

6. Systematic listing of a large number of proposed health research options. Research priorities will usually be set under two types of circumstances. In the first scenario, a funding agency/government will aim to distribute its

Table 44-3. *Example of yes/no questions that can be used to assess likelihood whether proposed health research options satisfy the chosen priority-setting criteria.*

CRITERION 1: ANSWERABILITY

1. Would you say the research question is well framed and endpoints are well defined?

2. Based on: (i) the level of existing research capacity in proposed research; and (ii) the size of the gap from current level of knowledge to the proposed endpoints; would you say that a study can be designed to answer the research question and to reach the proposed endpoints of the research?

3. Do you think that a study needed to answer the proposed research question would obtain ethical approval without major concerns?

CRITERION 2: EFFECTIVENESS

1. Based on the best existing evidence and knowledge, would the intervention which would be developed / improved through proposed research be efficacious?

2. Based on the best existing evidence and knowledge, would the intervention which would be developed / improved through proposed research be effective?

3. If the answers to either of the previous two questions is positive, would you say that the evidence upon which these opinions are based is of high quality?

CRITERION 3: DELIVERABILITY

1. Taking into account the level of difficulty with intervention delivery from the perspective of the intervention itself (e.g. design, standardizability, safety), the infrastructure required (e.g. human resources, health facilities, communication and transport infrastructure) and users of the intervention (e.g. need for change of attitudes or beliefs, supervision, existing demand), would you say that the endpoints of the research would be deliverable within the context of interest?

2. Taking into account the resources available to implement the intervention, would you say that the endpoints of the research would be affordable within the context of interest?

3. Taking into account government capacity and partnership requirements (e.g. adequacy of government regulation, monitoring and enforcement; governmental intersectoral coordination, partnership with civil society and external donor agencies; favourable political climate to achieve high coverage), would you say that the endpoints of the research would be sustainable within the context of interest?

CRITERION 4: MAXIMUM POTENTIAL FOR DISEASE BURDEN REDUCTION

1. Taking into account the results of conducted intervention trials, or for the new interventions the proportion of avertable burden under an ideal scenario, would you say that the successful reaching of research endpoints would have a capacity to remove 5% of disease burden or more?

2. To remove 10% of disease burden or more?

3. To remove 15% of disease burden or more?

CRITERION 5: EFFECT ON EQUITY

1. Would you say that the present distribution of the disease burden affects mainly the underprivileged in the population?

2. Would you say that the underprivileged would be the most likely to benefit from the results of the proposed research after its implementation?

3. Would you say that the proposed research has the overall potential to improve equity in disease burden distribution in the long term (e.g. 10 years)?

annual budget in the most rational way, without having already received any specific funding proposals. It will need to define its funding priorities and launch the calls for research proposals, while deciding in advance how much funding will be made available for each call. In the second scenario, an existing source of funding (such as a donor agency or a national ministry) will receive demands for research support from many research groups. The sum of their demands will greatly exceed the available funds.

In both scenarios, it is useful to systematically list (or categorize) all the competing research options. In the first scenario, this systematic list will ensure that all apparent research options are given a fair chance to compete against each other. In the second scenario, the systematic categorization will expose avenues of research in which there is fierce competition and those in which there seems to be no research capacity or research interest. The number of possible health research options is endless and limited only by imagination of all living researchers. Theoretical framework that enables systematic listing of such an endless spectrum of options is rather complex (1,4). However, the CHNRI methodology developed a process of systematic listing of all competing research options that respects that theoretical framework, but is also practical and intuitive. In both scenarios, the way we propose that all competing health research options should be listed (or categorized, if they have already been proposed for funding) was already shown in **Table 43-2** in previous chapter.

There is different *"depth"* of health research. The most fundamental categorization of all health research is shown in the first column, which we call *"research domains"*. There are three main domains: (i) health research to assess burden of health problem (disease) and its determinants; (ii) health research to improve performance of existing capacities to reduce the burden; and (iii) health research to develop new capacities to reduce the burden. All imaginable health research options should fall under one of those *"domains"*.

The next level of *"depth"* are broad *"research avenues"*, shown in the second column. Within each of those avenues, large number of *"research options"* can be envisaged (the third column). In practice, prioritization in health research investments will usually be made between the competing *"research options"*, as they correspond to 3-5-year research projects. That is a concept that both investors and researchers are familiar with and the level at which investment prioritization is already taking place (competition for research grants).

Finally, there is an even more specific level of *"depth"* of health research, which we call *"research questions"*. Each *"research option"* will propose to answer a number of *"research questions"*. These are very specific lines of research that correspond to a title of a single research article, which is another concept the researchers are familiar with.

In some instances, e.g., when the process is conducted as a mainly theoretical exercise to identify the most important specific questions that should be investigated within a given context, the prioritization using CHNRI methodology can be performed between the competing research questions. **Table 43-2** is an example of how research options (or questions) should be categorized before they are scored against the relevant criteria in order to be prioritized for investments. It should also be stressed that this step is not really necessary to identify priorities and can even be skipped, but it has an advantage of ensuring that the process is systematic, that it gives a fair chance to all types of health research, and that it exposes areas of fierce competitiveness and also of low interest and capacity.

7. Pre-scoring check of all competing health research options. Once that all competing research options have been systematically listed, technical experts should read them all again very carefully before the scoring. The experts need to ensure that scoring of all proposed research options against all proposed criteria should be possible. If problems are envisaged, research options should be reworded to enable their structured scoring by the experts.

The easiest way to do this is by keeping in mind the simple framework shown in **Figure 44-1**. The research options (or questions) must always suggest what is the new knowledge that they intend to generate. Also, it should be possible to envisage an uninterrupted link between this knowledge and its proposed effect on disease burden reduction through translation and implementation.

8. Scoring of health research options using the chosen set of criteria. At this stage, technical experts are expected to use their knowledge and experience to systematically score research options against the criteria chosen by process managers. The more experts agree to participate in the scoring, the more reliable is the outcome of the process. The experts should score all research options independently of each other. Each technical expert scores each research option by answering three questions per each criterion about that particular option. The answers to each question are simply: *"I agree"* (1 point), or *"I disagree"* (0 points). There will be cases in which technical experts will not feel informed enough to answer some questions. In all such cases, they should leave those answers blank (*"no answer"*). Furthermore, when technical experts are sufficiently informed to answer the question, but can *"neither agree nor disagree"*, they are allowed to enter a score of 0.5 (half a point). In this way, such choice is distinguished from *"no answer"*.

When finished with scoring, each technical expert should submit his/her own scores to the process management team independently from other experts. This will ensure that the overall scores represent a measure of their collective optimism toward each of the scored research options.

9. Calculating intermediate scores for each health research option. Each research option will first achieve its intermediate scores. The number of intermediate scores equals the number of selected criteria, as each intermediate score informs process managers on likelihood that the research option would satisfy a specific criterion (e.g., answerability, effectiveness, equity, etc). Once all the scores from all technical experts are submitted to process managers, intermediate scores for each criterion can be easily computed. **Table 44-4** presents how this should be done. In this simple example, 12 competing research options (options 1–12) are being scored, only one criterion is used (criterion 1), research options are assessed by three scoring technical experts (TE1–3) based on three related questions (question 1–3). In reality, there will be more research options, criteria, and scoring technical experts, but all the principles of calculating the intermediate scores will remain exactly the same as shown in **Table 44-4**.

The intermediate scores are computed by adding up all the informed (i.e., non-blank) answers ("1," "0," or "0.5"). The achieved sum is then divided by the number of received informed answers. Blanks are left out of the calculation in both numerator and denominator. All intermediate scores for all research options will, therefore, be assigned a value between 0 and 100%. In this way, the methodology deals with missing answers because it should not be expected that all technical experts would be sufficiently informed on each possible research option to score it against each possible criterion.

In the hypothetical case shown in **Table 44-4**, the values for intermediate score 1 (for criterion 1) ranged from 31% (option 11) to 78% (option 4). These figures now represent a measure of collective optimism among technical experts toward the likelihood that each of the proposed research options would satisfy the priority-setting criterion 1. They can now be prioritized and ranked according to this criterion based on the scores they received. Some of the expected advantages of this approach in comparison with other priority-setting methodologies are its transparency, limitation of personal biases through a structured survey, a systematic process with very specific outcomes and intuitive quantitative scores (3,4). The concerns over subjectivity of this approach are discussed in the concluding paragraph, where possible biases and limitations of the methodology are addressed.

Table 44-4. *An example of scoring of 12 hypothetical proposed research options (RO) by three technical experts (TE1-TE3) using a single criterion and computation o intermediate score for that criterion.*

	CRITERION 1										
	Question 1			Question 2			Question 3			Calcu-lation	Criterion Score
	TE1	TE2	TE3	TE1	TE2	TE3	TE1	TE2	TE3		
RO1	1	1	0	1	1	0	1	1	–	sum (6) / answers (8)	6/8 = 0.75
RO2	0	0.5	1	0.5	–	1	1	1	1	sum (6) / answers (8)	6/8 = 0.75
RO3	0	–	1	0.5	0	0	1	1	–	sum (3.5) / answers (7)	3.5/7 = 0.50
RO4	0.5	1	0	1	0.5	1	1	1	1	sum (7) / answers (9)	7/9 = 0.78
RO5	1	1	0	0	0	0.5	1	1	1	sum (5.5) / answers (9)	5.5/9 = 0.61
RO6	1	0	0	0	0.5	0	0	1	1	sum (3.5) / answers (9)	3.5/9 = 0.39
RO7	1	0.5	1	0	0	1	1	1	1	sum (6.5) / answers (9)	6.5/9 = 0.72
RO8	1	0.5	1	0	0	0	1	1	1	sum (5.5) / answers (9)	5.5/9 = 0.61
RO9	1	0	1	0	–	0.5	0	1	1	sum (4.5) / answers (8)	4.5/8 = 0.56
RO10	0	1	1	0	–	1	1	0.5	1	sum (5.5) / answers (8)	5.5/8 = 0.69
RO11	1	0.5	0	0	–	0	1	0	0	sum (2.5) / answers (8)	2.5/8 = 0.31
RO12	1	1	0	0	1	1	0.5	1	1	sum (6.5) / answers (9)	6.5/9 = 0.72

10. Obtaining further input from stakeholders. One of the biggest challenges in prioritizing health research investments is involving relevant stakeholders and the wider community in the process (7). The term "*stakeholders*" refers to all individuals and/or groups who have interest in prioritization of health research investments. Stakeholders will therefore comprise a large and very heterogeneous group. Examples of stakeholders include research funding agencies (e.g., governmental agencies, private organizations, public-private partnerships, international and regional organizations, taxpayers of a certain region), direct recipients of the funding (e.g., researchers and research institutions), users of the research (e.g., policy makers, industry, or the general population of a country), and any other group with interest in prioritization process (e.g., advocacy groups, journalists and media, lawyers, economists, experts in ethics, and many others). To ensure legitimacy and fairness of priority setting decisions in health research investments, involvement of a wide range of stakeholders is recommended.

Stakeholders from the wider community are usually not included in the process because they lack sufficient technical expertise. The CHNRI methodology developed a strategy of involving the stakeholders in the process regardless of their technical expertise. This can be done by modifying intermediate scores (which are entirely based on the structured input from technical experts) according to the stakeholders' system of values. In this way, the final research priority score for each research option will contain the input from both technical experts and the stakeholders. Although the stakeholders do not have enough technical expertise to score research options according to chosen priority-setting criteria, they can still score the chosen criteria. This is expected to reveal how much each criterion matters to them relative to the others. In this way, the wider group of stakeholders may still substantially influence the final outcome of the process. The stakeholders can: (i) define minimal score (threshold) for each intermediate score (criterion) that needs to be achieved to consider any research option a funding priority; and (ii) allocate different weights to intermediate scores, so that the overall score is not a simple arithmetic mean of the intermediate scores, but rather the weighted mean that reflects relative values assigned to each criterion by the stakeholders.

Thresholds will prevent investments in research options that dramatically fail any of the criteria to which stakeholders are particularly sensitive, regardless how well these research options were scored against other criteria. Weights will ensure that some intermediate scores, which relate to priority setting criteria that are seen as more important, would influence the value of the final score more than the others. Values for thresholds and weights can be obtained through a simple survey conducted among the appropriate group of representatives of the stakeholders (*"larger reference group"*). **Table 44-5** shows an example. Further details are available in the article by Kapiriri et al (8).

11. Adjusting intermediate scores taking into account the values of stakeholders. The managers of the process need to compute average thresholds and weights for each criterion based on the suggestions obtained from the survey in a larger reference group of stakeholders. They need to check if all intermediate scores for all research options pass all the suggested thresholds. Research options that fail to pass all the thresholds should be disqualified at this stage and not considered funding priorities.

Then, every intermediate score received by each research option should be multiplied by the average weight (amount of assigned US$) suggested by the larger reference group of stakeholders. The products represent *"weighted intermediate scores"*. These scores will be used to compute an overall score (see next step), which will reflect both the input from technical experts and the stakeholders. The actual size and composition of the larger reference group of stakeholders will depend on the context. Small reference group of stakeholders is appropriate when several major donors to any health research-funding organization want to influence priority setting process. They can set very specific thresholds and weights for each criterion. Large and diverse reference group of stakeholders is more appropriate for priority setting for health research on problems of regional or global importance.

12. Calculating overall priority scores and assigning ranks. Intermediate scores for each research option that are based on the scores received from technical experts will range between 0%–100%. At that point, the managers of the process can simply agree that all criteria that they initially chose for priority setting are equally important (because all of them are needed to get from new knowledge to decrease in disease burden). In that case, an overall research priority score (RPS) will be a simple mean of all intermediate scores.

In a hypothetical example shown in **Figure 44-2**, research option received five intermediate scores from technical experts: 60%, 80%, 70%, 60%

Table 44-5. *An example of a simple questionnaire that can be used to survey different stakeholders and obtain their input into the CHNRI process.*

Below are the criteria that can be used to set priorities in health research investments.

– In the "threshold" column, please enter the minimum acceptable score (on a scale 0–100) for each criterion that should be achieved by proposed health research to receive funding support.

– In the "weight" column, please distribute a total of $ 100 to the 5 proposed criteria to reflect how much does each criterion matter to you.

CRITERION	THRESHOLD	WEIGHT
Answerability (Likelihood that the research will indeed reach its proposed endpoints)		
Effectiveness (Likelihood that the results of the research will have effect against the disease)		
Deliverability (Likelihood that the results of the research will be delivered to those who need them)		
Maximum impact (Likelihood that the research can influence a substantial share of disease cases)		
Equity (Likelihood that the results of the research will improve health inequities in the population)		

and 80%, respectively. This would mean that its overall RPS can be computed as follows:

$$RPS = (60\%+80\%+70\%+60\%+80\%)/5 = 70\%$$

However, if stakeholders were also involved and a survey was undertaken among them to include their values in the process, it could provide hypothetical average thresholds for the five criteria (50%, 50%, 40%, 20%, and 60%, respectively), and also hypothetical average weights (US $15, $15, $15, $30, and $25, respectively). In this case, the initial check will establish that all thresholds have been passed and that the research option from the example below remains in the contest for the funding. Then, the weights are applied as shown below and the overall RPS is corrected to 69.5%. After computing weighted RPS for all research options that passed all the thresholds, the options can be ranked by priority according to their achieved RPS.

13. Performing an analysis of agreement between scorers. Scoring performed by technical experts is both independent and transparent to process managers. Therefore, the CHNRI methodology offers the potential to expose the points of the greatest agreement and the greatest controversy among the experts. Identification of these points should allow more focused discussion on the priorities after the completion of the process. In this way, in addition to the information on how each research option complies with the chosen priority-setting criteria, investors and policy makers are informed about the amount of agreement between the experts on each research option.

The level of agreement can be assessed for each specific research option using agreement statistics (κ). This calculation becomes extremely complicated when the number of scorers exceeds 2 and the number of rating categories exceeds 2. We suggest that all observations where the expert reviewer chose 0.5 (*"knowledgeable, but the answer is indeterminate"*) should first be recoded as missing values, restricting the number of rating categories to 2 and making the calculation of the κ statistics more meaningful. The decision to choose 0.5 is nearly equivalent to choosing to leave the answer field blank, since in both situations the expert reviewer is revealing that his or her answer to the question is unknown.

Kappa value should be computed for each research question as a measure of the level of agreement among the scorers. When the number of scorers is variable across subjects, statistical significance testing cannot be performed. Interpreting κ statistics is arbitrary, and the greater the κ, the greater the level of agreement. Further details on calculation of κ can be found elsewhere (9).

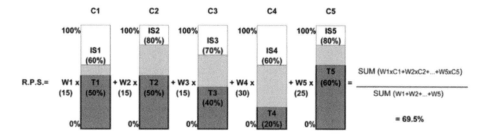

Figure 44-2. *Calculation of overall research priority score (RPS) based on 5 hypothetically chosen priority setting criteria (C1-C5); values W1-W5 are factors by which each criterion is weighted (computed as average weights for each criterion obtained from the survey among stakeholders – see Step XI); in dark green, achieved intermediate scores (IS1-IS5) for each research option (see Step X); in red, the required thresholds for intermediate scores for each criterion (computed as average thresholds for each criterion obtained from the survey among stakeholders – see Step XI). The final "research priority score" (RPS) for each proposed research option is defined as their weighted average: [W1 × IS1 + W2 × IS2 + … + Wn × ISn / (W1 + W2+ … + Wn). In the hypothetical case below, the overall RPS should equal (15 × 0.6 + 15 × 0.8 + 15 × 0.7 + 30 × 0.6 + 25 × 0.8) / 100 = 69.5%.*

14. Linking computed research priority scores with investment decisions. There are two main scenarios in which process managers will link research priority scores with investment decisions. The first one is designing an investment strategy before actual investments are made. The second one is modifying an already existing investment portfolio to reduce risk and/or increase returns on investments.

In the first scenario, a donor agency or organization will conduct an informative CHNRI process to define its priorities before it commits to funding and launching of the calls for grant proposals. In this case, we argue that investing in health research is fundamentally not much different than investing in stocks of different companies on the stock market. Rather than making investment decisions by comparing companies, investors in health research will be choosing between many groups of health researchers and their research grant proposals. Seen in this way, investors in health research should learn from the vast experience and literature on investment in financial markets (10).

Among many analogies, *"high risk"* health research investment is the one with very uncertain (or unlikely) answerability, transferability (usefulness) or potential impact on disease burden reduction. *"High profit"* health research investment is the one offering very high reduction in disease burden if successful. There will be investments in health research that offer lower *"profits"*, but also at lower *"risks"* (such as research on improvement of existing interventions);

and also *"high-risk high-profit"* investment options (e.g., research to develop new and non-existent vaccines against malaria or AIDS).

There is always a risk and a potential profit associated with any investment. The risk preference of the investors will therefore represent an important determinant of their investment strategy. For a rational investor, the probability of success always needs to be balanced against the probability of failure. The preferences of both those who tend to seek or to avoid risk have costs in terms of reduced expected profits, which is easy to demonstrate with standard expected utility theory (11). While this theory does not normatively qualify some preferences as better than others, a common suggestion is that rational actors who are sufficiently large for risk pooling should base investment decisions on preferences that are risk-neutral, as this strategy leads to highest profits in the long run (11,12). This implies that an unbalanced investment portfolio, in which large majority of investments are in *"low-risk low-profit"* health research options or in *"high-risk high-profit"* options, is neither rational nor responsible. However, because there is very little accountability for poor investment decisions in health research and their evaluation in terms of benefits for the society, we are witnessing an increasing trend of global research portfolio becoming unbalanced and favoring *"high-risk high-profit"* health research options (12).

In an alternative scenario, international funding agency or national government has already been funding health research for several years and would like to improve the mix of supported research options. In this case, a classical *"Program Budgeting and Marginal Analysis"* would be appropriate: (i) identifying funding cut-off points and RPSs for funded research options; (ii) comparing research options that have no allocated funding to existing funding programs; (iii) assessing relative value of each priority using the same criteria; (iv) releasing resources from existing programs to support additional new priority research areas (13). All decisions that need to be made within this scenario are based on: (i) defining RPS and cost of each research option, either already supported or proposed as an alternative; (ii) maximizing the sum of RPS values of supported research options within a given fixed budget; (iii) if the sum of RPS scores within an existing program is lower than the sum of the alternative, resources should be shifted from the existing into the new research options.

15. Feedback and revision. CHNRI methodology is a process which does not end with definition of health research priorities and allocation of funding. The investments are expected to lead to changes in the context over time in terms of disease burden. Other components of the contexts may also change substantially, from stakeholders' system of values to limits in space or risk management preferences. All these changes can be accounted for by: (i) adding further research options to the list; (ii) adding additional criteria; (ii) re-scoring all research options in the redefined context; and (iii) revising thresholds and weights placed on intermediate scores. In this way, the research investment portfolio will continuously be adjusted to the context and aim to reduce the existing disease burden most cost-effectively and in an equitable way.

16. Conclusion. Some of the possible advantages of CHNRI's research priority-setting methodology include: (i) transparent presentation of the context and criteria in the priority setting process; (ii) management of the process by investors themselves over its entire duration; (iii) structured way of scoring, which should limit specific interests or personal biases; (iv) involvement of non-technical stakeholders in priority setting; (v) the flexibility of the process provided by adding or subtracting the criteria; (vi) potential to revise weights and thresholds based on the changes in the context; (vii) simple presentation of the strengths and weaknesses of each competing research option; (viii) possibility to rank research options according to each individual criterion; (ix) a simple quantitative outcome that is easy to present, justify, and explain to policy-makers; (x) exposure of the points of the greatest agreement and controversy. Although the proposed guidelines are based on wide consultations and extensive review and assessment of previous approaches, the CHNRI method will eventually benefit from independent validation in various settings in the future. It will be even more challenging to define the real impact of the process on shifting global research priorities. That is the ultimate goal of CHNRI method and the one that will leverage support for health research to make more impact on the disease burden in the real world.

Still, the methodology is not free of several possible biases. Although the advantages mentioned above represent a serious attempt to deal with many issues inherent to a highly complex process of research investment priority setting, there are still concerns over the validity of the CHNRI approach and related biases. One of them is related to the fact many possible good ideas (*"research investment options"*) may not have been included in the initial list of research options that was scored by the experts, and to the potential bias toward items that get the greatest press. The spectrum of research investment options listed initially in this exercise was derived through a systematic process, but it is not endless and it cannot ever cover every single research idea. Specific research methodologies (i.e., randomized clinical trials) are not mentioned because the research questions listed in that exercise are unlikely to be answered by a single well-defined study. Therefore, the CHNRI process aims to achieve reasonable coverage of the spectrum of possible ideas.

Another concern over the CHNRI process is that its end product represents a possibly biased opinion of a very limited group of involved people. In theory, a chosen group of experts can have biased views in comparison with any other potential groups of experts. However, the number of people who possess enough experience, expertise, and knowledge on the issue to be able to judge a very diverse spectrum of research questions is rather limited. If one thinks of this *"pool of technical experts"* as the whole population that could theoretically be used to solicit expert opinion on the questions that need to be asked, we then propose selection of a *"sample"* from that population, based on their track record. The larger and the more diverse this sample is, the less likely it is that there would be considerable differences in the composition of the initial list of questions (or results of the scoring process) if some other group of experts had been selected.

Acknowledgement: Originally published as: Igor Rudan, Jennifer L. Gibson, Shanthi Ameratunga, Shams El Arifeen, Zulfiqar A. Bhutta, Maureen Black, Robert E. Black, Kenneth H. Brown, Harry Campbell, Ilona Carneiro, Kit Yee Chan, Daniel Chandramohan, Mickey Chopra, Simon Cousens, Gary L. Darmstadt, Julie Meeks Gardner, Sonja Y. Hess, Adnan A. Hyder, Lydia Kapiriri, Margaret Kosek, Claudio F. Lanata, Mary Ann Lansang, Joy E. Lawn, Mark Tomlinson, Alexander C. Tsai, Jayne Webster on behalf of Child Health and Nutrition Research Initiative (CHNRI): Setting priorities in global child health research investments: Guidelines for implementation of the CHNRI method. Reprinted with permission from Edinburgh University Global Health Society under Creative Commons Attribution License (Croat Med J 2007; 126:237-240). Child Health and Nutrition Research Initiative (CHNRI) of the Global Forum for Health Research was supported by The World Bank in conducting this work.

References

1. Rudan I, El Arifeen S, Black RE. A systematic methodology for setting priorities in child health research investments. In: A new approach for systematic priority setting. Dhaka: Child Health and Nutrition Research Initiative, 2006.
2. Leroy JL, Habicht JP, Pelto G, Bertozzi SM. Current priorities in health research funding and lack of impact on the number of child deaths per year. Am J Public Health 2007; 97:219–223.
3. Rudan I, Gibson J, Kapiriri L, Lansang MA, Hyder AA, Lawn J, et al. Setting priorities in global child health research investments: assessment of principles and practice. Croat Med J 2007; 48:595–604.
4. Rudan I, El Arifeen S, Black RE, Campbell H. Childhood pneumonia and diarrhoea: setting our priorities right. Lancet Infect Dis 2007; 7:56–61.
5. Tomlinson M, Chopra M, Sanders D, Bradshaw D, Hendricks M, Greenfield D, et al. Setting priorities in child health research investments for South Africa. PLoS Med 2007; 4:e259.

6. Chisholm D, Flisher AJ, Lund C, Patel V, Saxena S, Thornicroft G, et al. Scale up services for mental disorders: a call for action. Lancet 2007; 370:1241–1252.

7. Ham C, Robert G (eds). Reasonable rationing: international experience of priority setting in health care. New York, NY: McGraw-Hill, 2003.

8. Kapiriri L, Tomlinson M, Chopra M, El Arifeen S, Black RE, Rudan I. Setting priorities in global child health research investments: addressing values of stakeholders. Croat Med J 2007; 48:618–627.

9. Cicchetti DV, Feinstein AR. High agreement but low kappa: II. Resolving the paradoxes. J Clin Epidemiol 1990; 43:551–558.

10. Graham B. The intelligent investor. New York: Harper Collins, 2003.

11. Elbasha EH. Risk aversion and uncertainty in cost-effectiveness analysis: the expected-utility, moment-generating function approach. Health Econ 2005; 14:457–470.

12. Arrow KJ, Lind RC. Uncertainty and the evaluation of public investment decisions. Am Econ Rev 1970; 60:364–378.

13. Mitton CR, Donaldson C. Setting priorities and allocating resources in health regions: lessons from a project evaluating program budgeting and marginal analysis (PBMA). Health Policy 2003; 64:335–348.

CHAPTER 45.

Setting health research priorities using the CHNRI method: Involving funders

In 2007 and 2008, the World Health Organization's Department for Child and Adolescent Health and Development (later renamed as WHO MNCAH – Maternal, Newborn, Child and Adolescent Health) commissioned five large exercises to define research priorities related to the five major causes of child deaths for the period up to the year 2015. The exercises were based on the CHNRI (Child Health and Nutrition Research Initiative) method, which was just being introduced at the time (1,2). The selected causes were childhood pneumonia, diarrhoea, birth asphyxia, neonatal infections and preterm birth/ low birth weight (3–7). The context for those exercises was clearly defined: to identify research that could help reduce mortality in children under five years of age in low and middle income countries by the year 2015. The criteria used in all five exercises were the "*standard*" CHNRI criteria: (i) answerability of the research question; (ii) likelihood of the effectiveness of the resulting intervention; (iii) deliverability (with affordability and sustainability); (iv) potential to reduce disease burden; and (v) effect on equity (3–7).

The five criteria used by the scorers were intuitive as they followed the path from generating new knowledge to having an impact on the cause of death. They were chosen with a view to identifying research questions that were most likely to contribute to finding effective solutions to the problems. However, after the five exercises – all of which were published in respected international journals (3–7) – the WHO officers were left with an additional question: how "*fundable*" were the identified priorities, i.e. how attractive were they to research funders? More specifically, should another criterion be added to the CHNRI exercises, which would evaluate the likelihood of obtaining funding support for specific research questions?

To answer these questions, coordinators of the CHNRI exercises at the WHO agreed that it would be useful to invite a number of representatives from large funding organizations interested in child health research to take part in a consultation process at the WHO. The process aimed to explore funders' perspectives in prioritization of health research. The funders would be presented with the leading research priorities identified through the CHNRI exercises and asked to discuss any potential variation in their likelihood of being funded. If all the leading priorities were equally attractive to funders and likely to attract funding support, this would indicate that the *"standard"* CHNRI criteria were sufficient for the process of prioritization. However, if there were large differences in attractiveness of the identified research priorities to funders, then adding another criterion to the exercise – *"likelihood of obtaining funding support"*, or simply *"fundability"* – would be a useful addition to the standard CHNRI framework.

1. The meeting with the funders (Geneva, 27-29 March 2009). In March 2009, MNCAH invited 40 representatives from funding organizations, including the Bill and Melinda Gates Foundation, the Wellcome Trust, National Institutes of Health USA, Department for International Development UK, Save the Children, INCLEN, EPICENTRE, UNICEF, USAID, PATH, Ministry of Science and Technology of India, Ministries of Health of Zambia, Pakistan and Brazil, Global Forum for Health Research, Trinity Global Support Foundation, Children's Investment Fund Foundation, Osaka Research Institute for Maternal and Child Health. Eventually, 16 representatives of funding agencies agreed to take part in the exercise under the condition of anonymity. Moreover, it was understood that their input would not necessarily be the official position of their respective funding agencies, nor would it create any form of funding obligation.

CAUSE OF DEATH (1 / 5) - e.g. PNEUMONIA		
NAME:		
ORGANIZATION:		

	RANK?	US$?
RESEARCH QUESTION 1		
RESEARCH QUESTION 2		
RESEARCH QUESTION 3		
RESEARCH QUESTION 4		
RESEARCH QUESTION 5		
RESEARCH QUESTION 6		
RESEARCH QUESTION 7		
RESEARCH QUESTION 8		
RESEARCH QUESTION 9		
RESEARCH QUESTION 10		

Figure 45-1. *A questionnaire that was given to 16 funder representatives at the meeting to obtain information useful to understanding funding attractiveness of different research priorities.*

Having explained the aims of the consultation meeting to the representatives of funding agencies, the 16 participants were presented with a list of the top 10 research priorities for each of the five major causes of child deaths: pneumonia, diarrhea, birth asphyxia, neonatal infections and preterm birth/low birth weight (3–7). This set of 50 research priorities represented roughly the top 5% of all the research ideas submitted for scoring during the CHNRI exercises. The WHO coordinators (RB and JM) explained each of the 50 leading research priorities to the 16 donor representatives. Then, the 16 donor representatives were provided with the list of research priorities and asked to individually identify those that were most likely to receive funding support from their respective organizations.

Funding attractiveness was measured in two ways. Firstly, funder representatives were asked to rank the identified research priorities according to their likelihood to receive funding support under an organization's current investment policies and practices. Secondly, funding attractiveness was measured by asking funder representatives to distribute a theoretical US$ 100 among the research priorities that seem most fundable. Results were used to facilitate discussion on what makes a research question attractive (or unattractive) for funding support. The scoring sheet that was given to meeting participants is shown in **Figure 45-1**. While they did not need to provide their name or organization, they were asked to assign ranks 1–10 to the ten research priorities identified for each of the five causes of death (column 1), and also to distribute a hypothetical US$ 100 to different research priorities in concordance to the likely funding support that they may obtain.

Sixteen participants scored the identified research priorities according to the instructions (**Figure 45-1**). The average ranks across the 16 participants (1 = most likely to be funded; 10 = least likely to be funded) assigned to the 50 research priorities ranged from 3.7 to 7.2. The average US$ amount assigned to research priorities ranged from US$ 20.1 to US$ 2.5. There was general consistency between ranks and the US$ assigned to research priorities.

Importantly, the analysis of the collective input based on the 2nd column (i.e., assigned US$), presented in **Figure 45-2**, clearly shows that there was a rather substantial departure of the assigned funds from that expected at random: if all research priorities were equally likely to obtain support from the funders, then all the bars would be extending only to the line that represents an investment of US$ 10.0. Furthermore, four research priorities (8%) clearly stood out from the rest (8). It was agreed that they might provide a starting point from which MNCAH Department could concentrate its efforts. These four research priorities are shown in **Table 45-1**.

2. An analysis of the exercise with funder representatives. The results were analysed after the first day of the meeting and presented to donor representatives at the beginning of the second day of the meeting. An open discussion was held with participants to understand and interpret the results of their collective input. Participants agreed that the most important criteria for research prioritisation differed between researchers and funders. Researchers tended to value answerability, effectiveness, deliverability, impact on the burden and equity. Funders were also interested in the clarity and specificity of research ideas, value for money, novelty, international competitiveness of the groups proposing the research, linkages to broader societal issues, and complementarity with other long–term strategic investments that were already made. An important point in the discussion was that researchers and research funders, especially those in the private sector, often speak quite different languages. Researchers need to be clear on what their goals are and communicate these in more readily understood terms. This point is particularly important because it implies that the CHNRI exercises' research priorities that were identified as most likely to generate useful new knowledge may not be considered equally relevant by the funders. This should certainly be taken into account when presenting and discussing the results of the CHNRI exercises.

Moreover, there seem to be important differences between the categories of funders in the criteria that they use to decide on research priorities. Generally, all investors in health research are concerned with answerability of the proposed research ideas in an ethical way, feasibility and value for money. However, some may be particularly interested in potential for forming partnerships between researchers and industry to increase the translation of findings and their application. Ministries and international organizations appeared more interested in deliverability, affordability and sustainability of the resulting interventions, local and national research capacities to carry out the proposed research ideas, and whether a research question is linked to an ongoing public debate or an important societal issue. Industrial donors may be primarily motivated to generate patents and translate research results into commercial products. Finally, society as a whole may be more concerned with issues of safety and equity and ask whether implementation of research results would widen the existing socio-economic gaps.

Transparency of research priority setting processes must, therefore, begin with those who invest. Perceived returns on investments in health research should be clearly stated at the beginning of the process. They may be defined as reduction in disease burden wherever public money is being invested. Investors from industries may see patentable products as their preferred returns.

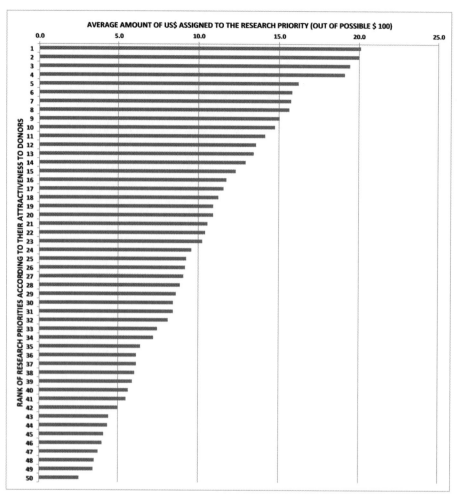

Figure 45-2. *The results of the collective input from 16 funder representatives, showing large differences in funding attractiveness between 50 research priorities. (No substantial differences in funding attractiveness would be indicated by equality of the scores on the horizontal axis at the 10.0 US$ line).*

Non-profit organizations may be primarily interested in increased media attention for their agenda. The context in which investment prioritization takes place is thus primarily defined by expected returns of the funders. Moreover, their investment styles may be balanced and responsible (suggested for those investing public funds), risk–averting (which may be preferred among some industrial partners) or risk–seeking and biased towards high risk – high profit avenues of health research (which may be typical for some industry and not-for-profit organizations).

Table 45-1. *The four research priorities (8%) that were identified as positive outliers in terms of their likelihood to obtain funding support.*

- Evaluate the quality of community workers to adequately assess, recognize danger signs, refer and treat acute respiratory infections (ARI) in different contexts and settings.
- What are the barriers against appropriate use of oral rehydration therapy?
- What are the feasibility, effectiveness and cost of different approaches to promote the following home care practices (breastfeeding, cord/skin, care seeking, handwashing)?
- What are the feasibility, effectiveness and cost of a scheme of routine home visits for initiation of supportive practices, detection of illness and newborn survival?

Apart from funders' perceived returns and their investment styles, the population, geographic area and disease burden of interest, the time frame in which returns are expected is an important defining component of the overall context. Priorities can differ substantially if the overall context is one of great urgency to tackle a problem, or whether decisions are made on very long–term, strategic investments.

3. Conclusions. The meeting with research funders organized by the WHO MNCAH department in March 2009 was exceptionally useful in understanding that funders certainly have their own views on what represents an attractive funding option. These views are not generalizable and may differ between categories of funders. Moreover, funders' perspectives are often quite different from those of researchers, or wider stakeholder groups. It is important to involve funders early in the process of setting research priorities, such as the CHNRI process, to encourage their ownership of the results. Funder–supported criteria must be taken into account, in addition to those preferred by the researchers and wider stakeholders. Otherwise, the outcomes of research prioritization exercises may have very limited impact on funders' decision making.

The key value of the CHNRI method to funders lies in its ability to transparently lay out the potential risks and benefits associated with investing in many competing research ideas, drawing on collective knowledge of the broad research community. Results of the CHNRI process represent an attempt on the part of researchers to communicate their views and opinions to funders in a way that is easily understood, transparent, replicable and intuitive. It provides useful additional information that funders may, or may not take into account when deciding on their own research agenda. From a methodological perspective, finding appropriate and effective ways of involving funders in future CHNRI exercises, communicating the outcomes clearly, and securing their commitment to acknowledge the results of the CHNRI process remain considerable challenges. An even greater challenge in future years will be to develop tools that can detect and evaluate the impact of CHNRI exercises on funder decision making and any change in funding priorities as a direct result of the CHNRI process. This should be particularly relevant to those who make decisions about investing public funds, whose primary agenda should be improving public health in the most cost–effective way – a target that CHNRI exercises should serve quite well.

Acknowledgement: *Originally published as: Igor Rudan, Sachiyo Yoshida, Kit Yee Chan, Simon Cousens, Devi Sridhar, Rajiv Bahl and Jose Martines: Setting health research priorities using the CHNRI method: Involving funders. Reprinted with permission from Edinburgh University Global Health Society under Creative Commons Attribution License (Journal of Global Health 2016; 1:010301). JM and RB organized the consultation at the World Health Organization and IR moderated the consultation process. We sincerely thank the representatives of the funding agencies for taking part in the consultation process and providing useful information under the condition of anonymity. SY, RB and JM are the employees of the World Health Organization. Their views expressed here do not necessarily represent the views of the Organization.*

References

1. Rudan I, Chopra M, Kapiriri L, Gibson J, Lansang MA, Carneiro I, et al. Setting priorities in global child health research investments: universal challenges and conceptual framework. Croat Med J 2008; 49:307–317.
2. Rudan I, Gibson JL, Ameratunga S, El Arifeen S, Bhutta ZA, Black M, et al. Setting priorities in global child health research investments: guidelines for implementation of the CHNRI Method. Croat Med J 2008; 49:720–733.
3. Rudan I, El Arifeen S, Bhutta ZA, Black RE, Brooks A, Chan KY, et al. Setting research priorities to reduce global mortality from childhood pneumonia by 2015. PLoS Med 2011; 8:e1001099.
4. Fontaine O, Kosek M, Bhatnagar S, Boschi-Pinto C, Chan KY, Duggan C, et al. Setting research priorities to reduce global mortality from childhood diarrhoea by 2015. PLoS Med 2009; 6:e41.
5. Bahl R, Martines J, Ali N, Bhan MK, Carlo W, Chan KY, et al. Research priorities to reduce global mortality from newborn infections by 2015. Pediatr Inf Dis J 2009; 28(Suppl 1): S43–8.
6. Lawn JE, Bahl R, Bergstrom S, Bhutta ZA, Darmstadt GL, Ellis M, et al. Setting research priorities to reduce almost one million deaths from birth asphyxia by 2015. PLoS Med 2011; 8:e1000389.
7. Bahl R, Bhandari N, Bhutta ZA, Biloglav Z, Edmond K, Iyengar S, et al. Setting research priorities to reduce global mortality from low birth weight by 2015. J Glob Health 2012; 2:010403.
8. Anonymous. Consultation Proceedings: Identifying priorities for child health research to achieve Millennium Development Goal 4. DRAFT April 30, 2009. Geneva: World Health Organization, 2009, pp. 1–29.

CHAPTER 46.

Setting health research priorities using the CHNRI method: Involving stakeholders

When decisions on investments into health research are made, the term *"stakeholders"* refers to all individuals and/or groups who have interest in prioritisation of those investments. The stakeholders will therefore comprise a large and highly heterogeneous group. Some apparent examples may include research funding agencies (e.g. governmental agencies, private organisations, public-private partnerships, international and regional organisations, taxpayers of a certain region), direct recipients of the funding (e.g., researchers, and research institutions), beneficiaries of the research (e.g. policy makers and the general population of a country), and any other group with interest in prioritisation process (e.g. advocacy groups, journalists and media, lawyers, economists, experts in ethics, and many others).

Two fundamental characteristics of any acceptable and successful priority setting process are legitimacy and fairness (1). In order to ensure the legitimacy and fairness of the priority setting decisions in health research investments, involvement of a wide range of stakeholders (and / or eliciting their values) is needed. Health research priorities are presently mainly driven by technical experts (2–5). The results of prioritisation are therefore in danger of being mostly influenced by their personal views, with minimal input from representatives from the wider community who also may have interest in the process but lack the technical expertise. Since the values and criteria important to scientists and technical experts may vary remarkably from those of the other relevant stakeholders (6-8), the relevance of eliciting wider stakeholders' input is increasingly being acknowledged (9–11). However, the main challenge is to develop a systematic, flexible and repeatable strategy on how this can be achieved in different contexts.

The literature on priority setting for health interventions identifies two main strategies: (i) stakeholders' values may impact decisions through procedural processes (by having access to the decisions and the rationales behind the decisions, and by having the authority to deliberate on the decisions and influence the final outcome); (ii) stakeholders' values can be directly elicited using quantitative methods (through surveys where respondents rank, weigh or rate their values) and qualitative methods (involving individual interviews,

Delphi technique, complaints procedures or group discussions, concept mapping, citizen's jury and public meetings) (12). The main challenges in those attempts have mainly been the lack of capacity for some stakeholders to engage in meaningful deliberations (13) and how to practically incorporate the elicited stakeholders' values in decision-making (12,14). This paper presents our suggestions and experiences on how the values and interests of large and diverse group of stakeholders could still be incorporated in decisions on health research investment priorities.

1. Systematic methodology for setting priorities in health research investments. Child Health and Nutrition Research Initiative (CHNRI) has recently presented the main concepts underlying systematic methodology for setting priorities in health research investments (9–11). It is a flexible methodology that firstly defines all criteria relevant to priority setting in a given context. In the second step, technical experts are responsible for systematic listing of research options and for scoring all those options against all the defined criteria using simple and discriminative set of questions. This eventually leads to all research options receiving several different intermediate scores, each addressing one important criterion relevant to priority setting. These intermediate scores could, for example, address the criteria of answerability of research options in ethical way, efficacy and effectiveness of resulting interventions, deliverability, affordability and sustainability of resulting interventions, maximum potential for disease burden reduction and predicted impact on equity (9–11). The final research priority score, which describes the overall value of each research option when all criteria are taken into account, is then computed as the average of the intermediate scores. Research priority score then becomes a basis for ranking the competing research options and for combining their value with their proposed cost to achieve the optimal mix of investments within a fixed funding budget. Up to this point, priority setting process is based on profound understanding and knowledge of technical details and scientific literature. Hence, it is not proposed to involve non-technical stakeholders in the computation of these intermediate scores.

2. Strategies within CHNRI's methodology for addressing stakeholders' values. The intermediate scores assigned to each research option during the process described above can still be modified to include the values of non-technical groups of stakeholders before the final research priority score is computed. The wider group of stakeholders may: (i) define minimal score (threshold) for each intermediate score (criterion) that needs to be achieved to consider any research option a funding priority; (ii) allocate weights to intermediate scores so that the final research priority score is not their simple arithmetic mean, but rather the weighted mean that reflects relative values assigned to each criterion. In this way, some intermediate scores (priority setting criteria) would influence the value of the final score more than the others. The concept of introducing thresholds prevents investments into research options that dramatically fail one of the important criteria, regardless how well they fare when scored against other criteria. The concept of weights is graphically presented in **Figure 46-1**.

The concept of pre-defined thresholds on each of the criteria prevents funding of proposed research option if it largely fails one important criterion, regardless how well it complies with all other criteria. In the first exercise presented in the results section, stakeholders' representatives were asked to draw a horizontal line on a vertical bar ranging between 0 and 100 (as in **Figure 46-1**) to define where they would like to see minimum thresholds for compliance with each of the relevant criteria. Their suggestions were then turned into quantitative values and the average of these values was chosen as the threshold. In the second exercise thresholds were derived post-hoc, as the lowest 10% of the scores on any given criteria.

The concept of weights complements the concept of thresholds. The scoring performed by technical experts, which eventually leads to intermediate scores, is based on the assumption that all criteria are mutually independent and equally important (**Figure 46-1**). The concept of weights makes some

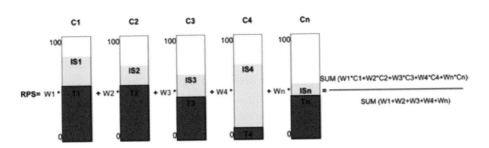

Figure 46-1. *Graphical presentation of the concept of thresholds and weights (T1-Tn and W1-Wn). A priority-setting tool below addresses n key priority setting criteria (e.g. answerability, effectiveness, deliverability, maximum potential for disease burden reduction and impact on equity); intermediate scores for this particular research options had values IS1-ISn. Input from stakeholders resulted in values W1-Wn, i.e. factors by which each criterion's value (intermediate score) is weighted, and threshold scores (T1-Tn) needed to be met within each criterion in order for the proposed research option to be considered a priority. The final "research priority score" (RPS) for each proposed research avenue is defined as their weighted average: [W1 x (Criterion 1 score) + W2 x (Criterion 2 score) + ... + Wn x (Criterion n score)] / (W1+...+Wn)*

intermediate scores more important than the others, which is determined by the stakeholders. In this way, their system of values is reflected in assigning different weights to criteria used for priority setting before the final priority score is computed for each research option. Numerical values for these weights can be obtained through survey conducted among the appropriate group of representatives of the stakeholders (termed *"larger reference group"* in further text, LRG).

In this paper, we specified thresholds and weights needed to address stakeholders' values within CHNRI methodology using three different versions of a questionnaire. We aimed to assess stakeholders' values for priority setting in global health research investments. We tested questionnaires that presented different levels of complexity and details of the questions that stakeholders' representatives would be asked. We also aimed to evaluate different strategies of turning their responses into numerical thresholds and weights.

3. Design of questionnaires used to assess stakeholders' values. We tested three different versions of questionnaires (**Table 46-1**). The simplest version asked five simple questions that captured the essence of each of the criteria relevant to priority setting that were highlighted by CHNRI's previous work on conceptual framework for the methodology (9-11). The questions were short and they used layman's terms. The intermediate version of the questionnaire (**Table 46-1**) listed some technical terms that described each of the five criteria relevant to priority setting (9–11). These terms required some understanding of public health concepts and they were therefore used in a smaller group of stakeholders' representatives (details on composition of larger reference groups are given in further text). Finally, the most complex version was tested in a relatively small group of highly motivated people with good understanding of the issues related to health research investments, aiming to obtain deeper understanding of the elicited weights.

In the simplest version of the questionnaire, output from stakeholders' representatives were simple ranks of the five listed criteria in ascending order, with the first indicating the most important criterion (ranks ranged from 1 to 5). An average of the individually suggested rank for each of the five criteria was computed. Then, if all five criteria were valued exactly the same, their average rank would be 3.0. Therefore, any increase from this expected value towards the theoretical maximum of 5.0 indicated lower assigned importance to the criterion, while any decrease towards the theoretical minimum of 1.0 indicated greater assigned importance. Dividing the expected average rank (3.0) by the observed (i.e. obtained) average rank gave us numerical weights for the five criteria. These weights can theoretically range between 3.0 (which is the expected average rank of 3.0 divided by theoretically most favourable average rank of 1.0) and 0.6 (which is the expected average rank of 3.0 divided by theoretically the least favourable average rank of 5.0). In this way, intermediate scores for criteria that were seen as more important by stakeholders' representatives were assigned greater weight (of up to 3 times), while the weight of the criteria that were considered less important by the LRG could be reduced in importance (up to 40% reduction).

In the other two versions of the questionnaire, stakeholders' representatives were asked to allocate 100 US$ (this amount was set arbitrarily because it is intuitive) across the five criteria. The amount allocated to each criterion reflected its relative importance to the stakeholders. Eventually, every criterion then had its average "*value*" expressed in US$. All intermediate scores could then be multiplied with average value of weights (in US$), added up and then divided by 100 (US$). This gave the final research priority score, which again had a value between 0 and 100.

4. Composition of larger reference group of stakeholders' representatives. The CHNRI methodology proposes that the process of setting priorities in health research investments should involve two main groups: (i) technical working group (TWG), which consists of technical experts (mainly scientists) who assign a value (the intermediate score) to each proposed health research option by judging its likelihood to address each of the criteria relevant to priority setting; (ii) larger reference group (LRG), which should comprise representatives of all other stakeholders not represented in the TWG. The initiators of the priority setting process (e.g., funding agencies, national governments, international agencies) should be responsible for gathering this larger reference group of stakeholders bearing in mind the aim of the exercise and general context.

In our paper, where the context was defined as global health research and relevant policies were already set by UN's Millennium Development Goals (15), we used three different groups of stakeholders' representatives – all of whom particularly suitable to administration of the respective version of the questionnaire. This composition is presented in detail in the examples given below in the results section and further discussed in the discussion section of this paper.

5. Exercise 1: Internet-based survey of the affiliates to the Global research priority setting network. Between March and May 2006 thirty affiliates to the Global research priority setting network agreed to participate in a piloting test and to represent the reference group of stakeholders for global childhood mortality issues (addressing the UN's Millennium Development Goal

4). Respondents included researchers, policymakers and health practitioners with interest in the field of priority setting in health care from high, low and middle income countries. They were sent the simplest form of the questionnaire (**Table 46-1**, *Version 1*) and asked to simply rank the criteria from 1st to 5th by the order of their importance and to return their ranks. They were also asked to set thresholds on each of the five criteria. The results of this exercise are presented in **Table 46-2**.

The respondents placed the greatest weight (1.75) to maximum potential for disease burden reduction, while the weights for the remaining four criteria were similar to each other and smaller than 1.00. The highest threshold was placed on the criterion of answerability in an ethical way (54/100), while the lowest was placed on maximum potential for disease burden reduction (39/100) (**Table 46-2**).

6. Exercise 2: Interview-type survey in identified group of stakeholders in South Africa. This example differs from the first and third one because it refers to the exercise conducted at the national level, rather than global one (11). It is presented here to demonstrate how, when recruiting larger reference group of stakeholders' representatives, context can be of particular importance. In South Africa, given its apartheid history and the history of health systems organization and management, when identifying participants in the larger

Table 46-1. *Three versions of questionnaire that can be presented to larger reference group members, depending on the size and background of larger reference group membership and the desired level of complexity and amount of information that wishes to be captured.*

Version 1 (the simplest form)
Please assign relative importance to the following 5 criteria*:
• That the new or improved health intervention is likely to indeed be developed through proposed research investment • That, if developed, it is likely to have a real and true effect against the disease that it aims to tackle • That, if developed, it is likely to be delivered to most of those who are in need for it • That, if developed, it has a potential to make substantial share of the disease cases disappear • That, if developed, it is likely to become available to all segments of the society equally
Version 2 (intermediate complexity)
Please assign relative importance to the following 5 criteria*:
• Answerability and Ethics • Efficacy and Effectiveness • Deliverability, affordability and sustainability • Maximum potential for disease burden reduction • Equity in achieved disease burden reduction

Version 3 (the most complex)

Please assign relative importance to the following 5 criteria*:

- The proposed research questions will be answerable in an ethical way:

  (Please explain further the relative importance of answerability and ethics to each other within this criterion)

  – Answerability: the research is likely to lead to discovery of new knowledge

  – Ethics: the research would achieve its aims in an ethical way

- The proposed research will create new knowledge that would increase the efficacy and effectiveness of child health and nutrition interventions

  (Please explain further the relative importance of efficacy and effectiveness to each other within this criterion)

  – Efficacy: The research would yield information on impact of the intervention on disease/disability in child health and nutrition under ideal conditions, such as the randomised controlled trials

  – Effectiveness: The research would yield information on impact of the intervention on disease/disability in child health and nutrition when implemented in the *real world* context

- The proposed research will create new knowledge that would improve deliverability, affordability and sustainability of child health and nutrition interventions in the given context

  (Please explain further the relative importance of deliverability, affordability and sustainability to each other within this criterion)

  – Deliverability: The intervention based on proposed research will be deliverable (infrastructure: basic intervention design, communication and transport infrastructure, need for human resources) in the context

  – Affordability: The intervention based on proposed research will be affordable (available resources in place to implement the intervention) in the context

  – Sustainability: The intervention based on proposed research will be sustainable (government capacity and partnership requirements, ease of delivery and usage characteristics) in the given context

- The proposed research will lead to new knowledge that would expand the magnitude of impact of child health and nutrition interventions on human potential through the reduction of mortality, disease and promotion of mental, physical and cognitive development

- The proposed research will lead to new knowledge that would improve child health and nutrition interventions in a way that they would become more likely to benefit the most vulnerable populations (e.g. the poor, visible minorities, children of female headed house holds, orphans) in the given context

---

* The way this particular question is phrased will depend on the way in which their responses would afterwards be turned into numerical weights; this question could be posed either as asking LRG members to rank the 5 criteria from 1st to 5th in order of importance, or to distribute US$ 100 by those 5 criteria respecting their relative importance.

reference group it was very important to recognize the ideological environment within which the study was being conducted. While gender and wealth inequities were central, equity in this context also referred to attempts to redress the racial determination of access to health care and services.

In May 2006, LRG members were recruited. Participants were identified using different strategies and included: (i) participants at a local public health conference; (ii) academicians (from disciplines ranging from history to psychology and public health) from the three universities in the Western Cape Province and one from the University of Kwazulu-Natal; (iii) workers at the Medical Research Council and the Human Sciences Research Council in Cape Town; (iv) *"lay people"*, including child and youth care workers, teachers, social workers, a statistician, a health journalist; and (v) members of the public. Detailed description of this group of stakeholders' representatives was presented by Tomlinson and colleagues (11). These stakeholders used the version of the questionnaire of intermediate complexity (**Table 46-1**, *Version 2*). Their output is presented in **Table 46-2**.

Predictably, the greatest weight in this specific context was placed upon the criterion *"predicted impact on equity"* (1.30), while the weights for the remaining four criteria were similar to each other and close to 1.00. It was decided that thresholds should not be determined in the same way as in the first exercise, but rather by excluding all research options that found themselves in bottom 10% for any of the five criteria (**Table 46-2**).

7. Exercise 3: Interview-type survey at the international conference on child health. In June 2006, the most complex version of the questionnaire (**Table 46-1**, *Version 3*) was administered by trained university students to twenty participants at the conference related to international child health held in Washington, DC, USA. Respondents included mostly female program implementers with a couple of students, researchers and fundraisers. Respondents were also asked to evaluate the process and suggest any other important criteria that may not have been included in the questionnaire. In this exercise, they were asked to allocate US$ 100 to the presented criteria and sub-criteria deemed as relevant to health research priority setting. Their output is presented in **Table 46-2**.

Three respondents allocated 0 dollars to criterion 2 (efficacy and effectiveness), criterion 4 (maximum potential for disease burden reduction) and criterion 5 (predicted impact on equity). One respondent allocated all US$ 100 to criterion 4. When the average allocations were computed, the highest allocation (US$ 32.89) went to criterion 3 (deliverability, affordability, sustainability) and the smallest allocation (US$ $19.20) went to criterion 2 (efficacy and

Table 46-2. *Suggested weights and thresholds by the representatives of the stakeholders. The simple version of the questionnaire was used to survey the members of the global research priority setting network; the intermediate version for a diverse group of national-level stakeholders from South Africa; and the most complex one to the participants at the conference related to international child health held in Washington, DC, USA.*

Criterion	Mean rank (1–5) / investment (US$)	Mean suggested weight	Mean suggested threshold
SIMPLE VERSION OF THE QUESTIONNAIRE			
Question related to answerability and ethics	3.14	0.96	54/100
Question related to efficacy and effectiveness	3.50	0.86	47/100
Question related to deliverability, affordability and sustainability	3.36	0.89	42/100
Question related to potential for disease burden reduction	1.71	1.75	39/100
Question related to predicted impact on equity	3.29	0.91	41/100
Intermediate version of the questionnaire			
Answerability and ethics	3.72	0.80	bottom 10%
Efficacy and effectiveness	2.75	1.09	bottom 10%
Deliverability, affordability and sustainability	2.94	1.02	bottom 10%
Maximum potential for disease burden reduction	3.28	0.91	bottom 10%
Predicted impact on equity	2.31	1.30	bottom 10%
Complex version of the questionnaire			
Efficacy and effectiveness	19.20 US$	0.192	N/A
Deliverability, affordability and sustainability	32.89 US$	0.329	N/A
Maximum potential for disease burden reduction	24.21 US$	0.242	N/A
Predicted impact on equity	23.94 US$	0.239	N/A

effectiveness). Criteria 4 and 5 received almost the same allocation (US$ 24.21 and US $23.94 respectively). Respondents proposed some additional criteria including popular/political support, government commitment and cultural acceptability (which criteria may be included in the criterion of deliverability and sustainability).

8. Discussion. This paper presents a strategy of involving a variety of stakeholders who lack technical expertise into decision-making process on investments into health research. The process of research priority setting is clearly complex and multi-dimensional and it should be perceived as legitimate and fair by those affected by the decisions (1). CHNRI recently presented a new systematic methodology for setting priorities in health research investments that highlighted five different broad and mutually independent dimensions (*"lenses"*) through which competing research options could be viewed as priorities over each other (**Figure 46-1**) (8–10). The methodology takes into account all those criteria when assigning a value to each proposed research option, and it can flexibly introduce more criteria or leave some of the proposed ones out. Each research option is scored against each of the criteria to derive intermediate scores that transparently highlight its strengths and weaknesses (8). Those intermediate scores are initially determined by people with technical expertise, but then subjected to thresholds and weights set by large group of stakeholders. The thresholds and weights reflect stakeholders' own systems of values and their definition does not require technical expertise (**Figure 46-1**).

Delegating the representatives of stakeholders into the larger reference group should involve systematic listing of the different groups of the relevant stakeholders. These may include research funding agencies, direct recipients of the research funds, beneficiaries of the research and any other group with interest in prioritisation process (16). When convening this group, there should be clear agreement upon the rationale and the relative importance of each stakeholder group. The relative importance may be reflected in either the group's sample size or the weight put on their responses relative to the others'. The actual size and composition of the group would depend on the research options to be considered and the available resources including time. Stakeholders can be represented by a reasonably small or very large reference group, depending on the context. For example, the group may comprise of only 10 persons (e.g., main individual donors to a private charity who want to participate in decision-making on how their money is invested) or more than a thousand people (e.g., in the case of addressing research to avert global child mortality, where everyone from members of public in developing countries, public and private donor foundations, to the UN, WHO and UNICEF officials represent the potential stakeholders).

Small reference group of stakeholders is appropriate when several major donors to any health research-funding organisation want to influence priority setting process. They can set very specific thresholds and weights for each criterion. Large and diverse reference group of stakeholders is more appropriate for priority setting for health research on problems of regional or global importance. In the latter case, the size and diversity of the representatives of stakeholders may lead to regression of thresholds to the mean, regardless of the criteria. In this case a different approach is proposed, by setting a threshold at bottom 10% or 20% of values of all scored research options for any of the criteria. In this way, stakeholders will set the overall level of tolerance towards underachieving in any single criterion. They may even set such percentile-based thresholds for each criterion individually (**Figure 46-1**).

It should be stressed that intermediate scores upon which weights and thresholds are placed do not exactly represent likelihood that the research option would fulfil the criterion in question. They are abstract numbers that measure collective optimism of technical experts about that likelihood. Therefore, when thresholds are being set by larger reference group of stakeholders as specific cut-off points on a scale 0-100, it may be very difficult to predict them intuitively. In all such cases, we advise that those who set thresholds should be made aware of the distribution of the values of intermediate scores, without linking these values to specific research options. In this way, more useful thresholds can be suggested. Otherwise, it is likely that some thresholds may not disqualify any option (and therefore be redundant), or may disqualify unreasonable proportion of scored research options. In our first exercise, it became apparent that thresholds can not be set in advance intuitively, given the reasons above. In our second exercise we felt that it would be more appropriate to understand the outcome first, and then set these thresholds *"post hoc"*, so we applied the statistical approach based on lowest 10%. In the third exercise we dropped the thresholds altogether, although the statistical approach from the second exercise could still be applied.

The first version of the questionnaire tested in this paper is highly recommended for use in very large reference groups, involving representatives from different backgrounds and levels of education. The second (intermediate) version may not be suitable for some members of the larger reference group of stakeholders, some of whom may lack the appropriate background or literacy levels to clearly understand the proposed concepts. However, if a survey involves people with the appropriate knowledge, our view is that this questionnaire should be more useful. This is because in the second version the questions correlate more directly to the chosen criteria for priority setting, whereas in the first version they were translated into layman's terms, but in this *"simplification"* there is always a concern that the essence of the criterion was slightly distorted and that the stakeholders are not understanding all the questions in the same way. Finally, the most complex form of the questionnaire should only be used in exceptional cases such as: (i) when the larger reference group is formed by a relatively small number of highly motivated people with a good understanding of the issues related to health research investments, (ii) For the purpose of qualitative research on the stakeholders' values where this form of questionnaire could provide more detailed information, providing a deeper understanding of the elicited weights. In our exercise, the first group was an experimental group and they had no moderator to their exercise, so we needed to keep the questionnaire as simple as possible and presented them with the simplest form. In the second group, members of the public formed a minority of the group (up to 10%) and they were moderated through the exercise, so they were able to join the survey although it was a more demanding one. In the third group, the background of the stakeholder groups justified the use of the most complex form.

When turning the input from the stakeholders into useful quantitative values, the first version of the questionnaire was the simplest and it worked very well in practice. Still, it should be recognized that it has conceptual shortcomings. There is no clear theoretical justification for limiting the weights for intermediate scores to values between 0.6 and 3.0. In view of this limitation, we recommend the second approach (distribution of US$ 100) wherever possible. This approach places no limits on the values of the weights. In extreme cases, some criteria (intermediate scores) may be assigned an average weight of zero by the larger reference group of stakeholders and thereby be excluded from influencing the final priority score.

Some important lessons were also learned through interviewing stakeholders' representatives in different contexts. In South Africa, where stakeholders were gathered from within national boundaries, equity was ranked higher than some of the most popular criteria in similar contexts (7,17). This underscores the importance of eliciting local values (18,19). Given the variations in individual values in this context, technical experts who were deriving intermediate scores recommended that the choice of representatives of the stakeholders should be systematic to ensure representation from all relevant stakeholders (11). The feedback from stakeholders' representatives attending large international health conference in Washington, USA, where the most complex form of the questionnaire was administered, included comments that the interview should be guided by trained research assistants. Suggestions were made to delineate the criteria especially in contexts where the individual criteria may be valued differently. Finally, since the five proposed criteria were not exhaustive, there should always be provision for respondents to give suggestions for criteria that may be relevant to their local context.

Conclusion. This paper addresses one of the most pressing issues in health research priority setting globally – the lack of involvement of stakeholders other than the scientists in decision-making process on investments. This paper presents how this can be achieved through introducing a large reference group of stakeholders' representatives that complement the work of technical experts. The representatives of stakeholders are enabled to assign greater value to some of the priority-setting criteria defined by technical experts. This adds a dimension of public opinion to the rational scientific assessment of the research options derived by technical experts. Thresholds and weights set in this way are transparent and can be later challenged or revised based on a feedback. The change may be prompted by the outcomes of priority setting process or because of the changes in dynamic social, political or economic context. While this paper provides some progress in including stakeholders' values in decision making, there are still the unresolved problems of how the proposals put forward can be operationalized in the real world (20). Future work should focus on these areas.

Acknowledgement: Originally published as: Lydia Kapiriri, Mark Tomlinson, Jennifer Gibson, Mickey Chopra, Shams El Arifeen, Robert E. Black and Igor Rudan on behalf of Child Health and Nutrition Research Initiative (CHNRI): Setting priorities in global child health research investments: addressing values of stakeholders. Reprinted with permission from Croatian Medical Journal under Creative Commons Attribution License (Croat Med J 2007; 48:618-627). We wish to express our gratitude to the individuals from Global Priority Setting Network, participants of the conference in international health in Washington, DC, USA (May 2006), students of the Johns Hopkins Bloomberg School of Public Health in Baltimore, USA, and a group of stakeholders representatives from South Africa who either helped to organize or conducted the survey among the stakeholders, or agreed to participate in pilot testing of the methodology and kindly provided their personal views and opinions.

References

1. Daniels N, Sabin JE. Setting limits fairly: Can we learn to share medical resources? Oxford: Oxford University Press, 2002.
2. Global Forum for Health Research. The 10/90 report on health research. Global Forum for Health Research: Geneva, 1999.
3. Varmus H, Klausner R, Zerhouni E, Acharya T, Daar AS, Singer PA. Grand challenges in global health. Science 2003; 302:398–399.
4. Ghaffar A, de Francisco A, Matlin S (eds). The combined approach matrix: a priority-setting tool for health research. Global Forum for Health Research: Geneva, 2004.
5. Costello A, Filippi V, Kubba T, Horton R. Research challenges to improve maternal and child survival. Lancet 2007; 369:1240–1243.
6. Kapiriri L, Norheim OF. Criteria for priority-setting in health care in Uganda: exploration of stakeholders' values. Bull World Health Organ 2004; 82:172–179.
7. Kapiriri L, Arnesen T, Norheim OF. Is cost-effectiveness analysis preferred to severity of disease as the main guiding principle in priority setting in resource poor settings? The case of Uganda. Cost Eff Resour Alloc 2004; 2:1.
8. Arnesen T, Kapiriri L. Can the value choices in DALYs influence global priority-setting? Health Policy 2004; 70:137–149.
9. Rudan I, El Arifeen S, Black RE. A systematic methodology for setting priorities in child health research investments. In: Child Health and Nutrition Research initiative (CHNRI) (eds): A new approach for systematic priority setting. Dhaka: CHNRI, 2006.

10. Rudan I, El Arifeen S, Black RE, Campbell H. Childhood pneumonia and diarrhoea: Setting our priorities right. Lancet Inf Dis 2007; 7:56–61.

11. Tomlinson M, Chopra M, Sanders D, Bradshaw D, Hendricks M, Greenfield D, et al. Setting priorities in child health research investments for South Africa. PLoS Med 2007; 4:e259.

12. Kapiriri L. Public accountability in priority setting: the case of Uganda (Ph D Thesis). Bergen: University of Bergen, 2003.

13. Mullen P. Public Engagement in health care priority setting: are the methods appropriate and valid? In: Coulter A, Ham C (eds): The global challenge of health care rationing. Philadelphia: Open University Press, 2000.

14. Baltussen R, Niessen L. Priority setting of health interventions: the need for multi-criteria decision analysis. Cost Eff Resour Alloc 2006; 4:14.

15. http://www.unmillenniumproject.org/goals/index.htm; Accessed: 1 Sep 2007

16. Nilstun T. Priority setting, justice, and health care: conceptual analysis. Croat Med J 2000; 41:375–377.

17. Ubel PA, Loewenstein G. Distributing scarce livers: the moral reasoning of the general public. Soc Sci Med 1996; 42:1049–1055.

18. Hermans H, den Exter A. Priorities and priority-setting in health care in the Netherlands. Croat Med J 1998; 39:346–355.

19. Ljubic B, Hrabac B. Priority setting and scarce resources: case of the Federation of Bosnia and Herzegovina. Croat Med J 1998; 39:276–280.

20. Nuyens Y. Setting priorities for health research: lessons from low and middle-income countries. Bull World Health Organ 2007; 85:319–321.

CHAPTER 47.

Global health research priorities: Mobilizing the developing world

The paper focuses on two questions: (i) how can we set research priorities in a transparent, systematic, fair and legitimate way; and (ii) how can we mobilize low and middle-income countries to take more ownership in defining their own research policies, rather than merely being passive recipients of international aid for research and development?

The Child Health and Nutrition Research initiative (CHNRI) started as an initiative of the Global Forum for Health Research in Geneva, Switzerland. Its aim was to develop a tool that could assist decision making, consensus development and priority setting in health research investments to improve child health and nutrition. CHNRI noted the absence of a practical and systematic tool that could assist priority setting in health research investments. It aimed to develop a methodology that could address support for different instruments of health research to achieve better balance between fundamental research, translation research and implementation research. The application of CHNRI methodology should maximize the potential of health research to reduce disease burden and gradually reduce inequities that exist between support for research on the health problems of the rich and the poor.

The CHNRI methodology was being developed between 2005 and 2007 through 12 consecutive meetings of a trans-disciplinary panel of experts led by Professors Igor Rudan (University of Edinburgh, UK), Shams El Arifeen (International Centre for Diarrhoeal Disease Research, Bangladesh (ICDDR,B) in Dhaka, Bangladesh) and Robert E. Black (Johns Hopkins University, Baltimore, USA). With funding support from The World Bank, they gathered 15 multi-disciplinary experts from the fields of international health, health research policy, paediatrics and child health, economics and management science, political science, law and ethics, along with programme leaders from low and middle-income countries and members of international organizations. They worked together to address a number of key challenges related to multi-dimensional problem of setting priorities in health research investments (see **Table 43-1**).

They firstly reviewed and addressed the current principles and practice of research priority setting (1). They concluded that there were no methods or tools available in a form of algorithm that could enable systematic, transparent, legitimate and fair, scientifically rigorous and replicable process of priority setting. They identified key stakeholders and proposed including them all in the priority-setting process: investors in health research, community of health researchers and members of general public (2).

The investors were expected to carefully define the context and the criteria for health research priority setting. The context is defined by transparency about expectations on returns from investments in health research (e.g. maximum cost-effectiveness in disease burden reduction), the style of investment (e.g. risk averting or *"high-risk high-profit"*), population of interest that would benefit from the investments (e.g. children of a single country), the focus of investments in health research (e.g. a single disease or an overall burden) and time frame within which the *"returns"* are expected (short, medium or long term).

The investors were also expected to agree transparently on the set of five criteria that would discriminate between many competing research options. CHNRI's *"standard"* set of criteria follows a simple framework in which five dimensions of each proposed research option are assessed: (i) likelihood that the proposed health research would be answerable; (ii) likelihood that it would result in an effective health intervention; (iii) likelihood that this intervention would be deliverable, affordable and sustainable; (iv) the maximum potential of intervention to reduce disease burden; and (v) likelihood that the research would reduce inequity. In the next step of the CHNRI process, large number of researchers would be invited to contribute hundreds of their ideas towards a systematic conceptual framework, so that all dimensions of health research (descriptive, fundamental, translational and implementation research) are represented and that all the questions have a similar level of *"depth"* (e.g., a 3-year research project).

Once a list of a manageable number of ideas – *"research investment options"* (usually up to 200 of them) – is consolidated by removing all overlapping ideas, dozens of researchers are invited by the internet to submit their scores for each research option. This gives each competing research option a score for each of the five criteria. The scores measure *"collective optimism"* of all scoring researchers on a scale 0-100. In the final step, a very large number of members of general public set different thresholds and weights for each of the five criteria, so that the overall score also includes the value system of a wider community – which may give more weight to e.g. likelihood of effectiveness, or the impact on equity. The final output of CHNRI process is a list which ranks up to 200 research investment options by the 5 transparent criteria and the overall score – from the most to the least attractive for investment support

(3). CHNRI published this conceptual framework (3) and detailed guidelines for implementation of the priority-setting methodology (4,5).

Fundamentally, the CHNRI methodology combines two main ideas. The first is *"principal component analysis"*, a statistical technique which reduces a very complex system with many dimensions (in this case, possible criteria for prioritization) to a small number of relatively independent *"principal components"* which still capture a sizeable proportion of variation in the system. By defining a set of 5 criteria, CHNRI process effectively reduces a notoriously complex and multi-dimensional task of priority setting, which could be approached through an almost infinite number of *"lenses"*, into an exercise where the five most important – and reasonably independent – criteria for priority setting are clearly defined. They can even be weighted afterwards, in order of their importance to the users. The second idea is known as the *"Wisdom of crowds"*, the collective opinion of a group of individuals. It has been shown that the collective average of many independent guesses is nearly always closer to the truth than a single expert judgement.

The advantages of the CHNRI process include its systematic nature, transparency, well defined (a priori) context and criteria chosen for discriminating between research investment options, a highly structured way in which relevant information is obtained from the scorers, independent scoring that limits influence of strong-minded individuals on the rest of the scorers, its informative and intuitive quantitative output, ability to expose points of greatest agreement and controversy, low implementation cost and replicability. In the past three years the CHNRI methodology became an increasingly popular tool. A growing number of papers, based on the implementation of CHNRI methodology, are being published in leading international peer-reviewed journals (6–20). The impact of those papers, measured by both citations and media coverage, is growing fast.

The applications of CHNRI methodology proved helpful to systematically list and transparently score a very large number of research options in very diverse areas of health research. It has been used to define national-level priorities for child health research in South Africa (6). At the global level, the CHNRI methodology was used to define research priorities for mental health research issues (7,8) primary health care (9), zinc deficiency in children (10), people with disabilities (11), implementation research at the community level (12) and stillbirths (13). The World Health Organization's Department for Child and Adolescent Health and Development used the CHNRI methodology to identify research priorities for the five main causes of child deaths that could contribute to accelerated progress towards the Millennium Development

Goal 4. Several hundreds of international technical experts participated in this exercise co-ordinated by the WHO between 2008 and 2009 and they defined immediate research priorities for childhood pneumonia (14), diarrhoea (15), neonatal infections (16), birth asphyxia (17) and preterm birth/low birth weight (18). This large effort was followed by a meeting of up to 40 donor organizations at the WHO in March 2009 and a range of follow-up activities to address the priorities through health research at the national level.

The CHNRI methodology is not free of possible biases. Many good ideas ("*research investment options*") may not get included in the initial list of research options that is scored by the experts because the CHNRI process only aims to achieve a manageable coverage of the spectrum of all possible research options, which is endless. Another concern is that the final list of priorities may represent a biased opinion of a very limited group of researchers involved in the scoring process. However, the number of people globally who possess enough experience, expertise and knowledge on the research areas of interest to be able to judge a very diverse spectrum of research questions is typically rather limited. Given that the "*sample*" of the experts chosen for most exercises is getting larger and more diverse for each new exercise thanks to the widespread internet use, this continuously improves the validity of the process (19,20).

Further progress with the implementation of the CHNRI methodology is expected in several areas: (i) the method has recently been implemented by international expert panels in the areas of prematurity and stillbirths, child development, emergency situations and refugee crisis, and several others; (ii) the World Health Organization is currently planning the CHNRI exercise with the governments of 5 large countries (including Pakistan, India, Egypt and Bangladesh) to define priorities for implementation research and health systems and policy research, and Pakistani government has already piloted the CHNRI methodology; (iii) Bill and Melinda Gates Foundation have funded several grants based on CHNRI methodology approach in which they sought advice on the emerging health interventions and technologies that deserve attention; (iv) a modified CHNRI methodology is being developed to address priorities among the emerging health technologies, and also health care investment priorities; (v) a user-friendly "*CHNRI software*" is also being developed, and it should allow large groups of international experts to perform CHNRI exercise and express their collective optimism towards competing health research priorities over the internet in a fast, cheap and effective way, hoping to promote the CHNRI methodology as a widely applicable tool for consensus development in any area of research. I believe that this tool will find application within many low and middle-income countries and assist them to pull together their own experts and actively define their priorities for research and development in the coming years.

Acknowledgement: Originally published as: Igor Rudan: Global health research priorities: Mobilizing the developing world. Reprinted with permission from Elsevier (Public Health 2012; 126:237–40).

References

1. Rudan I, Gibson J, Kapiriri L, Lansang MA, Hyder AA, Lawn J, et al. Child Health and Nutrition Research Initiative (CHNRI). Setting priorities in global child health research investments: assessment of principles and practice. Croat Med J 2007; 48:595–604.

2. Kapiriri L, Tomlinson M, Gibson J, Chopra M, El Arifeen S, Black RE, et al. Child Health and Nutrition Research Initiative (CHNRI): setting priorities in global child health research investments: addressing the values of the stakeholders. Croat Med J 2007; 48:618–627.

3. Rudan I, Chopra M, Kapiriri L, Gibson J, Lansang MA, Carneiro I, et al. Setting priorities in global child health research investments: universal challenges and conceptual framework. Croat Med J 2008; 49:307–317.

4. Rudan I, Gibson JL, Ameratunga S, El Arifeen S, Bhutta ZA, Black M, et al. on behalf of Child Health and Nutrition Research Initiative (CHNRI). Setting priorities in global child health research investments: guidelines for implementation of the CHNRI Method. Croat Med J 2008; 49:720–733.

5. Rudan I, El Arifeen S, Black RE, Campbell H. Childhood pneumonia and diarrhoea: setting our priorities right. Lancet Inf Dis 2007; 7:56–61.

6. Tomlinson M, Chopra M, Sanders D, Bradshaw D, Hendricks M, Greenfield D, et al. Setting priorities in child health research Investments for South Africa. PLoS Med 2007; 4:e259.

7. Chisholm D, Flisher AJ, Lund C, Patel V, Saxena S, Thornicroft G, et al. Lancet Global Mental Health Group. Scale up services for mental disorders: a call for action. Lancet 2007; 370:1241–1252.

8. Tomlinson M, Rudan I, Saxena S, Swartz L, Tsai AC, Patel V. Setting investment priorities for research in global mental health. Bull World Health Organ 2009; 87:438–446.

9. Walley J, Lawn JE, Tinker A, De Francisco A, Chopra M, Rudan I, et al. Primary health care: making Alma Ata a reality. Lancet 2008; 372:1001–1007.

10. Brown KH, Hess SY, Boy E, Gibson RS, Horton S, Osendarp SJ, et al. Setting priorities for zinc-related health research to reduce children's disease burden worldwide: an application of the Child Health and Nutrition Research Initiative's research priority-setting method. Public Health Nutr 2009; 12:389–396.

11. Tomlinson M, Swartz L, Officer A, Chan KY, Rudan I, Saxena S. Research priorities for health of people with disabilities: an expert opinion exercise. Lancet 2009; 374:1857–1862.

12. George A, Young M, Bang A, Chan KY, Rudan I, Victora CG, et al. GAPPS expert group on community based strategies and constraints. Setting implementation research priorities to reduce preterm births and stillbirths at the community level. PLoS Med 2011; 8:e1000380.

13. Pattinson R, Kerber K, Buchmann E, Hani C, Friberg I, Belizan M, et al. for the Lancet Stillbirth Series Steering Committee. Stillbirths: how can health systems deliver for mothers and babies? Lancet 2011; 377:1610–1623.

14. Rudan I, El Arifeen S, Bhutta ZA, Black RE, Brooks A, Chan KY, et al, the WHO/CHNRI Expert Group on Childhood Pneumonia. Setting research priorities to reduce global mortality from childhood pneumonia by 2015. PLoS Med 2011; 8:e1001099.

15. Fontaine O, Kosek M, Bhatnagar S, Boschi-Pinto C, Chan KY, Duggan C, et al. Setting research priorities to reduce global mortality from childhood diarrhoea by 2015. PLoS Med 2009; 6:e41.

16. Bahl R, Martines J, Ali N, Bhan MK, Carlo W, Chan KY, et al. Research priorities to reduce global mortality from newborn infections by 2015. Pediatr Inf Dis J 2009; 28(Suppl. 1):S43–48.

17. Lawn JE, Bahl R, Bergstrom S, Bhutta ZA, Darmstadt GL, Ellis M, et al. Setting research priorities to reduce almost one million deaths from birth asphyxia by 2015. PLoS Med 2011; 8:e1000389.

18. Bahl R, Bhandari N, Bhutta ZA, Biloglav Z, Edmond K, Iyengar S, et al. Setting research priorities to reduce global mortality from low birth weight by 2015. J Global Health 2012; 2:30–35.

19. Rudan I, Kapiriri L, Tomlinson M, Balliet M, Cohen B, Chopra M. Evidence-based priority setting for health care and research: tools to support policy in maternal, neonatal, and child health in Africa. PLoS Med 2010; 7:e1000308.

20. Rudan I. The complex challenge of setting priorities in health research investments. Indian J Med Res 2009; 129:351–353.

Index